'ABDU'L-BAHÁ IN AMERICA

'ABDU'L-BAHÁ IN AMERICA

ROBERT H. STOCKMAN

Bahá'í PUBLISHING
Wilmette, Illinois

Bahá'í Publishing
401 Greenleaf Avenue, Wilmette, Illinois 60091-2844
 Published 2012
Printed in the United States of America on acid-free paper ∞

18 17 16 15 4 3 2

Library of Congress Cataloging-in-Publication Data

Stockman, Robert H., 1953–
'Abdu'l-Bah? in America / by Robert H. Stockman.
p. cm.
Includes bibliographical references.
ISBN 978-1-931847-97-1
1. 'Abdu'l-Bah?, 1844–1921—Travel—North America. 2. Bahai Faith—North America. I. Title.
BP393.S76 2012
297.9'3092—dc23
2012005096

Cover design by Andrew Johnson
Book design by Patrick Falso
Photograph of 'Abdu'l-Bahá reproduced with the permission of the
Bahá'í International Community

To Lua and Nabil and the next century of American Bahá'ís

CONTENTS

'Abdu'l-Bahá

PREFACE

One approaches the vast subject of 'Abdu'l-Bahá's eight-month sojourn in North America, even after a century of hindsight, with trepidation. This was not the visit of a sixty-seven-year-old foreign tourist bent on seeing new places or a religious teacher hoping to cement his fortune and reputation; rather, it was the effort of an almost indescribable man, whose impact on people was superhuman, and who used his newfound freedom from forty years of imprisonment and privation to share his Father's message of the oneness of humanity and the principles of universal peace with as many North Americans as possible. His exhausting yet exhilarating 239-day trek from coast to coast took him to fifty cities and towns, where he delivered up to four talks a day—about four hundred total—to approximately ninety-three thousand people.*

On some days, one hundred fifty persons sought private meetings with him. Their accounts are full of tears of joy, intimate conversation—sometimes with a minimum of words spoken—prophetic utterances, and even epiphanies and apparent miracles, such as release from grief and healing from physical illness. Prominent men and women flocked to

* "Table of Talks Given by 'Abdu'l-Bahá in North America," author's personal papers. The table was assembled by combing various sources. Whenever possible, available attendance information was recorded; in other cases it was estimated.

hear him, invited him into their homes, and asked him to speak at some of their most prestigious venues. His commitment to racial and ethnic equality during an era of legal discrimination and widespread prejudice was demonstrated in talks at an African American church, university, and conference; a Japanese-American church; and a Syrian relief society; and by his encouragement of the first interracial (Black/White) marriage in the American Bahá'í community. His championing of the full equality of women and the inevitability of their acquiring the right to vote was controversial and was often featured in headlines about him. His devotion to the poor brought him to visit four hundred homeless men at the Bowery Mission in New York City and speak at six other settlement houses. His desire to give solace to the sick prompted him to travel for hours to visit ill persons far from the crowd of admirers demanding his attention. Jaundiced newspapermen withheld their cynical barbs and praised his wisdom, genuineness, sincerity, and love. Clergymen turned their pulpits over to him after introducing him to their flocks with great warmth and high praise.

Because of the continued expansion of the Bahá'í Faith, a thorough study of 'Abdu'l-Bahá's journey becomes important for those wishing to know more about this new religion. The Founder of the Faith, Bahá'u'lláh (1817–92), was born in Iran and spent most of His life in exile in the Ottoman Empire. He passed away outside the small city of Acre, in what is today Israel. His claim to be a Messenger of God was expressed in the form of a vast array of books, prayers, and letters—some eighteen thousand works—that described the nature of God and revelation, depicted the spiritual nature of human beings and the need for their continual spiritual and ethical refinement, proclaimed the oneness of humanity and its implications for racial and sexual equality, and outlined principles for the construction of a world civilization. Before His passing, He appointed His eldest son, 'Abdu'l-Bahá (1844–1921) as His successor, gave 'Abdu'l-Bahá the authority to interpret His texts, and made him Head of the Faith. He established a Covenant with His followers that stated that 'Abdu'l-Bahá was a divinely guided figure and that the Bahá'ís should obey him.

'Abdu'l-Bahá took up the reins of leadership immediately and was soon coordinating efforts to take the Bahá'í Faith to the United States and Europe. Americans had first heard about Bahá'u'lláh at the World's Parliament of Religions in Chicago in 1893, but when 'Abdu'l-Bahá arrived nineteen years later, knowledge about him was limited, and American Bahá'ís numbered only a thousand or two. Since then, the Bahá'í Faith has sunk its roots deep into American culture, has well over a hundred fifty thousand adherents, and is emerging from obscurity. Academic study of its development is becoming more widespread, and public interest is growing—hence the need for a book such as this one.

After a century of researching 'Abdu'l-Bahá, Bahá'ís have not found all the literary sources relating to his trip, though the expanding resources of the World Wide Web present new opportunities for finding rare articles in rural newspapers and references in personal papers. The information already available is staggering: *The Promulgation of Universal Peace,* a collection of his discourses, has 140 talks; the diary of his companion, Maḥmúd-i-Zarqání, describes almost every major event—though sometimes he's off by a day or even two—and many private scenes and frank comments by 'Abdu'l-Bahá; Juliet Thompson's diary intimately records his visit to New York and Washington; Agnes Parsons's diary covers Washington and Dublin, New Hampshire; Howard Colby Ives offers a hundred perceptive pages scattered throughout his memoir; Allen Ward's *239 Days* provides a day-to-day summary of 'Abdu'l-Bahá's trip; the Bahá'í periodical *Star of the West* has contemporary news and lightly edited transcriptions of his talks; over 350 newspaper and magazine articles are available; a score of books have chapters or sections about his visit, including Hasan Balyuzi's important biography, *'Abdu'l-Bahá: The Centre of the Covenant of Bahá'u'lláh*; the

Ella Cooper Papers in the National Bahá'í Archives in Wilmette, Illinois, have hundreds of pages of unpublished talks by and conversations with 'Abdu'l-Bahá; and hundreds of pages of other unpublished telegrams, letters, diaries, and memoirs reside in the National Bahá'í Archives. The total number of works published about 'Abdu'l-Bahá's visit may exceed three thousand pages. The crucial source that remains untapped is the archive of the Bahá'í World Centre in Haifa, Israel, where 'Abdu'l-Bahá's own correspondence is located but is not yet available to researchers. At some point, once this information becomes available, it may force many revisions of our understanding of his North American sojourn.

Equally important to the problem of sources is the interpretation one brings to them. In his epochal history, *God Passes By,* Shoghi Effendi Rabbani (head of the Bahá'í Faith from 1921 to 1957, its authorized interpreter, and grandson of 'Abdu'l-Bahá) provides several short passages with incisive judgments about 'Abdu'l-Bahá's purpose, key efforts, and effectiveness. The Bahá'í World Center has offered additional overview in its insightful review of the twentieth century, *Century of Light.* But individual Bahá'ís have rarely ventured to analyze 'Abdu'l-Bahá's journey.

When 'Abdu'l-Bahá's feet touched these shores, he had already composed a Will and Testament that outlined how the Bahá'í community would be organized after his death, but little has been written concerning how his plan for the organization of the Faith may have shaped what he did and said in 1912. His other fundamental contribution to the Faith's future was a series of fourteen letters to the North American believers called Tablets of the Divine Plan, penned in 1916 and 1917. They summoned the American Bahá'ís to take the Bahá'í message to every part of their country and to the entire planet, providing both specific countries, territories, and cities where it had to be established and practical advice about how to disseminate it. 'Abdu'l-Bahá's 1912 journey constituted preparation for the monumental assignments in Tablets of the Divine Plan, preparation that one can see stretching back nearly a decade further, when ʻAbduʼl-Bahá directed the first American Baháʼís to undertake teaching trips within the United States and internationally.

In addition to these concerns of the internal consolidation and development of the Baháʼí community, no matter how important they may be, there are other questions to consider, such as the impact ʻAbduʼl-Bahá had on American culture and values, his influence on African Americans and women, and his insights about the issues of race, gender, and world peace. A full exploration of those matters must await the painstaking study of the historical context; this work can only offer preliminary observations.

There is also the matter of how Americans became attracted to non-Christian religions and how the growth of the American Baháʼí community relates to the growth of Hindu and Buddhist convert communities, which were founded by visiting Asian religious teachers. Most Americans initially saw little difference between the Asian religious teachers and ʻAbduʼl-Bahá; they were unaware of the Baháʼí understanding of ʻAbduʼl-Baháʼs station, and at first had no experience of his personality or teachings. Their expectations of him were shaped by their earlier experiences. Protap Chunder Mozoomdar, a Hindu religious leader, preceded him by almost thirty years; Swami Vivekananda, Anagarika Dharmapala, and Soyen Shaku (Hindu, Theravada Buddhist, and Zen Buddhist respectively) by almost twenty; Inayat Khan (who introduced Sufism to America), by a year and a half. A comparison of ʻAbduʼl-Baháʼs travels with their tours of North America highlights many similarities and differences, some of which were caused by the changing times and others by their differing personalities, goals, and resources. One notable conclusion is that ʻAbduʼl-Bahá was far more successful at attracting to his religion European Americans (not to mention African Americans, who were significantly attracted to the Baháʼí Faith but were not addressed by the others). ʻAbduʼl-Baháʼs success was fostered by twenty years of correspondence with American Baháʼís and was no doubt assisted by the more open attitudes toward non-Christian religions that the earlier Asian religious visitors helped to create.

In order to explore 'Abdu'l-Bahá's visit from all these various angles, the book must serve a diversity of readers. The Bahá'ís constitute the bulk of the book market and naturally are the group most interested in a study of this sort, but my colleagues in the field of religious studies need a good survey and analysis of what is an important and neglected event in American religious history, and there are many members of the public who will want to know about 'Abdu'l-Bahá's character and the way he taught the Bahá'í Faith to others. To satisfy all these audiences is a challenge of high order; to please them may be impossible; but to ignore one in favor of the others would weaken the entire work, for the priorities and needs of all three ultimately are complementary.

One major issue I have wrestled with repeatedly is how to treat the talks of 'Abdu'l-Bahá. While 'Abdu'l-Bahá's writings are regarded as divine in origin and authoritative in nature, any utterances of his are not so viewed, unless 'Abdu'l-Bahá reviewed the transcript of the talk for accuracy and approved it. Very few of the talks used in this book fall in that category; they are unauthenticated and therefore less reliable renderings of his words. 'Abdu'l-Bahá spoke in Persian and was simultaneously interpreted in English. In many cases, a Persian-language secretary took notes or wrote down as best he could the spoken Persian text. Since no formal shorthand existed for the Persian language, it is not known how well the Persian texts were recorded, especially if 'Abdu'l-Bahá spoke about biblical terms and persons with which the transcriber may not have been familiar (and therefore would record more slowly). Some of the Persian texts were then revised by 'Abdu'l-Bahá in written form for publication.

In many cases, the English translations were also recorded, sometimes by professional stenographers using shorthand, sometimes in note form. When the English transcriptions don't agree with the Persian, we don't know whether the English texts include commentary added by the English-language interpreter, whether the Persian texts are missing something 'Abdu'l-Bahá really said, or whether 'Abdu'l-Bahá chose to excise something from the Persian transcripts when they were being prepared for publication. The English transcriptions also went through multiple revisions; the original handwritten notes (which are no longer extant, as far as I know) were typed up, many were edited for publication in *Star of the West,* and then in many cases Howard MacNutt took the *Star of the West* pages, hand-edited them (some of these still exist in the archives), had the result typeset, and published them in two volumes, titled *The Promulgation of Universal Peace*, in 1922. A few other talks that 'Abdu'l-Bahá regarded as particularly important were revised for English-language publication within weeks of their delivery by 'Abdu'l-Bahá's English-language secretaries, in consultation with him. The second edition of *Promulgation*, published in 1982, includes at least one new translation of a talk from the Persian-published version. Eleven Persian texts of his talks have also been published in authorized English translations in *Maḥmúd's Diary.*

Considerable work is necessary to locate the various drafts of the texts and translations and compare them before we have a comprehensive and complete picture of 'Abdu'l-Bahá's spoken message to the West. Because of my limited Persian, the book rarely uses the Persian sources. When researching, discussing, and quoting 'Abdu'l-Bahá's talks, I have used authorized English translations from the Persian when they are available. If they are not available, I have used the oldest English translations I could find, usually found in *Star of the West* magazine or the Ella Cooper Papers. They have a spontaneous, colloquial, and occasionally frank feel to them. Their accuracy and authenticity cannot be checked, but they often contain Persian turns of phrase that are unidiomatic in English, which indicate that they are a fairly reliable record of the interpreter's rendering of 'Abdu'l-Bahá's words. Unfortunately, they can also be unclear. The translations in *The Promulgation of Universal Peace* have been my last resort; they are clearer and in elegant, formal language, but often Howard MacNutt has inferred meaning that might not have been intended.*

As for spelling, the word *Bahá'í* (including the accents) was standardized among Bahá'ís by Shoghi Effendi in 1923, but before that date, it appeared in a variety of forms (*Behai, Bahai, Bahaism, Bahaist*), and after that date, numerous spellings have persisted in the academic community based sometimes on technical transliteration systems and other times on archaic spellings that the authors adopted for obscure reasons. This book will preserve the original spellings in documents, when quoting them, and in names (such as *Bahai Temple Unity*). It will use anglicizations of Middle Eastern names if they were adopted by the individuals under discussion. Otherwise, this work will follow the standard Bahá'í transliteration system, simply because it has by far the most momentum and, because of the World Wide Web, its use is spreading.

A word must also be offered about the term *American.* In 1912 the Canadian Bahá'í community numbered in the dozens and was in close connection with the thousands of Bahá'ís south of the border. The Canadians participated in the election of the Bahai Temple Unity Executive Board in 1909, the Bahá'í coordinating body for North America, and remained a part of the "national" organization of the Bahá'í Faith in North America until 1948. 'Abdu'l-Bahá treated Canada as part of the greater

* When Howard MacNutt produced the first edition of *Promulgation of Universal Peace* in the years 1919–22, in most cases he started with a copy of *Star of the West* magazine, pulling apart the various pages and editing on them or rewriting them by hand. His editing for smoothness and clarity often introduced interpretations of 'Abdu'l-Bahá's meaning. He kept the *Star of the West's* order even when it was not chronological; for example, the three talks 'Abdu'l-Bahá gave on April 30 (published in *Star of the West,* vol. 3, no. 4) start with his evening address to the Bahai Temple Unity convention, which was the last of the three chronologically.

North American Bahá'í community, and the word *American* was often used to include them.

This volume can hope to provide only preliminary observations based on the third of the addresses of 'Abdu'l-Bahá available in English. Time will bring about many revisions, clarifications, and nuances about the content and meaning of 'Abdu'l-Bahá's talks. The footnotes provide all the information that was available to me regarding variant texts, so that readers can make their own study of the talks and future researchers will have a foundation for the next stage of research.

ACKNOWLEDGMENTS

No work like this is possible without advice from people with various types of expertise. I have benefited greatly from the assistance of and conversations (oral and electronic) with Kurt Asplund, Amin Banani, Kenneth Bowers, Roger Dahl, Manuchehr Derakhshani, Rhett Diessner, Amín Egea, Betty Fisher, Paula Freedman, Ladjamaya Green, Kurt Hein, Jan Jasion, Eric Kreitzer, Firuz Kazemzadeh, Louis Maani, Marlene Macke, Bill Mahoney, Bijan Ma'sumian, Jesse McBride, Mike McMullen, J. Gordon Melton, John A. Milne, Tim Moore, Guy Emerson Mount, Ali Nakhjavani, Lil Osborn, Carol Rutstein, Darius Sohrab, Peter Terry, Duane Troxel, Lewis Walker, and David Weigert. My colleagues on the Tarikh listserv (which brings some two hundred people together to discuss Bahá'í history) provided new information, corrected errors, exposed misinterpretations, fleshed out theories, generated brainstorming sessions, and hashed out variant interpretations of aspects of the visit and its context. Among those on Tarikh who have assisted me were Loni Bramson, Chris Buck, Steve Cooney, Sen McGlinn, Brent Poirier, and Phillip Tussing. Jonathan Menon, Gayle Morrison, Anne Perry, and Christopher White read through much or all of the manuscript with great care and caught all sorts of vague phrases. Conversations with a wide range of friends on my Facebook page offered new ideas and much encouragement. Finally, Chris Martin at Bahá'í Publishing has provided excellent and careful editing of the manuscript.

My wife and children have suffered through the researching, writing, and editing phases of the book with minimal complaints, and I am grateful for their patience and sacrifice. Watching my eight-year-old son, Nabil, and my thirteen-year-old daughter, Lua, say their Bahá'í prayers, read their Bahá'í books, and gradually mature in their understanding of their Faith has been an inspiration and encouragement to me in this project. As the first century after 'Abdu'l-Bahá's visit draws to a close, I dedicate this book to them and everyone else who will explore the meaning of his visit over the next hundred years.

1

THE FIRST DAY

On the morning of Thursday, April 11, 1912, the White Star Line's passenger ship *Cedric* steamed toward the wharves of New York Harbor. Standing on the upper deck, wearing a long, black oriental cloak flapping in the breeze, with light tan robes underneath and a turban of pure white over his gray locks, was 'Abdu'l-Bahá Abbás, the sixty-seven-year-old head of the Bahá'í Faith. According to a journalist and Bahá'í, Wendell Phillips Dodge, who boarded the ship with other journalists when the customs agents went on board, he was a "strongly and solidly built" man of medium height, though he "seemed to be much taller," weighing about 165 pounds (75 kilograms) and pacing the deck, "alert and active in every moment, his head thrown back and splendidly poised upon his broad, square shoulders":

> A profusion of iron grey hair bursting out at the sides of the turban and hanging long upon the neck; a large, massive head, full-domed and remarkable wide across the forehead rising like a great palisade above the eyes, which were very wide apart, their orbits large and deep, looking out from under massive overhanging brows; strong Roman nose, generous ears, decisive yet kindly mouth and chin; a creamy white complexion, beard same color as his hair, worn full over

> the face and carefully trimmed at almost full length—this completes an insufficient word picture of this "Wise Man Out of the East."[1]

As the ship passed the Statue of Liberty, 'Abdu'l-Bahá is reported to have "held his arms wide apart in salutation" and to have said, "There is the new world's symbol of liberty and freedom. After being forty years a prisoner, I can tell you that freedom is not a matter of place. It is a condition. Unless one accept dire vicissitudes he will not attain. When one is released from the prison of self, that is indeed a release."[2]

It is noteworthy that 'Abdu'l-Bahá did not comment about the nature of America when gazing at the quintessential symbol of the American republic, but about the nature of true freedom. He commented on a more mundane symbol of America some minutes later, as the ship approached the wharf, but even then, the "rugged sky line" of lower Manhattan's skyscrapers seemed to convey a spiritual message to him: "These are the minarets of Western World commerce and industry, and seem to stretch heavenward in an endeavor to bring about this Universal Peace for which we are all working, for the good of the nations and mankind in general." As he exclaimed to the Bahá'ís later that day, "I am very much pleased with the City of New York. Its entrance, its wharves, the buildings and the broad avenues are all magnificent and beautiful. Truly I say it is a wonderful city. As New York has made wonderful progress in material civilization, I hope that spiritually it may also advance in the realm of God."[3]

When the customs officials boarded the ship, they were accompanied by a group of journalists anxious to be the first to interview 'Abdu'l-Bahá. In the last three decades, Americans had become accustomed to visiting "oriental" teachers. Journalists often found opportunity to focus on the exoticism of foreigners or the strangeness of "heathen" religions. They may have known that he was the head of an independent religion with a substantial following in America, but they would not have known anything about the high station Bahá'u'lláh had given him, his role as authoritative interpreter of Bahá'u'lláh's texts, or his position as the Center of Bahá'u'lláh's Covenant. Even many American Bahá'ís were unaware of these aspects of the Bahá'í teachings. One task 'Abdu'l-Bahá set out to accomplish, over the next few months, was to deepen the Bahá'ís in them.

'Abdu'l-Bahá accommodated the journalists in his stateroom; it was his first of many informal press conferences in America, and they became a standard feature of his arrival in any North American city. His Persian answers to their questions were translated into English by one of his attendants, Ameen Fareed. To the inevitable question of why he had traveled to America's shores, he replied that he had come "to visit the peace societies of America because the fundamental principles of our Cause are universal peace and the promotion of the basic doctrine of the oneness and truth of all the divine religions." He had already been invited to speak to the Lake Mohonk Peace Conference in mid-May, a prestigious annual gathering of peace leaders, as well as thirteen churches and at two Bahá'í conferences. His reply provides a summary of two of the major themes 'Abdu'l-Bahá spoke about again and again: world peace and the oneness of religion. When asked how world peace could ever be achieved, he stressed the impact of the terrible evils of war, giving as examples the destruction wrought by Italy in its ongoing military campaign to wrest Tripolitania from the Ottoman Turks.[4]

A third major theme was prompted by another question: "To be a Bahai simply means to love all the world, to love humanity and to try to serve it; to work for Universal Peace, and the [*sic*] Universal Brotherhood," he explained to a reporter.[5] But lest people think that 'Abdu'l-Bahá's approach to humanity was all love and no substance, his response to a question about women's suffrage was unambiguous, bold, and controversial:

> The modern suffragette is fighting for what must be . . . One might not approve of the ways of some of the more militant suffragettes,

> but in the end it will adjust itself. If women were given the same advantages as men, their capacity being the same, the result would be the same. . . . The world in the past has been ruled by force, and man has dominated over woman by reason of his more forceful and aggressive qualities both of body and mind. But the scales are already shifting—force is losing its weight and mental alertness, intuition, and the spiritual qualities of love and service, in which woman is strong, are gaining ascendancy.[6]

He spoke at length about the importance of educating women and girls. Over the next eight months, 'Abdu'l-Bahá's support of woman's suffrage garnered many headlines. He also offered the reporters some humor, for which he was well known:

> An enquirer, about to set off to Jerusalem, was one day discussing with Abdul-Baha the subject of pilgrimage:
>
> "The proper spirit," said 'Abdul-Baha in his quaint way to the enquirer, "in which to visit places hallowed by remembrances of Christ, is one of constant communion with God. Love for God will be the telegraph wire, one end of which is in the Kingdom of the Spirit, and the other in your heart."
>
> "I am afraid my telegraph wire is broken," the enquirer replied.
>
> "Then you will have to use wireless telegraphy. . ." said Abdul-Baha, laughing heartily.[7]

After the *Cedric* docked, about noontime, the journalists thanked 'Abdu'l-Bahá and left him to file their stories. Mountfort Mills and Howard MacNutt, who were the two-man reception committee in charge of planning his visit, boarded to confer with him. Several hundred Bahá'ís awaited 'Abdu'l-Bahá at the pier, some having traveled hundreds of miles to meet him. A public spectacle seemed inevitable, something 'Abdu'l-Bahá personally disliked and that might lead to sensationalist publicity, so he sent word that the Bahá'ís should depart for the home of Edward and Carrie Kinney, where he would meet them at 4pm. Before disembarking, he distributed gifts to many of the crew who had served him throughout the eighteen-day voyage from Alexandria; 'Abdu'l-Bahá was always a master host, even when he was a guest.

When he disembarked from the *Cedric*, the crowd had dispersed, but a few lingered. Juliet Thompson (1873–1956) was a professional artist and devoted Bahá'í who had made a pilgrimage to Acre to meet 'Abdu'l-Bahá in 1909 and had traveled to France in 1911 to see him there. Her love for 'Abdu'l-Bahá was unbounded. As she reports in her diary,

> Everyone obeyed [the request to leave] at once except Marjorie, Rhoda, and myself! Marjorie, who loves the Teachings but has never wholly accepted them, said "I can't leave till I've seen Him. I *can't.* I WON'T!" So, though we followed the crowd to the street, we slipped away there and looked around for some place to hide. Quite a distance below the big entrance to the pier we saw a fairly deep embrasure into which a window was set, with the stone wall jutting out from it. Here we flattened ourselves against the window, Rhoda (who is conspicuously tall) clasping a long white box of lilies which she had brought for the Master. Just in front of the entrance stood Mr. Mills' car, his chauffeur in it. Suddenly it rolled forward and, to our utter dismay, parked directly in front of us. Now we were caught: certain to be discovered. But there was no help for it, for Marjorie still refused to budge till she had seen the Master.
>
> Then, He *came*—through the entrance with Mr. MacNutt and Mr. Mills, and turned and walked swiftly toward the car. In a panic we waited.

A few nights ago Marjorie and I had a double dream. In her dream, I was out in space with her. In mine, we were in a room together and the Master had just entered it. He walked straight up to Marjorie, put His two hands on her shoulders and pressed and pressed till she sank to her knees. And while she was sinking, she lifted her face to His and everything in her seemed to be dying except her soul, which looked out through her raised eyes in a sort of agony of recognition.

Today, after one glance at the Master, this was just the way she looked.

"Now," she said, I *know*."

As the Master was stepping into the car, He turned and—*smiled* at us.[8]

Mr. Mills drove 'Abdu'l-Bahá and his three companions to the Hotel Ansonia, an elegant, modern seventeen-story apartment hotel at the corner of Broadway and 79th Street, where they checked into a four-room suite on the seventh floor.* After a cup of tea and a rest, they were ready to go to the home of the Kinneys at 780 West End Avenue, on the Upper West Side of Manhattan between Broadway and Riverside Park. The Kinneys were comfortable, though not wealthy, and leased an elegant house. By all accounts, the several hundred visitors strained it to the bursting point.† But it did not matter; "what a wonderful meeting it was!" reported Maḥmúd-

* Maḥmúd-i-Zarqání, *Maḥmúd's Diary,* 38, says he was on the seventh floor, but Kate Carew, in the *New York Tribune,* May 5, 1912, says he was on the fifth floor, room 111.

† Juliet Thompson, in her diary, p. 234, says "several hundred" attended, but the *New York Sun,* April 12, 1912, reports that three hundred were in the Kinney home, and the *New York World,* April 12, 1912, says 150. The house had about 1,300 square feet on the first floor, consequently people would have been packed pretty tightly together.

i-Zarqání (c. 1875–1924). "The friends* were so full of joy and happiness that it seemed the very walls were immersed in rapture and ecstasy." Howard Colby Ives, a Unitarian minister at the Brotherhood Church in Jersey City, New Jersey, and a friend of the Bahá'í Faith,† left this account:

> The press of eager friends [Bahá'ís] and curious ones was so great that it was difficult even to get inside the doors. I have only the memory of an impressive silence most unusual at such functions. In all that crowded mass of folk, so wedged together that tea drinking was almost an impossibility, though the attempt was made, there was little or no speech. A whispered word; a remark implying awe or love, was all. I strove to get where I could at least see Him. All but impossible. At last I managed to press forward where I could peep over a shoulder and so got my first glimpse of 'Abdu'l-Bahá. He was seated. A cream colored fez upon His head from under which white hair flowed almost to His shoulders. His robe, what little I could see of it, was oriental, almost white. But these were incidentals to which I could pay little attention. The impressive thing, and what I have never forgotten, was an indefinable aspect of majesty combined with exquisite courtesy. He was just in the moment of accepting a cup of tea from the hostess. Such gentleness, such love emanated from Him as I have never seen. Remember that at that time I had no conviction, almost, I might say, little or no interest in what I came later to understand by

* The use of "friends" to refer to Bahá'ís is a common one and is a translation of various Arabic and Persian terms rather than a borrowing of Quaker practice.

† Ives later became a Bahá'í.

the term His "station." I was an onlooker at a scene concerning the significance of which I was totally ignorant.[9]*

Juliet Thompson's recollection was of crying, not of silence:

He was sitting in the center of the dining room near a table strewn with flowers. He wore a light pongee 'abá. At his knees stood the Kinney children, Sanford and Howard, and His arms were around them. He was white and shining. No words could describe His ineffable peace. The people stood about in rows and circles—several hundred in the big rooms, which all open into each other. In the dining room many sat on the floor, Marjorie and I included. We made a dark background for His glory. Only our tears reflected Him, and almost everyone there was weeping just at the sight of Him. For at last we saw divinity incarnate. Divinely He turned His head from one child to the other, one group to another. I wish I could picture that turn of the head—an oh, so tender turn, with that indescribable heavenly grace caught by Leonardo da Vinci in his Christ of the Last Supper (in the study for the head)—but in 'Abdu'l-Bahá irradiated by smiles

* A map of the Kinneys' neighborhood made in 1898–99 can be found in the New York Public Library and is digitized (accessed January 23, 2011). It shows a house of about 1,300 square feet per floor located on a 19-foot-11 inch by 100-foot lot with a back yard about twenty-four feet long. Juliet Thompson says the first floor was "open the entire length of the house" (*Diary of Juliet Thompson,* 371), so the entire space would have been available that day. It is feasible that 250 or 300 people could fit into such a house and they would be packed so tightly that it was hard to drink tea without having one's cup jostled, as Ives reports. I am grateful to Eric Kreitzer for finding the map for me.

> and a lifting of those eyes filled with glory, which even Leonardo, for all his mystery, could not have painted. The very essence of compassion, the most poignant tenderness is in that turn of the head.[10]

The crush was difficult on everyone, and the house became quite warm, so 'Abdu'l-Bahá spoke for only a few minutes:

> How are you? Welcome! Welcome!
>
> After arriving today, although weary with travel, I had the utmost longing and yearning to see you and could not resist this meeting. Now that I have met you, all my weariness has vanished, for your meeting is the cause of spiritual happiness.
>
> I was in Egypt and was not feeling well, but I wished to come to you in America. My friends said, "This is a long journey; the sea is wide; you should remain here." But the more they advised and insisted, the greater became my longing to take this trip, and now I have come to America to meet the friends of God. This long voyage will prove how great is my love for you. There were many troubles and vicissitudes, but, in the thought of meeting you, all these things vanished and were forgotten. . . . As New York has made such progress in material civilization, I hope that it may also advance spiritually in the Kingdom and Covenant of God so that the friends here may become the cause of the illumination of America, that this city may become the city of love and that the fragrances of God may be spread from this place to all parts of the world. I have come for this. . . I am very happy to meet you all here today. Praise be to God that your faces are shining with the love of Bahá'u'lláh. To behold them is the cause of great spiritual happiness. We have arranged to meet you every day at the homes of the friends. . . .

> I will see you again. Now I will greet each one of you personally. It is my hope that you will all be happy and that we may meet again and again.[11]

With that, the formal meeting ended. 'Abdu'l-Bahá greeted people—especially the children—for quite a while, then said good-bye and returned to his hotel. The New York Bahá'ís had had their first memorable encounter with the one they called "the Master." Some non-Bahá'ís, like Ives, had perceived something extraordinary in the face and bearing of the head of the Bahá'í Faith. The adulation from the sober businessmen, pensive seekers, and starry-eyed artists must have presented a fascinating but puzzling sight. As Ives wrote, "What was it that these people around me had which gave to their eyes such illumination, to their hearts such gladness? . . . I did not know, but I wanted to know as I think I had never known the want of before."[12]

2

"MY INVITATION TO AMERICA WILL BE THE UNITY OF THE BELIEVERS"

"The Master" who so intrigued New Yorkers that day had been, in effect, a Bahá'í all his life. He was born on the evening of May 22, 1844, in Tehran, the capital of Persia. At about the same time, in the southern Iranian city of Shiraz, a young siyyid—a descendant of the Prophet Muḥammad—was announcing to a man who was to become His first disciple that He was the Promised One of Islam, sent by God to deliver a new revelation to humanity. The siyyid took on the title of the Báb (the Gate) and gradually proclaimed His message, in spite of fierce opposition by the Iranian clergy. A religion was born that night, as well as a baby boy, who was given the name *'Abbás*. (The title *'Abdu'l-Bahá* was not to be introduced for another forty-eight years.)

One of the Báb's early followers was an aristocrat from northern Iran named Mírzá Ḥusayn-'Alí (1817–92), the father of New York's future illustrious visitor. When the baby was just a few months old, Ḥusayn-'Alí accepted the Báb and dedicated His energies and prestige to the propagation of the Bábí Faith.* He immediately emerged as one of the most prominent Bábí leaders. The boy was four when His father took the title of *Bahá'u'lláh* ("The Glory of God"), by which He was to be known the rest of His life. When 'Abbás was six, the Báb was executed by firing squad, and the Bábí Faith torn apart by fierce persecution. When 'Abbás was eight, Bahá'u'lláh was thrown in an underground prison, the Black Pit, for four months, where He had a revelatory experience that marked the beginning of His mission.

In 1853—before 'Abbás's ninth birthday—Bahá'u'lláh led His family out of Iran to an involuntary exile in Baghdad. The boy acquired whatever education he could in his studious but impoverished household. In his late teens, he emerged as his father's chief assistant and ambassador. Ten years later, the almost nineteen-year-old 'Abbás witnessed his father publicly declare Himself a divine Messenger and the Promised One to succeed the Báb. Over the next decade, most of the scattered and persecuted Bábís became Bahá'ís, followers of Bahá'u'lláh.

The Ottoman Turkish government, displeased by the growth of what they viewed as an Islamic heresy, exiled Bahá'u'lláh and His family from Baghdad to a series of other cities, eventually settling them in Acre, a pestilential prison-city on the Mediterranean coast in what today is northern Israel. There, 'Abbás greeted Bahá'í pilgrims, met with government officials, and handled family affairs. Early on, Bahá'u'lláh commanded family and followers to call 'Abbás *Áqá*, an honorific that was translated into English as *the Master*. He often referred to him in writings as *the Most Great Branch*. In Bahá'u'lláh's copious writings—over eighteen thousand unique works

* An eloquent account of Bahá'u'lláh's conversion to the Bábí Faith is presented in David Ruhe, *Robe of Light: The Persian Years of the Supreme Prophet Bahá'u'lláh, 1817–1853* (Oxford: George Ronald, 1994), 60–62.

are extant—which outlined in great detail His teachings, He designated the Most Great Branch His successor and delegated to him the authority to lead the Faith and interpret Bahá'u'lláh's own revelation.[1]

The Ministry of 'Abdu'l-Bahá, 1892–1921

Bahá'u'lláh passed away on the night of May 29, 1892, at age seventy-four, leaving 'Abbás as head of the Bahá'í Faith. To designate his complete servitude to Bahá'u'lláh, he took the title of *'Abdu'l-Bahá*, which means *servant of Bahá*. One of his first acts as head of the Faith was to oversee the efforts of a Lebanese Christian convert to the Bahá'í Faith, Ibrahim Kheiralla, to teach the Bahá'í Faith in the United States. Kheiralla had left for the West just weeks after Bahá'u'lláh's passing; by 1894, five Americans had become Bahá'ís in Chicago.

While the vast majority of Bahá'ís immediately accepted 'Abdu'l-Bahá as head of the Bahá'í Faith, his half brother, Muḥammad-'Alí, became intensely jealous, intrigued against 'Abdu'l-Bahá, sought to undermine his authority, and built up a small following. He spread falsehoods about 'Abdu'l-Bahá to government officials that caused them to order, in August 1901, that he remain confined to the city of Acre. At first, 'Abdu'l-Bahá said nothing about his half brother's disloyalty, but in order to protect the Bahá'ís from disunity, he began to educate them about the written Covenant that Bahá'u'lláh left to the Bahá'ís following His passing. The requirements of this Covenant explicitly included obedience to 'Abdu'l-Bahá and indicated that anyone opposing him was breaking the Covenant, an act with grave spiritual consequences. The Iranian Bahá'í community, in consequence, ignored Muḥammad-'Alí and the few Covenant-breakers who followed him. The early American Bahá'í community, which numbered some 1,500 by 1899, was soon caught up in the conflict as Kheiralla, sensing that he would be given greater leadership authority by Muḥammad-'Alí, turned away from 'Abdu'l-Bahá and broke the Covenant.

While some American Bahá'ís followed Kheiralla, most recognized that personal ambition was his chief motive and rejected him. From 1899 to 1904, 'Abdu'l-Bahá sent a series of four Persian teachers to the United States to deepen the community's understanding of Bahá'u'lláh's teachings, which heretofore had been limited by lack of translated texts and experienced believers. They explained Bahá'u'lláh's Covenant and 'Abdu'l-Bahá's position as Center of the Covenant. Muḥammad-'Alí sent his son, Shua Ullah Behai, to America to help Kheiralla, but 'Abdu'l-Bahá told the American Bahá'ís to ignore him, which the vast majority did. Until 'Abdu'l-Bahá's arrival in America stirred Kheiralla and Shua Ullah to action, they had sunk into obscurity. Many American Bahá'ís knew nothing about them.

While the Bahá'í communities of Kenosha, Wisconsin, and Chicago did not recover the numbers they had lost over the next decade, New York did. Cincinnati, Philadelphia, the San Francisco Bay area, and Hudson County, New Jersey continued to grow. New communities were established in Baltimore; Boston; Buffalo; Cleveland; Denver; Eliot, Maine; Los Angeles; Milwaukee; Minneapolis-St. Paul; Montreal; Muskegon, Michigan; Portland; Seattle; Spokane; and Washington, D.C.

Some 110 books, articles, and pamphlets about the Bahá'í Faith—including thirty-six scriptural works, twenty-two introductory works, and nineteen pilgrims' notes*—were published in English between 1900 and 1911, providing the growing community with a rich literature.† Bahá'í

* Pilgrim's notes are records of 'Abdu'l-Bahá's utterances. Unless 'Abdu'l-Bahá subsequently reviewed the notes for accuracy—which he rarely did—they are not considered authoritative statements of the Bahá'í teachings, nor are they Bahá'í scripture.

† A bibliography of Bahá'í publications, 1896–1912, appears in Stockman, *The Bahá'í Faith in America, vol. 2,* 418–27.

holy days came to be understood and commemorated starting in 1901, the nineteen-day Feast* was begun by 'Abdu'l-Bahá and spread to North America by 1907, and Bahá'í hymns—both original works and modifications of Protestant classics—were published as early as 1903. 'Abdu'l-Bahá directed American Bahá'ís to travel to Iran, Central Asia, India, and Burma to teach the Faith, and to settle in Germany and Iran. He called on Americans to elect local consultative bodies but left the details—how many members to elect, how often to elect them, and the procedures to follow in the electing—to the local American communities.

In 1903, 'Abdu'l-Bahá approved Chicago's request to build a House of Worship and gently turned down other similar requests so that everyone would back Chicago's effort, converting it into a national project that culminated in 1909 in the election of the Bahai Temple Unity, a North American-elected Bahá'í consultative body. The arrival of American Bahá'í women in Iran to provide educational and medical services—whose presence tended to underline emphatically the Bahá'í principle of equality of women and men—helped to prompt the Washington, D.C. Bahá'ís to organize the Persian American Educational Society, a nonprofit organization that funneled American expertise and funds to Iranian Bahá'í schools and clinics.[2] American Bahá'ís gave scholarships so that poor Persian Bahá'í children could go to Bahá'í schools in Iran; at the same time, Persian Bahá'ís donated money to help build the Bahá'í House of Worship being planned in Wilmette, Illinois, twelve miles from downtown

* 'Abdu'l-Bahá inaugurated a "Feast" once per Bahá'í month—which has nineteen days—where Bahá'ís gather for a devotional program and socializing. Discussion of community business was added as a third portion of Feast by Shoghi Effendi in the 1920s. Bahá'ís do not customarily gather for a weekly devotional service the way churches do.

Chicago. The financial exchanges built ties between these two very different communities—one of Muslim cultural background, the other of Christian origin—and helped them gradually get to know each other and collaborate. American and Persian Bahá'ís rubbed shoulders in Acre when they went on pilgrimage to pray at Bahá'u'lláh's shrine, see the places associated with His life there, and meet 'Abdu'l-Bahá.

In spite of his confinement to the walled city of Acre, 'Abdu'l-Bahá maintained a steady correspondence involving thousands of letters to the American Bahá'ís and continued to receive pilgrims. Many hoped that 'Abdu'l-Bahá would move to the United States, where he would be free; in 1901, the Chicago Bahá'í governing council even organized a "supplication," which was signed by 370 Bahá'ís, inviting him to move to the United States permanently. But 'Abdu'l-Bahá rejected the offer and remained in Acre, where he could protect the Faith's sacred texts, holy places, and relics.[3]

In the summer of 1908, however, the Young Turks Revolution liberated all political prisoners. 'Abdu'l-Bahá was now a free man. He did not leave the Holy Land because he had a major project to complete; on the northern slope of Mount Carmel, he had begun constructing a mausoleum for the remains of the Báb, which had been transferred to Acre secretly from Iran years before and concealed in his sister's room. On March 21, 1909, with the basic form of the mausoleum complete, he was able to inter the Báb's remains. Over the next year, he ensured the continuity of many aspects of his work in his absence, so that on August 29, 1910, he was able to leave Acre for Egypt.

'Abdu'l-Bahá's Travels to Egypt and the Occident, 1910–11

The plan was to remain in Egypt a month and then head for Europe, but 'Abdu'l-Bahá needed more time to rest; forty-two years of imprisonment and house arrest, interrogations, the immense pressure of running an international religious community, and the stress of dealing with malicious relatives had taken their toll. Furthermore, the trip proved not to be as restful as expected, as this item from the April 28, 1911, issue of *Star of the West* indicated:

> A daily newspaper, *The Valley of the Nile,* in its issue of March 22nd, presents a full page concerning the life and teachings of Abdul-Baha. It is a noteworthy fact that all the prominent people of Egypt are beginning to feel his spiritual presence and call upon him to receive instruction. The news of the looking forward of the American Bahais to the coming of Abdul-Baha to that country has reached here [Egypt] and it is hoped that all the friends may attain to this blessing and that the Center of the Covenant may travel to the West. Not only are the American Bahais anxious to have Abdul-Baha in their midst, but the friends of every country are supplicating him to visit them. Now that he is free the believers are not satisfied with Tablets and Messages, but they long to have him personally.[4]

The Egyptian Bahá'ís wanted to meet him, the newspapers wanted to interview him, and notables sought his company. Even Europeans met him; Major Wellesley Tudor Pole (1884–1968), a British aristocrat, became a Bahá'í or a close sympathizer, and the Russian-Polish playwright Izabella Grinevskaia visited him. As a result, 'Abdu'l-Bahá stayed almost a year, first in Port Said, then Alexandria, then Cairo.

As the article above notes, 'Abdu'l-Bahá's departure for Egypt stirred hopes that he would visit North America. Not all were in favor; Agnes Parsons (1861–1934) notes that some American Bahá'ís felt "it would be very incongruous for Him to visit this western country. That this would be a very inappropriate setting for Him."[5] Presumably they imagined a cynical press and indifferent public poking fun at his robes, oriental mannerisms, and foreign ways of speaking. But some Bahá'ís wrote, begging him to come. In December 1910, in a tablet to "the members of the Assembly of Bahais of America," 'Abdu'l-Bahá said that after "our purpose is realized" in Egypt, "perhaps We shall journey to other parts." But he added that

> If the beloved of God in all America strive for unity and harmony, attain perfect love and accord, and act according to the divine teachings and the precepts of the Blessed Perfection [Bahá'u'lláh], this will prove a magnet attracting Abdul-Baha so that perchance He may journey to America.
>
> But, until . . . all the believers in America become united and harmonious, My coming to America will be hindered, nay, impossible.[6]

The Bahá'ís in Washington, D.C. spearheaded a nationwide effort during the 1911 Bahá'í fast (March 2–20) asking the Bahá'ís to pray a certain prayer and sign a "supplication" inviting 'Abdu'l-Bahá to come to America. More than 850 sent their signatures to the Bahá'ís of Washington, who forwarded them to 'Abdu'l-Bahá.[7] Non-Bahá'ís wrote letters as well; Russell Conwell, the chief pastor of Baptist Temple in Philadelphia, had met 'Abdu'l-Bahá in Acre in 1906 and cabled him while he was in Egypt, inviting him to speak in his church. Aware that he might be traveling to America in the future, in August 1911, 'Abdu'l-Bahá initiated correspondence with Mr. Albert Smiley, the founder of the Lake Mohonk Conference on International Arbitration:

> The details of the Conference of Peace and Arbitration which is organized under your presidency has been read in the papers of the

East and the West and the utmost joy and fragrance was produced; that, praise be to God, in the continent of America, under the presidency of a glorious personage, the Conference of International Peace is convened. . . . Therefore, although this longing one has no acquaintance with your honor, but this great cause and this eminent effort of yours became the cause of my having infinite love for you while absent. Consequently I am engaged in writing you this epistle. . . . To be brief, as His Highness Baha'o'llah in this period of man has planted a fruitful tree in the garden of the oneness of the human race, and as your honor is engaged in reality to irrigate this garden, therefore I found it necessary to express my gratitude and happiness to you, so that your good name may be spread not only in Persia but throughout all Oriental countries and the people of the East may remember your name with great respect. I hope that the principles of international peace and universal reconciliation may be established firmly among the individual members of humanity and its fragrance may be spread throughout all the regions.

I beg of you to accept the expressions of my highest consideration.[8]

Clearly, 'Abdu'l-Bahá was preparing for the trip as well. To make sure the American Bahá'ís prepared for him, he wrote several tablets in response to the letters he received. In April, 1911, he replied to the supplication in a tablet to the Bahá'ís of America:

. . . . Now Abdul Baha . . . has hastened to the country of Egypt . . . . All the newspapers wrote innumerable articles. Some gave the utmost praise; others raised a great cry, saying: "The arrival of this personage in this land will shake the pillars of Religion and will shatter to pieces ancient customs and conventions. He attracts every one he meets and when he loosens his tongue in any meeting, it creates faith in the hearts of the deniers." The papers are still writing detailed articles and will continue to do so.

Now the friends and the maid-servants in America have written innumerable letters and all of them are pleading that Abdu'l-Baha make a trip to that country. Their supplications and entreaties are insistent. In view of the difference among the friends and the lack of unity among the maid-servants of the Merciful, how can Abdul-Baha hasten to those parts? Is this possible? No, by God!

If the friends and the maid-servants of the Merciful long for the visit of Abdu'l-Baha, they must immediately remove from their midst differences of opinion and be engaged in the practice of infinite love and unity. No Bahai must open his lips in blaming another one, he must regard backbiting as the greatest sin of humanity, for it is clearly revealed in all the Tablets of Baha'o'llah that backbiting and faultfinding are the fiendish instruments and suggestions of Satan and the destroyers of the foundation of man. A believer will not blame any soul among the strangers, how much less against the friends. Faultfinding and backbiting are the characteristics of the weak minds and not the friends. . . . If ye are yearning for my meeting, and if in reality ye are seeking my visit, ye must close the doors of difference and open the gates of affection, love and friendship. Ye must pulsate as one heart, and throb as one spirit. . . .

Verily, verily, I say unto you, were it not for this difference amongst you, the inhabitants of America in all those regions would have, by now, been attracted to the Kingdom of God, and would have constituted themselves your helpers and assisters. . . .

I beg of God to confirm you in union and concord that you may become the cause of the oneness of the kingdom of humanity. Live and act in accord with the Divine Teachings, be abstracted from all

> the attachments of the human world, characterized with merciful characteristics, release yourselves from the nether world, become heavenly souls, spiritual beings and the angels of Paradise.[9]

To another Bahá'í, he added a practical concern:

> Thou hast invited me to America . . . . I have the utmost yearning to meet all of you; but unless the conditions which have been previously mentioned are realized, my trip to those parts would be difficult, for it would produce no results.[10]

Disunity among the American Bahá'ís would indeed undermine his message—it was primarily a message of unity, after all—and would turn off inquirers. The American Bahá'ís were not split into competing organizations—unlike the Theosophists and many other new religious movements—nor did they have discernible factions, nor were there subgroups with names. There were, however, clear dissonant tendencies. On the one hand, there were Bahá'ís who understood and followed the distinctive Bahá'í practices: reciting the obligatory prayers, fasting during the March fasting period, attending Bahá'í worship programs (which were often weekly, on Sunday), voting in Bahá'í elections, and serving on the elected Bahá'í consultative bodies and their committees. A few, aware of the Bahá'í law against consumption of alcohol, even gave up alcoholic beverages.*

* Bahá'u'lláh revealed three daily obligatory prayers, of which the individual is to choose one to recite daily. Two of them were published in an American Bahá'í prayer book, with limited explanation about their use, in 1905 (see Stockman, *The Bahá'í Faith in America, Early Expansion, 1900–1912,* vol. 2, 235). The Bahá'í fast involves abstinence from all eating and drinking from sunrise to sunset from March 2 through

On the other hand, there were Bahá'ís who viewed Bahá'u'lláh's revelation as providing the world with a new antisectarian spirit that could reform and leaven existing religious and political institutions. The teachings were guidelines for reforming the world, and 'Abdu'l-Bahá was the exemplar of such teachings. Such Bahá'ís tended to oppose the organization of local Bahá'í communities on the grounds that organization would kill the Bahá'í spirit or separate Bahá'ís from churches and other spiritual organizations; they complained about the sectarian spirit of Bahá'í hymns; they advocated maintaining ties with churches and metaphysical groups. Some of them mixed Bahá'í teachings with metaphysical ideas, such as channeling guidance from the next world.[11] Some looked at practices like obligatory prayer and fasting as unfortunate holdovers from Islam.

Many Bahá'ís were uncommitted to these two tendencies; some may even have been unaware of them, because many Bahá'ís were isolated geographically, had access to little of the literature, or had been adherents a short period of time. In addition to these two tendencies, there were also personal clashes among various Bahá'ís, who often had unconventional or individualistic personalities, which could disrupt unity as much as arguments over the teachings and their application.*

March 20. A few American Bahá'ís were fasting as early as 1903, and in 1906, 486 Bahá'ís sent a supplication to 'Abdu'l-Bahá noting that they were fasting during the fasting period (see ibid., 108–9). The prohibition of alcohol consumption was followed by some American Bahá'ís by 1907 (see ibid., 255–56) but was not widely known for three more decades.

* Juliet Thompson tells how one Bahá'í went all the way to Thonon, France, to complain to 'Abdu'l-Bahá about Howard MacNutt, a prominent New York Bahá'í. Before the complainant had a chance to say anything, 'Abdu'l-Bahá asked her to convey a message to the New York Bahá'ís about the utmost importance of harmony, unity, and love among them. This made it impossible for her to deliver her complaint. See Thompson, *The Diary of Juliet Thompson,* 181–83.

A love of and devotion to 'Abdu'l-Bahá was central to the experience of being a Bahá'í, and this tended to submerge disagreements about other matters. As many as could afford it took the expensive trip to Acre to meet him, a trip that typically took at least two months and might yield only three or four days with the Master. They invariably returned with incredible stories of his love, kindness, concern for the poor, and spiritual discernment. They told their stories in Bahá'í meetings and published them in the form of literature called pilgrim's notes, which were eagerly read by others. Their narratives shaped the ways 'Abdu'l-Bahá was received and perceived in America; for example, newspaper articles often refer to him as a Prophet (often with a capital P) of the biblical sort, unlike teachers from South Asia. His white beard and Middle Eastern clothing reinforced this impression.

Those unable to travel to Acre wrote letters to 'Abdu'l-Bahá; by 1912, he may have written as many as three thousand letters (called *tablets*) to American Bahá'ís, advising them about personal difficulties, revealing prayers for them to say, naming their children (for sometimes Bahá'ís made such requests), resolving disputes between believers, clarifying misunderstandings about the Bahá'í teachings, and urging them to dedicate themselves to the Faith and teach it to others. He advised larger Bahá'í communities to organize a *mahfil-i-rawhání* (spiritual assembly), but there was uncertainty over the meaning of the term—even how to translate it—opposition to organization in general, and opposition to the election of women—who were the majority of the community members—to Bahá'í consultative bodies. Consequently, 'Abdu'l-Bahá's advice often wasn't implemented, and if it was, the resulting body had limited authority. 'Abdu'l-Bahá rarely called on the American Bahá'ís to recite the obligatory prayers or to fast; he left the observance of these practices for a future time.

Before 'Abdu'l-Bahá left Egypt for Europe, he is not known to have written to the European Bahá'ís calling on them to be unified, as he had to the Americans. His one tablet to the British Bahá'ís, dated May 9, 1911, was filled with encouragement and praise and said nothing about a visit. Europe's Bahá'í communities were vastly smaller than America's. Stuttgart had perhaps two score Bahá'ís, London and Paris a dozen each, Manchester a handful. There were no Bahá'í elected consultative bodies at all. It is not known whether any of the European Bahá'ís said the obligatory prayers, fasted, or observed the Bahá'í holy days or the nineteen-day Feast (which were fairly widespread in the United States after 1907).* Lil Abdo's doctoral dissertation on the British Bahá'ís makes it clear that they were more firmly embedded in churches and social reform movements than the American Bahá'ís and generally did not regard Bahá'u'lláh as establishing a separate religion. Thus 'Abdu'l-Bahá's European visit occurred under very different circumstances than his later trip to North America.[12]

Departing Alexandria on August 11, 1911, he arrived in Marseilles and traveled to Hotel du Parc, located in the French resort town of Thonon-les-Bains on the southern shore of Lake Geneva, by August 21. There he received a steady stream of American, French, and Persian visitors. The Americans included Juliet Thompson, whose diary provides a valuable and enthusiastic window into his New York sojourn, and Horace Holley, a new Bahá'í of great talent whose commitment to the Faith was greatly strengthened by meeting him. Hippolyte Dreyfus and Laura Dreyfus-Barney, two of Europe's most dedicated Bahá'ís—who both spoke Persian and had translated many Bahá'í works into English and French—met with 'Abdu'l-Bahá to help plan the next steps of his journey. Persian visitors included Zillu's-Sultán, eldest son of Náṣiri'd-Dín-S͟háh, Iran's late king,

* The spread of the nineteen-day Feast in the United States is described in Stockman, *The Bahá'í Faith in America,* vol. 2, 244–47.

now in exile in nearby Geneva, Switzerland. Zillu's-Sultán had been responsible for the deaths of many Bahá'ís, including the King of Martyrs and the Beloved of Martyrs, two famous and devoted Bahá'ís. He mumbled "miserable excuses," but 'Abdu'l-Bahá forgave him and invited him to bring his two sons and spend the day, which he did.[13]

Departing Thonon-les-Bains, 'Abdu'l-Bahá took a train to London, arriving on September 4. His month-long stay in Britain included his first public talk in the West on Sunday, September 10, in London's City Temple, a nonconformist congregationalist church that was a center of many progressive causes, including women's suffrage and socialism. 'Abdu'l-Bahá's presentation after the sermon was brief—just eight minutes—and unannounced. Over two thousand were present.[14] His talk in St. John's Church, Westminster, was covered by *The Christian Commonwealth,* a progressive Protestant periodical edited by members of City Temple. On that occasion, he was introduced by the pastor, Albert Basil Orme Wilberforce (1841–1916), Canon of Westminster Abbey and Chaplain to the House of Commons. A grandson of William Wilberforce, one of the chief campaigners for the abolition of slavery and the slave trade, he inherited an involvement in liberal causes such as temperance and women's suffrage and had an interest in Eastern religions and spiritualism.

'Abdu'l-Bahá also traveled briefly to Bristol for a stay at the Clifton Guest House, a hotel owned by the family of Wellesley Tudor Pole. Nearly every day, a large crowd flocked to visit him at the house of Mrs. Sara Louisa Blomfield, where he stayed in London. "In all the arrangements for the comfort of the numerous guests, Miss Beatrice Platt, Dr. Lutfullah Hakim, and my daughters, Mary and Ellinor, were occupied from morning till night," Mrs. Blomfield states in her book about his visit. "They also took notes of the addresses of 'Abdu'l-Bahá, and made appointments for interviews with Him."[15] The visitors included

> ministers and missionaries, Oriental scholars and occult students, practical men of affairs and mystics, Anglican-Catholics and Nonconformists, Theosophists and Hindus, Christian Scientists and doctors of medicine, Muslims, Buddhists, and Zoroastrians. There also called: politicians, Salvation Army soldiers, and other workers for human good, women suffragists, journalists, writers, poets, and healers, dressmakers and great ladies, artists and artisans, poor workless people and prosperous merchants, members of the dramatic and musical world, these all came; and none were too lowly, nor too great, to receive the sympathetic consideration of this holy Messenger, who was ever giving His life for others' good.[16]

Among them was Annie Besant (1847–1933), head of the Theosophical Society, who invited 'Abdu'l-Bahá to address the society at its London headquarters. He also addressed the Brahmo-Somaj and the Muslim community, the latter at the Woking Mosque. He met Emmeline Pankhurst (1858–1928), founder of a militant suffrage movement that used prison hunger strikes and eventually arson to win votes for women; he assured her that "women would very shortly take their rightful place in the world," though he did not approve of her tactics.[17]

'Abdu'l-Bahá left London for Paris on October 3. His Paris sojourn lasted two months and was the first of three visits to that city, which would be his residence longer than any other Western locality. He soon rented a flat at 4 avenue de Camoëns, a short walk from the Eiffel Tower. The Theosophical Society invited him to speak, and it was there, in October 1911, when he gave a talk listing ten Bahá'í principles, one of his first talks with that approach to explaining the Faith. He left Paris for Egypt on December 2. Many Americans had hoped he would come straight to North America, but 'Abdu'l-Bahá contemplated "a long visit" to Washington, Chicago, "even to

California."[18] For that, he needed some rest and time to prepare for the trip properly. He did not leave Egypt for New York until March 25, 1912.

Before 'Abdu'l-Bahá left France for Egypt, he told Ahmad Sohrab, a young Bahá'í serving as his secretary and interpreter, who had already lived in the United States for a decade, to return to America and help prepare for his arrival. "The forces are gathering and when Abdul Baha arrives in America He will have such a reception . . . as to astonish the world," predicted Sohrab. He listed seven invitations 'Abdu'l-Bahá had already received:

> The Society of Ethical Culture with Felix Adler President has invited the Master. Isn't that wonderful! . . . 2d. New York Peace Society (the strongest and the most influential society that today exists). 3d International Peace Forum. . . 6th Mayor of Boston. 7th the Japanese Peace Society Newyork [*sic*], etc. Now don't you think that is a good showing? I have tablets [letters from 'Abdu'l-Bahá] and autographed photographs of Abdul Baha for these people and will have personal interviews with all of them. . . . I am really astonished beyond belief how God has opened these doors. . . . We are going to have a harvest time.[19]

Asian Teachers in America

Sohrab was under the impression that 'Abdu'l-Bahá's reception would be unprecedented, perhaps because his spiritual station and his status as the first head of an independent religion to visit America were unique. But at least three prominent "Oriental" teachers had preceded him to America, all of whom served as leaders or spokesmen of Hindu or Buddhist groups, as well as a dozen less well known Asian savants. Their travels shaped the expectations that Americans had about Asian religious visitors such as

'Abdu'l-Bahá and explains why he was sometimes compared to "swamis." The places they visited, the audiences they spoke to, and the subjects they addressed also illuminate 'Abdu'l-Bahá's sojourn.

The first major figure was Protap Chunder Mozoomdar (1840–1905), a prominent figure in the Brahmo Samaj, an important early Hindu nationalist movement. Mozoomdar visited the same parts of the country as 'Abdu'l-Bahá—New England, New York, Washington, D.C., greater Chicago, and San Francisco—between August 28 and November 24, 1883, a trip of about a third the duration of 'Abdu'l-Bahá's. Mozoomdar spoke in over sixty Unitarian churches and a few Congregationalist churches, a narrowly focused audience. The purpose of his trip was to raise awareness of India's needs, partly to seek funds for Brahmo charitable efforts, and to correct misunderstandings about Hinduism. He did not seek to establish a Hindu movement in the United States. He frequently spoke about Jesus, for he had just published a highly respectful book about Him from a Hindu perspective, *The Oriental Christ*.[20]

On his second American trip, Mozoomdar spoke at the World's Parliament of Religions in Chicago in September 1893 about Hinduism and the Brahmo Somaj, then went to Indianapolis, Buffalo, Boston, New York City, and Washington, reportedly delivering over two hundred talks in three months.[21] He returned to the United States for five weeks in May and June 1900, mostly visiting Unitarian churches and organizations in Massachusetts, though he also traveled to New York City and Washington, D.C. He spoke at the American Unitarian Association annual conference in Boston, just as 'Abdu'l-Bahá did in 1912.

Anagarika Dharmapala (1864–1933), the emerging main spokesman for Buddhism in the British colony of Ceylon (modern Sri Lanka), spoke at the Parliament and went on a three-month tour of the United States, to which he returned in 1896–97. Dharmapala raised money for Buddhist schools and stimulated interest in Buddhism, which was already on the rise as a result of books about the tradition, a journal started by an American convert, and lectures about it. Dharmapala's second U.S. trip included meditation classes for up to several hundred people at once.[22]

Soyen Shaku, a Japanese Zen master, followed his time at the Parliament with a series of tours of the United States, and he encouraged several of his students, notably D. T. Suzuki, to lecture in America as well, thereby creating a number of Buddhist sympathizers. Paul Carus, an Illinois scientific naturalist, published books about religions and included many articles about it in his journal, *Open Court*. One observer estimated that about the year 1900, "at most a thousand or two" Americans were "engaged in a conversation" about Buddhism. But only two were formally inducted into a lay Buddhist order.[23] It was a small start for formally organized Buddhism in America; much smaller than the effects of 'Abdu'l-Bahá's visit on the American Bahá'ís.

Best known is Swami Vivekananda (1863–1902), head of the Rama Krishna Mission, a Hindu organization. He spoke repeatedly at the Parliament and crisscrossed the United States for two and a half years, lecturing on Hinduism, critiquing "Christian civilization," and criticizing missionaries for attempting to Christianize India. Vivekananda's aggressive speaking style, his eloquent English accented with a slight brogue, and his impressive education in Western philosophy made him a formidable and controversial speaker, which may explain why his travels in the United States are described by scholars of religion more than anyone else's, and why the word "swami" entered the vocabulary of Americans. Vivekananda spoke to opera house audiences, women's clubs, and Unitarian churches. Unlike 'Abdu'l-Bahá, he was rarely invited to speak in a mainline Protestant place of worship; he criticized them too frankly. He often sold tickets to his talks to cover his own traveling costs—he had no money and no sponsors—and to raise money for the Ramakrishna Mission's schools, orphanages, and poor relief efforts, for the Mission was actively involved in social and economic development efforts.

Vivekananda created a community of American converts, the Vedanta Society. The group had perhaps a hundred members when he left America. The early followers were nearly all wealthy, educated, European Americans (in contrast to the Bahá'ís, who were drawn from the middle and working classes as well). The Vedantists suffered from internal controversies that sometimes shattered their unity; their membership of 190 in 1916 was less than half the membership reported in 1906. A few Bahá'ís had connections with the Vedanta Society, but 'Abdu'l-Bahá was never invited to speak to any of their groups. However, the larger liberal "post-Protestant" religious groups—in 1916 the United States had 86,000 Unitarians, 29,000 Spiritualists, and 5,400 Theosophists—were interested in his message.[24]

Creating a Bahá'í Community in America, 1894–1912

Mozoomdar, Dharmapala, and Vivekananda were largely dependent on the Unitarians for an audience, funding, and logistical support. This was not true of 'Abdu'l-Bahá. His audience was much broader and included Congregationalists, Universalists, Methodists, Episcopalians, northern Baptists, and Reform Jews. The American Bahá'ís raised $16,000 to cover the cost of his North American trip, but he returned the money and consistently refused all offers of financial assistance while in the Occident.[25] He received a steady flow of contributions from the Bahá'ís of Iran and the Middle East, enabling him to cover the travel expenses of himself and his entourage—which sometimes included as many as eight others—and make contributions to churches and charities. Logistical support was available in the form of a very active American Bahá'í community, comprising between 1,000 and 2,500 members in 1912—depending on whether one counted only the actively committed or included those who occasionally participated in Bahá'í events—and located in at least twenty-five communities in fifteen states, the District of Columbia, and one Canadian province. Some had been Bahá'ís as long as eighteen years; over one hundred had met 'Abdu'l-Bahá during their pilgrimages to Palestine.*

Chicago and New York had had functioning Bahá'í consultative bodies since 1900. In 1909, a continental coordinating body, the Bahai Temple Unity, had been elected to build a House of Worship in Wilmette, a Chicago suburb. The Temple Unity scheduled its annual convention for April 27 to May 2, 1912, and anticipated 'Abdu'l-Bahá's participation. Since 1910, a Bahá'í periodical, *Star of the West,* had been published once a Bahá'í month (that is, every nineteen days). It had become the principal medium uniting America's Bahá'ís and often included a Persian section, which gave it international importance. The Bahá'ís had widespread contacts with churches, metaphysical groups, suffrage groups, peace organizations, Esperantists, and progressive-minded people.

Three young Persians—Ali-Kuli Khan, Ahmad Sohrab, and Ameen Fareed—had resided in the United States over a decade, had mastered English, and were translating Bahá'u'lláh's works and 'Abdu'l-Bahá's tablets into English. Khan, whose marriage to Florence Breed is considered the

---

* There was no definition of Bahá'í membership in 1912; consequently, there was no clear demarcation between an adherent and a sympathizer. The definition of a Bahá'í "community" was also fluid in 1912, but there were active Bahá'í groups in the following places: Montreal, Quebec; Eliot, Maine; greater Boston; New York City; Buffalo; northern New Jersey; Philadelphia; Pittsburg; Baltimore; Washington, D.C.; Cleveland; Cincinnati; Muskegon and Fruitport, Michigan; greater Chicago; Kenosha, Wisconsin; Racine; Milwaukee; Minneapolis-Saint Paul; Denver; Oakland, California; San Francisco; Los Angeles; Portland; Seattle; and Spokane. This does not included small groups (less than a dozen members) in a dozen or more other localities. For a list of 105 American Bahá'ís who met 'Abdu'l-Bahá while on pilgrimage before his 1912 visit to America, see *Bahá'í Centenary,* 141–42.

first Iranian-American intercultural marriage, was appointed Iran's chargé d'affairs in Washington, D.C., in 1910. Sohrab had spearheaded formation of the Persian-American Educational Society, the Washington-based nonprofit organization that supported the Iranian Bahá'í community's clinic and its growing network of schools. Their annual meeting, on April 18–20, 1912, also anticipated 'Abdu'l-Bahá's presence.*

Consequently, 'Abdu'l-Bahá could look forward to active assistance during his North American sojourn, and the outline of his first month's activities was set by the various invitations he had received even before the *Cedric* docked in New York harbor.

The bigger question was what 'Abdu'l-Bahá could challenge the American Bahá'ís to do for their new faith. That was very much dependent on their response to his visit. Some years earlier, he had drafted a Will and Testament in which he appointed his grandson, Shoghi Effendi Rabbani (1897–1957) to be Guardian of the Bahá'í Faith and head of the community after his passing. No one yet knew this. Shoghi Effendi (fifteen years old in March, 1912) left for North America with 'Abdu'l-Bahá, but physicians, including Dr. Ameen Fareed, turned him back at Naples on the grounds that his eyes were infected.†

'Abdu'l-Bahá's undisclosed Will also specified that Bahá'ís were eventually to elect delegates locally who would then elect nine-member National Spiritual Assemblies, and that the members of the National Spiritual

* For more information on the Persian American Educational Society, see Stockman, *Bahá'í Faith in America,* vol. 2, 354–58. Regarding Bahá'í schools in Iran, see Moojan Momen, "Baha'i Schools in Iran," in Dominic Parviz Brookshaw and Seena B. Fazel, *The Baha'is of Iran,* 94–121.

† Ruḥiyyih Rabbání, in *The Priceless Pearl,* 19–20, says there was nothing wrong with Shoghi Effendi's eyes or those of two other members of 'Abdu'l-Bahá's entourage, who were turned back on the same grounds, and that Dr. Ameen Fareed, another member of 'Abdu'l-Bahá's party who also was a physician, made the allegation in order to strengthen his own position with 'Abdu'l-Bahá.

Assemblies, assembled in an electoral college, would elect the nine-member Universal House of Justice, the supreme worldwide Bahá'í legislative body that Bahá'u'lláh had ordained.* The Bahá'í concept of unity was not possible without an organizational structure to actualize and channel it. Patiently overcoming the resistance some American Bahá'ís had to organization proved to be one of 'Abdu'l-Bahá's priorities.

'Abdu'l-Bahá had already witnessed the Americans' zeal for spreading religion. He had encountered numerous American Christian missionaries and had seen the same dedication and energy in the American Bahá'í teachers whom he had directed to Iran, India, and Burma. He had encouraged numerous American Bahá'ís to teach their faith all across their country or to take it to their friends and neighbors, and he had seen the great success that had resulted. They were ready for a challenge to spread their Faith internationally, after the follow-up work for his trip was over.† Some American Bahá'ís must have wondered what seeds he would sow and how many of them the American Bahá'ís would bring to a bountiful harvest in the future.

* The Will and Testament of 'Abdu'l-Bahá was first publicly read in January 1922, a few weeks after his death, and was subsequently published in English.

† I allude here to the Tablets of the Divine Plan, a series of fourteen letters addressed to the Bahá'ís of North America in 1916 and 1917, in which 'Abdu'l-Bahá summoned them to take the Bahá'í Faith to the entire globe.

3

"HIS WISDOM IS SURELY NOT HIS OWN"

'Abdu'l-Bahá inaugurated his eight-month sojourn in North America with a nine-day visit to New York on April 11–19, 1912. It was his first visit to the city, to which he frequently returned; he spent more time in New York City than in any other North American locality. The nine days were packed with interviews and meetings and generated some controversy. He is known to have spoken twice at his hotel, four times in public places, and nine times in the homes of Bahá'ís, to an estimated audience of 4,700.* In addition, every day dozens, scores, "sometimes one hundred fifty in one morning," thronged to the Hotel Ansonia to meet him privately. They are not counted among those attending his talks. Finally, at least fifteen newspaper articles in New York and thirty-six more in papers from around the United States resulted from his stay. Wendell Phillips Dodge's

* The number of talks by 'Abdu'l-Bahá was determined from information in *Maḥmúd's Diary, The Promulgation of Universal Peace,* newspaper articles, and other sources. The attendance figure for most larger gatherings has been published in newspaper articles and diaries; attendance at other meetings has been estimated based on the likely size of the place and information about similar gatherings.

interview with 'Abdu'l-Bahá and the telegram of his arrival, spread by the Associated Press, appeared in at least twenty-three papers.* Articles with headlines such as "ABDUL BAHA ABBAS, HEAD OF NEWEST RELIGION, BELIEVES IN WOMAN SUFFRAGE AND DIVORCE," and "ABDUL BAHA IN EPISCOPAL PULPIT," and "Abdul Baha, Dazed by City's Rush, Calls New York a Beehive" spread information about him to hundreds of thousands of New Yorkers.[1]

The Personality of 'Abdu'l-Bahá

During the nine-day period, 'Abdu'l-Bahá introduced many of the themes, by both word and deed, on which he would focus throughout his North American visit. But in particular, the period proved to be an opportunity for individuals and the public to get to know him. In order to describe the impact of his "vibrant personality . . . astonishingly potent" in both its "charm and strength" on others, one must present the full spectrum of experiences and select some metaphorical lenses through which to view them. A common term that could be used to describe `Abdu'l-Bahá is *charismatic.* Max Weber (1864–1920), one of the founders of sociology, described charismatic individuals as "holders of specific gifts of the body and spirit; and these gifts have been believed to be supernatural, not accessible to everybody." He notes that charismatic individuals are often conceived as having a "divine mission" and that their authority is in contrast to "any kind of bureaucratic organization of offices" or any regulated "career."

* Amin Egea has assembled a collection of over seven hundred newspaper articles about 'Abdu'l-Bahá's travels in the United States, Canada, and Europe. The United States National Bahá'í Archives has about two hundred. Duane Troxel has searched the Web and found another hundred fifty or so and has made them available to me. Between Troxel's work, the archives, and a scattering of other sources, I am aware of 358 newspaper articles that appeared in the United States and Canada between April 10 and December 5, 1912.

Charismatic authority "is never a source of private gain for its holders in the sense of economic exploitation by the making of a deal" or "in the form of pecuniary compensation." Sociologists H. H. Gerth and C. Wright add that "a genuinely charismatic situation is direct and inter-personal." It is often "spontaneous."[2]

A related notion to the charismatic individual is *genius*. W. E. H. Lecky (1838–1903), an Irish historian, broadened the concept and applied it to leaders of human conduct thus:

> There arise from time to time men who bear to the moral condition of their age much the same relations as men of genius bear to its intellectual condition. They anticipate the moral standard of a later age, cast abroad conceptions of disinterested virtue, of philanthropy, or of self-denial that seem to have no relation to the spirit of their time, inculcate duties and suggest motives of action that appear to most men altogether chimerical. Yet the magnetism of their perfections tells powerfully upon their contemporaries. An enthusiasm is kindled, a group of adherents formed, and many are emancipated from the moral condition of their age.[3]

Lecky's idea stresses the moral dimension of genius. It resonates with recent work in developmental psychology about the unfoldment of the nature of personal faith. Faith is a complex response to the world similar to trust. It can be simple and pure in the case of children or complex and rich in the case of older adults. James Fowler (1940–), a Harvard-trained developmental psychologist and Methodist clergyman, built on Eric Erikson's stages of human development, Jean Piaget's theories about child development, and Lawrence Kohlberg's research on the development of human moral reasoning to outline six stages in the development of personal faith. The sixth and highest stage is "Universalizing Faith":

> Stage 6 is extremely rare. The persons best described by it have generated faith compositions in which their felt sense of an ultimate environment is inclusive of all being. They have become incarnators and actualizers of the spirit of an inclusive and fulfilled human community. They are "contagious" in the sense that they create zones of liberation from the social, political, economic, and ideological shackles we place and endure on human futurity. Living with a felt participation in a power that unifies and transforms the world, Universalizers are often experienced as subversive of the structures (including religious structures) by which we sustain our individual and corporate survival, security, and significance. Many persons in this stage die at the hands of those whom they hope to change. . . . The rare persons who may be described by this stage have a special grace that makes them seem more lucid, more simple, and yet somehow more fully human than the rest of us.[4]

The liberation theologian Dorothée Soelle (1929–2003) further comments on the idea of a "zone of liberation" as the psychic space someone creates "in which the words 'mine' and 'yours' lose their meaning."[5]

Weber, Lecky, Fowler, and Soelle provide ideas that help us interpret accounts of meeting 'Abdu'l-Bahá. Howard Colby Ives, the Unitarian minister, describes his gentleness, love, and courtesy in accepting a cup of tea. For Juliet Thompson, the artist and devoted Bahá'í, he was "contagious" in terms of his compassion and poignant tenderness. He "kindled enthusiasm" in many because of the "magnetism" of his "perfections." These are examples of ways 'Abdu'l-Bahá was an "incarnator" of "inclusive community."

Ives was to experience 'Abdu'l-Bahá in an even more "direct and personal" way the next day. On Friday morning, April 12—'Abdu'l-Bahá's first full day in New York City—Ives arrived at the Hotel Ansonia at 9am, hoping for a private meeting. He had arisen very early to reach the city from a distant suburb and was disappointed to find the large reception room already filled. His secret hope—divulged in February to his friend Mountfort Mills, one of New York's most active Bahá'ís—was to have a meeting without an interpreter, even though Ives spoke no Persian and 'Abdu'l-Bahá's English was very limited. At the time, Mills dissuaded him on the grounds that such an interview would be of no use, but Ives reported that he replied, "If He at all approaches in the spiritual discernment what I hear and read of Him, we would get closer together, and I might have a better chance of understanding, even if no words were spoken. I am very tired of words."[6]

Ives sat by the reception room window, ignoring the others, wrapped up in his own thoughts, until 'Abdu'l-Bahá came out of his private room with a party to say good-bye to them. Everyone turned to watch him. He looked around, his eyes met Ives's, and he beckoned Ives to come in next. Ives wrote:

> Startled gives no hint of my sensations. Something incredible had happened. Why to me, stranger unknown, unheard of, should He raise that friendly hand? I glanced around. Surely it was to someone else that gesture was addressed, those eyes were smiling! But there was no one near and again I looked and again He beckoned and such understanding love enveloped me that even at that distance and with a heart still cold a thrill ran through me as if a breeze from a divine morning had touched my brow![7]

Ives followed 'Abdu'l-Bahá to the meeting room. There, to the surprise of both Ives and the interpreter, 'Abdu'l-Bahá waved everyone away. Ives continued:

I was absolutely alone with 'Abdu'l-Bahá. The halting desire expressed weeks ago was fulfilled the very moment our eyes first met.

Still holding my hand 'Abdu'l-Bahá walked across the room towards where, in the window, two chairs were waiting. Even then the majesty of His tread impressed me and I felt like a child being led by his father. . . His hand still held mine and frequently His grasp tightened and held more closely. And then, for the first time, He spoke, and in my own tongue: Softly came the assurance that I was His very dear son.

What there was in these simple words that carried such conviction to my heart I cannot say. Or was it the tone of voice and the atmosphere pervading the room, filled with spiritual vibrations beyond anything I had ever known, that melted my heart almost to tears? I only know that a sense of verity invaded me. Here at last was my Father. What earthly paternal relationship could equal this? A new and exquisite emotion all but mastered me. My throat swelled. My eyes filled. I could not have spoken had life depended on a word. I followed those masterly feet like a little child.

Then we sat in the two chairs by the window: knee to knee, eye to eye. At last He looked right into me. It was the first time since our eyes had met with His first beckoning gesture that this had happened. And now nothing intervened between us and He looked at me. He looked at me! It seemed as though never before had anyone really seen me. I felt a sense of gladness that I at last was at home, and that one who knew me utterly, my Father, in truth, was alone with me.

As He looked such play of thought found reflection in His face, that if He had talked an hour not nearly so much could have been said. A little surprise, perhaps, followed swiftly by such sympathy, such understanding, such overwhelming love—it was as if His very being opened to receive me. With that the heart within me melted and the tears flowed. I did not weep, in any ordinary sense. There

> was no breaking up of feature. It was as if a long-pent stream was at last undammed. Unheeded, as I looked at Him, they flowed. He put His two thumbs to my eyes while He wiped the tears from my face; admonishing me not to cry, that one must always be happy. And He laughed. Such a ringing, boyish laugh. It was as though He had discovered the most delightful joke imaginable: a divine joke which only He could appreciate.
>
> I could not speak. We both sat perfectly silent for what seemed a long while, and gradually a great peace came to me. Then 'Abdu'l-Bahá placed His hand upon my breast saying that it was the heart that speaks. Again silence: a long, heart-enthralling silence. No word further was spoken, and all the time I was with Him not one single sound came from me. But no word was necessary from me to Him. I knew that, even then, and how I thanked God it was so. Suddenly He leaped from His chair with another laugh as though consumed with a heavenly joy. Turning, He took me under the elbows and lifted me to my feet and swept me into his arms. Such a hug! No mere embrace! My very ribs cracked. He kissed me on both cheeks, laid His arm across my shoulders and led me to the door.
>
> That is all. But life has never been quite the same since.[8]

Ives left the meeting a man both confused and at peace, for "I began to see, dimly indeed but clearly enough to give me hope, that even if I could not know myself, I knew with certainty that heights far beyond ever before dreamed attainable lay before me and could be reached."[9] He did not become a Bahá'í right away—that took another year—but he had become a moth attracted to the flame; he attended every talk by 'Abdu'l-Bahá that he could.

The interview's most remarkable aspects are its silence and interiority. Much of Ives's description revolves around the various emotions that welled up within him during the interview. These emotions were driven partly by 'Abdu'l-Bahá's remarkable social intuition, his facial expressions, body language, and minimal command of English. Yet, what Ives experienced also came about because the magnetism of 'Abdu'l-Bahá's perfections—echoing Lecky—had made him contagious and had given Ives a new vision of the world. 'Abdu'l-Bahá impressed Ives as "more fully human"—as a "Father" (the capital letter is Ives's), yet as someone with a "boyish laugh." As we shall see, 'Abdu'l-Bahá loved to hold hands with people, embrace and kiss them, laugh, and urge them to be happy.

Not everyone had an experience like Ives'. Stanwood Cobb (1881–1982), an educator who became a Bahá'í in 1906 while studying at Harvard Divinity School, invited his boss, Porter Sargent, who was "a confirmed, positive atheist . . . but an idealist, a humanitarian, a man of great vision for humanity, and somewhat of a genius," to meet 'Abdu'l-Bahá while in Paris in 1913. Sargent apparently enjoyed the meeting and afterward described 'Abdu'l-Bahá to Cobb, much to his "shattering disappointment," as a "dear, kind, tired old man." Cobb concluded that people saw 'Abdu'l-Bahá's spiritual side to the degree of their own spiritual receptivity and to the extent 'Abdu'l-Bahá chose to reveal it: "Anyone who had looked into the large reception room [in Agnes Parsons's house in Washington, D.C.], as I did, and had seen 'Abdu'l-Bahá sitting in the corner and exchanging funny stories with the [Ottoman] ambassador, would have seen in 'Abdu'l-Bahá's facial expressions no trace of spiritual power. For He was not here for primarily spiritual purposes, but to play a social part."[10]

Thus we see a wide range of reactions to 'Abdu'l-Bahá displayed by the people who met him. Jeffrey Parsons, a wealthy Washingtonian whose wife, Agnes, was one of that city's most active Bahá'ís, never became a Bahá'í himself. He described 'Abdu'l-Bahá as "the most perfect gentleman I have ever known." The word "gentleman," according to Ives, "connoted all which he [Parsons] held most admirable" as a man of wealth and culture.

Percy Stickney Grant, a prominent Episcopal clergyman and Rector of the Church of the Ascension, whose pulpit was the site of 'Abdu'l-Bahá's first talk in New York City, said to Howard MacNutt, "You can't help but love the old gentleman," and to Juliet Thompson he added, "The Master compels one's love and esteem. What He radiates is peace and love." Clearly, Grant felt 'Abdu'l-Bahá's magnetism. Many clergy sought private meetings with 'Abdu'l-Bahá in every city he visited, perhaps because they had heard of his remarkable charisma.[11]*

Hudson Maxim (1853–1927) a prominent American scientist and inventor of a variety of explosives and weaponry, whose brother invented the first self-powered machine gun and founded a gun and ammunition factory, apparently felt none of 'Abdu'l-Bahá's magnetic appeal. He had no problem arguing with him about issues of war and peace. On April 15, 1912, Maxim came to the Hotel Ansonia to meet him, coincidentally arriving at the same moment as Mr. W. H. Short, secretary of the New York Peace Society. The men were a physical as well as ideological contrast to each other; Maxim was missing his left hand because an 1894 explosives experiment had blown it off. The stenographic notes of the conversation with Maxim (hereafter H. M.) include the following:

> H. M. "Fewer are killed in modern engagements than in the battles of ancient times; the range is longer and the action less deadly."
>
> A. B. "How about the war between Japan and Russia?"
>
> H. M. "Less men are killed in war in a year now than are killed by our industries through preventable accidents."
>
> A. B. "War is the most preventable accident."

---

* Thompson, *Diary of Juliet Thompson,* 329, says that 'Abdu'l-Bahá received a large number of invitations to talk in churches; reportedly twelve in his first few days in New York, plus one telegraphed to his ship when it passed Gibraltar. *Mahmúd's Diary* records many meetings with clergy as well.

H. M. "The short sword was more deadly in battle than the quick firing gun, for the reason that massed men come together in hand to hand conflict and the slaughter was fearful. . . . In ancient times many thousands would have been overtaken and killed. War is no more dangerous now than automobiling."

A. B. " . . . In modern warfare there are bombs which kill men like stripping leaves from a tree. An Egyptian general who had served in war against England was accused of cowardice at a meeting in Syria. He asked those present, 'Have you ever seen an English shell? When you see one explode among troops you will be excused for defeat and cowardice.'"

H. M. [Making diagram.] "The effect of a bomb is not so great as expected. Most of its force is expended upward into the air. . . . If its explosive energy could be expended in the right direction, it would do plenty of killing."

A. B. "The greatest intelligence of man is being expended in the direction of killing his fellow man. The discovery of high explosives, perfecting of death dealing weapons of war, the science of military attack, all this is a wonderful manifestation of human intelligence; but it is in the wrong direction. You are a celebrated inventor and scientific expert whose energies and faculties are employed in the production of means for human destruction. Your name has become famous in the science of war.

Now you have the opportunity of becoming doubly famous. You must practice the science of peace. You must expend your energies and intelligence in a contrary direction. You must discover the means of peace; invent guns of love which shall shake the foundations of humanity. . . . This work and accomplishment will be more wonderful than all you have done heretofore. . . . Then will your name be recorded in the pages of history with a pen of gold. No man

> in history will equal you in fame and greatness. You will be doubly renowned. God will be pleased with you and from every standpoint of estimation you will be a perfect man."[12]

One sees in the transcript that 'Abdu'l-Bahá refused to argue; he asks a question, uses a clever quip, and tells a story to make his points, praises the "wonderful manifestation of human intelligence" that Maxim demonstrates, and exhorts Maxim to turn his talents in a new direction, appealing to the man's desire for fame.

Maxim, however, was an exception; many found it exceedingly difficult to disagree with 'Abdu'l-Bahá. One day, 'Abdu'l-Bahá was expounding on a Christian doctrine to Howard Colby Ives, and he found it so contrary to received Christian teaching and his ministerial training that he remonstrated with 'Abdu'l-Bahá: "How is it possible to be so sure? No one can say with certainty what Jesus meant after all these centuries of misinterpretation and strife." 'Abdu'l-Bahá replied that no, it was quite possible to know, driving Ives, in his impatience, to reply flatly, "That I cannot believe." He continued:

> I shall never forget the glance of outraged dignity the interpreter cast upon me. It was as though he would say: "Who are you to contradict or even to question 'Abdu'l-Bahá!" But not so did 'Abdu'l-Bahá look at me. How I thank God that it was not! He looked at me a long moment before He spoke. His calm, beautiful eyes searched my soul with such love and understanding that all my momentary heat evaporated. He smiled as winningly as a lover smiles upon his beloved, and the arms of His spirit seemed to embrace me as He said softly that I should try my way and He would try His.
>
> It was as though a cool hand had been laid upon a fevered brow; as though a cup of nectar had been held to parched lips; as though a key

> had unlocked my hard-bolted, crusted and rusted heart. The tears started and my voice trembled, "I'm sorry," I murmured.[13]

Perhaps the most intriguing interview with 'Abdu'l-Bahá was by Mary Williams (1869–1961), a caricaturist who wrote under the pen name of Kate Carew. The Barbara Walters or Katie Couric of her generation, she published a newspaper interview with a famous person every Sunday, complete with sketches of the subject.* On the afternoon of April 19, she went to the Ansonia Hotel to interview 'Abdu'l-Bahá. While waiting, she drew a word portrait of some of the others in the reception room:

> An enthusiastic, plump, middle aged little person, gowned in a very worldly manner, haloed with a new spring hat, whose artificial aigrettes had the real optimistic slant, was telling the stranger seated near of a domestic disturbance. Of course it had to do with a cook.
>
> There was a pretty girl on a narrow seat. You felt she must have lots of oversoul. She wore a sad, withdrawn look as of one who lives on the heights. A stout man, baldish, with a fringe of hair on his neck, had the remaining two thirds of the seat, lolling against her, and turning up his eyes to gaze into hers, which were, in turn, turned up. They were very much in the picture. Some suburbanites stared their way admiringly, wishing they could do it.
>
> Suddenly there was a stir, murmurs of "The Master." Many stood up, a few rushed from the room, among them the Enthusiast. . . .
>
> I blinked my eyes. Everybody in the room was standing, breathlessly expectant. I rose mechanically.

* For a good example of her work, see her interview with the Wright Brothers at http://www.wright-brothers.org/History_Wing/Aviations_Attic/Carew_Interview/Carew_Interview.htm.

> Abdul Baha entered.
>
> He is scarcely above medium height, but so extraordinary is the dignity of his majestic carriage that he seemed more than the average stature.
>
> He wore, over biscuit colored velveteen trousers girded with white, a long, full robe of grayish wool. The Panama fez was wound with white folds.
>
> While slowly making the round of the room his soft, penetrating, faded eyes studied us all, without seeming to do so.
>
> One and another he termed "my child"—and they were not all young who responded to this greeting. . . .
>
> A blushing young woman introduced her escort—"Master, we have just been married."
>
> Such a look of joy illumined the face that in repose looks like a sheet of parchment on which Fate has scoured deep, cabalistic lines.
>
> He did not want to leave them. He held their hands a long time, then turned and blessed the young man.
>
> My dears, if that young man ever thinks of straying from the path of loyalty, methinks the pressure of that hand will weigh heavily on his soul.
>
> He patted several people on the cheek . . . I got a nice, paternal little pat which has made me feel, oh, so much more like folks.[14]

'Abdu'l-Bahá spoke briefly to those gathered, then took questions. Carew notes that

> [His] words, even repeated by an interpreter, are so fraught with the Baha's wonderful personality that they seem never to have been uttered before. His meaning is not couched in any esoteric phrases. Again and again he has disclaimed the possession of hidden lore. Again and again he has placed the attainments of the heart and soul above those of the mind.

> After a few more questions and answers the meeting is declared adjourned. Abdul Baha rises and passes into the inner room, where he gives some private hearings.
>
> No one starts to go. He has actually made New York people forget the dinner hour.
>
> That in itself is a victory, I think. Don't you?[15]

Carew waited patiently until Ameen Fareed escorted her to 'Abdu'l-Bahá's room, where she found "the Baha seated in a comfortable easy chair at the bay window":

> The Master looks very spirituelle. He is in a relaxed attitude, sometimes "going into the silence." So much more akin to the spirit world than this does he seem that I find myself often addressing Dr. Fareed personally, referring to him in the third person.
>
> "Do you think our luxury degenerate," I ask, "as in this great hotel?"
>
> Abdul Baha strokes his long white beard. "Luxury has a limit. Beyond that limit it is not commendable. There is such a thing as moderation. Men must be temperate in all things."
>
> "Does the attention paid at present in this country to material things sadden you? Does it argue to you a lack of progress?"
>
> "Your material civilization is very wonderful. If only you will allow divine idealism to keep pace with it there will be great hope for general progress."
>
> . . . . "Do you believe in woman's desire for freedom?"
>
> He adjusts his turban—a frequent mannerism.
>
> "The soul has no sex."
>
> "In a supreme moment, as in that of the Titanic disaster, should both sexes share the danger equally?"

"Women are more delicate than men. This delicacy men should take into consideration. That is their obligation. If the time ever comes when the average woman is a man's equal in physical strength there will be no need for this consideration; but not until then."

As he says this he shakes the wonderful, full-domed head and the singsong recitation has a note of great sweetness.

I thought of his childhood, passed among such unspeakable scenes of distress—early matured into knowledge of sin and sorrow. I marveled at his childlike simplicity, which is combined with a sort of ageless, spiritual wisdom. I asked:

"Is it possible for us ever to rid ourselves of our grown-up illusions and become, as Christ said, 'as little children'?"

"Certainly. There is such a thing as innocence due to ignorance, due to weakness. It is innate in the child to be simple, but when a person becomes matured there should be such thing as innocence of knowledge, of strength. . . ."

. . . . Is there any way of making this life in a commercial city less crude for the young boy or girl?"

"It would be well to get them together and say 'Young ladies, God has created you all human: isn't it a pity that you should pass your energy along animalistic lines? God has created you men and women in order that you may acquire his virtues. . ."

"There are so many temptations put in their way," I murmur.

The Abdul Baha looks very sympathetic, but his singsong tones are relentlessly firm.

"Let them try a little of the delicacy of the spiritual world, the sweetness of its perfection, and see which life is preferable. . . ."

I notice a trembling of the eyelids and that the gestures of arranging his turban and stroking his beard were more nervously frequent. Dr. Fareed answered to my inquiry "Shall I go now?"

> "He has been giving of himself to everyone since 7 o'clock this morning. I am a perfect physical wreck, but he is willing to go on indefinitely."[16]

'Abdu'l-Bahá invited Kate Carew to accompany him to his next meeting. As with Howard Colby Ives, 'Abdu'l-Bahá took her hand and walked with her through the corridors of the hotel, with his entourage, to the waiting automobile:

> Can you imagine your Aunt Kate and Abdul Baha going to it [Mr. Mills's automobile], hand in hand, through the Ansonia corridors?
>
> Perhaps the [hotel] guests didn't gurgle and gasp! Perhaps!
>
> I did feel rather conspicuous, but I braced myself with the thought of the universal brotherhood and really got along fairly well.
>
> When we were seated in the machine, each inch of space taken by some member of the suite, I caught myself thinking what an amusing little anecdote I might make of this happening. Just then the Master said to me in a gentle but firm voice: "Remember, you press people are the servants of the public. You interpret our words and acts to them. With you is a great responsibility. Please remember and please treat us seriously."
>
> Often during the interview I had felt like saying: "You dear old man! You fine old gentleman!" I felt more than ever like it now.
>
> As if anyone could hold up that pure white soul to ridicule.[17]

Again we see several common features; as in the Ives interview, 'Abdu'l-Bahá anticipates his guest before the latter can speak; as in the Maxim interview, he always tries to agree with his guest to the extent possible, building on the guest's comments and carrying them a step further. As the others noted, 'Abdu'l-Bahá was magnetically likable and very directly personable, holding hands with visitors and looking them directly in the eyes. Like Parsons and Grant, Carew refers to 'Abdu'l-Bahá as a "gentleman" and is impressed by his genuineness and sweetness; a comparison of her slightly jaded descriptions of the people waiting to meet 'Abdu'l-Bahá with her comments about him shows the extent to which she was impressed by him. Like Ives, she finds him both childlike and venerably wise.

The *Sacramento Bee,* in an article six months later, offered a similar evaluation: "He. . . was most simple and unassuming in manner. His style of delivery is entirely unaffected and purely conversational, and he is sparing of gesture. Both in voice and expression of countenance he is pleasant, and he gives one the impression of being entirely sincere."[18]

Thornton Chase, the first American Bahá'í, was particularly amazed by the reaction of journalists to 'Abdu'l-Bahá: "there is evidently a certain strength, sincerity, righteousness, wisdom, knowledge, and nobility manifesting from him, as an aura of spiritual power, that even our flippant and calloused news men are restrained by it." He commented that Kate Carew, "a noted cynic and cartoonist" was tempted to poke fun at 'Abdu'l-Bahá after one or two "unconventional situations" and decided not to: "There you see it. The purifying, uplifting effect He has upon even a Kate Carew."[19]

Harry Randall (1863–1929) had an unexpected one-on-one encounter with 'Abdu'l-Bahá in May. A skeptical Boston businessman of Catholic and Episcopal background and descendant of the pilgrims, Randall also had a spiritual side; he had studied Swedenborgianism and Christian Science, and at one time Swami Vivekananda explained yoga to him and cooked his supper over the coals of Randall's fireplace. He also hired a Harvard professor to tutor him weekly in history and religion.[20]

In 1911, he attended a Bahá'í meeting and began to study the Bahá'í Faith a little. He was asked whether he wanted to meet 'Abdu'l-Bahá and declined: "What do I want to meet another oriental for? I've met Vivekananda and all the great orientals that have come to this country, and

I don't want to meet any more."* But when 'Abdu'l-Bahá was in Boston, Randall attended one of his talks. According to his daughter, he thought, "Well, He really is a saint. Now this is the first one I've met, whom I thought really lived what he preached." But he had no plan to investigate further. Leaving the lecture, however, he overheard one of 'Abdu'l-Bahá's secretaries ask where one could purchase grape juice for 'Abdu'l-Bahá on a Sunday. Randall volunteered to find some and take it to his hotel room. There, much to his surprise, he was asked to take it to 'Abdu'l-Bahá. 'Abdu'l-Bahá was sitting in a chair, eyes closed. Randall placed the juice on a table near him, who said (apparently in English), "Be seated." Randall did not want to, but complied and sat while 'Abdu'l-Bahá continued to repose silently. At first Randall got angry, but after ten minutes or so he thought, "Here I am in the presence of a tired old man and I cannot remain reposeful for ten minutes. What good has my study of all the religions of the world done for me?" After that he relaxed and became at peace. Finally after another twenty minutes 'Abdu'l-Bahá "rose and held my hands and looked into my face and stroked me, all in silence for some time. Then He spoke in Persian and my mind heard this in English: 'Great is the power of the intellect but it is dead without love. It needs the vivifying fragrance of love to make it a servant of God.' He then blessed me and said 'Be happy.'"[21]

Like Ives, Randall's experience was direct, one-on-one, and personal. A day or two later he wrote a letter to his wife, who was convalescing in California, and summarized his experience. Once again, the description was of someone paradoxically childlike and venerably old: "I found 'Abdu'l-Bahá a wonderful little man, or rather a child of great sweetness and love. His wisdom is surely not His own, for He sees your character or state, and

* Sometimes the typescript is identical word for word with passages in Randall-Winckler, *William Henry Randall;* at other times it has significant additional information or differs in detail.

just gives you a lift by some gentle suggestions and you feel like holding His hand and telling Him all you know. In fact, I didn't feel that I knew anything or cared. I just felt love—words were unnecessary."[22]

'Abdu'l-Bahá in New York, April 11–19, 1912

'Abdu'l-Bahá's ability to reach an audience was demonstrated in the fifteen talks he gave during his first eleven days in New York. On Friday, April 12, after a morning of private interviews with Howard Colby Ives and many others, he went to Howard MacNutt's house at 935 Eastern Parkway, Brooklyn, where he met hundreds of people. His talk began by emphasizing the spiritual atmosphere present in the gathering: "the light of the spirit shining in your faces brings me rest and reward. In this meeting the divine susceptibilities are radiant. This is a spiritual house, the home of the spirit. There is no discord here; all is love and unity."[23] 'Abdu'l-Bahá connected His observation about the spiritual atmosphere to the "divine Prophets" who "came to establish the unity of the Kingdom in human hearts." He gave the example of Jesus Christ, whose goal also was "to establish the unity of the Kingdom in human hearts":

> Only a few were attracted to Him. They were not the kings and rulers of His time. They were not rich and important people. Some of them were catchers of fish. Most of them were ignorant men, not trained in the knowledge of this world. One of the greatest of them, Peter, could not remember the days of the week. All of them were men of the least consequence in the eyes of the world. But their hearts were pure and attracted by the fires of the Divine Spirit manifested in Christ. With this small army Christ conquered the world of the East and the West. Kings and nations rose against Him. Philosophers and the greatest men of learning assailed and blasphemed His Cause. All were defeated and overcome, their tongues silenced, their lamps

extinguished, their hatred quenched; no trace of them now remains. They have become as nonexistent, while His Kingdom is triumphant and eternal.[24]

'Abdu'l-Bahá then brought the story up to the present by talking about the Báb and Bahá'u'lláh:

> Praise be to God! The light of unity and love is shining in these faces. These spiritual susceptibilities are the real fruits of heaven. The Báb and Bahá'u'lláh over sixty years ago proclaimed the glad tidings of universal peace. The Báb was martyred in the Cause of God. Bahá'u'lláh suffered forty years as a prisoner and exile in order that the Kingdom of love might be established in the East and West. He has made it possible for us to meet here in love and unity. Because He suffered imprisonment, we are free to proclaim the oneness of the world of humanity for which He stood so long and faithfully. He was chained in dungeons, He was without food, His companions were thieves and criminals, He was subjected to every kind of abuse and infliction, but throughout it all He never ceased to proclaim the reality of the Word of God and the oneness of humanity. We have been brought together here by the power of His Word—you from America, I from Persia—all in love and unity of spirit. Was this possible in former centuries? If it is possible now after fifty years of sacrifice and teaching, what shall we expect in the wonderful centuries coming?
>
> Therefore, let your faces be more radiant with hope and heavenly determination to serve the Cause of God, to spread the pure fragrances of the divine rose garden of unity, to awaken spiritual susceptibilities in the hearts of mankind, to kindle anew the spirit of humanity with divine fires and to reflect the glory of heaven to this gloomy world of

> materialism. When you possess these divine susceptibilities, you will be able to awaken and develop them in others.[25]

The talk epitomizes a common pattern in his addresses to the public or to a mixed Bahá'í and non-Bahá'í audience: start with a simple observation—an event in the newspapers, an introductory remark, even the weather—transition to a spiritual principle, relate that principle to Jesus and the Bible, connect the subject to Bahá'u'lláh, and close with an exhortation for his audience to internalize the principle and express it in their lives, thereby bringing the audience from the commonplace to Bahá'u'lláh and to a spiritual principle via their Christian heritage.

That evening, he spoke to about two hundred people at Miss H. Phillips's spacious studio at 39 West Sixty-seventh St., Manhattan. The audience was perhaps mostly Bahá'í, for the talk seems aimed at Bahá'ís: "The affairs of this world are to be accounted as nothing compared to the joy and heavenly happiness of meeting the friends of God. . . Tonight I am in the greatest happiness . . . Your meeting here is surely an evidence that you are upholding the Cause of God, that you are aiding and assisting in establishing the Kingdom of God."[26]* He exhorted them to arise and teach this new Faith:

* The version in *Star of the West* 3, no. 8 (Aug. 1, 1912): 3–4, was edited by Howard MacNutt, and the only changes he made when producing *The Promulgation of Universal Peace* were to regularize spelling and punctuation, so I have used the latter version. The Persian notes of the talk, published in *Majmu'ih-i-Khatábát-i-Hazrat-i-'Abdu'l-Bahá* (Talks of 'Abdu'l-Bahá), vol. 2, p. 8, are much longer, and the English appears to be a loose précis of the talk. This highlights the difficulty of determining exactly what 'Abdu'l-Bahá said. The Persian notes also have two obvious errors: the talk is described as occurring at "Mr. Phillips," and the date is given as April 11, in the afternoon. *Maḥmúd's Diary* (p. 39) also says the talk was on April 11, but in the evening. Maḥmúd has 'Abdu'l-Bahá's arriving in New York one day too early, and his diary entries are often off by a day.

With hearts set aglow by the fire of the love of God and spirits refreshed by the food of the heavenly spirit you must go forth . . . quickening the hearts of men by the call of glad tidings, the light of God in your faces, severed from everything save God. Therefore, order your lives in accordance with the first principle of the divine teaching, which is love. Service to humanity is service to God. Let the love and light of the Kingdom radiate through you until all who look upon you shall be illumined by its reflection. Be as stars, brilliant and sparkling in the loftiness of their heavenly station. Do you appreciate the Day in which you live?

. . . These are the days of seed sowing. . . . He who sows a seed in this day will behold his reward in the fruits and harvest of the heavenly Kingdom. . . . All who sow such a seed and plant such a tree according to the teachings of Bahá'u'lláh shall surely witness this divine outcome in the degrees of its perfection and will attain unto the good pleasure of the Merciful One. . . . Know ye then the value of these days.

Awake ye to the realization of this heavenly opportunity. Strive with all the power of your souls, your deeds, actions and words to assist the spread of these glad tidings and the descent of this merciful bounty. You are the reality and expression of your deeds and actions. If you abide by the precepts and teachings of the Blessed Perfection, the heavenly world and ancient Kingdom will be yours—eternal happiness, love and everlasting life.

Consider me—in the years of my advanced age, burdened with physical infirmities—crossing the wide ocean to look upon your faces. It is my hope that through the life of the spirit you may all become as one soul, as one tree adorning the rose garden of the Kingdom. It is my hope that the endless treasures of the bestowals of God may be yours here and hereafter. It is my prayer that the

> Supreme Concourse may be illumined by your brilliant lights shining forever in the heavens of eternal glory.[27]

'Abdu'l-Bahá's exhortation was for unity among the Bahá'ís, personal transformation, and a devotion to spreading the word of Bahá'u'lláh to others. But he did not call for the establishment of a Bahá'í community, for the strengthening of Bahá'í organization, for the observance of distinctive Bahá'í practices such as obligatory prayer and fasting, or for people to leave the churches. He sought to inspire; the rest he reserved for later.

On Saturday, April 13, he again spoke in two houses, those of Alexander Morten and Mountfort Mills. We do not have an account of the latter address, but the former was a public talk; he spoke about how each divine Messenger brought a new springtime to religion, the springtime brought by Christ two thousand years ago, and the springtime brought by Bahá'u'lláh today, again roughly following the pattern of the talk at the MacNutt house. He closed with an exhortation to personal transformation:

> I hope that each and all of you may become like unto verdant and green trees so that through the breezes of the divine spring, the outpouring of heaven, the heat of the Sun of Truth, you may become eternally refreshed; that you may bear blossoms and become fruitful; that you may not be as fruitless trees. Fruitless trees do not bring forth fruits or flowers. I hope that all of you may become friends of the paradise of Abhá, appearing with the utmost freshness and spiritual beauty. I pray in your behalf and beg of God confirmation and assistance.[28]

The meeting also had an amusing incident; when the interpreter, Ahmad Sohrab, couldn't remember the proper English translation for *tábistan,* 'Abdu'l-Bahá himself supplied it: *summer,* eliciting a ripple of laughter from the audience. After the talk, 'Abdu'l-Bahá was so exhausted he looked ill, so he went upstairs to rest. But people streamed up the stairs and into the room to meet him anyway, and he refused to close the door to keep them out. When a woman came in with a baby, he took it and pressed it to his heart. "Beautiful baby! Little chicken!" he said in English, then explained through the interpreter that "little chicken" was a favorite Turkish expression for children.[29] Sometimes he had to receive visitors in bed because he had no energy left to sit.

On Sunday, April 14, 'Abdu'l-Bahá spoke for the first time in a public location. He chose the Church of the Ascension, Fifth Avenue and Tenth Street. The Rector, Percy Stickney Grant (1860–1927), was a prominent, Harvard-educated, controversial Episcopal clergyman who was known for his support for Socialism, the labor movement, and many social reform movements. He was also a close friend of Juliet Thompson, who was in love with him, a love 'Abdu'l-Bahá discouraged after he met Grant. 'Abdu'l-Bahá invited Grant to meet him on Friday—without Thompson—to talk about the service. According to Thompson, the 11am Sunday service was set up specially, with a prophetic passage from the Old Testament and I Corinthians 13:12 as the two scriptural texts, even though others were normally prescribed for that day.[30] After the second reading, as the choir sang the hymn "Jesus Lives!" Grant walked to the vestry room, escorted 'Abdu'l-Bahá into the church, hand in hand, and seated him in the bishop's chair, behind which hung a "victor's wreath," an oval of laurel leaves. Grant's "broad, catholic, beautiful" introduction echoes the common contemporary stereotypes about the spiritual East and materialistic West:

> It is to be our privilege this morning to listen to one who has come out of the East; a new and great herald of good-will. He comes with a plan of construction and reconstruction, and bears a message of peace and love to all mankind. Abdu'l Baha is a Master of the things of the

> Spirit. . . . He comes from that part of the world where men meditate; where contemplation was born. He teaches the fundamental unity of all religions, a truth in which this congregation believes profoundly, and we welcome here one who may help the material fervor of the Occident to gain a new peace by the infiltration of the harmonies of the Orient. . . .
>
> Some will ask, "What has he done to prove his sincerity?" An exile from his native land from the age of nine, a prisoner for forty years;—these are the badges of Abdu'l Baha's sincerity. We are going to listen in the fashion of the East and listen to a great student.[31]

'Abdu'l-Bahá's talk followed the format of many of his public talks: reference to a common event, statement of a spiritual theme—the oneness of humankind and universal peace, in this case—a connection to Jesus Christ, a connection to Bahá'u'lláh, then a closing exhortation:

> In his scriptural lesson this morning the revered doctor read a verse from the Epistle of St. Paul to the Corinthians, "For now we see through a glass, darkly; but then face to face."
>
> The light of truth has heretofore been seen dimly through variegated glasses, but now the splendors of Divinity shall be visible through the translucent mirrors of pure hearts and spirits. The light of truth is the divine teaching, heavenly instruction, merciful principles and spiritual civilization. Since my arrival in this country I find that material civilization has progressed greatly . . . but spiritual civilization has been left behind. Material civilization is like unto the lamp, while spiritual civilization is the light in that lamp. . . .
>
> Jesus Christ came to teach the people of the world this heavenly civilization and not material civilization. He breathed the breath of the Holy Spirit into the body of the world and established an

illumined civilization. Among the principles of divine civilization He came to proclaim is the Most Great Peace of mankind. Among His principles of spiritual civilization is the oneness of the kingdom of humanity. . . .

Today the world of humanity is in need of international unity and conciliation. To establish these great fundamental principles a propelling power is needed. It is self-evident that the unity of the human world and the Most Great Peace cannot be accomplished through material means. . . .

All the Prophets have come to promote divine bestowals, to found the spiritual civilization and teach the principles of morality. . . . Bahá'u'lláh appeared in that country [Persia] and founded the spiritual civilization. He established affiliation among the various peoples, promoted the oneness of the human world and unfurled the banner of the Most Great Peace. . . .

I find a strong movement for universal peace emanating from America. It is my hope that this standard of the oneness of the world of humanity may be upraised with the utmost solidity so that the Orient and Occident may become perfectly reconciled and attain complete intercommunication, the hearts of the East and West become united and attracted, real union become unveiled, the light of guidance shine, divine effulgences be seen day by day so that the world of humanity may find complete tranquillity, the eternal happiness of man become evident and the hearts of the people of the world be as mirrors in which the rays of the Sun of Reality may be reflected. . . .[32]

When the collection plate was passed around, 'Abdu'l-Bahá made a generous contribution. Grant asked him to give the closing benediction, so he rose, raised his hands, closed his eyes, and prayed, a kneeling clergyman arrayed on either side of him. The recessional hymn was "Christ our Lord has risen again."[33]

According to Maḥmúd, the Bahá'ís were "elated" by the program, though Juliet Thompson's reaction could best be described as "rapturous":

> How can words tell what I realized, or *thought* I realized, at that incomparable service?
>
> This church has been my cross for years . . . Was I seeing, this morning, divine results for the pain? . . . . Here in this pulpit, with all his great force, his disturbing magnetism, and the fire of his eloquence, Percy Grant had opposed my unshakable belief, thundering denunciation of "the subtle" "the Machiavellian Oriental" (God forgive me for quoting this)—of the slumbering and superstitious Orient—the Orient that brought the West "nothing but disease and death"—determined to conquer this Faith of mine which made me resistant to him. He had even gone so far as to openly name "the Bahá'í sect" in his pulpit and to warn his flock against it.
>
> And *now,* framing that matchless head of the Master, who sat there so still in His Glory, hung the victor's wreath! Oh for words vivid and sublime enough to make you *see* Him sitting there, in the very spot where He had been so violently denied![34]

'Abdu'l-Bahá thanked Grant, shook hands with many in the crowd, and made a special effort to meet Grant's mother before he left the church. Maḥmúd describes an almost biblical scene of the audience listening to 'Abdu'l-Bahá "spellbound." After the service ended, a woman came forward, tears pouring from her eyes, and grabbed the hem of 'Abdu'l-Bahá's robe, "so overcome she could not speak." 'Abdu'l-Bahá "calmed her with loving words of assurance. It was a great day and a most impressive meeting," Maḥmúd added, "Not one of the two thousand people was disappointed and everyone left smiling in warm appreciation."[35]

Maḥmúd's glowing assessment proved hasty, because the next day he reported that the decision to sit 'Abdu'l-Bahá in the bishop's chair had violated church law and that other Episcopal clergy were scandalized. They wrote critically of Grant's act, resulting in an exchange in the newspapers. The Episcopal bishop of New York called on 'Abdu'l-Bahá, partly to apologize for the controversy and prevent any hurt feelings.[36] The controversy did not die down but became a national concern for the Episcopal Church when *The Churchman,* the denomination's weekly newspaper, published a critical editorial in its April 27, 1912 edition:

> Abdul Baha does not profess to be a Christian. What right, then, has he to preach in a Christian church? Still further, what right has the rector of one of our parishes to commit his people to the religious instruction of a teacher who does not believe in the Christian religion? In the Epistle for the same Sunday St. James writes: "He that believeth not God hath made Him a liar, because he believeth not the record that God gave of His Son. . . . He that hath the Son hath life; and he that hath not the Son of God hath not life." The Apostle does not mince words. Abdul Baha, however, excellent may be the morality which he preaches . . . does not pretend to believe in this record; and yet he is invited to preach in a church in which this Epistle has been read as part of the divine service. . . . A canon of this church ordains that "no minister in charge of any congregation of this church. . . shall permit any person to officiate therein without sufficient evidence of him being duly licensed or ordained to minister in this Church. . . . ." When tested by this canon the action of the

> rector of the Church of the Ascension has the appearance of a flagrant breach of the law of the Church. Tested by the Epistle for the day, it has the appearance of an affront to the inspired record.[37]

The controversy was echoed in Baltimore, where the bishop insisted 'Abdu'l-Bahá would never preach in any Episcopal church in that city when he visited.[38] But otherwise, few church publications took notice of 'Abdu'l-Bahá's North American sojourn.

'Abdu'l-Bahá's day was not over after the talk at the Church of the Ascension. That afternoon, he spoke to the "Union Meeting of Advanced Thought Centers"—described by a New York newspaper as a meeting of the New Thought Society—at Carnegie Lyceum.[39] It again followed the standard public format: an opening, a transition to a spiritual principle—in this case, the oneness of humanity—the example of Christ, the example of Bahá'u'lláh in uniting diverse peoples in one Bahá'í community, and a closing exhortation:

> I have come from distant lands to visit the meetings and assemblies of this country. In every meeting I find people gathered, loving each other; therefore, I am greatly pleased. The bond of union is evidenced in this assembly today, where the power of God has brought together in faith, agreement and concord those who are engaged in furthering the development of the human world. . . .
>
> All the Prophets have striven to make love manifest in the hearts of men. Jesus Christ sought to create this love in the hearts. He suffered all difficulties and ordeals that perchance the human heart might become the fountain source of love. Therefore, we must strive with all our heart and soul that this love may take possession of us so that all humanity—whether it be in the East or in the West—may be

> connected through the bond of this divine affection; for we are all the waves of one sea; we have come into being through the same bestowal and are recipients from the same center. . . .
>
> In the Orient there were great differences among races and peoples. They hated each other, and there was no association among them. Various and divergent sects were hostile, irreconcilable. The different races were in constant war and conflict. About sixty years ago Bahá'u'lláh appeared upon the eastern horizon. He caused love and unity to become manifest among these antagonistic peoples. He united them with the bond of love; their former hatred and animosity passed away; love and unity reigned instead. It was a dark world; it became radiant. A new springtime appeared through Him, for the Sun of Truth had risen again. . . .
>
> I have come here with this mission: that through your endeavors, through your heavenly morals, through your devoted efforts a perfect bond of unity and love may be established between the East and the West so that the bestowals of God may descend upon all and that all may be seen to be the parts of the same tree—the great tree of the human family. For mankind may be likened to the branches, leaves, blossoms and fruit of that tree.[40]

One wonders what the audience thought of the talk, which was seemingly devoid of practical suggestions and was focused on broad, spiritual principles. Samuel Graham Wilson, a Presbyterian missionary to Iran who wrote several anti-Bahá'í works, described 'Abdu'l-Bahá's talks as "tame and full of platitudes." But such a view missed 'Abdu'l-Bahá's point. America in 1912 was dominated by white Protestants, most of whom believed that God had fitted them and their country for the special mission of spreading Christianity and Christian civilization to the entire world. As such, they viewed themselves as a race, and their country as a nation and culture, as superior. One historian of the period has described the resulting dominant cultural assumption as the "conflation of race, religion, and progress"; that white and Christian (meaning Protestant, to most) equaled true civilization. Even Unitarians and Theosophists exhibited some of these attitudes. The principle of the oneness of humanity that 'Abdu'l-Bahá was espousing was a direct challenge to such assumptions. When 'Abdu'l-Bahá described the hatred and separation that existed among the people of the east and the harmony Bahá'u'lláh brought to them, he was telling the story of separate peoples, each with their own assumptions of superiority, coming together as equals when they became Bahá'ís. It is hardly surprising that a Presbyterian missionary to Iran would miss 'Abdu'l-Bahá's point. If one applies the analytical frame of reference offered by Lecky, it would seem that Wilson was not able to "anticipate the moral standard of a later age" or the "duties" it "inculcated." In the upcoming weeks, 'Abdu'l-Bahá would begin to lay out the moral standards and their duties progressively but subtly in his talks. Possibly members of the New Thought movement, which had sought to go beyond Christianity and explore the truths of other faiths, might be more open to a new approach to religion and progress.[41]

The next four days—Monday through Thursday, April 15 through 18—'Abdu'l-Bahá met with individuals during the day and spoke at the home of a Bahá'í at night. On Tuesday and Wednesday, the crush of visitors was so great at the Hotel Ansonia that he spoke to the crowds there as well. One of these talks was particularly important and is often quoted: He spoke about the four ways people can know things—through sense perception, reason, religious tradition, and inspiration—and noted that all four epistemological paths were ultimately faulty. Only through the promptings of the Holy Spirit could perfect knowledge be attained.[42]

Many clergy visited and asked 'Abdu'l-Bahá to speak at their Sunday services, but he had to postpone their invitations because he was leaving for Washington on Saturday.[43] 'Abdu'l-Bahá had requested that a racially integrated meeting be held; hence, on Wednesday evening, whites and blacks together were invited to the Kinney residence for a talk and refreshments. This was the first time 'Abdu'l-Bahá's related his emphasis on the oneness of humanity to the American race problem. His comments anticipated many principles he enunciated later: ". . . the blessings of the colored and white people under the creative effect and influence of the outpouring of the Sun of Reality resemble the gathering of roses of variegated colors. This difference of color adds charm and beauty, and is conducive to the wealth of their splendor." After speaking, 'Abdu'l-Bahá helped cook dinner for the crowd.[44]

Friday, April 19—'Abdu'l-Bahá's last full day in New York City—began with a meeting with Kahlil Gibran (1883–1931). He was a neighbor of Juliet Thompson and had heard of 'Abdu'l-Bahá through her. Because Gibran was from Mount Lebanon, he was able to converse with 'Abdu'l-Bahá in Arabic. It was the first of at least three meetings between the men. Gibran was very impressed: "He is a very great man. He is complete. There are worlds in his soul. And oh what a remarkable face—what a beautiful face—so real and so sweet." Eventually Gibran asked and received permission to sketch 'Abdu'l-Bahá, for he was an accomplished artist as well. Gibran told Juliet Thompson that when he wrote *Jesus, Son of Man* (1928), his second most famous work, "he thought of 'Abdu'l-Bahá all through." Two renowned Gibran scholars have come to the same conclusion in a book they coauthored; that 'Abdu'l-Bahá was the "inspiration and template for his unique portrait of Christ" in *Jesus, Son of Man*. Gibran once exclaimed of 'Abdu'l-Bahá, "for the first time I saw a form noble enough to be the receptacle for the Holy Spirit."[45]

In the afternoon, 'Abdu'l-Bahá went to the theatre to see a play, *The Terrible Meek,* about Jesus Christ, which made him weep. At 5pm, he spoke at Earl Hall, Columbia University. Perhaps because of the secular, academic nature of the institution, 'Abdu'l-Bahá chose not to refer to Jesus Christ or Bahá'u'lláh, as was his wont in other settings, although he did mention the Manifestations of God and "the Gospel and the other Holy Books." He began with a basic observation based on the Aristotelian-inspired philosophy that dominated traditional nineteenth-century science in the Middle East:

> If we look with a perceiving eye upon the world of creation, we find that all existing things may be classified as follows: first, mineral—that is to say, matter or substance appearing in various forms of composition; second, vegetable—possessing the virtues of the mineral plus the power of augmentation or growth, indicating a degree higher and more specialized than the mineral; third, animal—possessing the attributes of the mineral and vegetable plus the power of sense perception; fourth, human—the highest specialized organism of visible creation, embodying the qualities of the mineral, vegetable and animal plus an ideal endowment absolutely absent in the lower kingdoms—the power of intellectual investigation into the mysteries of outer phenomena.[46]

While the classification of creation into animal, vegetable, and mineral types would have been familiar to an audience at al-Azhar University in Cairo, it would not have been current at Columbia. But 'Abdu'l-Bahá moved next to modern science, praising very extensively its powers to discover the secrets of nature. He noted that "man through the possession of this ideal endowment of scientific investigation is the most noble product of creation, the governor of nature. He takes the sword from nature's hand and uses it upon nature's head." He then transitioned to the spiritual principle he wished to stress:

As material and physical sciences are taught here and are constantly unfolding in wider vistas of attainment, I am hopeful that spiritual development may also follow and keep pace with these outer advantages. . . .The most important principle of divine philosophy is the oneness of the world of humanity, the unity of mankind, the bond conjoining East and West, the tie of love which blends human hearts.

Therefore, it is our duty to put forth our greatest efforts and summon all our energies in order that the bonds of unity and accord may be established among mankind. For thousands of years we have had bloodshed and strife. It is enough; it is sufficient. Now is the time to associate together in love and harmony. . . . God has created us all human, and all countries of the world are parts of the same globe. We are all His servants. He is kind and just to all. Why should we be unkind and unjust to each other? He provides for all. Why should we deprive one another? He protects and preserves all. Why should we kill our fellow creatures? If this warfare and strife be for the sake of religion, it is evident that it violates the spirit and basis of all religion. All the divine Manifestations have proclaimed the oneness of God and the unity of mankind. They have taught that men should love and mutually help each other in order that they might progress. Now if this conception of religion be true, its essential principle is the oneness of humanity. The fundamental truth of the Manifestations is peace. This underlies all religion, all justice. The divine purpose is that men should live in unity, concord and agreement and should love one another. Consider the virtues of the human world and realize that the oneness of humanity is the primary foundation of them all. Read the Gospel and the other Holy Books. You will find their fundamentals are one and the same. Therefore, unity is the

> essential truth of religion and, when so understood, embraces all the virtues of the human world. Praise be to God! This knowledge has been spread, eyes have been opened, and ears have become attentive. Therefore, we must endeavor to promulgate and practice the religion of God which has been founded by all the Prophets. And the religion of God is absolute love and unity.[47]

It is interesting to note that Columbia had a graduate program in anthropology—the first in the United States—led by Franz Boas, the father of modern anthropology, whose scientific approach to cultures had begun to debunk racist conceptions about the inferiority of other ethnicities and cultures and thus supported the oneness of humanity in its own way. Whether any Columbia University anthropologists attended the talk is not known. But many in the audience apparently were fascinated. When the meeting ended, 'Abdu'l-Bahá made himself available to meet people in another room in the building. So many came to talk to him that a tour of the campus had to be canceled.

He returned to the Hotel Ansonia to meet with the crowd of inquirers accumulating there, which included Kate Carew, whose interview has already been described. He had no time to rest; the interviews continued until he had to leave for the Bowery Mission to meet the impoverished men who went there for meals and hope. 'Abdu'l-Bahá had devoted a significant part of his life in the prison city of Acre to helping that city's poor; he distributed alms at his home weekly and made visits to people to provide them food, often at night to preserve his anonymity and their dignity. Juliet Thompson had arranged for the Bowery meeting; two months earlier, she had been invited to tell the men there about the Bahá'í Faith, and had mentioned that 'Abdu'l-Bahá was coming to America. The pastor in charge asked the men to stand if they would like to invite him to visit, and the entire audience stood. In preparation, 'Abdu'l-Bahá gave Juliet Thompson and Edward Getsinger each a thousand French francs—worth about $250—to change into quarters. Both brought heavy bags with them.[48]

'Abdu'l-Bahá arrived with a large party in Mills's automobile and walked into the Bowery holding Kate Carew's hand. He was welcomed by the three to five hundred men present and spoke to them about poverty:

> Tonight I am very happy, for I have come here to meet my friends. I consider you my relatives, my companions; and I am your comrade.
>
> You must be thankful to God that you are poor, for Jesus Christ has said, "Blessed are the poor." . . . Jesus Himself was poor. . . . When Jesus Christ appeared, it was the poor who first accepted Him, not the rich. Therefore, you are the disciples of Jesus Christ . . . Jesus Christ said so; Bahá'u'lláh said so. While Bahá'u'lláh was in Baghdád, still in possession of great wealth, He left all He had and went alone from the city, living two years among the poor. . . . God has not said that there are mansions prepared for us if we pass our time associating with the rich, but He has said there are many mansions prepared for the servants of the poor, for the poor are very dear to God.
>
> So, my comrades, you are following in the footsteps of Jesus Christ. Your lives are similar to His life; your attitude is like unto His; you resemble Him more than the rich do. Therefore, we will thank God that we have been so blessed with real riches. And in conclusion, I ask you to accept 'Abdu'l-Bahá as your servant.[49]

Maḥmúd says that "even those who were not poor became envious at 'Abdu'l-Bahá's description of the station of poverty."[51] 'Abdu'l-Bahá explained he wished to serve the poor and asked the men to line up. Juliet Thompson describes the scene with her characteristically passionate prose:

At the end of the aisle the Master paused, calling Edward [Getsinger] and me and asked us to stand on each side of Him, with our bags. He was wearing His pongee 'abá and was very shining in white and ivory, His Face like a lighted lamp.

Then down the aisle streamed a sodden and grimy procession: three hundred men in single file. The "breadline." The failures. Broken forms. Blurred faces. How can I picture such a scene? That forlorn host out of the depths, out of the "mud and scum of things"—where nevertheless "something always, always sings." And the Eternal Christ, reflected in the Mirror of "The Servant," receiving them all, like prodigal sons? stray sheep? No! Like His own beloved children, who "resembled Him more that the rich resembled Him."

Into each palm, as the Master clasped it, He pressed His little gift of silver: just a symbol and the price of a bed. Not a man was shelterless that night. And many, many, I could see, found shelter in His Heart. I could see it in the faces raised to His and in His Face bent to theirs.

Those interchanged looks—what a bounty to have witnessed them—to have such a picture stamped on my mind forever!

As the men filed toward Him, the Master held out His hand to the first, grasped the man's hand and left something in it. Perhaps five or six quarters. . . the completely destitute ones received the most. The man glanced up surprised. His eyes met the Master's look, which seemed to be plunging deep into his heart with fathomless understanding. He, this poor derelict, must have known very little of even human love or understanding; and now, too suddenly, he stood face to face with Divine Love. He looked startled, incredulous—as though he couldn't believe what he saw; then his eyes strained toward the Master, something new burning in them, and the Master's eyes answered with a great flash, revealing a more mysterious, a profounder love. A drowning man rescued, or—taken up into heaven? I saw this repeated scores of times. Some of the men shuffled past, accepting their gift ungraciously, but most of them responded just as the first did.

Who can tell the effect of those immortal glances on the lives and even, perhaps, at the death of each of these men? Who knows what the Master *gave* that night?[51]

Kate Carew reported a similar scene:

Think of it! Some one actually coming to America and distributing money. Not here with the avowed or unavowed intention of taking it away.

It seems incredible.

Possibly I may be a little tired of mere words, dealing in them the way I do, but that demonstration of Abdul Baha's creed did more to convince me of the absolute sincerity of the man than anything else that had happened.

And it was all done so unostentatiously, so gracefully, without any fuss or fume.

The Master stood, his eyes always turned away from the man facing him, far down the line, four or five beyond his vis-à-vis, so that when a particularly desperate looking specimen came along he was all ready for him, and, instead of one quarter, two were quietly pressed into the calloused palm.

I had said good night on the platform, so my last view of Abdul Baha was as he stood at the head of the Bowery Mission line, a dozen or more derelicts before him, giving to each a bit of silver and a word of blessing.

> And as I went out into the starlight night I murmured the phrase of an Oriental admirer who had described him as The Breeze of God.[52]

'Abdu'l-Bahá invited everyone in his party back to the Hotel Ansonia for supper. On their way upstairs, they met the "little chambermaid" who took care of 'Abdu'l-Bahá's suite. She had previously told Juliet Thompson that she thought he was "a great Saint." 'Abdu'l-Bahá asked her to hold up her apron and emptied the remaining quarters—about eighty—into it. She was surprised, and the Americans explained to her that they were the leftovers from his visit to the Bowery, where he had given the rest to the men. "I will do the same with this money," she declared, "I will give away every cent of it." Her decision to imitate his selflessness was a fitting end of his last day in New York City, and was yet another example how "the words 'mine' and 'yours' lose their meaning" in the presence of 'Abdu'l-Bahá.[53]

4

THE ONENESS OF HUMANKIND

'Abdu'l-Bahá's eight days in Washington, D.C., while outwardly similar to his visit to New York, were qualitatively different. It was far more intense, involving eight public talks and twelve talks in the homes of Bahá'ís to a cumulative audience of about 10,500. Among his audiences were a Unitarian Church, a Universalist Church, an African American literary society at an African American Methodist Episcopal Church, a Theosophical group, an Esperanto association, the members of the Persian-American Educational Society, and the faculty and students at Howard University. The talks were more varied in subject than those in New York, but race unity was an important theme. Newspaper articles about his visit totaled at least twenty-one.* Because local Bahá'ís had some excellent contacts with government officials and the socially prominent, 'Abdu'l-Bahá met senators, Congressmen, a Supreme Court justice, an Italian duke, several ambassadors, the Treasurer of the United States, the inventor Alexander Graham Bell, labor

* This is based on the 350 articles available to me in the National Bahá'í Archives in Wilmette and from Dr. Duane Troxel.

leader Samuel Gompers, and Admiral Robert Peary (who had led an expedition to reach the North Pole).* He also sat briefly for a portrait by the well-known portrait artist, F. Carl Smith (1868–1955).[1]

Central to his Washington visit were three Bahá'ís. Agnes Parsons (1861–1934) became a Bahá'í about 1908, apparently after an earlier interest in Christian Science. In 1910, she went on pilgrimage to meet 'Abdu'l-Bahá in Acre. While there, anticipating the possibility of his visit to Washington, she invited him to stay in her new house. She had wide-ranging contacts among the city's elite. Not only did she invite everyone she knew to meet 'Abdu'l-Bahá, but she insisted on hosting him—which he agreed to only with reluctance—and made her house available for large meetings every afternoon. When the Georgian-style house was built in 1910, she included a 25' x 50' function room by the front door in order to hold large events; its reported capacity was 150. Juliet Thompson described the "very long white ballroom" as having "an unusually high mantel—the mantel, as well as the ceiling and the paneled walls, delicately carved with garlands. At the windows hang thin silk curtains the color of jonquil leaves. . . . In front of the mantel, a platform had been placed for the Master and every day it was banked with fresh roses, American Beauties."[2]

Of similar importance was Ali Kuli Khan (1879?–1966), an Iranian Bahá'í who came to the United States in 1901 to serve as interpreter for the older Persian Bahá'í teachers 'Abdu'l-Bahá had sent. Khan stayed and

* Elbert Hubbard, in an article he wrote, "A Modern Prophet," published in a book of his essays titled Hollyhocks and Golden Glow, accessible at http://books.google.com/, states that 'Abdu'l-Bahá visited the White House and that the Supreme Court and House of Representatives adjourned when he was in Washington. It is not known where Hubbard acquired this misinformation, which was repeated in Allan Ward, *239 Days,* p. 37, and thus received considerable circulation. The article in Hollyhocks and Golden Glow is an amplification of his article in Hearst's Magazine, July 11, 1912, with considerably more exaggeration and misinformation.

married Florence Breed; theirs was the first Persian-American marriage in the Bahá'í community. Florence was from a wealthy New England family; her mother Alice had been one of Swami Vivekananda's Boston-area hosts in the 1890s and later became one of New England's first Bahá'ís. Khan translated a dozen of Bahá'u'lláh's most important works into English, some of which remained in print into the 1970s. In 1910 he was appointed Iran's chargé d'affairs in Washington, there being no ambassador at the time. As a result, he was able to host important receptions for 'Abdu'l-Bahá in the Persian Legation (the equivalent of an embassy) and invite many prominent diplomats to meet him. Khan was also able to obtain an invitation for 'Abdu'l-Bahá to visit the White House, but President Taft's plans changed, and the visit never occurred. He also helped to arrange for 'Abdu'l-Bahá to be invited to speak to the United States Congress, but the invitation arrived too late to be carried out.[3]

The third significant figure was Louis G. Gregory (1874–1951), an African American lawyer and descendant of slaves. He became a Bahá'í in Washington in June, 1909. The Bahá'í community in that city had a handful of white Bahá'ís who, understanding the implications of the Bahá'í teaching on the oneness of humanity, had begun to teach the Faith to African Americans. Gregory wrote to 'Abdu'l-Bahá in 1909 and received a tablet in reply that encouraged him to "become . . . the means whereby the white and colored people shall close their eyes to racial differences and behold the reality of humanity." He became active in the Washington, D.C., Bahá'í community and encouraged that community to integrate its meetings, even though many white Bahá'ís and the city's social conventions opposed such action. In February, 1911, he was elected to serve on the "Working Committee," the consultative body that coordinated Bahá'í efforts in Washington.[4]

In 1911, Gregory went on pilgrimage—the second African American Bahá'í to do so—and 'Abdu'l-Bahá asked him repeatedly about American racism. 'Abdu'l-Bahá encouraged him to confront racial divisions with love and patience and added that "if you have any influence to get the races to intermarry, it will be very valuable."[5] Gregory met a devoted British Bahá'í, Louisa Mathew, on the pilgrimage, and they became friends. 'Abdu'l-Bahá's advice to her was that she should visit America, and when her health delayed her departure, he invited her to accompany him to New York, which required her to take a train from Paris to Naples to join his party when the *Cedric* docked in that city. Once 'Abdu'l-Bahá's trip to Washington was confirmed, Gregory began to arrange for him to speak at African American venues in the capital where Gregory had good contacts.

Washington, April 20–28, 1912

'Abdu'l-Bahá arrived in Washington at 1:33pm on Saturday, April 20, after a five-hour train ride. He asked that the time of his arrival not be publicized so as to avoid a scene at the station. Awaiting him were Charles Mason Remey and Joseph Hannen—two prominent Washington Bahá'ís who were officers in the Persian-American Educational Society—and the Khan family, Ali-Kuli, his wife Florence, and their three children, Rahim (7), Marzieh (4), and baby Hamideh. Rahim and Marzieh presented 'Abdu'l-Bahá with flowers, then the party squeezed into an automobile and a horse-drawn carriage to ride to Mrs. Parsons's house, with four-year-old Marzieh riding the whole way on 'Abdu'l-Bahá's lap.[6] Out of obedience to 'Abdu'l-Bahá's wishes, a house had been rented for him and his party, but he agreed to honor Mrs. Parsons's request and stay at her home; his party went to the rented place.

'Abdu'l-Bahá rested—the day before had been exhausting, and the train ride had provided little comfort—but people kept calling at the house to see him, so his speech to the last session of the Orient-Occident Unity Conference, sponsored by the Persian-American Educational Society, was delayed. The hall at the Public Library, which normally holds four hundred, was filled with six hundred persons, with another hundred standing outside, unable to get in. According to Joseph Hannen, when 'Abdu'l-Bahá arrived, "the audience rose at once and remained standing until he bade them to be seated. His address, delivered at once, was received with close interest, and at its close the Conference was adjourned." Five reporters were present. Maḥmúd recorded in his diary that "it was amazing to witness how spontaneously these people paid Him respect, even though most were not Bahá'ís."[7]

'Abdu'l-Bahá's talk began with practical observations about the complementary nature of the American and Iranian economies but quickly turned to the theme of the materially civilized West and the spiritually civilized East that he had discussed on other occasions:

> Tonight I am most happy . . . . I see a group of people here assembled on whose faces I perceive the light of God. And this I consider as an evidence of the possibility of uniting the East and the West; of establishing a perfect bond between Persia and America. For . . . the Persians there is no better country as a contributory government than America; and for America there is no better mart than that of Persia, for there is a virgin soil for her commerce. . . in Persia all the mineral resources are still latent beneath the soil. And I hope that this American democracy may be instrumental in developing this hidden wealth, and the perfect amity and a bond of unity may be established between the American Republic and the Persian Government. Whether it be material bonds or spiritual bonds, may they both be well established. May the material civilization of America find a great efficacy and establishment in Persia and the spiritual civilization of Persia find currency in America.[8]

He then turned to his perennial theme of the oneness of humankind, but with an extra twist, possibly an allusion to the intercultural marriage of Ali-Kuli Khan and Florence Breed:

> The created beings of this world can some of them live solitary and alone. . . . But man—it is impossible for him to live solitary and without cooperation. . . . Thus through cooperation we find the happiness of life. . . . If two villages were to be united on a cooperative basis, if they should observe intercourse and cooperation, surely their advancement will be assured. . . . In the country of Persia there shall be established material civilization and advancement, and the doors for American commerce will be opened wide. But above and beyond all this, there shall be a great love and a fountain of affection established between these two peoples. For His Holiness, BAHA'O'LLAH, proclaimed to the world the solidarity and oneness of the world of humanity. He has addressed humanity saying, "Ye are all leaves of one tree and the drops of one sea." The world of humanity may be expressed as one family, and all mankind represents one human unit—one family. It is therefore hoped that the American nation, this revered nation of America, may be united and cemented well with Persia. May they become one race. May they have the same susceptibilities. May the bonds of amity, unity and accord be firmly established.[9]

He closed his remarks with a prayerful exhortation about the future of America:

> It is my utmost hope and desire that the utmost amity and greatest bond of unity may be established between America and Persia; and it is self evident that you will cooperate with me, and I know this is your

> hope also. We shall, therefore, offer supplication to the Threshold of God, so that perchance a great love may take possession of the hearts of men and unite the nations of the world. . . . all this is made possible and feasible through your efforts, until this American democracy may be the first nation to hoist the banner of international peace. May it be the first nation to promulgate the universality of mankind. May it be the first nation to upraise the banner of the Most Great Peace. . . Truly, this is a great nation. Liberty has reached its utmost degree. It is a revered nation. The intentions are all good; they are indeed worthy of being the people to raise the tabernacle of this great peace and to hoist the standard of the oneness of humanity. I supplicate to God and I will ask aid and confirmation in your behalf![10]

Hannen notes that "practically the entire audience remained to shake his hand."[11]

The next day, Sunday, 'Abdu'l-Bahá spoke twice. The first gathering was the Washington Bahá'ís' Sunday school at 11:15am, attended by two hundred people. He seems to have still been reflecting on the international gathering of the night before:

> If we offer a hundred thousand thanks to the Threshold of God for this love which has obtained between the Orient and the Occident, we shall fail to sufficiently express our gratitude. If all the powers of the world were desirous of bringing about this love and unity between the East and the West, they would prove incapable. If they wished to establish this unity it would have proven an impossibility. But His Holiness, BAHA'O'LLAH, has accomplished this through the Holy Spirit, and this unity is indissoluble. It shall stand to time everlasting, and day by day shall it increase. Ere long, it shall take hold of the world, and eventually the hearts of all the nations of the

> world will be brought together thereby. The world of humanity shall become the manifestation of the Lights of God, and the Bestowals of God shall surround all. From the standpoint of material civilization, and from that of spiritual civilization, extraordinary progress shall be accomplished. In this cycle there shall be such progress along the lines of civilization as to be unparalleled in the history of the world. For the world of humanity has heretofore been in the state or stage of infancy. Now it is beginning, or it is in the process of attaining maturity. Just as the human organism attaining the period of maturity, attains a great development,—the intellectual faculties ripen to the fullest extent, in one year of this period there is accomplished a tremendous, unprecedented development, likewise the world of humanity, having reached the period of maturity, will accomplish a tremendous upward progress, and that power, which is the depository of God in the human realities, that Universal power like unto the intellectual faculty of man, will reveal tremendous development.[12]

After passing before each row and shaking hands with everyone, he lunched at the house of Mrs. Alice Barney-Hemmick, who was the mother of Laura Barney, a prominent Parisian Bahá'í. Mrs. Parsons asked him to watch a friend of hers dance at 3pm, but was concerned that modern dance might be too risqué and therefore not approved by him. 'Abdu'l-Bahá replied, "I've done almost everything, but I've never watched dancing," and agreed. Afterward "He said it was very good and blessed her work."[13]

The second talk was to one thousand people at the Universalist Church, Thirteenth and L Streets. Hannen notes that the church was filled to capacity an hour before the service began and that the Reverend John van Schaick, Jr. (1873–1949), a prominent Universalist minister and Social Gospeler, introduced 'Abdu'l-Bahá with a "most glowing tribute to his life and teachings."[14] 'Abdu'l-Bahá's lengthy address could potentially be titled "recognizing the oneness of religion and striving for the unity of humanity." Perhaps alluding to the term "universalist" in the church's name, he began by praising the church's principles:

> What the minister of the Church delineated before us just now testifies to his high sense of morality and his efforts to serve the world of humanity. It is truly praiseworthy and deserves commendation for it opposes the ingrained prejudices of man. These prejudices have kept the human world in a state of chaos for the past six thousand years. . . . Now it is enough! We must investigate the truth. We must pass by these vain imaginings. Praise be to God that we are all the servants of one God. We are all under the protection of His favors and are recipients of His bestowals. . . .[15]

'Abdu'l-Bahá then moved on to talk about Jesus Christ and the prophets of God and alluded to Bahá'u'lláh:

> All the Prophets of God came for the education of humanity in order that the immature souls might become mature and to establish love and amity among mankind. The Prophets have not come to this world to cause discord and enmity. . . . The teachings of the Prophets were solely directed to educate humanity in order to subdue the animal side so that persons under the yoke of nature may find salvation and the heavenly aspect may rule victorious. This divine aspect is the bounty of the Holy Spirit, it is the second birth. He who possesses the divine aspect is a well-wisher of mankind and is most kind to all. He will entertain no enmity toward any Faith and will not belittle any religion, for the foundations of the religions of God are one. If we refer back to these foundations, we shall become united. But if we turn toward imitations, we shall be at variance,

> for imitations differ but the foundations of the divine religions are one and the same. Imitation leads to differences and trouble but the foundations of the divine religions cause love and union.
>
> Christ once said, "When he, the Spirit of Truth, is come, he will guide you into all truth." He also said, "There are many things which you cannot bear hearing now, but when the Spirit of Truth is come, he will expound all truth unto you." Now is the century in which the Spirit of Truth has spoken and has revealed the whole truth. He has laid bare the truth of the religion of Christ and has redeemed people from superstitions so that the edifice of ignorance and enmity may be destroyed and the foundation of love may be established . . . . I ask you, did God create us for love or for enmity? Surely He has created us for love and friendship. . . I hope that the people of the East and the West shall be quickened by the breath of the Holy Spirit, in this, the blessed century of Bahá'u'lláh, and become united, that all may cling to the essential reality of the divine religions—that truth is one and that it is indivisible and not multiple. When all investigate the truth, all will be united, the light of the oneness of humanity will shine and universal peace will come into being. I will now pray on your behalf.[16]

Reverend van Schaick had previously explained that the usual order of service would not be followed, and 'Abdu'l-Bahá's talk would be the entire program that Sunday. When 'Abdu'l-Bahá finished, van Schaick "made a strong appeal" that everyone shake 'Abdu'l-Bahá's hand, and the entire audience responded. Parsons noted that this took "quite a long time" and Maḥmúd quoted 'Abdu'l-Bahá as saying afterward "the people of the church pressed my hand to such a degree that it is now aching."[17]

'Abdu'l-Bahá had earned some well-deserved rest, but he had no time; there was a tea with a large number of people afterwards. At dinner, Mr.

Parsons asked him whether he would like to see the Library of Congress building some evening. 'Abdu'l-Bahá replied, to Parsons's surprise, "Let us go tonight."[18] Parsons was a librarian in the Prints Division and thus was able to give him a tour of the stacks as well as the magnificent, domed Reading Room.

Monday was no less full; Maḥmúd says that 'Abdu'l-Bahá spoke three times: once at a private home, once in the Parsons's ballroom (where he commented about the sinking of the *Titanic* and the passengers on that ill-fated ship whom he had met on the *Cedric*), and once at a dinner party at the Parsons.

In many ways, Tuesday was the pivotal day of his visit. At noon, 'Abdu'l-Bahá went to Howard University, America's premiere historically black university, to address the thousand students plus the faculty and guests, some 1,600 total. His talk focused on how the oneness of humanity transcends race:

> Today I am most happy, for I see here a gathering of the servants of God. I see white and black sitting together. There are no whites and blacks before God. All colors are one, and that is the color of servitude to God. . . .
>
> In the realm of existence colors are of no importance. Observe in the mineral kingdom colors are not the cause of discord. . . . The world of humanity, too, is like a garden, and humankind are like the many-colored flowers. . . . Now ponder this: Animals, despite the fact that they lack reason and understanding, do not make colors the cause of conflict. Why should man, who has reason, create conflict? . . .
>
> White and black are the descendants of the same Adam; they belong to one household. In origin they were one; they were the same color. . . . These colors developed later due to climates and regions; they have no significance whatsoever. Therefore, today I am very

happy that white and black have gathered together in this meeting. I hope this coming together and harmony reaches such a degree that no distinctions shall remain between them, and they shall be together in the utmost harmony and love.

But I wish to say one thing in order that the blacks may become grateful to the whites and the whites become loving toward the blacks. If you go to Africa and see the blacks of Africa, you will realize how much progress you have made. Praise be to God! You are like the whites; there are no great distinctions left. But the blacks of Africa are treated as servants. The first proclamation of emancipation for the blacks was made by the whites of America. How they fought and sacrificed until they freed the blacks! Then it spread to other places. The blacks of Africa were in complete bondage, but your emancipation led to their freedom also—that is, the European states emulated the Americans, and the emancipation proclamation became universal. It was for your sake that the whites of America made such an effort. Were it not for this effort, universal emancipation would not have been proclaimed.

Therefore, you must be very grateful to the whites of America, and the whites must become very loving toward you so that you may progress in all human grades. Strive jointly to make extraordinary progress and mix together completely. . . .

I hope that you attain to such a high degree—and this is impossible except through love. You must try to create love between yourselves; and this love does not come about unless you are grateful to the whites, and the whites are loving toward you, and endeavor to promote your advancement and enhance your honor.[19]

Maḥmúd notes that the audience repeatedly interrupted the talk with applause. Hannen reports that "when both white and colored people were present, Abdul-Baha seemed happiest. The address was received with breathless attention by the vast audience, and was followed by a positive ovation and a recall." To hear a man, regarded by many people as white, address a largely black audience in this way was thrilling.* No doubt many were contemplating 'Abdu'l-Bahá's courage in defying the color line and rejecting deep-seated racial stereotypes and prejudices. His call to "mix together completely" was no doubt an allusion to, among other things, interracial marriage. Possibly 'Abdu'l-Bahá's exhortation to be grateful to whites was shocking, but it was an integral part of his call for building love between the races, for gratitude and appreciation create bonds and lead to reciprocal love in a way that accusations and anger do not. Twenty-seven years later, Shoghi Effendi, 'Abdu'l-Bahá's grandson and Guardian of the Bahá'í Faith, echoed and elaborated on his grandfather's advice in *The Advent of Divine Justice.*[20]

Exhortation was followed by demonstration. Leaving Howard University, 'Abdu'l-Bahá went to the Persian Legation for a luncheon with a group of distinguished Bahá'í guests, "some prominent in the social and political life of Washington." About an hour before the meal was to be served, Louis Gregory arrived; 'Abdu'l-Bahá had summoned him for a private meeting. When lunch was announced, Gregory unobtrusively headed for the door, since he had not been invited to the meal. 'Abdu'l-Bahá led the others to

---

* More research is necessary to determine whether 'Abdu'l-Bahá was perceived as "white" in 1912 or not. The term was legally important but vaguely defined because United States citizenship at that time was open to whites and blacks, but not Asians. A 1915 court case ruled that Syrians were white and could become citizens; a 1923 case that went to the Supreme Court ruled that Punjabis were not white and could not; two court cases in the 1940s reached contradictory conclusions as to whether Arabs were white; no court had ruled whether Iranians were white. See GhaneaBassiri, *A History of Islam in America,* 155–59.

the dinner table, where everyone found their seat; the seating had been carefully set up to follow diplomatic protocol. Everyone sat, but 'Abdu'l-Bahá then rose and said to Ali-Kuli Khan "Where is Mr. Gregory? Bring Mr. Gregory!" Khan hurried off to retrieve Gregory before he left the building. Meanwhile, 'Abdu'l-Bahá rearranged the seating to open up the seat at his right—the place of honor—for the African American lawyer. Once Gregory joined them, "He stated He was very pleased to have Mr. Gregory there, and then, in the most natural way as if nothing unusual had happened, proceeded to give a talk on the oneness of mankind."[21]

Washington was a thoroughly segregated city at the time. Gregory himself later wrote that 'Abdu'l-Bahá "made everyone feel perfectly at ease by his genial humor, wisdom, and outpouring of love."[22] 'Abdu'l-Bahá had made his point.

The luncheon was followed by a 3pm reception that included Admiral Robert Peary, Alexander Graham Bell, Mabel Thorp Boardman (head of the American Red Cross), Ottoman Ambassador Yusuf Ziya, and Duke Pompeo Litta-Visconti-Arese, a prominent Italian nobleman with an American wife. Admiral Peary was still being celebrated for his greatest feat, his 1909 expedition to reach the North Pole, and reportedly that day looked like a "blown up balloon." "'Abdu'l-Bahá spoke charmingly to him and congratulated him for his discovery," Juliet Thompson recalled, and then thanked him for discovering "that *nothing* was to be found there; and so, in relieving the public mind, he had rendered a great service." Peary was nonplussed and no longer looked so self-important. But Clara Rodelheim Sulzer was impressed and told her husband, Congressman William Sulzer, who arranged a private meeting with 'Abdu'l-Bahá later. Before leaving the Legation, 'Abdu'l-Bahá spoke briefly to the African American servants and shook hands with all of them.[23]

The reception was followed by 'Abdu'l-Bahá's usual 5pm talk at Mrs. Parsons's house to a packed crowd. The Ottoman ambassador came with him, and they entered "hand in hand"; he had become quite impressed by 'Abdu'l-Bahá. "Today I have been speaking from dawn until now, yet because of love, fellowship, and desire to be with you, I have come to speak again briefly," 'Abdu'l-Bahá began. He talked about the *Titanic* disaster again—he could have been on the ship, and that week Congress was holding hearings with survivors about the disaster—about the infinite worlds of God after this life, and the unpredictability of this life. He barely had time to eat before heading to the Metropolitan African American Episcopal Church, 1518 M Street NW, downtown Washington. There he was to address the Bethel Literary and Historical Society, "the leading colored organization in Washington," founded in the 1850s, in which Louis Gregory had been a leader. The church itself had a distinguished history; the congregation had been founded in 1838, and the church building, which seats 2,300 exclusive of the balcony section, was built 1880–86. Frederick Douglass, the great African American abolitionist, attended its services regularly. His funeral was held there in 1895.[24]

Hannen notes that "the audience taxed the capacity of the edifice in which the meeting was held."[25] His talk was reminiscent of the one at Columbia; he started with a general observation, turned to the power of science and investigation, and exhorted the audience to pursue the unification of the human race. Unusual, however, was its stress on the importance of liberty to human progress:

> As I stand here tonight and look upon this assembly, I am reminded curiously of a beautiful bouquet of violets gathered together in varying colors, dark and light. This is an evidence and indication that the United States of America is a just and free government, for I see black and white seated together in perfect harmony and agreement. Hearts are united. . . . This evening I will speak to you upon scientific subjects.

The virtues of humanity are many, but science* is the most noble of them all. The distinction which man enjoys above and beyond the station of the animal is due to this paramount virtue. It is a bestowal of God; it is not material; it is divine. . . . Science is the first emanation from God toward man. . . . All blessings are divine in origin, but none can be compared with this power of intellectual investigation and research, which is an eternal gift producing fruits of unending delight. . . .

How shall we utilize these gifts and expend these bounties? By directing our efforts toward the unification of the human race. We must use these powers in establishing the oneness of the world of humanity, appreciate these virtues by accomplishing the unity of whites and blacks . . .

And now as I look into your faces, I am reminded of trees varying in color and form but all bearing luscious and delectable fruits, fragrant and delightful to the inner and outer senses. The radiance and spirituality of this meeting is through the favor of God. . . . You are living upon the great continent of the West, enjoying the perfect liberty, security and peace of this just government. . . . in this human world there is no greater blessing than liberty. You do not know. I, who for forty years have been a prisoner, do know. I do know the value and blessing of liberty. For you have been and are now living in freedom, and you have no fear of anybody. Is there a greater blessing than this? Freedom! Liberty! Security! These are the great bestowals of God. Therefore, praise ye God! I will now pray in your behalf.[26]

---

* According to Alice Ives Breed, 'Abdu'l-Bahá "never uttered the word science" in the talk; her son-in-law, Ali Kuli Khan, said "the word should have been translated 'knowledge.'" See Breed to Thornton Chase, May 1, 1912, p. 3, Chase Papers.

No account of the audience's reaction to the talk has been found. One is struck by the fact that 'Abdu'l-Bahá emphasized not the appalling legal and social limitations placed on his black audience—limitations of which he was aware—but their freedom to progress, their rational and scientific capacities, and their innate gifts on which their development as individuals and as a community depended. Rather than dwelling on the unjust restrictions placed on them by their "just government," he emphasized their relative advantages and the potential of their government to help them. This was typical of 'Abdu'l-Bahá's talks.

At the conclusion of the talk, 'Abdu'l-Bahá was approached by a reporter who asked him about criticisms of "Bahaism" by Rev. Peter Z. Easton, a prominent Protestant missionary to Iran who had interviewed 'Abdu'l-Bahá in London and who wrote that "Bahaism is not Christian; on the contrary, it is essentially anti-Christian" because it is "pantheistic" and puts "this anti-Christ [Bahá'u'lláh] in the place of God and Father of our Lord." 'Abdu'l-Bahá responded that "like the mirror reflects the warmth and rays of the sun, so does Christ reflect the love of God." The reporter from *The Washington Herald* followed up with Easton, who rejected such a simple answer and added, "I am firmly convinced that strong utterances should be made to awaken American Christians to the truth of Abdul Baha's propaganda. I greatly fear that this cult of Bahaism may find fruitful ground in the United States, and I am anxious to raise my voice and urge Christians to crush it in its infancy."[27] 'Abdu'l-Bahá's success was beginning to generate opposition.

Wednesday, April 24 was also a full day, with a meeting with the Bahá'í children in the morning, various private meetings with individuals and families, the usual 5pm reception at the Parsons's, and a 9pm talk at the home of Mrs. Andrew J. Dyer, an African American whose husband may have been white. The Dyer home had been the site of racially integrated meetings every Wednesday for some time; the African American Bahá'ís went there, and some whites went as well. Over one hundred people attended. 'Abdu'l-Bahá likened the interracial gathering to "a beautiful cluster of precious jewels—pearls, rubies, diamonds, sapphires. It is a source of joy and delight. Whatever is conducive to the unity of the world of mankind is most acceptable and praiseworthy; whatever is the cause of discord and disunion is saddening and deplorable." He offered a parallel "in the world of minds and souls" where "fellowship, which is an expression of composition, is conducive to life, whereas discord, which is an expression of decomposition, is the equivalent of death." He noted that "sheep, black and white, associate without discord. . . . Therefore, in the world of humanity it is wise and seemly that all the individual members should manifest unity and affinity. In the clustered jewels of the races may the blacks be as sapphires and rubies and the whites as diamonds and pearls." He promised that "when the racial elements of the American nation unite in actual fellowship and accord, the lights of the oneness of humanity will shine, the day of eternal glory and bliss will dawn, the spirit of God encompass, and the divine favors descend. . . . This is the blessing and benefit of unity; this is the outcome of love. This is the sign of the Most Great Peace; this is the star of the oneness of the human world. Consider how blessed this condition will be." Solving America's race problem was a step in the unity of humanity, and race unity in the United States was itself a sign of the "dawn" of the Most Great Peace (a term referring to a world not only free from war, but in a state of justice and unity).[28]

'Abdu'l-Bahá left the Dyer home in a state of "joy and happiness" and headed to yet another meeting, in the home of Alexander Graham Bell. Bell held gatherings in his home every Wednesday evening, to which prominent scientists and literary figures were invited. It was "one of the intellectual high spots in Washington," noted Theodore Spicer-Simson (1871–1959), a prominent sculptor, who created a portrait medallion of 'Abdu'l-Bahá. Spicer-Simson was present that evening and met "Abdu'l Baha, a slight, striking-looking bearded man picturesquely gowned in Persian turban and cloak, a lovable character and very charming." Bell asked various men present to speak about their discoveries or inventions, and Ali Kuli Khan gave a short summary of the Bahá'í Faith. Then 'Abdu'l-Bahá spoke. Lee McClung, the Treasurer of the United States, was supposed to speak next, but declined, saying, "'Abdu'l-Bahá has spoken, I cannot." At midnight, the entire party retired to the dining room for dinner.[29]

Theosophists, then Esperantists met 'Abdu'l-Bahá at Mrs. Parsons's house at two separate meetings on Thursday; to the latter, he spoke about the Bahá'í principle of a universal language to supplement the ethnic tongues. In the afternoon, he attended a reception in his honor at the Ottoman embassy sponsored by Ambassador Yusuf Ziya. The ambassador praised 'Abdu'l-Bahá highly to the gathering and afterward said to Juliet Thompson, with tears in his eyes, "Truly, He is a Saint." Subsequently, the ambassador visited with 'Abdu'l-Bahá often. It was quite a turnaround; Istanbul had advised him not to assist Ali Kuli Khan in the effort to arrange a White House visit for 'Abdu'l-Bahá and warned him to "avoid having relations" with 'Abdu'l-Bahá, lest it damage diplomatic relations with Iran and Russia.[30]

After the reception at the Turkish embassy, 'Abdu'l-Bahá gave his customary 5pm address at Mrs. Parsons's. For the first time in America, he spoke about the Bahá'í Faith having a series of teachings; he spoke of the "first teaching" of Bahá'u'lláh being "the duty incumbent upon all to investigate reality," the "second teaching of Bahá'u'lláh" being the oneness of the "world of humanity," and the "third teaching" being that "religion which is not in accordance with established science is superstition." He promised that "the other principles I shall illustrate at another time."[31] In the coming months, Americans would hear about more Bahá'í principles.

Friday saw three more public meetings, at All Saints Unitarian Church in the morning, Mrs. Parsons's in the late afternoon, and in the Continental

Hall of the Daughters of the American Revolution at 9pm. The latter gathering of nearly three thousand people, sponsored by the Orient-Occident Unity Society, included Samuel Gompers, president of the American Federation of Labor, one of America’s largest groups of unions, and Mrs. Matthew T. Scott, president of the Daughters of the American Revolution. The talk is not published, but Maḥmúd said it was about the “equality of rights for men and women.” Hannen added that “it had not been contemplated to have such a large meeting that evening, but the interest became so intense that it was deemed necessary.”[32]

As the crowd exited the hall, it encountered a lone “prophetic evangelist” passing out anti-Bahá’í pamphlets; “of the many of this class of false Christs and Elijahs who have carried off the lame sheep from the churches, none is more deceptive than this one from the Holy Land, known as Abdul Baha.” He even threw a bundle of the pamphlets into ‘Abdu’l-Bahá’s carriage.[33] This was not the last anti-Bahá’í action in the city. On Sunday, April 28, the Reverend Dr. James S. Montgomery of Metropolitan Memorial Methodist Church gave a sermon about “The Popular Appetite” deploring the “tendency of people nowadays to flock behind a sensational leader of so-called ‘New Thought’ religion”:

> I have watched the efforts of Abdul Baha, head of the ‘universal’ cult with distress. While I must conclude that the Bahai movement is born in sincerity, for men do not die merely for opinions and whims, and that Abdul is doubtless sincere. . . I do hope that a sojourn in this country will cause him to see the light, and that he will return to his Eastern home a greater man. The incarnation of Jesus Christ, the keystone of our holy faith, is unknown to the teachings of Abdul. This is to deny the foundation stone on which Christianity must rest. . . It would be well if some of those who have listened to Abdul’s lectures

> would take the role of teacher themselves, and convert to Christ this remarkable priest of the 'universal cult.'[34]

One is impressed that even this sermon, while regarding 'Abdu'l-Bahá as mistaken, recognizes his sincerity and "remarkable" qualities. 'Abdu'l-Bahá later privately commented about the sermons and pamphlets against him in Washington, saying that he "never gave any thought to these things, never mentions them nor the names of those who attack him."[35]

Saturday, April 27 was relatively quiet in that it had only one event, an "elegant reception" for three hundred dignitaries and government officials at Mrs. Parsons's house. The day was packed with private meetings, including with relatives of President Howard Taft. This meeting may have been in lieu of the invitation to the White House that 'Abdu'l-Bahá had received for 12:30 the next day, which President Taft had to cancel because of a political trip to Massachusetts.[36]

On Sunday, 'Abdu'l-Bahá met with the Treasurer of the United States, the head of the Patent Office, the chargé d'affaires of Switzerland, and a British diplomat. At 1:25pm, he boarded a train for Chicago.[37] An outside observer would have been impressed by the results of his visit; in spite of his age and the exhausting schedule, he had had ample opportunities to explain his father's teachings. The *Chicago Defender,* Chicago's premier black newspaper, printed a glowing report of 'Abdu'l-Bahá's impact:

> His visit to Washington has been a triumphal march. He has met and conquered southern prejudices. He made addresses at Metropolitan A. M. E. church, at Howard University, and at many white churches and halls and was listened to by many thousands of people of both races, who applauded his propaganda of the fatherhood of God and the brotherhood of man.

> He was the guest of one of Washington's wealthiest women, one who moves in the most exclusive social circles at the capital, and yet her house has been thrown open to rich and poor and black and white. Southern people whose hearts were once filled with the most bitter prejudices against their brothers in black, have publicly acknowledged their change of heart and now treat the colored people as brother indeed.[38]

Chicago, April 29–May 6, 1912

From Washington, the Baltimore and Ohio train passed through Harper's Ferry, Pittsburgh, Youngstown, Akron, and Nappanee. It was supposed to arrive Monday morning, but apparently it had a breakdown and arrived that night.* Because he had been unable to sleep on board, 'Abdu'l-Bahá settled into a suite at the Plaza Hotel at the corner of North and Clark Streets on the north side of downtown Chicago facing Lincoln Park. After resting, he addressed a crowd of Bahá'ís.

Tuesday, his first full day in Chicago, was packed with momentous events. He began by meeting reporters and giving them a talk outlining seven principles of the Bahá'í Faith: investigation of truth; unity of mankind; harmony of science and religion; religion must be a cause of unity; the abolition of religious, racial, patriotic, and political prejudices; universal peace; and equality of rights for men and women.[39] At the conclusion, he

* The train 'Abdu'l-Bahá probably took (assuming the departure time of 1:25pm is correct) can be found in the *Official Railroad Guide* for January 1910, 485. Presumably the 1912 schedule had not changed significantly. Maḥmúd (*Maḥmúd's Diary,* 67) says 'Abdu'l-Bahá's train reached Chicago after dark, rather than 9:45am as scheduled, and the Bahá'ís were at the train station all day looking for him, suggesting a delay of about twelve hours. Also see "Bahaist Chief Missing," *Chicago Daily News,* April 29, 1912, clipping in Bahá'í National Archives.

gave each journalist an apple; he often gave people fruit, flowers, and other small gifts. His visit resulted in at least six local newspaper articles.

He traveled to the house of Mrs. Corinne True, one of Chicago's most dedicated Bahá'ís, to meet her mortally ill son, Davis, age 25, who died of tuberculosis later that day.[40] From there he went to Hull House, one of the first settlement houses in the United States, established to provide social and educational services to immigrants and the impoverished. Jane Addams, founder of Hull House and one of Chicago's most distinguished residents, invited him and welcomed him to the podium. There, he addressed several hundred blacks and whites about racial unity:

> The question of the colored and the white is one in which both, as regards the material, are one . . . Their points of contact are numerous, for the colored and the white are both human . . . . and both are endowed with intelligence. . . . And as regards you here in this country, there is another point of importance, namely, patriotism. That is common to both. And from the standpoint of language, you share that, both of you speak one tongue, and you have in common the same civilization. And now, with these numerous points of partnership or contact and the one point of difference, which is of the least importance, that of color, are you going to allow this least of differences, namely, that of color to separate you? . . . God is not pleased, nor is any intelligent man pleased, nor is any reasonable man willing to have any difference because of that.
>
> But there is need of a great, powerful agent which can overcome all these prejudices. A power which nothing in the world can withstand, and which may overcome all other powers, and that great power is the Love of God, which power can overcome all forces, and I hope that that one power may eradicate this one point of difference and may unite you all, so that hereafter there shall be no distinction. His

> Holiness BAHA'O'LLAH has proclaimed to the world the Oneness of the world of humanity. He has caused the various nations and divergent sects and creeds to unite, and He has declared that the difference in color in the human kingdom is similar to the differences of the flowers, the variegated flowers in a garden. If you enter a garden, you will see yellow flowers, white flowers, black, variegated flowers, the red flower for example, in the utmost of delicacy and beauty, radiant, and each one through difference lends a charm to the other. Hence this difference in the human kingdom is similar to that. If you were to be ushered into a garden where all the flowers were of the same hue or color, how monotonous it would be!
>
> Therefore he has said that the various colors of human kind, one white, one black, one yellow, one red, lend a harmony of color and beauty to the whole. Therefore all must associate with one another, even as flowers consort harmoniously together in a given garden.[41]

Before leaving Hull House, 'Abdu'l-Bahá spontaneously gave away quarters to some unemployed laborers and children, just as he had done at the Bowery.[42]

Later that day, 'Abdu'l-Bahá went to Handel Hall to address the 750 people gathered to attend the closing session of the fourth annual conference of the National Association for the Advancement of Colored People. W. E. B. Du Bois, editor of the N.A.A.C.P. journal *The Crisis,* noted that "a thousand disappointed people were unable even to get standing room in the hall" and the rest experienced "the calm sweet universalism of Abdul Baha." 'Abdu'l-Bahá was originally scheduled to open the conference on Sunday evening when the theme was "Our Common Humanity," but at that time he was leaving Washington, D.C. He seems to have preferred speaking at the end of conferences; he spoke at the closing session of the Orient-Occident Unity Conference and of the Bahai Temple Unity

Convention, perhaps because he did not want his continued presence to distract people from the event. In his talk, 'Abdu'l-Bahá reflected on the verse from Genesis 1:26, "Let us make man in our image, after our likeness":

> This statement indicates the fact that man in some particular is of the image and likeness of God; that is to say, the Perfections of God, the Divine Virtues, have become reflected or revealed in the human reality. Just as the effulgence and the light of the sun, when cast upon a mirror, is reflected fully, gloriously, if the mirror be polished, so likewise the virtues of Divinity are possible of reflection in the human reality. And this makes it evident that man is the most noble of God's creatures. . . .
>
> Let us find out just where and how he is the image and likeness of the Lord, and what is the standard or criterion whereby he can be measured. The criterion or the standard can be no other than the Divine virtues within men, which are Divine and after His image. Therefore every man who is imbued with the Divine qualities, who reveals the heavenly perfections and heavenly morals, who is an expression of the praiseworthy attributes, ideal in nature, is verily an image and likeness of God. If a man should possess wealth, can we call him an image and likeness of God? Or is human honor the criterion whereby he can be called the image of God? Or can we apply a color test as a criterion, and say such and such an one is colored with a certain hue and he is, therefore, in the image of God? Can we say, for example, a man who is green in hue is an image of God? Or can we make another distinction, saying that one who is white is any more an image of God? Is simply the white color a criterion whereby man is to be judged? And shall we make a sweeping statement like that? Or is it reasonable for us to choose the dark color,

> supposing we say a colored man is, after all, the image and likeness, just because of his color, or the red-skinned man, shall he be the image and likeness of God? Or shall we declare the yellow race to be a creation and therefore an image and likeness of God? Can we say simply that so and so is yellow in color, therefore he must be an image and likeness of God? Hence we come to the conclusion that colors are of no importance. Colors are accidental in nature.[43]

It is clear from the *Chicago Defender's* article that the talk was well received:

> That wonderful teacher of peace and the brotherhood of man, Abdul Baha, of Persia, made his first appearance at the Hull House.
>
> In both his addresses at Hull House and Handel hall, Abdul Baha very eloquently showed the folly of discrimination on the account of the only point of difference between men, that of the color of the skin.
>
> A garden of flowers, all of one color, would be monotonous and by no means beautiful.[44]

From the N.A.A.C.P. conference, 'Abdu'l-Bahá went straight to the Bahai Temple Unity conference's closing session. Over one thousand people awaited his arrival. While the details of the talk will be given in the next chapter, an important theme of the talk was the role of houses of worship in establishing unity between races and nations. He offered a glorious vision of the unity of humankind:

> The ages of darkness have passed away and the century of light has arrived. The imaginary prejudices are in the process of dispersion and the Light of Unity is shining. The difference which exists among the

> nations and the peoples is soon to pass away, and the fundamentals of the Divine Religious, which are no other than the solidarity and the oneness of the human race, are to be established. For six thousand years the human race has been at war. It is enough! Now let them, for a time at least, consort in amity. They entertained enmity formerly. Let them for a period exercise love. For six thousand years have they negated each other. Each nation considering the other as infidel. It is sufficient! We must all know that we are the servants of One God; that we are turning to One God; that we have one Kind Father; that we have one Divine Law; that we have one Reality; that we have one Desire. Thus may we live in the utmost of amity and love together, and for this love, for this amity, the Favors and Bounties of God shall surround us; the world of humanity will be reformed; the human kind will find a new life, eternal light shall shine; merciful and Heavenly morals shall become manifested.[45]

Eight days of talks about the oneness of the races of humanity, which started with the talks at Howard University and Metropolitan A. M. E. church, had reached their conclusion. The Bahá'ís had been offered a new understanding of their religion's message, an example of how to implement it, and some of the concrete steps necessary for achieving unity. Furthermore, thousands of blacks and whites who were not Bahá'ís had heard parts of the vision in talks or had read details in newspapers, and were influenced as well. One was Robert Abbott, publisher of the *Chicago Defender,* the city's leading black newspaper and the most influential African American publication in the United States. He attended 'Abdu'l-Bahá's talk at Hull House, met 'Abdu'l-Bahá, and was impressed. He began to associate closely with the Bahá'ís and formally joined the Bahá'í Faith in 1934. Ida B. Wells, a prominent African American activist in the city, who was also on the program of the N.A.A.C.P. conference, was attracted to the Bahá'í teachings and briefly associated herself with the Chicago Bahá'í community in 1919. Without 'Abdu'l-Bahá's influence, the American Bahá'í community never would have been able to attract Alain Locke, one of the premier black intellectuals of the early twentieth century and a founder of the Harlem Renaissance, to the Bahá'í Faith in 1918.[46]

W. E. B. Du Bois, one of the two or three most influential African Americans in the country, met 'Abdu'l-Bahá in New York and Chicago and was impressed by him. As editor of *The Crisis,* the leading African American monthly (circulation 22,500 nationwide), he featured 'Abdu'l-Bahá as the "Man of the Month" in the May 1912 issue—the column almost exclusively focused on African Americans—and reprinted a digest of the Hull House and N.A.A.C.P. talks in the June issue. His contact with the Bahá'í community deepened when his wife, Nina Gomer Du Bois, became a Bahá'í in 1936. When 'Abdu'l-Bahá died, Du Bois commented in *The Crisis* that "Two men sit high before the world today—Eugene Debs and Abdul Baha. One is free of chains that never should have bound him—the other of Life which he tried to free of race and national prejudice."[47]

A measure of 'Abdu'l-Bahá's impact on the attitudes of whites toward blacks occurred that very day. On Tuesday afternoon, possibly while 'Abdu'l-Bahá was speaking at the N.A.A.C.P. convention, the delegates of the Bahai Temple Unity held their annual election for the nine members of the Executive Board. The vote produced a tie for the ninth position between Louis Gregory and Dr. Frederick Nutt of Chicago. Both men resigned in favor of the other, and the convention voted unanimously to accept Dr. Nutt's resignation.[48] The Bahai Temple Unity delegates—probably 99% of whom were white—had elected an African American to their national governing board, which was responsible for building the Bahá'í House of Worship in Wilmette, Illinois, and otherwise coordinating the affairs of the Bahá'í Faith in North America. It was a momentous, rare, and historic event.

No doubt 'Abdu'l-Bahá was very pleased by Mr. Gregory's election and the victory over prejudice that it represented. But evidence shows that he had a yet greater victory over prejudice in mind. While in New York or Washington, 'Abdu'l-Bahá had given Louisa Mathew a white flower and told her to give it to Louis Gregory. The two had become friends while on pilgrimage the year earlier. "By looking at me in a peculiar way [He] conveyed his meaning to me, that he wished me to marry Mr. Gregory," Mathew later recalled. She continued:

> Curiously enough, after this love began to grow in my heart & the desire for marriage whereas before I only liked Mr. Gregory as a friend. Later Abdul Baha said before Dr. Getsinger, Fareed & others in the train to Chicago to me "How are you & Mr. Gregory getting along?" Startled I answered "What do you mean, we are good friends?" To which He replied emphatically & with His face wreathed in mischievous smiles "You must be *very* good friends."
>
> Before He left Chicago I asked Abdul Baha plainly one morning early if I had understood aright that he wished Mr. Gregory & myself to marry. He said "yes." He did wish it. "I wish the white & the colored to marry," He added.
>
> Then on my intimating that as a woman I could do nothing to bring it about He asked "Do you love him, would you marry him if he asked you?" & I replied "yes." Then He said "if he loves you he will ask you." Later in the morning as I learned some time afterwards, He told Louis it would give Him much pleasure if he & I would marry, which came as an utter surprise to Louis who had no thoughts of marriage. Abdul Baha said "What is the matter? Don't you love her?" "Yes, as a friend," Louis said. "Well, think of it," said Abdul Baha, "& let me know; . . . marriage is not an ordinance & need

> not be obeyed, but it would give me much pleasure if you & Miss Mathew were to marry."[49]

Another account of the event is provided by Ghodsiyeh Khanum Ashraf, a Persian Bahá'í woman attending college in the United States. According to her, Louisa Mathew asked her to serve as interpreter on the day in Chicago when Louisa came to 'Abdu'l-Bahá because she didn't want a man to be interpreting for her. Ashraf says that Louisa "was determined to fight racism in America," so she "requested permission to attain the presence of 'Abdu'l-Bahá and asked Him to order the learned black gentleman, Louis Gregory, to marry her."[50] Presumably her determination to fight racism was itself a result of 'Abdu'l-Bahá's talks and His prior hints to her.

Ashraf was present when 'Abdu'l-Bahá spoke to Louis Gregory as well. "When he was permitted to leave and shook my hand, it felt ice-cold," she noted. "He left the Master's presence as if he had been struck by lightning. Later, he told me that it took him two hours to regain his composure. During those hours, he had walked aimlessly in streets and that he had passed a huge test in his life."[51]

Louis and Louisa married less than five months later, on September 27, in New York City. Their marriage lasted until their deaths almost four decades later. It was a testimony to 'Abdu'l-Bahá's insight into character, the power of his extraordinary personality, and Louis and Louisa's faith in him. At the time, their marriage was illegal in twenty-five of the country's forty-eight states and unacceptable to a majority of people everywhere. It was controversial even among the Bahá'ís, who were willing to accept the principle of the oneness of humanity in the abstract but could not imagine that the world was ready for its most radical implications. But to 'Abdu'l-Bahá, it was a question of consistency and the courage of one's convictions. The interracial marriage of the Gregorys did more than perhaps any other event in 'Abdu'l-Bahá's visit to drive home his message: humanity is one, and differences of race are ultimately superficial. Thus it can be seen as the act that was paradigmatic of his entire message. Indeed, in Shoghi Effendi's list of 'Abdu'l-Bahá's accomplishments during his epochal North American trip, "last but not least" was "the exemplary act He performed by uniting in wedlock two of His followers of different nationalities, one of the white, the other of the Negro race."[52] Over the next century, thousands of Bahá'ís were inspired to follow them.

5

"THE TEMPLE IS ALREADY BUILT"

On the evening of Tuesday, April 30, 'Abdu'l-Bahá stood before over a thousand people gathered for the closing public session of the Bahai Temple Unity convention in Drill Hall, Masonic Temple, downtown Chicago.[1] Of all the audiences he faced on his North American trip, it was one of the most complicated to address, for the audience was the most varied. It included in its ranks a spectrum of involvement or interest in the Bahá'í Faith.

At one end of the spectrum were "the involved": those who outwardly identified themselves as Bahá'ís and were active in various ways: they said Bahá'í prayers, fasted during the fasting period, attended Bahá'í worship services, took their children to Bahá'í religious classes, voted in local Bahá'í elections, subscribed to *Star of the West* magazine, or actively told others about the Faith and encouraged them to investigate it. No one of these various activities was necessarily definitive of their commitment. Because obligatory prayers or the fast were not emphasized, some Bahá'ís did not know about them, although others did both. Some voted in local Bahá'í elections, while others lived in places with no elected organization because it was not a required feature of a Bahá'í community. Some communities deemphasized Bahá'í devotional meetings so that Bahá'ís could attend church services, while other communities had a long tradition of Sunday morning worship in a rented hall, with a piano accompanying them as they sang Bahá'í hymns—dozens had been composed—or Christian hymns stripped of overtly Christian references to, for example, Jesus or the Trinity.

If there was one defining characteristic of the involved, it was their active response to 'Abdu'l-Bahá's constant exhortation to teach the Bahá'í Faith to others. They were the ones finding people such as Howard Colby Ives and Harry Randall, going to their homes to talk to them about the Bahá'í teachings, inviting them to Bahá'í meetings, patiently answering their questions, and providing them with literature to read. If this group can be subdivided, one would look at locally versus nationally involved Bahá'ís. The latter knew many Bahá'ís outside their own communities, sometimes had the means or time to go on pilgrimage to Palestine, and often were the ones corresponding with others, writing pamphlets and books, and telling the local Bahá'ís about national news and trends, especially the plan to build a Bahá'í temple outside Chicago. Construction of the temple was the purpose of the Bahai Temple Unity, a continental organization that held an annual convention, attended by delegates from local Bahá'í communities.

'Abdu'l-Bahá's audience that night included the bulk of the nationally active believers—numbering perhaps a few hundred—and a few hundred more believers from Chicago and the vicinity. Together, they may have constituted half of the people present. The hall also contained a large number of friends of Bahá'ís and members of the general public who wanted to know more; they constituted a group one could call "the interested." Some were attracted, perhaps even partially committed; they liked some teachings but disliked others; they were attracted to the Master but did not want him to replace the Master already in their hearts, Jesus Christ; they saw in the eyes of the Bahá'ís the spark of faith and the flame of commitment but were hesitant or afraid to light the fire of faith in their hearts; they felt the commonsense nature of some Bahá'í teachings, but the rational bent to their personality prevented them from committing to abstract metaphysical ideas.

The involved and the interested: in their various levels of commitment, they made up the audience that evening. They could not be differentiated from each other based on whether they were "Christian" or not because many involved Bahá'ís felt they had not left Christianity behind when accepting Bahá'u'lláh and 'Abdu'l-Bahá. Some continued to attend church services irregularly; in New York, Juliet Thompson sometimes attended Percy Stickney Grant's Episcopal Church of the Ascension, and later many active New York Bahá'ís attended St. Marks. It would be another two decades before the Bahá'ís were asked to renounce church membership. 'Abdu'l-Bahá did not require it, and because Bahá'í communities were still loosely organized, they often could not provide a good substitute for the experience of belonging to a church. But this is not to say that all Bahá'ís had dual membership. Some had been unchurched when they became Bahá'ís, and they made the Bahá'í community the center of their religious efforts. Other Bahá'ís were "post-Christian" in that they had been active in Theosophy, New Thought, or esoteric Masonic groups before becoming Bahá'ís and had no interest in churches. Most of the involved Chicago Bahá'ís did not retain active membership in churches, and archival records do not preserve the names of any churches they attended regularly. Some attended metaphysical groups as observers, but the Chicago House of Spirituality, the community's elected governing body, made a distinction between the Bahá'í Faith and these other groups and did not consider themselves one of the metaphysical organizations in the city.*

* In 1904 and 1906 the House of Spirituality was asked to send an official representative of the Faith to participate on the New Thought Executive Committee, a committee that conducted quarterly meetings of all the New Thought groups in Chi-

Finally, in 1912 there was no process of formal enrollment, and thus there was no formal boundary defining membership in the Bahá'í community. An enrollment process was not put into place until more than a decade later. Consequently, the involved and the interested were not easy to differentiate; someone interested one year might become involved during the next, then cease involvement the year after because of disaffection over a teaching or sheer lack of time. When the United States census asked the Bahá'ís to report their membership, as it did in 1906 and 1916, each local Bahá'í community used its own definition. Internally, Bahá'ís had a sense of who were "the workers" for the Cause, and when asked to provide a list of "workers," the total tended to be about a thousand.* While this was a small number compared to Christian denominations, it was comparable to other metaphysical and non-Christian groups. It was several times larger than the Vedantists, who suffered from the occasional lapse of their local congregations, and it was several times smaller than the Theosophists, who suffered from occasional internal controversy and schisms.

Standing before the thousand people that night, 'Abdu'l-Bahá was certainly aware of the presence of the involved and the interested in all their gradations. He would have recognized the faces of scores or hundreds of Bahá'ís from meetings in New York and Washington and from the pilgrimages some Americans had made to see him overseas. He would have recognized the curious from their quizzical or detached expressions or their cautious retreat to the rear wall of the hall. But who was there mattered less to him than how to serve them, regardless of their involvement or

cago. The House of Spirituality decided that the Faith was not a New Thought group and therefore official representation was not appropriate, but individual Bahá'ís could attend informally. See Stockman, *The Bahá'í Faith in America, vol. 2,* 398–99.

* For details about the number of Bahá'ís in the United States, 1899 to 1936, see Stockman, *The Bahá'í Faith and American Protestantism*, 26–34.

interest. As 'Abdu'l-Bahá had stated on his first day in the United States, he had come to promote "the fundamental principles of our Cause . . . universal peace and the promotion of the basic doctrine of the oneness and truth of all the divine religions."[2] This was not shorthand for "converting people to the Bahá'í Faith"; while he did want people to accept Bahá'u'lláh and dedicate their lives to Him, he also wished to spread Bahá'u'lláh's principles—which revolve around the oneness of humanity—to the entire world and thus to help leaven human society with principles that would better civilization. He had dual goals.

One of 'Abdu'l-Bahá's techniques for attracting people both to Bahá'u'lláh and to His principles was the construction of what one scholar has called a "polyreligious world." In such a world, "the same religious beliefs and practices were subject to widely varied meanings," allowing them to help "bridge individual differences in ethnicity, race, and religion."[3] A key aspect of a polyreligious world is the polyvalence of religious terms and symbols, in other words, that they have different meanings to different peoples. By utilizing polyvalence, 'Abdu'l-Bahá was able to speak to the involved and the interested at once and inspire them in different ways.

His address that evening could be titled "Temples and the Oneness of Humanity." By conjoining the purpose of the Bahai Temple Unity—to build a House of Worship for North America's Bahá'ís—with the need to unite humanity and establish universal religion, he neatly brought the organization's goal to the service of wider, universal themes:

> Among the institutes of the Holy Books is that of the foundation of Holy Edifices. That is to say, an edifice is to be built in order that humanity might find therein a place of meeting, and this is to be conducive to unity and fellowship amongst them. The real Temple is the very Law of God, for to that all humanity must resort, and that is the Center of Unity for all mankind. That is the collective center.

> That is the cause of accord and unity of the hearts. That is the cause of solidarity of the human race. That is the source of the life eternal. Temples are the symbols of that uniting force, in order that when the people gather there in a given edifice of God, in the house and of God, they may recall the fact that the law has been revealed for them and that that law is to unite them.[4]

As he so often did after an opening statement of his general theme, 'Abdu'l-Bahá acknowledged the Christian ethos permeating nearly any North American gathering, and from the New Testament he extracted the perfect reference for the occasion: "Jesus Christ, addressing Peter, said, "Thoù art Peter, and upon this rock I will build my church" (Matt. 16:18). He noted that this referred to Peter's faith:

> This faith of thine, O Peter! is the very cause of uniting the various nations and summoning them to unite, and shall be the bond uniting the hearts. It shall be a cause of uniting the world of humanity. In brief, the purpose of places of worship and edifices for adoration is simply that of unity in order that various nations, divergent races, varying souls, may gather there and among them amity, love and accord may be realized. The original purpose is this. That is why His Holiness BAHA'U'LLAH has commanded that a place be built for all the religionists of the world; that all religions and races and sects may gather together; that the Oneness of the human world may be proclaimed; that all the human race is the servant of God, and that all are submerged in the Ocean of God's Mercy.[5]

For the "interested" the vision of all peoples uniting in a single building to worship their God was, no doubt, very appealing; it was reminiscent of Isaiah 2:3-4: "Come ye, and let us go up to the mountain of the LORD, to the house of the God of Jacob; and he will teach us of his ways, and we will walk in his paths: for out of Zion shall go forth the law, and the word of the LORD from Jerusalem. And he shall judge among the nations, and shall rebuke many people: and they shall beat their swords into plowshares, and their spears into pruning hooks: nation shall not lift up sword against nation, neither shall they learn war any more."[6]

But what did 'Abdu'l-Bahá mean when he said that "a place be built for all the religionists of the world; that all religions and races and sects may gather together"? Did they have to become Bahá'ís? Would the Bahá'í temple have religious services sponsored by other groups, or even separate chapels for them, as some Bahá'ís thought? Or would the building be open for silent prayer by all and for Bahá'í worship using the scriptures of the world's religions, but not for services by other faiths, as was actually the case after it was completed? 'Abdu'l-Bahá did not address such questions in his address that night, although he had already resolved similar questions for the Bahá'í temple under construction in Ashkhabad, Russian Central Asia; it did not have separate worship spaces, but one large one, and it did not provide facilities where Muslims could perform ablutions (as would be required if they were to say their obligatory prayers), nor did it have places where Eastern Orthodox Christians could store holy relics or Jews the Torah. 'Abdu'l-Bahá had spoken in a similar fashion two weeks earlier to the Bahá'ís of New Jersey when he said that Bahá'u'lláh established "unity and agreement" among the "many different communities. . . religions, sects and denominations" of Iran, meaning not that Iran was now a united society, but that within the Bahá'í community, Bahá'ís of many different backgrounds were in agreement and unity.[7]

'Abdu'l-Bahá saw the Mas͟hriqu'l-Ad͟hkár as not just a building, but a universal symbol of unity: "The world of existence may be likened to this place [the Mas͟hriqu'l-Ad͟hkár]. . . . Just as the external world is a place where various peoples of different hues and colors, of various faiths and denominations, meet; just as they are submerged in the same Sea of Favors; likewise all may meet under the dome of the Mashrak-el-Azkar and adore the One God in the same spirit of truth, for the ages of darkness have passed away and the century of light has arrived."[8] After offering a vision of a world to come where war and racism are annulled, he turned to the theme of service to others:

> there are some people who are as children. They are ignorant, and with the utmost love are we to educate them in order that they may become wise. They are sick; they are ill. We must tenderly care for them and treat them until they become well. Their morals are unpraiseworthy. We must train them in order that they may become imbued with morals commendable. Otherwise we are all the servants of One God, and we are beneath the Protection and Providence of One God. These are the Institutes of God and the Foundations of the Mashrak-el-Azkar, or His Temple. The outer edifice is a symbol of the inner. May the people be admonished thereby![9]

He concluded his address with a prayer, the one known by Bahá'ís as "The Prayer for America." The audience applauded vigorously and sang "The Temple Song" by Louise Waite. 'Abdu'l-Bahá presented two thousand French francs to the Temple fund. After two more songs, the program concluded, "though the hour was early."[10]

Laying the Cornerstone, May 1, 1912

People perhaps needed the extra sleep, for the next morning many of them headed to a "wooded and grass covered" knoll in Wilmette, not far from the place where the newly excavated North Shore Channel entered Lake Michigan, to attend the laying of the cornerstone of the Bahá'í temple. The elevated train line was not yet extended to Wilmette, making it difficult to reach the site without an automobile or taxi. A "brilliant white tent, pitched to guard against the threatening rain," was erected on the southeastern part of the plot. The tent contained three circles of seats numbering three hundred, broken by nine aisles leading to the large open center; outside the seats was a broad perambulatory able to accommodate another hundred or two unable to find seats. The tent was set up like a temporary Mas<u>h</u>riqu'l-A<u>dh</u>kár.[11]

'Abdu'l-Bahá was expected to arrive at 11am, when the program was scheduled to begin, but he chose to meet with people who had stopped at the Plaza Hotel to visit, including the four-person editorial board of *Star of the West* magazine, whom he encouraged to continue their work. Here, as in many other cases during his journey, he followed the promptings of the spirit rather than adhering to a schedule, and he gave an impromptu talk on the role of America to others who arrived to see him. When he reached the temple site by taxi at 1pm, he sent one of his Persian attendants to find Corinne True, the "mother of the temple," who had dedicated her life to finding the site, convincing Bahá'ís to buy it, and raising the funds to pay the mortgage. The taxi took 'Abdu'l-Bahá and Mrs. True to the bridge over the North Shore Channel and parked there for a few minutes while he presumably offered her some words of comfort and condolence about the passing of her son, Davis, the day before. 'Abdu'l-Bahá and Corinne True walked to the tent and entered it from the north end.[12]

'Abdu'l-Bahá went straight to the central area of the tent and addressed the gathering about the historic and spiritual significance of the building they were about to commence:

> Thousands of Mashrak-el-Azkars, which mean the Dawning Points of Praise for all religionists, will be built in the world. In the Orient

and in the Occident of the world will they be built. But this Mashrak-el-Azkar being the first one in the Occident, has great importance. . . . In Ishkabad, Caucasus, Russia, the Mashrak-el-Azkar has the same great importance, being the first one built there. In Persia there are many Mashrak-el-Azkars. Some have been houses which have been rented for that purpose. Others have given their homes entirely for that purpose, and in some places temporary and small places have been built therefor. . . but the great Mashrak-el-Azkar was founded in Ishkabad. Because it is the first Mashrak-el-Azkar, hence it possesses the superlative degree of importance. All the friends of Ishkabad agreed and put forward the greatest effort. . . . Hence such a tremendous edifice was built. A colossal effort was put forward. Notwithstanding their contributions to that Mashrak-el-Azkar, they have, as you know, contributed to you here in this city. Now that one is almost complete, that is to say, with all its gardens. That Mashrak-el-Azkar is centrally located. It has nine avenues, nine gardens, nine fountains, so it is nine on nine, all nines. It is like a beautiful bouquet. Just imagine an edifice of that beauty in the center, very lofty, surrounded centrally by gardens, variegated flowers, with nine avenues interlacing nine gardens, nine ponds and nine fountains, and see how delightful it must be! That is the way it should be. It is matchless, most beautiful! Such is the design. And now they are at work building a Hospital and a School for Orphans and a Home for the Cripples and a large Dispensary and a Hospice. They are now planning, thinking of these things. When that, God willing, shall be completed, it will be a Paradise![13]

Thus 'Abdu'l-Bahá stated the basic design elements of the building to be erected in Wilmette—a building not yet designed—and emphasized that it was the second most important Bahá'í House of Worship in the world.* He also described a future when the Bahá'í communities would be numerous enough to build thousands of houses of worship; it was yet another indication that the Bahá'í teachings were not just an inspiration for reforming the existing faiths, but also the basis for a new community.

After his address, he led the crowd out of the tent and to the center of the grounds to lay the first stone. At that time, no one knew exactly where the building would be built or how large it would be, so the act was symbolic. This was not how the program was supposed to go; 'Abdu'l-Bahá departed from the official plans. A cubical limestone block with a broken corner lay nearby, transported from a building site near downtown Chicago in September 1908 by Nettie Tobin, a devoted Chicago Bahá'í, with the help of an old Persian Bahá'í, a series of reluctant streetcar conductors, and, at one point, a broken old cart. Perhaps the construction workers had consented to her taking the stone because it was defective. Her effort would eventually assume epic proportions in the minds of many Bahá'ís, whose thoughts would turn to Matthew 21:44: "The stone which the builders rejected, the same is become the head of the corner: this is the Lord's doing, and it is marvelous in our eyes."†

'Abdu'l-Bahá called for the stone to be brought to the spot he had selected at the center of the property—fulfilling, as it were, the prophecy of the

* The Bahá'í House of Worship in Ashkhabad (or I<u>sh</u>qábád, according to the standard Bahá'í system of transliteration) was confiscated by the Soviet government in 1928, converted into an art gallery in 1938, and very badly damaged by a severe earthquake in 1948. It was torn down by the government in 1963. See "The Razing of the Ma<u>sh</u>riqu'l-A<u>dh</u>kár of 'I<u>sh</u>qábád," *The Bahá'í World: An International Record, vol. XIV, 1963–1968* (Wilmette: Bahá'í Publishing Trust, 1974), 479–80.

† Not all approved of the stone hauling; Thornton Chase, an early Chicago Bahá'í, commented negatively about Tobin's effort to haul the stone to Wilmette. See Thornton Chase to Mrs. A. M. Bryant, October 2, 1908, quoted in Stockman, *The Bahá'í Faith in America, vol. 2,* 301.

verse. A woman presented him with a golden trowel to lay the stone, but it proved utterly inadequate to cut through the tough prairie grass covering the ground. A Bahá'í ran to a nearby farm house and fetched an axe. 'Abdu'l-Bahá "took it and like an athlete swung it high in the air and after several blows, cut through the resisting turf."[14] While 'Abdu'l-Bahá enlarged the hole with the trowel, Dr. Ameen Fareed urged the audience to sing Bahá'í hymns. At that point another Bahá'í ran up with a shovel borrowed from a nearby crew extending the El tracks, allowing the excavation to proceed more easily.

Corinne True suggested that a woman be asked to enlarge the hole, so 'Abdu'l-Bahá asked Fareed to call Lua Getsinger forward. After she worked on the hole with the shovel, Corinne True contributed with the axe, then Louise Waite with the shovel, followed by an honorary representative of various groups: Bahá'ís of Zoroastrian background, of Muslim background, Bahá'í women of the East, Persians, Syrians, Egyptians, Indians, Japanese, South Africans, English, French, Germans, Dutch, Norwegians, Swedes, Danes, Jews, and American Indians. Two active Bahá'ís of American and Canadian background, respectively—Harlan Ober and Grace Robarts—excavated the hole on behalf of their countries.* The oneness of humanity was graphically represented by the people who prepared the hole to receive the stone.

The excavation completed, 'Abdu'l-Bahá scooped out handfuls of earth and presented them to various people as souvenirs of the ceremony. On behalf of all the peoples of the earth, he rolled the stone into the hole,

* The list of persons and groups represented is assembled from Mahḥmúd-i-Zarqání, *Maḥmúd's Diary*, 72; Jaxon, "Dedication of the Mashrak-el-Azkar Site," 6, and Louise Waite, "My Visits with and Instructions from Abdul Baha while He was in Chicago from April 30th to May 6th 1912," 6–7; Elizabeth Robarts, "Reminiscences of 'Abdu'l-Bahá," untitled typescript, National Bahá'í Archives, Wilmette, IL, 10.

pushed dirt around it with the trowel, and pounded it down with the shovel. Finally, he stated, "The Temple is already built."[15]

That ended the dedication ceremony. 'Abdu'l-Bahá soon departed for Chicago, leaving the assembled Bahá'ís and their friends to explore the grounds, just breaking out in the verdure of early spring, or to sit together in the circles of chairs and contemplate their next steps. They faced the daunting task ahead, as a tiny band, devoid of extremely wealthy members, of paying for the acres of land in a rapidly developing affluent suburb, selecting the design of a monumental structure, raising it, and completing the magnificent gardens and fountains 'Abdu'l-Bahá had envisioned. The task would challenge the growing North American community for four decades, absorb millions of dollars of contributions, and push them to develop the most capable Bahá'í organization in the world, an organization that would also be called on to win many significant victories for the Bahá'í Faith. The building of the Temple would serve as an important catalyst in the construction of the Bahá'í Administrative Order, a system ordained by Bahá'u'lláh and already detailed in 'Abdu'l-Bahá's Will and Testament for organizing the Bahá'í community. As such, the dedication ceremony proved to be one of the signal events of 'Abdu'l-Bahá's ministry and one of the most important events in North American Bahá'í history.

6

ENUNCIATING THE BAHÁ'Í PRINCIPLES

Throughout the month of May, 'Abdu'l-Bahá had many opportunities to elaborate on the teachings of the Bahá'í Faith. He gave at least fifty-five talks in eleven different cities in the Midwest and East Coast to a combined audience of some fifteen thousand people.[1] The diverse audiences—peace associations, women's groups, Unitarian and Protestant churches, denominational conferences, Theosophists, universities—provided many opportunities to explain different aspects of Bahá'í beliefs. In many cases, he had time to touch on only one aspect of the Bahá'í teachings.

The central piece—the key to putting the entire puzzle together—was the oneness of humanity. The phrase is deceptively simple—by the early twentieth century, no one seriously argued that the different races of humanity were different species, for example. But as 'Abdu'l-Bahá's talks at Hull House, Howard University, the Metropolitan A.M.E. Church, and the N.A.A.C.P. convention indicated, the oneness of humanity meant that the differences of race ultimately were superficial, and his encouragement of the courtship of Louis Gregory and Louisa Matthew made clear that intermarriage was a radical, symbolic demonstration of this truth. His talk at the Bahai Temple Unity convention April 30 noted that all religions had always stood for unity and that places of worship were meant to symbolize that unity.

Chicago, May 2–6, 1912

'Abdu'l-Bahá's subsequent talks provided other pieces of the jigsaw puzzle. On May 2, he gave no less than five talks in downtown Chicago elaborating on important aspects of the oneness of humanity. In the gaps between talks, he met privately with individuals, including Corinne True and her daughters, whom he consoled for the loss of Davis, whose funeral was also held that day.[2]

The first public talk came after a busy morning of "successive waves of visits from friends and inquirers" which included "learned men, scientists, engineers and government officials."[3] The crowd grew so large that 'Abdu'l-Bahá addressed them in the Hotel Plaza's large parlor, which seated 150. He spoke about consultation:

> In this Cause the question of consultation is of the greatest importance. But the spiritual consultation, not physical consultation. In France I visited the Senate, the Parliament. I did not like their system at all, for consultation must have for its aim the arrival at truth and not opinionated opposition. When there shall be opposition or inimical opinion, it is very bad. I found that they altercated, by worthless or useless altercations, each one presenting a certain angle or a certain word, someone would oppose him, and then there was a turmoil, and it happened that while I was there two of them got up and had a fight. I said, this is not parliamentary consultation. This is a fiasco![4]

'Abdu'l-Bahá emphasized that the purpose of consultation was the investigation of truth, an extremely important Bahá'í principle in its own right because the oneness of humanity implies the ability and right of all human beings to contribute to the collective decision-making processes of society. 'Abdu'l-Bahá described the conditions for proper consultation: that one should offer contributions to the group humbly, "with utmost serenity, sobriety, soberness of temperament"; that one should first "weigh the opinion previously expressed"; that one should accept "immediately" the position of another if one finds it to be "better," rather than being "willful" in holding to one's own position. The purpose is "unity" and "truth"; should "opposition" and "dispersion" result, it is "very bad." Consultation "must be spiritual, in the utmost love." He then gave as an example of true consultation a conversation among a group of Jesus's disciples (not found in the Bible or early Christian texts) after the crucifixion.[5]

Considering that the Bahai Temple Unity Convention had just ended, it is possible that the talk was aimed at improving the decision-making processes within the Bahá'í community. The Chicago Bahá'ís had begun to discuss and practice consultation some ten years earlier, but the concept had not yet spread much beyond that city.[6] The use of an example from early Christianity does not necessarily indicate that a non-Bahá'í audience was intended.

Later that morning, he spoke to another gathering in his hotel. He referred to the fog enveloping the city that morning, which hid the sunrise. He noted that the sun represented God and that the different points along the horizon from which it rose every day were the Messengers of God. After a time, "the dawning point is being worshipped instead of the sun itself." He called on his audience to "make use of intelligence and reason so that you may dispense the dense clouds" of superstition and imitation and "hold to the Reality of all of the prophets."[7] In this way, 'Abdu'l-Bahá taught aspects of the oneness of religions, which all come from the same source through different Prophets, who adapt their message to their cultural and historical context.

'Abdu'l-Bahá then went to the Hotel La Salle to meet with the Federation of Women's Clubs. Louise "Shahnaz" Waite (1867–1939), a prominent Chicago Bahá'í and composer of Bahá'í hymns, arranged the invitation. A thousand people, mostly women with some men, from all over Illinois were present. 'Abdu'l-Bahá arrived after the luncheon was finished. As he entered the room, "they all instantly arose to their feet and stood until he motioned them to be seated." The inevitable subject of his talk was the equality of women, another implication of the oneness of humanity. He began with a simple observation about the sun awakening the potentialities of the earth through its light and heat and used it as an analogy for "the inner and ideal Sun of Truth, the Word of God," which awakens human potentialities: "One of the great things which was hidden in the realm of existence was the potential capability or capacity of womankind. Through the light of the Sun of Reality in this age of illumination, the light and capability of womankind has become manifest to the extent that the equality of man and woman is an established fact."[8]

He spoke of woman poets, philosophers and warriors "who exhibited their valor and courage on the battlefield," and Ṭáhirih, the great Bábí poetess. At one point, he was asked, "What is the difference between man and woman?" He answered:

> At most it has been this: That woman has not had the opportunities which man has so long enjoyed, especially education. She has not had military tactics. If she cannot go on the battlefield and kill, is that a shortcoming? Supposing she has not used a gun, nor worked the cannon. If we present a cannon to a woman and ask her to fire it and she should fail, is that an imperfection? At most we can say such is a compliment or praise to her, that in the hardness of the heart she is, inferior to man! If we say to womankind, Come along and kill people, they will say—I cannot do it. Now that is not a shortcoming! But be it known that if womankind had been trained according to military tactics, I believe that they could kill as many too. But God forbid womankind to learn military tactics! May they

> never make up their minds to take up the gun. Because that is not a glory. Home-making and joy-creating and comfort-making are truly glories of man! Man should not glory in this, that he can kill people. Man should glory in this, that he can love.[9]

'Abdu'l-Bahá essentially identifies the loving qualities of women—of human beings—as better suited to the world that is coming than the militaristic qualities perfected by males. 'Abdu'l-Bahá even engages in an analysis of gender-specific language that dominated English in 1912:

> When we find that the word "man" is used as a generic name it applies to all creatures, especially humankind; for example, in the Bible the statement is made that "man is created after our own image and likeness,"—that does not mean that the female was not created. That applies to her as well as to man. "We have created man after our own image and likeness." You may be interested to know that in Persian and Arabic there are two words distinct, which in English are translated "man"; in Persian and Arabic there is this distinction, when the word "man" is used in one sense it means both man and woman, and the pronoun is referable to both, whereas there is a word which distinguishes the male and the female. . . . In Hebrew it is the same.[10]

He called for equal treatment and superior encouragement of women:

> That which God has not created, that distinction which He has not made, we must not observe. It is a superstition. The thing which is to be considered, however, is this: that womankind must be more highly educated. They must have equal opportunities with men. There must be no difference whatsoever between their education. And until this reality, namely, the equality between the male and the female in the

> human kingdom, is fully established, is fully realized, the highest attainment for society is not made possible. Supposing womankind is inferior to man in a certain degree, even if that be the case that is not to be considered, because this very distinction is going to create discord and trouble. . . . [rather] We must declare that their capacity is greater. When man endeavors to educate a person, he should inspire him with hope and ambition so the susceptibilities for progress may increase. He should not be told that he is inferior or weaker in qualities. . . . In short, my hope is that in the five continents where this is not fully established, it may be established and the banner of equality may be raised.[11]

He closed his address by saying that "Until the two are equal in strength, the oneness of humanity cannot be realized. And the happiness of humankind will not be a reality. God willing, this is to be so."[12]

The notions about the role of women that prevailed in the late nineteenth and early twentieth century United States tended to focus on idealized female qualities related to domestic life—women as homemakers and therefore as nurturers, educators, civilizers of children, and creators of a peaceful environment. Feminists extended these qualities into the public arena, arguing in favor of *virtuous womanhood*: that women should also serve as teachers, nurses, and other nurturing professions, and become involved in voluntary associations for the peaceful advancement of society.[13] While 'Abdu'l-Bahá did stress woman's peaceful qualities and the value of "home-making and joy-creating and comfort-making" (without specifying that they were women's work) one is struck by the radical call for equality in his speech and its grounding in the oneness of humanity. Women are as capable as men to learn "military tactics," but the greater glory is for men to learn to love their fellow humans.

The meeting was followed by a Bahá'í women's reception at the same hotel, also said to have had a thousand present. Chicago's Bahá'í women had had an organization since 1901; it had been a major source of impetus for the construction of the House of Worship and had occasionally clashed with the all-male House of Spirituality (the community's coordinating body) over policy; and it was entertaining out-of-town Bahá'í women who had stayed on after the Bahai Temple Unity convention to hear the Master.[14] Probably many women from the first reception attended as well.

'Abdu'l-Bahá's talk to the Bahá'í women's reception was much briefer. He did not mention equality of the sexes but developed his comments about the importance of education—an essential effort to bring about the oneness of humanity in fact—by discussing the divine education brought by God's messengers versus the education brought by ordinary people. Bahá'u'lláh, he said to them, is "your teacher, your instructor . . . He is the teacher of the Orient and Occident. He is the very teacher of the world of divinity . . . of spirituality . . . the very Sun of Truth."[15] 'Abdu'l-Bahá offered no references to Jesus or previous Messengers of God. Perhaps one purpose of the talk was to consolidate the faith of those who were already involved in Bahá'í activities.

From the La Salle Hotel, 'Abdu'l-Bahá rode a mile back to his own hotel to meet with and speak to the overflow crowd accumulating there. His lengthy discourse focused on the order of nature and whether the order is "due to nature itself" as materialists claim or whether it is due to a "divine rule." Through various rational proofs he demonstrated that a Creator must exist.[16]

The large crowds flocking to hear 'Abdu'l-Bahá may reflect the newspaper coverage of his earlier talks and of his dedication of the temple site over the previous two days. The May 1 issue of the *Chicago Daily Tribune* included an editorial summarizing his "noble mission" as "universal brotherhood and peace, [and] inter-racial amity" and hoping that "possibly there will be a balm in Abdul Baha to soothe sore disturbed minds and iron out the kinks in [our] tempers." Therefore, he "is welcome in our midst."[17]

At least five people became active Bahá'ís as a result of 'Abdu'l-Bahá's time in Chicago. One person unexpectedly drawn to him was Ruth Moffett (1880–1978). When visiting Chicago from Wisconsin, she was standing on a train platform and saw 'Abdu'l-Bahá. "He looked at me, smiled and raised His hand," she later recalled. Curious, she found out more about him and attended one of his talks, but did not become a Bahá'í until 1919. She became a very active Bahá'í and traveled all across the United States in the 1930s, establishing Bahá'í communities in small and mid-sized cities. The young Harvard-trained minister at the Unitarian church in Bloomington, Illinois, Albert Vail, met 'Abdu'l-Bahá in Chicago; within three years he was a Bahá'í and writing scholarly articles about the Faith.[18]

Also seeking to meet 'Abdu'l-Bahá was an "association of Indians" residing in Chicago. Most were Hindu university students. On Friday morning, May 3, they came to the Plaza Hotel to meet him collectively. They read a greeting to him that described the Bahá'í Faith as "a source of uniting nations" and "a fulfillment of the teachings of our forefathers" and urged him to visit India. He spoke to them and the others present about divine civilization and spiritual education.* The talk impressed one Hindu in the audience, Dr. J. F. King, and apparently he became a Bahá'í.[18†] This may be the first talk of the day recorded in *The Promulgation of Universal Peace* where 'Abdu'l-Bahá condemns warfare in such places as Tripoli and added:

---

* This meeting may have occurred on Saturday, May 4th because Maḥmúd appears to have combined the events of two days together some time this week; he has 'Abdu'l-Bahá speaking at one church on Saturday, May 4, rather than Sunday, May 5.

† The article notes that King became a Bahá'í as a result of meeting 'Abdu'l-Bahá in Chicago "with a group of his fellow students" but does not give the date of the meeting. There is no other meeting with a group of Hindu students known.

> because I find the American nation so capable of achievement, and the American government the fairest of Western governments, its systems superior to others, my wish and hope is that the banner of peace may be raised first on this continent, that the standard of the Most Great Peace may here be unfurled. May the nation of America and its government unite in their efforts, in order that this light may dawn from this point and spread to all regions, for this is one of the greatest bestowals of God. In order that America may avail herself of this opportunity, I request that you strive and supplicate with heart and soul, devoting all your energies to this end, that the banner of International Peace in reality may be unfurled here, and that American Democracy may be the cause of the cessation of warfare in all other countries.[19]

The principle of the oneness of humanity, in the context of the Bahá'í teachings, implies the need for a global civilization and governing system, hence 'Abdu'l-Bahá's call for international reconciliation. He does not define the "Most Great Peace" in this talk, but elsewhere he and Bahá'u'lláh both describe it as a state of spiritual world civilization that would gradually evolve after international peace had been established. In subsequent weeks, 'Abdu'l-Bahá often expressed the hope that America would be the establisher of world peace.

'Abdu'l-Bahá's second talk of the day focused on the Prophets of God as the first educators of humanity. He gave the example of Jesus Christ and called for a "turning back to the original foundation. . . . His Holiness BAHA'O'LLAH has reiterated or re-established the quintessence of all the teachings of all the prophets. He has thrown out all the accessories; the quintessence thereof He has renewed."[20] At the time many religionists—Theosophists in particular, but some Hindus, Muslims, and Christians as well—emphasized the purity of the original faiths and called for people to look backward to the ideal ancestral forms. In actual fact, it was their modern interpretations and their idealizations of certain ancient forms that they advocated. 'Abdu'l-Bahá essentially replied that Bahá'u'lláh provided the standard for sifting through the ancestral faiths for the forms applicable to the modern day.

That evening, the Chicago Bahá'ís held a consultative meeting about the building of the House of Worship, which 'Abdu'l-Bahá attended and where he spoke briefly, though he intentionally avoided giving advice about the Bahá'í House of Worship, possibly because he didn't want to interfere with the local community's discussions. It may have provided the opportunity for 'Abdu'l-Bahá to speak privately to Dr. Frederick Nutt, who was President of the House of Spirituality. Nutt was a comparatively new Bahá'í who had served on the House of Spirituality for less than a year; he had received a tie vote with Louis Gregory for membership on the Bahai Temple Unity Executive Board a few days earlier. Nutt was in active communication with Ibrahim Kheiralla and his small group of Chicago followers, a fact that concerned 'Abdu'l-Bahá. Of further concern to 'Abdu'l-Bahá was the visit, some time during his stay, of a woman on behalf of Ibrahim Kheiralla, who said that if 'Abdu'l-Bahá invited Kheiralla to meet him, he would come. 'Abdu'l-Bahá replied that if Kheiralla came to him, he would meet him, because he never turned anyone away. But Kheiralla never came.[21]

On Saturday, May 4, after talking to scores of visitors at his hotel and taking a stroll in Lincoln Park—he did this just about every day and even visited the park's zoo one time—'Abdu'l-Bahá went to Northwestern University in Evanston, a Chicago suburb, to speak to the Theosophists at University Hall.* He discoursed about death as a transformation

* Honoré Jaxon even summarizes a talk 'Abdu'l-Bahá gave and includes photographs of the stroll, but does not specify which day the stroll occurred, though he says 'Abdu'l-Bahá's walk in the park was a "frequent occurrence," mornings or evenings.

from one form to another and about eternal life. He never mentioned reincarnation—a central Theosophical belief—but his entire talk described an alternative view of the afterlife and therefore was an implicit refutation of the belief.[22]

On Sunday, May 5, 'Abdu'l-Bahá met with thirty-five Bahá'í children and their parents at 8am. The children sang for him, then each came to him so that he could embrace them and stroke their hair affectionately. He whispered in English to each one to tell him her or his name. One child threw herself into his arms with great excitement. They sat in a circle again, and he addressed them, calling them his children. He then divided up a large bouquet and gave each child a flower. He also gave each an envelope of rose petals, presumably from the Holy Land. As he walked around the circle of children, he put his hand on each one and blessed them.[23]

Then he addressed the assembled adults. It was his last meeting with the Chicago Bahá'ís before returning east, and he did not know whether he would return. He had heard of disunity in the community and decided to stress the importance of strengthening their commitment to the Faith and their unity:

> I am going, but you must rise up to serve the Cause of God. Endeavor to keep your hearts sanctified and your intentions pure so that you may attract divine bounties. . . . This is the day in which only pure and chaste hearts can derive benefit from the eternal bounties and only pious souls can receive light from the ever-existent splendors. Praise be to God that ye believe in God, have faith in His words and are turned to His Kingdom. You have heard the voice of God and your hearts are delighted with the breezes of the Abhá paradise. Your intentions are good; your object is the will of God; and your desire is to render service to the Kingdom of God.

> Therefore, you must gird up your loins with unswerving determination, you must be united among yourselves and you must not be irritated by one another. . . . Your eyes must be turned always to the kingdom of God and not to the world of man. You must love His creation for His sake and not for your own. When you love one another for the sake of God you shall never be perturbed. . . . The eye that regards faults sees nothing but faults and the eye that overlooks faults is fixed on the Creator of the souls. It is He Who has created all, has nurtured all, has endowed all with life and spirit and has given to all eyes and ears. Thus all are the signs of His power and for His sake we must love all, and show kindness to all, assist the poor, render help to the weak, heal the sick and educate the ignorant.
>
> It is my desire that the union and harmony of the friends of Chicago may be an example for all the friends in America and that all creation may derive benefit from their behavior; that they may lead all. Then and only then shall the confirmations of the Abhá Kingdom and the bounties of the Sun of Reality encircle you.[24]

The visit culminated with a stroll in Lincoln Park together and a group photo.[25]

His next destination was Plymouth Congregational Church at 935 East Fiftieth Street. It had long had a reputation for openness; in November 1883, Protap Chunder Mozoomdar had preached there. The minister, Reverend Joseph A. Milburn, had considered going to Acre to meet 'Abdu'l-Bahá and went to see him several times after he arrived in Chicago. Milburn gave 'Abdu'l-Bahá a glowing introduction and offered his congregation a detailed account of the Bahá'í Faith's history and teachings. When 'Abdu'l-Bahá walked to the pulpit, "the congregation rose to their feet, and although they were in church, they greeted Him with prolonged applause and cheers of joy."[26]

'Abdu'l-Bahá began by praising the congregation "which is commemorating Him [God], whose members have no thought or aim save His good pleasure, and . . . the impartial investigation of reality." He asked his audience to consider the sun, the "center of illumination" of our solar system and our source of physical development. "Likewise," he said, "in the spiritual world . . . there must needs be a center" of illumination. It illuminates thought, morals, "and is the cause of the education of souls." That Center of Illumination "is the Manifestations of God in general." This sun of Truth "has its numerous dawning places" just as the phenomenal sun rises at different points along the horizon during the year.[27]

Furthermore, "just as the solar cycle has its four seasons, likewise the Sun of Reality has its distinct cycles." The religion founded by a Manifestation of God has a springtime when "tremendous motion takes place in the realm of thought and ideals," a summer of spiritual harvest, an autumn, and a winter when only "faint traces" remain of "the effulgences of that spiritual Sun." Then the cycle begins again with a new Manifestation; "the former spring is thus renewed and the world again becomes resuscitated, illumined, attains spirituality, and religion is organized, the hearts are turned to God, the summons of God are raised, and the life everlasting is vouchsafed. 'Abdu'l-Bahá did not mention Jesus or Bahá'u'lláh, as he was wont; the implication of the talk—that the Christian dispensation was in winter and a new spring had been brought by Bahá'u'lláh—was probably clear because Milburn had provided the necessary background. He closed thus:

> I hope that the lights of the Sun of Reality will illumine the whole world, so that no strife and warfare may remain, no bloodshed and

> battles may remain, so that fanaticism and religious bias may not remain . . . . Reality does not accept multiplicity; it is not divisible. All the Holy Manifestations of God have proclaimed and promulgated the same Reality; they have summoned people to the realm of Reality, and Reality is one. But imitations like unto the clouds or mists, have befogged the Sun of Reality. We must forsake these imitations in order that these mists and these clouds may be dispelled and may free the Sun of Reality. Thus may the sun shine most gloriously, then all the inhabitants of the world will be united, all the religions will become one, all the denominations will become united, all races will become unified, all nativities will become one fatherland, and all the degrees of humanity will be ushered beneath the same tabernacle and the same banner. . . . Consider the wars which disturb the world, consider the expressions of enmity and hatred! The presence of these wars indicate the fact that the heavenly civilization has not yet been established. If this heavenly civilization be promulgated all this dust will be dispelled, all these clouds will pass away, and the Sun of Reality, with greatest effulgence, with glory, will shine upon mankind.[28]

Maḥmúd describes the reaction of the congregation:

> The hearts of the listeners were so attracted that the church seemed to be filled with the Holy Spirit. The people crowded around 'Abdu'l-Bahá to the extent such that it became difficult for the Master and His companions to leave. Groups of people surrounded Him to shake His hand and to ask for His blessing. The most surprising thing about these meetings was that although most of the people had never before heard of the Bahá'í teachings, they were so attracted and fascinated that they would follow the Master in their cars from one meeting to another.[29]

'Abdu'l-Bahá lunched at the home of a Dr. Ford, returned to his hotel to meet visitors, went to the grave of Davis True with Mrs. True to offer prayers, then in the evening, went to All Souls Church. The minister, Jenkin Lloyd Jones (1843–1918), was one of the city's most distinguished clergy. In the 1870s and 1880s, his itinerant preaching doubled the number of Unitarian churches in the western United States; in 1877, he became the secretary of the Western Unitarian Conference; in 1878, he founded the leading Unitarian periodical in the west, *Unity*; he encouraged the ordination of women to the Unitarian clergy; he was general secretary of the committee that planned the World's Parliament of Religions in Chicago in 1893; he was a founder of the Chicago Peace Society; and he assisted Mozoomdar and asked Anagarika Dharmapala to preach from his pulpit. Service in the Union Army during the Civil War made him a lifelong pacifist. In 1898, he and his church, All Souls, left the Unitarian denomination—he had become a theist and had moved beyond a Christian focus. In 1905 the church built the Abraham Lincoln Center, a building that combined a worship facility with practical charitable agencies such as "a school of manual arts, a school of oratory, a printing and publishing company, a social center and a hospice." The Lincoln Center resembled the Mashriqu'l-Adhkár, which is also supposed to have auxiliary charitable agencies. Jones and his church were on a quest to find a creedless universal religion through study of the wisdom of all the world's traditions.[30]

Jones had extended an invitation to 'Abdu'l-Bahá to speak at his church through Louise Waite, who accompanied him to Lincoln Center and introduced him to Jones. Waite said her "heart ached at the cool manner in which Mr. Jones received Him, but Abdul Baha's God-like love melted the icy atmosphere." The seven hundred present were a racially mixed audience. 'Abdu'l-Bahá's lengthy talk began by noting that "divine religions were founded for no other purpose than the unification of humanity and the pacification of mankind." He noted that "Jesus Christ united the divergent peoples and the differing sects and denominations of the early days" and that Bahá'u'lláh "was enabled to unite peoples of various thoughts and various creeds and differing denominations" in "far-off Persia." He explained that divine revelation had two aspects: essential, concerned with "the realm of morals, with the spiritual susceptibilities, and the heavenly bestowals," and matters touching on "material conditions," such as the several laws about murder in "the days of Moses," which were swept away by Jesus.[31]

Since the "reality of the religions is one, and the difference is one of imitations," he pointed out that "the existing religions must give up the imitations in order that the Reality may enlighten them all, may unite humanity." He continued:

> The various nations of the world—the American, the English, the French, the German, all the continental nations, even the Turks and Persians, belong to the same Adam, belong to the same household—why should they have dissension? The surface of the earth is one nativity and that nativity was intended for all. God did not place these boundaries. Why should a matter which has not been originally destined by God, namely, the imaginary boundary lines placed by humankind, be made the bone of contention and the cause of differences? . . . we must forget all the imaginary causes of difference and refer to the very fundamentals of the divine religions in order that we may associate with perfect love and accord, considering humankind as one family, the surface of the earth as one nativity, and all races as belonging to one humankind, and let us live under the protection of God, attaining to the eternal happiness in this world and to the life ever lasting in the world to come.[32]

He then closed with a prayer that began "O Thou kind Lord! Thou hast created all humanity from the same stock." Maḥmúd said that "A great excitement was also created among the people of this church" and afterward "members of the audience came to Him to shake His hand and express their thanks and devotion." Jones apparently was pleased. He escorted 'Abdu'l-Bahá to his car, where 'Abdu'l-Bahá took him into his arms and kissed him on both cheeks.[33]

Overall, that Sunday's talks provided an excellent overview of the Bahá'í teachings regarding religion: that like humanity, it was ultimately one; that all religions had the same divine source; that the various divine teachers came to different peoples and cultures at different times with messages adapted to the context; that the revelation provided both timeless spiritual teachings and laws fitted to the times; that the religious traditions subsequently developed and flourished but gradually aged as interpretations of the original message clouded its light; that God then sent new Messengers, and that the latest one was Bahá'u'lláh.

The tension in the Bahá'í community over the strategy to follow in sharing this message with others was dramatically highlighted on Sunday as well. That morning, Louise Waite came to the Hotel Plaza to help prepare for the meeting with the Bahá'í children. But she also sought 'Abdu'l-Bahá's advice about the Bahá'í hymns she had composed and published, which were now being sung by Bahá'í communities throughout North America. Several had been sung at the Bahai Temple Unity convention and at the dedication ceremony in Wilmette. 'Abdu'l-Bahá had reviewed some of the hymns previously, had asked for some to be translated into Persian so the Bahá'ís in Iran could learn them, and had strongly encouraged her artistic work. As Waite writes,

> I thought of what Miss Alice Buckton had said about our Bahai hymn book—and the error of using the Names [of God, like Alláh-u-Abhá, a Bahá'í expression]—as I said [to 'Abdu'l-Bahá] "Shall I take the name 'Bahai' off of the book and not use the Names in [']Tell the

> Wondrous Story['] and [']Softly His Voice is Calling.['"] Abdul Baha asked Why? I said many thought they were a stumbling block to the people and one sister had particularly urged me to change the names and leave off "Bahai" which she said had "labeled us." Abdul Baha asked who this was and when I told Him He replied she is an earnest soul but young in the Kingdom, her work is in the churches and she is doing beautiful work but your work is to sing of the New Kingdom and to declare the Names. The people must learn to come under the banner of Baha Ollah and to be called Bahais. They must learn that these are universal terms of the Glory of God in this new cycle. Do not change anything unless I tell you. If anyone comes to you and says change this or that which you have written say to them show me a tablet from Abdul Baha commanding me to do so.[34]

What is significant about this passage is not 'Abdu'l-Bahá's encouragement of Louise Waite's work but his encouragement of Alice Buckton's. 'Abdu'l-Bahá's strategy seems to have been to move some of the public into the ranks of the "interested," some of the interested to the ranks of the "attracted," some of the attracted to the ranks of the "involved," and some of the involved—like Alice Buckton—to the ranks of the "consecrated." He sought to do this through the use of metaphors and examples, but he always sought to encourage. Buckton's work was "beautiful"; but she was "young in the Kingdom." Waite's work was to solidify Bahá'í identity through music, one of the most powerful media for strengthening and expressing faith.*

* As the Bahá'í community continued to become more sharply defined, Buckton (1867–1944) did not remain a Bahá'í. She moved to Glastonbury, England, purchased a sacred spring, and opened a retreat center and store. See Remey, Reminiscences of a Summer School, 39–42; "Alice Buckton," at http://www.glastonbury-pilgrim.co.uk/alice-buckton.php (accessed May 6, 2011).

Early on Monday, May 6, before 'Abdu'l-Bahá left for Cleveland, a reporter met with him to ask his reaction to a newspaper story that would appear in the Chicago *Examiner* the next day. His half-brother's son, Shua Ullah Behai, had called a "peace conference" in Chicago on June 15, where the "malcontents," as the article called them, wanted to ask 'Abdu'l-Bahá ten questions about the nature of his authority. 'Abdu'l-Bahá "smilingly denied knowledge of the questions to be asked, but said he would be glad to answer all that may be propounded," the journalist reported in the next day's paper.[35] The extensive publicity 'Abdu'l-Bahá's visit generated apparently stimulated Shua Ullah Behai and Kheiralla to offer the press any story they thought would gain them coverage, and several were published over the next few months. 'Abdu'l-Bahá devoted increased attention to the nature of Bahá'u'lláh's Covenant and to his own authority in his talks to the Bahá'ís.

Cleveland, May 6–7, 1912

On May 6, 'Abdu'l-Bahá took an 8:25am train, which passed through Toledo and arrived in Cleveland at 4:20pm. The dozen Bahá'ís in that city were ready; Grace Robarts, who had prepared 'Abdu'l-Bahá's residence in Chicago in advance, had come to Cleveland the day before. He went straight to the sanatorium and home of Dr. Charles M. Swingle, where he briefly addressed forty Bahá'ís and their friends and shared a buffet supper with them. He noted that "the American continent has advanced very much and in the future will advance greatly. It will lead all other nations spiritually, for its illumination is far reaching." 'Abdu'l-Bahá then went to the Hotel Euclid, where he met with reporters; his visit produced at least eight articles in the local papers. One subject they asked him about was the relationship between blacks and whites; his support of interracial marriage made headlines the next day. He addressed five hundred people at the hotel's hall about the great advances in material civilization, but also its dangers; he specifically mentioned the destructive power of the "smokeless gun," perhaps an allusion to Hudson Maxim, whom he had talked to in New York. He ended with a plea that America become the champion of world peace: "This American nation is a revered nation and presents great and deserved worthiness. I hope this fair government will stand for peace, so that warfare may not reign in the world, that the banner of peace shall be unfurled, and all nations shall be united together, which is the greatest attainment of the world of humanity. It is equipped to accomplish that which shall surely adorn the pages of history, become the envy of the world, and be blest in the East and the West because of its democracy. I hope it may be the cause thereof."[36]

Pittsburgh and Washington, May 7–11, 1912

After breakfast with a few Cleveland Bahá'ís, at 8am the next morning, he was on a train to Pittsburgh, where Martha Root (1872–1939), a devoted Bahá'í, had arranged for him to talk at the Hotel Schenley that night. Four hundred attended. He repeated his comments about the greatness of America's material civilization, its need for spiritual civilization, and the unity Bahá'u'lláh had brought to diverse people in Iran, and he enumerated seven teachings of the Bahá'í Faith: the importance of investigation of reality; the oneness of humanity; the oneness of religion and science; the adjustment of the economic standards of humanity; the abandonment of all prejudices; the equality of men and women; and education of all members of society. He added that "no matter how far the material world advances, it cannot establish the happiness of the human world. . . when the material civilization shall be linked with the spiritual or divine civilization, then happiness will be assured." Jesus Christ had summoned all to such a civilization through the "acquisition of good morals." The principles 'Abdu'l-Bahá had enunciated were, in effect, the "good morals" needed in the modern day.[37]

It was a significant talk because it was the first time 'Abdu'l-Bahá had enunciated a series of Bahá'í principles to a public audience in North America.* He did not just list principles, however; he set them in the context of the inadequacy of material civilization and the need for spiritual civilization. It was a point that, later, Bahá'ís did not always understand or emphasize when they explained the Faith's teachings.

After the talk, 'Abdu'l-Bahá met privately with leaders of thought. Five local newspaper articles were a product of his visit. At 9am the next morning, May 8, he was on his way to Washington, D.C. Twelve hours later, he was in the United States capital. Having already discharged his promise to Mrs. Parsons to stay in her residence, he rented a house at 1340 Harvard Street for three days. He continued to speak at the Parsons home every afternoon, however, and entertained a steady stream of visitors at the rented house. His talks were not transcribed. Maḥmúd says he spoke about economic issues, the rights and education of women, prophecies and signs indicating the coming of Bahá'u'lláh, and the principles of the Faith. On Friday, May 10, he visited a settlement house for children.[38]

New York City, May 11–14, 1912

The next day, he took the train for New York City, for a series of events had been planned there before he left for the Lake Mohonk Peace Conference. An apartment at the Hudson Apartment House, 227 Riverside Avenue, had already been prepared for him by Grace Robarts and Lua Getsinger with the help of various local Bahá'ís: Kate Ives, Carrie Kinney,

* As previously noted, he had enunciated seven principles to Chicago journalists on April 30 and three Bahá'í principles in Mrs. Parsons's house in Washington, D.C. on April 25. This was the longest list he had given in a public talk.

May Maxwell, and Juliet Thompson. Soon after his arrival, he spoke to a large crowd about the results of his thirty-one days in the United States:

> We have had no rest by day or night since we left you: either traveling, moving about or speaking; yet it was all so pleasantly done and we have been most happy. Praise be to God! Everywhere and all the time it has been "harakat" "harakat" "harakat" ("motion," "motion," "motion").
>
> The friends in America are very good. All the people we have met here are very good. They are polite, not antagonistic, although inquisitive. A small minority of them are prejudiced, yet even these have their good points. The American people have a real love for progressiveness. They are not content to stand still. They are most energetic and progressive. . . . The questions asked us have been opportune and to the point. The answers we gave have not been used for altercation and argument. We met savants and learned men and satisfied them with our explanations. . . . In brief, it would be difficult to find, in the aggregate of people we met, any one who was dissatisfied. Some scholastic minds aimed only at fruitless discussion. . . . not a single soul arose in opposition or went away disappointed. Yesterday we met . . . a Justice of the Supreme Court. There were many ladies of the Diplomatic Circle present. . . . There were also present at this meeting several Cabinet officers, United States senators, many from the Foreign Diplomatic Service, army and navy officials and other high dignitaries. . . . In Washington, also, we called a meeting of the colored and white people. The attendance was very large, the colored people predominating. At our second gathering this was reversed, but at the third meeting we were unable to say which color predominated. These meetings were a great practical lesson upon the unity of colors and races in the Bahai teaching. . . . God makes no

> distinction between the white and the black. If the hearts are pure both are acceptable unto Him. God is no respecter of persons on account of their color or race. All colors are acceptable to Him, be they white, black, or yellow. Inasmuch as from the standpoint of humanity both were created in the image of God, we must bring ourselves to realize that both are as one and both embody the Divine possibilities in humanity.[39]

He spoke at length about the unity of the races. Later, in private, he added to Juliet Thompson in even more frank words: "What does it matter if the skin of a man is black, white, yellow, pink, or green? In this respect animals show more intelligence than man. Black sheep and white sheep . . . do not quarrel because of differences of color."[40]

The next day being Sunday, a talk at a church had been arranged, the Unity Church in Montclair, New Jersey. Probably because of the church's name, 'Abdu'l-Bahá chose to speak about divine unity and the unity of religions. He spoke about the different religions stemming from the appearance of different Manifestations of God, Whom he likened to different mirrors, all of which reflected the light of the same sun perfectly. The difficulty that arose, however, was that people became attracted to the mirror rather than to the sun and refused to recognize a new mirror when it became manifest. He gave as examples Moses and Jesus, and the refusal of the people who accepted the first to later accept the second. He did not mention Bahá'u'lláh, but Rev. Edgar S. Wiers, in his introduction, had summarized the Faith and referred to Bahá'u'lláh's writings as "the New Gospel." Eight hundred were present, and many shook his hand afterward. 'Abdu'l-Bahá went to the house of one of the Bahá'ís in Montclair, Mr. Charles Edsall, for lunch with a large number of people, including Wiers and his wife, and promised to return to Montclair later. At Edsall's house, he commented that "wherever you go you hear" the expression "all right";

"You ask the bell boy at the hotel to do something and he responds 'All right'; you inquire as to the health of a friend and he answers 'All right' . . . I have never heard the expression used in any other country, and I believe it reflects the optimism of this great country." A reporter present wrote it up as an article, "Baha Likes 'All Right,'" for *The New York Times,* and it was syndicated all around the United States.[41]

'Abdu'l-Bahá returned to New York City for an 8pm meeting of the International Peace Forum at Grace Methodist Episcopal Church, West 104th Street. The Lake Mohonk Peace Conference was now only two days away, and presumably the New York Peace Society was sponsoring the forum because visitors had arrived who were on their way to Lake Mohonk. 'Abdu'l-Bahá addressed two thousand people about religion as a source of peace. He noted that religious warfare was contrary to the purpose of the Manifestations of God; that Moses had united and uplifted the twelve tribes of Israel, Jesus had spread peace across the Middle East, and Muhammad had civilized the wild tribes of Arabia. This was one of the first times he mentioned Muhammad in any detail. Other wars, he said, were caused by racial hatreds, but this is contrary to the truth that "all belong to one household"; the "false distinctions of race and native land, which are factors and causes of warfare, must be abandoned."[42] He referred to the terrible bloodshed then occurring as a result of the Italian campaign to wrest Tripoli from the Turks.

'Abdu'l-Bahá then described Bahá'u'lláh and His teachings for bringing about a world at peace, stressing the oneness of humanity. He concluded by urging his audience to make the United States the champion of world peace:

> All of us know that International Peace is good; that it is conducive to the general welfare of humanity and the glory of man; but we are in need of will, volition, and action. We must act. Inasmuch as this

century is a century of light, it has capacity for action. . . . When I came to America, I found this to be an exceedingly progressive country, the people in a state of readiness, the government a just one, and equality established to an extraordinary degree. Now inasmuch as the standard of International Peace must needs be hoisted, I hope that it may be hoisted upon this continent, for the American continent is more deserving, has greater capacity therefor, and is not like other countries. . . . Therefore it is my hope that you may be the cause, and that you may hoist this banner—for this banner will be hoisted. Raise it aloft, for you are deserving above all other nations. In the other countries there are many who are waiting for this summons, anxiously anticipating this call from some nation bidding all to the "Most Great Peace" for the people are distressed because of the excessive and irreparable damage of war. Thousands of the farmers are taxed and expenses collected for war. Every year the tax increases and the people have come to their end. Just now you can say Europe is a battlefield; like ammunition ready for a spark; and one spark can set aflame the whole world. Before these complications and colossal events happen, take a step and prevent it. . . . The foundation of all [religions] is One Reality and Reality is not multiple or divisible. For example, His Holiness Moses founded this Reality; His Holiness Jesus hoisted the tent of Reality, and the light of this Reality shone forth in all the religions. His holiness BAHA'O'LLAH proclaimed this Reality and promulgated the "Most Great Peace." . . . all the people who have accepted the teachings of BAHA'O'LLAH are peace lovers and are ready to sacrifice their lives and forfeit their fortunes for it. Now let this standard be hoisted in the West and many shall respond to the call. Just as America has become renowned because of her discoveries, inventions and skill; famous for the equity of her government and colossal undertakings—may she also become noted

> for the "Most Great Peace." Let this be her undertaking, and let it spread from her to other countries. And I pray for all of you that you may render this service to the world of humanity.[43]

The talk repeats his challenge that America become the leader in establishing world peace but adds that Europe was a powder keg that could "set aflame the whole world," something few expected to happen, two years before the sudden and shocking onset of World War One. Ahmad Sohrab summarized the result thus: "Wonderful meeting. . . the best yet. . . . The longest address he has ever delivered. People were weeping like children. Great effect. After him spoke a U. S. Senator. A great orator, Praised Abdul Baha's address. Referring to him as "His Holiness" "His Holy and Blessed Presence a great privilege." Last night['s] meeting a <u>spiritual victory</u>."[44]

'Abdu'l-Bahá offered a similar talk the next day to 1,800 people at a New York Peace Society reception in his honor. He went to the Hotel Astor in spite of exhaustion and a fever that confined him to bed all morning. Juliet Thompson begged him not to go, but he replied, "I work by the confirmations of the Holy Spirit. I do not work by hygienic laws. If I did I would get nothing done." His five lengthy introductions from prominent people underlined the significance of the occasion. Rabbi Stephen Wise (1874–1949), the master of ceremonies, referred to him as a "notable and deeply interesting teacher from the East." Mrs. Anna Garlin Spencer (1851–1931), the first woman ordained to the ministry in Rhode Island, feminist, suffragette, pacifist, and representative of the Ethical Cultural Society, spoke of the need to end racial prejudice, exploitation of one group by another, and religious bigotry, and referred to him as "our Prophet Friend." Percy Stickney Grant called for the audience to "get down below our discussion of Christian, Hebrew, Ethical Culture, whatever the discussion may be, to the spirit of life and of brotherhood. There we find we are all akin, there we find the fellowship of the great spirit of

Abdu'l Baha." Mr. Haozoun Hohannes Topakyan, the Persian Consul-General for New York City, called him a "Prophet of enlightenment and peace" and "the Glory of Persia."* William Jackson, Professor of Persian at Columbia University, spoke of his visit to the spot in Tabriz where the Báb, Bahá'u'lláh's forerunner, was martyred, referred to 'Abdu'l-Bahá as "his Successor," and said he "comes to us from the Orient to assure us that this Message of Peace is still being sounded and that we in the West and they in the East are really one in heart."[45]

In spite of a hoarse voice, 'Abdu'l-Bahá stressed the central importance of world peace—"peace is light, whereas war is darkness. Peace is life; war is death"—and talked about Bahá'u'lláh's teaching of the oneness of humankind and its importance in establishing peace in the world. He emphasized Bahá'u'lláh's sacrifice and the deaths of many Bahá'í martyrs to create conditions for peace in the world. He once again challenged "this revered democracy" to promulgate international peace and prophesied that its banner will be "unfurled here, permeating through the other countries from here."[46]

The talk was well received; Ahmad Sohrab telegrammed Agnes Parsons "WELL KNOWN MEN AND WOMEN GREETED ABDULHAHA [*SIC*] ENTHUSIASTICALLY A WONDERFUL REPRESENTATIVE MEETING." Even though he hadn't recovered from his illness, that evening he met twenty-five Japanese students and some Indian students at his apartment.[47]

---

* Topakyan's full name can be found in "Consul Topakyan Takes a Burglar," *The New York Times,* April 12, 1911, available at http://query.nytimes.com/.

Lake Mohonk, May 14–16, 1912

The next morning, 'Abdu'l-Bahá headed for Lake Mohonk, a resort built next to a lake on the crest of the Shawangunk Mountains some sixty miles from New York City. Albert K. Smiley (1828–1912), a Quaker, had established the resort hotel in 1869 and had started the Lake Mohonk Conference on International Arbitration, to which some of the country's most prominent statesmen were invited annually, in 1895. From the train station at New Paltz to the resort hotel, the road passed through seven miles of mountain scenery, which 'Abdu'l-Bahá and his party traversed by landau* in a most special way:

> he was so exhilarated by the beauty of nature, charming sceneries of mountains, valleys, plains and the verdant forest of trees and wild flowers that he ['Abdu'l-Bahá] burst into songs of happiness commanding others also to sing. Lua and Fareed sang some Persian songs written by Abdul Baha, then Mr. Mills being a good singer was asked to sing. All through the seven miles [*sic*] drive the party of four sung in whole and in turn while Abdul Baha out of the sheer joy applauded them. It was a never [*sic*] memorable incident which has seldom happened in the life of the Master and Doctor Fareed could not remember throughout all his service and travel with Abdul Baha of a similar occasion.[48]

'Abdu'l-Bahá settled into his room in the hotel—number 166—overlooking magnificent Mohonk Lake and went to the evening session to deliver a twenty-minute address to the 250 men and their wives in atten-

* A horse-drawn four-wheeled carriage with a top divided into two sections and a raised seat outside for the driver.

dance. He began by referring to all the wars that were being fought sixty years ago and the rancor that existed among the different ethnic and religious groups in Iran. At such a time Bahá'u'lláh appeared and proclaimed a series of principles to establish the oneness of humanity and world peace. 'Abdu'l-Bahá enunciated eight principles: the investigation of truth, the oneness of humankind, that "religion and science are twins," that religion should be a cause of unity in the world, that racial and other prejudices should be abolished, the equality "between mankind and womankind," the "readjustment of economic questions in the social body," and that "philosophy sufficeth not . . . the world of humanity is in need of the breath of the Holy Spirit."[49]

The speech was an elegant summary of points he had made in recent talks and was historic, considering the prestigious setting where it was delivered. Ahmad Sohrab was so thrilled by the response that he sent a telegram in typical "telegramese" to Agnes Parsons almost immediately: "Abdulhaha [*sic*] delivered address half an hour ago before large audience of Lake Mohonk conference on international arbitration on principles of Bahai movement created most profound impression actually fired hearts of listeners as soon as he finished there was most unforgettable satisfaction on faces such sensation has seldom seen few having heard of message his talk was like conflagration longest applause."[50]

Maḥmúd added that

> During the day most of the delegates had been engaged in materialistic issues. The highest level that their discussions had reached was the issue of the internal unity of countries and the problems of the United States of America. In the evening, however, they found themselves puzzled when they heard the eloquent, elegant address of the Master concerning the unity of all people, the reformation of the whole world and the Manifestation of the Greatest Name which

> would bring about the oneness of the world of humanity and the promulgation of the teachings of universal peace. . . . According to custom of the West, the audience applauded for a long time when He ceased speaking. They requested that He continue but because He was tired, He apologized and with a gesture of His hand bestowed kindness to all. One by one, dignitaries and delegates from many countries came to shake His hand. Some of them embraced Him and expressed their thanks. The president [Mr. Albert Smiley] again stood, offering thanks and spoke with great reverence on the importance of the teachings, praising and commending 'Abdu'l-Bahá on behalf of the audience. Mr. Smiley's wife then gave the Master a pendant especially made for the peace conference and thanked Him most joyfully.[51]

Rev. Frederick Lynch, at the Metropolitan Temple in New York, called it "the most remarkable address I have ever listened to." He summarized it as "full of this one thing, the unity of mankind. We are in this world,—one. When you get beneath the different languages, different nationalities, different races, different colors, different temperaments, after all, we are one."[52]

'Abdu'l-Bahá, however, was not so pleased with the audience's response. He commented to his interpreters immediately afterward:

> Once I wrote to the friends in Persia in regard to peace congresses and conferences, that if the members of the conferences for peace do not succeed in practicing what they say, they may be compared to those who hold a meeting to discuss and form firm resolutions about the sinfulness and harmfulness of liquors. But after leaving the meeting, they occupy themselves in selling liquors, and just as before they become engaged in their business. Now we must not only think

and talk peace but we must develop the power to practice peace, so that like unto the spirit in the body of the world, peace may permeate the whole world.[53]

The comment underscored 'Abdu'l-Bahá's strategy: to transform souls and strengthen the forces of love in the world, for they were the forces that could convert the principles into reality. The next day, to a crowd of young people who followed him on his walk around the Lake Mohonk grounds, he added, "It is very easy to come here, camp near this beautiful lake, on these charming hills, far away from everybody and deliver speeches on Universal Peace. These ideals should be spread and put in action over there, (Europe) not here in the world's most peaceful corner."[54]

He spoke at least one more time at the conference, but the talk is not recorded. The night before he left, he expressed the wish to give a Persian rug from his apartment to Mr. Smiley as a response to his kindness. Zia Bagdadi took up the challenge, hired a landau to take him to the nearest train station, hopped onto a freight train going to New York City, awoke the people staying in 'Abdu'l-Bahá's apartment at 2am to retrieve the rug, caught the first passenger train back to the vicinity of Lake Mohonk, and persuaded the mailman to give him a ride to the resort on the morning mail wagon, arriving at 10am, just as 'Abdu'l-Bahá was shaking Smiley's hand! The rug resembled one the Smileys had owned but had been burned up in a fire, so he was very pleased by the gift.[55]

New York City, May 17–22, 1912

When 'Abdu'l-Bahá returned to New York City, it was a good time to evaluate future plans. He had arrived in America with invitations to three large and important gatherings: the Persian-American Educational Society in Washington, the Bahai Temple Unity convention in Chicago, and the Lake Mohonk Conference on International Arbitration. All three were now discharged. Newspaper coverage had been extensive—over one hundred articles nationwide—and very positive. Several important invitations had subsequently come in and been discharged as well. Major speaking engagements were already set in Boston, and a promise had been extended to Montclair. He had tentatively planned to visit Boston, Montreal, and San Francisco by June, then head back across the Atlantic. The Bahá'ís on the West Coast were begging 'Abdu'l-Bahá to visit them—a few had made it to Chicago and New York—but he now realized how far away it was and how exhausting the trip might be. He also saw the great capacity and great need of the Bahá'í community of greater New York City and what he could do to consolidate the Bahá'í Faith in that area. He accepted an invitation to speak in Philadelphia in early June, but made no other plans to travel beyond greater New York. It was to be his base of operations for the next two months.[56]

The next two days were relatively quiet. 'Abdu'l-Bahá spoke in his apartment to crowds daily and met both Protestant clergy and a group of rabbis, but otherwise rested more than he had previously. The apartment was close to Riverside Drive where there was a park; sometimes he walked there alone, lay down, and slept in the grass, because that way "I come out of fatigue. My mind rests. But when I am not alone, surely I talk, and rest of body and mind cannot be gained."[57] While he rested a bit more, the landlord of the apartment building did not; the crowds had become a severe problem, and he asked 'Abdu'l-Bahá to leave. 'Abdu'l-Bahá moved temporarily to the house of the Kinneys, where he had delivered his first talk in America, while another residence was found.

On Sunday, May 19, he spoke in two churches; the Church of the Divine Paternity on Central Park West and the Brotherhood Church in Jersey City. At the first, he spoke about progressive revelation: "Abraham heralded reality. Moses promulgated reality. Christ established reality. Muhammad was the Messenger of reality. The Báb was the door of reality.

Bahá'u'lláh was the splendor of reality. Reality is one; it does not admit multiplicity or division." He again used the analogy of the seasons; each Messenger of God brought a new divine springtime. Onto this theme, which he had delivered to churches in Chicago, he grafted another recent theme: the principles brought by Bahá'u'lláh, of which he discussed four: the oneness of humanity, investigation of reality, the harmony of science and religion, and the purpose of religion as the creation of love and unity.[58]

The evening talk at the Church of the Brotherhood was one of his shorter addresses; it lasted about fifteen minutes, including translation. Howard Colby Ives, the Unitarian minister who first met 'Abdu'l-Bahá at the Kinney residence on the latter's first day in America, was the pastor and was unsalaried, because he was trying to create a new kind of church (he had a salaried position at another church as well). "I had requested of the Master that He speak rather longer than was His wont as I had the universal obsession that the worth of an address was in proportion to its length," Ives later explained. "That He spoke so briefly was undoubtedly with the endeavor to illustrate to me that a very few words, inspired by the Holy Spirit and aglow with wisdom celestial, were vastly more powerful than all the volumes of man-made sermons ever printed."[59] Much of Ives's experience, again, was nonverbal:

> It was an impressive, even to me a thrilling sight when the majestic figure of the Master strode up the aisle of the Brotherhood Church . . . . Here, in a setting of Western civilization, almost two thousand years from the dawn of Christian teaching, stood One whose Life and Word were the very embodiment of the essence of the message of good-will to all peoples which those nations which bear His name had seemingly forgotten. Here stood the living proof of the falsity of the assumption that East and West can never meet. . . . there was in that hall that evening an atmosphere of spiritual reality foreign to

> its past. It bore upon me almost unbearably and was reflected in the faces of many turned upon me as I rose to preface the talk of the Master with a few words of introduction. I can still see before me the rapt face of Lua Getsinger, one of the first of American believers in the divine revelation of Bahá'u'lláh, as her unwavering gaze dwelt upon 'Abdu'l-Bahá, and the faces of many others in the audience bore similar evidence to the unaccustomed atmosphere of holiness invading their souls.[60]

Ives introduced 'Abdu'l-Bahá briefly to the five or six hundred people present. 'Abdu'l-Bahá began by saying "because this is called the Church of Brotherhood, I wish to speak upon the brotherhood of mankind." He noted that various kinds of brotherhood existed, but "the real brotherhood is spiritual. . . . Material or physical association is based upon earthly interests, but divine fellowship owes its existence to the breaths of the Holy Spirit. Spiritual brotherhood may be likened to the light, while the souls of humankind are as lanterns. The incandescent lamps here"—he pointed to the electric lights in the hall—"are many, yet the light is one."[61] He noted that at first Bahá'u'lláh

> set forth the principles of physical brotherhood and afterward founded the spiritual brotherhood. He breathed such a spirit into the countries of the Orient that various peoples and warring tribes were blended in unity. Their bestowals and susceptibilities became one, their purposes one purpose, their desires one desire to such a degree that they sacrificed themselves for each other, forfeiting name, possessions and comfort. Their fellowship became indissoluble. This is eternal, spiritual fellowship, heavenly and divine brotherhood, which defies dissolution. Material civilization advances through the physical association of mankind. The progress you

> observe in the outer world is founded mainly upon the fraternity of material interests. Were it not for this physical and mental association, civilization would not have progressed. Now—praise be to God!—the indissoluble spiritual association is evident. . . . Souls have advanced to such a degree as to forfeit life and possessions for each other. Their spiritual perceptions have developed; their intelligence has quickened; their souls are awakened. The utmost love has been manifested. Therefore, it is my hope that spiritual fraternity shall unite the East and the West . . . . May it bind together individuals and members of the human family and be the cause of advancing minds, illuminating hearts and allowing divine bestowals to encompass us from all directions. May spiritual susceptibilities set hearts aglow with the message of glad tidings. May spiritual brotherhood cause rebirth and regeneration, for its creative quickening emanates from the breaths of the Holy Spirit and is founded by the power of God.[62]

The talk went on to praise material progress and civilization but noted that it "does not prevent nor remove warfare." He promised that this twentieth century "is the dawn, or beginning, of spiritual illumination" and that eventually "the human world will adapt itself to a new social form, the justice of God will become manifest throughout human affairs, and human equality will be universally established."[63]

Maḥmúd says that afterward "although all came to Him, one by one, to shake hands and depart, afterward when He went into an inner room of the church, a crowd of people, after receiving permission, came to see Him and were delighted to hear the blessed Master's explanations in response to their questions. All offered Him thanks and praise."[64]

Ives had a powerful reaction to the talk. "This was, indeed, a new type of brotherhood," he later wrote.

> Not a fraternal partnership, so to speak, which had as its objective a mutual sharing of the good things of the world more easily attained and more safely held by reason of this partnership. But rather a re-birth of man through a new baptism of the Holy Spirit, who by this rebirth found themselves actually conscious of a heavenly, spiritual, divine kinship which transcended any earthly relationship as the music of the spheres transcended earth's discordance. And as I gazed at the Master as I faced Him from the audience, it was not so difficult to imagine a world transformed by the spirit of divine brotherhood. For He Himself was that spirit incarnate. . . . His smile which seemed to embrace us with an overflowing comradeship; His eyes which flashed about the room as if seeking out each individual; His gestures which combined such authority and humility; such wisdom and humor, all conveyed to me, at least, a true human brotherhood. . . .[65]

For Ives, 'Abdu'l-Bahá's talk was not just a beautiful vision of a utopian world; instead, he saw the living embodiment of true human brotherhood before him.

On Monday, May 20, 'Abdu'l-Bahá met with a group of clergymen at the Kinney residence, where he spoke about Islam and attempted to correct some of the common misconceptions held by Christians. Maḥmúd says that "the ministers left humbly and joyfully, impressed by His explanations"; perhaps they, like others, found it difficult to argue with 'Abdu'l-Bahá because of his loving personality.[66] The meeting represents another stage in 'Abdu'l-Bahá's discussion of Islam, about which he had said little in his first days in America.

From the Kinneys, he went to the Metropolitan Temple to speak at a women's suffrage meeting. His presentation on the equality of women and men was perhaps the longest and most complete to date. He presented a long summary of the history of unequal treatment, noting that "in some countries men went so far as to consider women to belong to a sphere other than the human." But the conditions in past centuries "were due to woman's lack of education. They did not educate womankind at all, but left her in her undeveloped state. Naturally, womankind could not advance." In fact, "the education of womankind is more necessary and important than the education of man, for women are the educators of man when man is in the stage of infancy." Education is not the primary duty of the father, he added. If the educator is uneducated, the children will be poorly educated as well. "The mothers are the first educators of mankind; if they be imperfect, alas for the condition of man!" On this point, 'Abdu'l-Bahá was seven decades ahead of experts in social and economic development.[67]

'Abdu'l-Bahá offered a philosophical argument for equality as well: "The world of humanity consists of two factors: male and female. If one remains defective, the other necessarily will be defective; perfection cannot be obtained." He argued that women's suffrage was essential for the establishment of world peace:

> The mother bears the troubles of rearing the child. She undergoes the ordeals of birth and training. Therefore it is most difficult for mothers to send to the battlefield their dear ones, their offspring upon whom they have lavished such love and care. . . . With the utmost difficulty she has brought him to the age of maturity. How difficult then it is to sacrifice him upon the battlefield! . . . So it will come to pass that when womankind partake fully and equally in the affairs of the world in the great arena of laws and politics war will cease; for woman will prove the obstacle or hindrance to it.[68]

He spoke in detail about great women of the past—Queen Zenobia, Catherine I of Russia, and Queen Isabella of Spain—demonstrating what women can achieve. He describe the advancement of Iranian Bahá'í women, "who are the very pride and envy of the men." He concluded thus:

> If woman be fully educated and granted her prerogatives, she will attain to the accomplishment of wonderful deeds and prove herself the equal of man. For she is the coadjutor of man. Both are human, both are endowed with intelligence, both embody the virtues of humanity. In all human powers and functions they are partners. If in all degrees of human activity at present woman does not manifest her prerogatives, it is caused by lack of educational opportunity. Education, without doubt, will equalize her with man. . . . The absence of this equality is not becoming to man.[69]

Maḥmúd notes that "there was great excitement in the audience, and, as in other gatherings, the people were deeply moved and both men and women shook His hand."[70]

The next day was a time of farewells because 'Abdu'l-Bahá was leaving for Boston the next morning. He conducted two meetings and met with the Bahá'í children in the New York area. On Wednesday, he left for Boston at 10am.

Boston, May 22, 1912

He was greeted in Boston by a crowd of Bahá'ís at the station, who accompanied him to the Hotel Charles. At 8pm, he spoke at the 87th anniversary celebration of the American Unitarian Association, a weeklong affair for which 'Abdu'l-Bahá was considered one of the two principal speakers. It was not unusual for non-Unitarians to address the gathering; Protap Chunder Mozoomdar had done so in 1900. The program at Tremont Temple, attended by nearly one thousand Unitarian clergy and two thousand guests, was chaired by the lieutenant governor of Massachusetts, Robert Luce. He gave 'Abdu'l-Bahá a warm welcome and the audience "gave Him a prolonged standing ovation" when he rose to speak.[71]

'Abdu'l-Bahá began by talking about the vitality of motion and development for all things, including religion. He noted that "the divine Prophets have revealed and founded religion," but "gradually these heavenly teachings and foundations of reality have been beclouded by human interpretations and dogmatic imitations of ancestral beliefs." Because "human interpretations and blind imitations differ widely, religious strife and disagreement have arisen among mankind, the light of true religion has been extinguished and the unity of the world of humanity destroyed." If "the nations of the world forsake imitations and investigate the reality underlying the revealed Word of God, they will agree and become reconciled." In order to overcome the blind imitation of ancestral religious forms, "the fundamental reality of the divine religions must be renewed, reformed, revoiced to mankind":

> The seed of reality must be sown again in human hearts in order that a new tree may grow therefrom and new divine fruits refresh the world. . . . The spiritual brotherhood which is enkindled and established through the breaths of the Holy Spirit unites nations and removes the cause of warfare and strife. It transforms mankind into one great family and establishes the foundations of the oneness of humanity. It promulgates the spirit of international agreement and ensures universal peace. Therefore, we must investigate the foundation of this heavenly fraternity. We must forsake all imitations and promote the reality of the divine teachings. In accordance with these principles and actions and by the assistance of the Holy Spirit, both material and spiritual happiness shall become realized. Until all nations and peoples become united by the bonds of the Holy Spirit in this real fraternity, until national and international prejudices are effaced in the reality of this spiritual brotherhood, true progress,

> prosperity and lasting happiness will not be attained by man. This is the century of new and universal nationhood. Sciences have advanced; industries have progressed; politics have been reformed; liberty has been proclaimed; justice is awakening. This is the century of motion, divine stimulus and accomplishment, the century of human solidarity and altruistic service, the century of universal peace and the reality of the divine Kingdom.[72]

Maḥmúd says the audience applauded with "elation and joy." Edwin D. Mead, a vice president of the Free Religious Association and an Emerson scholar, reported one reaction of an audience member who was a "leading Unitarian": "After all, all that he said was simply what we have been hearing here all the time." Mead added this was a "noble thing" because it showed that in a totally different cultural and religious environment, the "first principles" of the forms of religion the Unitarians hold "loftiest" could develop and flourish.[73]

Howard Colby Ives reported a very similar reaction from other Unitarian clergy: "'A very interesting old gentleman,' several remarked to me afterwards, 'but he told us nothing new.'" 'Abdu'l-Bahá did tell them something new—that God had sent a new Messenger with a new revelation—but that did not appeal to an audience that had basically rejected belief in special divine Messengers, and the appealing parts of his message, such as votes for women, were often accepted by Unitarians. 'Abdu'l-Bahá did not mention the more radical aspects of the Bahá'í teachings to audiences that knew practically nothing about him, such as interracial marriage. Ives described the Unitarians' reaction as: "typical of most of the audiences He addressed. Truly, 'having ears we heard not.'" For Ives, the medium—'Abdu'l-Bahá himself—was as important as the message: "To me 'Abdu'l-Bahá's talk in the Brotherhood Church and the address before the Unitarian Conference in Boston marked a new phase in my spiritual journey from self to God. I had heard several of His public addresses before but never had I been near enough to Him to mark closely His demeanor. For it was not only His words, not nearly so much His accents and voice which now impressed me. There lay in His eyes a living flame which seemed to ignite a smouldering spark within me."[74]

Yet Ives recognized that not everyone became a believer as a result of experiencing 'Abdu'l-Bahá. He told the story of a Christian woman who "was not, and never became an avowed believer." She saw 'Abdu'l-Bahá at a private home in New York City and, "enthralled," was "overcome with emotion." When she later tried to describe 'Abdu'l-Bahá to a friend of hers, she could not; she was overcome and "could hardly speak for tears." All she could say was "Oh, you should have seen Him. You should have seen Him!"[75]

No doubt there were many who never became Bahá'ís and had this reaction. Others were attracted in various degrees to aspects of his message, such as the equality of all persons, the urgent need to work for world peace, or the holistic package of principles he outlined. By late May 1912, he had explicated many of the Bahá'í teachings he would discuss in his travels across North America. While he would continue to speak to large audiences and explain different aspects of the Bahá'í Faith, he was also prepared to go deeper and work further on the consecration of the core of his Father's followers.

7

THE CENTER OF THE COVENANT

'Abdu'l-Bahá's visit to greater Boston was relatively short—May 22–26, five days—possibly because he already had speaking engagements scheduled in New York. He gave eight major talks, and his visit was covered by at least twelve newspaper articles. While he spoke before the American Unitarian Association and the Free Religious Association, two huge associations of religious liberals, he did not speak in any churches, even though he was there on Sunday morning. Considering the number of Unitarian, Congregationalist, and Episcopalian churches in Boston, this is surprising.

Thursday, May 23 was a particularly busy day. 'Abdu'l-Bahá began with a visit to the "Greek Syrian Relief Society," an organization that assisted recent immigrants from the eastern Mediterranean. They met at Denison House, the third settlement house founded in the United States, patterned after Chicago's Hull House. After lunch with the society's members, he spoke to nine hundred people about poverty and detachment; before he left, he contributed "ten gold pounds (about $50)" to the poor. In the afternoon, he had an appointment at Clark University in Worcester, sixty miles west of Boston. The Boston area's colleges had long been open to Asian religious visitors; Vivekananda spoke at Harvard and Mozoomdar at Wellesley. 'Abdu'l-Bahá addressed as many as a thousand students and faculty about the importance of science and attended a reception at the college president's house.* He returned to Cambridge that evening for a gathering at the residence of Alice Breed, one of the most active Bahá'ís in the Boston area.† She had baked a birthday cake for 'Abdu'l-Bahá, complete with American, Persian, and English flags and sixty-eight candles, and had invited over a hundred guests. Since 'Abdu'l-Bahá was born on the day that the Báb inaugurated His mission in Iran, and the Declaration of the Báb was a Bahá'í holy day, some years earlier 'Abdu'l-Bahá had instructed the Bahá'ís not to celebrate his birthday. He had even expressed his objection explicitly to Alice's son-in-law. According to Marzieh Gail, Breed's granddaughter, "He did not stay for the festivities. . . . In His address He spoke only of the Báb's Declaration on this day, saying not a word about Himself. Afterward, Alice persuaded Him to step into the dining room and at least see the festive table and the cake, and take a little refreshment. He sat in the large, brocaded 'grandfather' chair but soon left." Maḥmúd adds that 'Abdu'l-Bahá lit the first candle on his cake and asked everyone else to take turns lighting the others.[1]

'Abdu'l-Bahá's remaining five Boston-area talks were delivered over the next three days. On Friday, May 24, he spoke to a thousand people at the Free Religious Association annual meeting and was received very warmly. The F.R.A. had welcomed non-Christians in the past; Dharmapala spoke to them in 1897, and Swami Abhedananda, one of Vivekananda's successors,

---

* 'Abdu'l-Bahá's Clark University address was published in the Persian pages of *Star of the West*; the author has a copy of an English translation made by some Worcester Bahá'ís.

† Alice Breed's daughter, Florence, was married to Ali Kuli Khan, Persian Counsul in Washington, D.C. In the 1890s Alice had been one of the main hosts for Swami Vivekananda when he had visited Boston.

in 1899.* From there 'Abdu'l-Bahá went to two houses, meeting crowds and speaking at each. On Saturday, May 25, he met with several small groups of clergy, journalists, and educators at his hotel and in the evening spoke to a thousand people at a farewell gathering organized by the Boston Bahá'ís. His topic was the signs of progress in the twentieth century, particularly the growing understanding of the oneness of religion and the oneness of humanity. On Sunday morning, before taking the train back to New York, he attended a meeting of the Golden Circle, the "largest Syrian society in America," apparently at the Syrian Roman Catholic (Melkite) Church near Denison House, where he spoke in Arabic. One woman threw herself at his feet and declared that the "spirit of Christ" was in him.[2]

New York City and Vicinity, May 26–June 8, 1912

From the Golden Circle meeting, he went to the train station, because he had a speaking engagement that afternoon at the Mount Morris Baptist Church, Fifth Avenue and 126th Street, New York. After the congregation sang the hymn "Nearer My God to Thee," 'Abdu'l-Bahá spoke on nearness to God.[3] It was the first talk of his two-month sojourn in greater New York City. The two months divide up, in turn, into five shorter periods: May 26–June 8; June 8–10, when he visited Philadelphia; June 11–20, when he was back in New York City; June 20–29, when he was in Montclair,

---

* 'Abdu'l-Bahá's talk at the Free Religious Association was published in *The Free Religions Association: Proceedings at the Forty-fifth Annual Meeting, Held in Boston, Mass., Thursday and Friday, May 23 and 24, 1912,* 85. As earlier noted, the talk in *The Promulgation of Universal Peace* attributed to May 24 was actually delivered to the American Unitarian Association on May 22. This can be determined by comparing the English language versions of the talks to the Persian versions and the summaries in *Maḥmúd's Diary.* Dharmapala's talk to them is mentioned in Schmidt, *Restless Souls,* 168; Abhedananda's talk in Jackson, *Vedanta for the West,* 51.

Newark, and West Englewood, New Jersey; and June 30–July 23, when he was back in New York City again.

During the first fourteen-day period, he delivered at least eighteen talks, seven of which have been preserved in English. One would particularly like to know what he said at New York University on May 30; Maḥmúd says the talk was about "scientific questions and divine philosophy." His talk to the Theosophists on that evening, the third of eight he would deliver to Theosophists in the United States, focused on international peace. He compared "the nations of the world to the members of a family" therefore "as strife and dissention destroy a family and prevent its progress, so nations are destroyed and advancement hindered." To remedy the existing human conditions, "a divine physician is needed." He spoke about the unity and peace brought by Jesus Christ and promised that the Holy Spirit would continually guide humanity, but apparently did not talk about Bahá'u'lláh.[4]

On May 31 'Abdu'l-Bahá went to Fanwood, a New Jersey suburb of New York City, where he gave three talks, in spite of the great heat and humidity. On June 2, he spoke at the Church of the Ascension in Manhattan for the second time, but at the "People's Forum" on Sunday evening rather than at the morning service. According to Juliet Thompson, "Bishop Burch had severely reprimanded" Percy Stickney Grant for 'Abdu'l-Bahá's first appearance "but an idiotic thing like that" only made Grant "more defiant." Grant's introduction was very lengthy and friendly, emphasizing the "warmth of personal affection" and "great satisfaction" in welcoming him back; "I assure him that we shall listen to every word that comes from his lips as proceeding from a soul which has lived nearly three score years and ten with the very central spiritual light of unity and has walked with God."[5]

Perhaps inspired by the nature of the Sunday evening forum, 'Abdu'l-Bahá noted that "the church is a collective center. . . . For this reason there have been churches and temples in all the divine religions; but the real Collective Centers are the Manifestations of God, of Whom the church or temple is a symbol and expression." 'Abdu'l-Bahá spoke of the unity that Jesus had wrought among the diverse peoples of the Mediterranean world. "Abraham, Moses, Jesus Christ, Muhammad were Collective Centers of Their day and time, and all arose in the East. Today Bahá'u'lláh is the Collective Center of unity for all mankind, and the splendor of His light has likewise dawned from the East." The idea of the spiritual East and material West was common at the time, but here 'Abdu'l-Bahá used it to refer to the East as the source of all religions, including the Bahá'í Faith.[6]

He spoke about the oneness of humanity and the "divine springtime" Bahá'u'lláh had brought to the world. Returning to the theme of material and spiritual civilization that appeared in many of his talks, he said that

> The degree of material civilization in the Occident cannot be denied; nor can anyone fail to confirm the spiritual civilization of the Orient, for all the divine foundations of human uplift have appeared in the East. . . . Therefore, you must assist the East in order that it may attain material progress. The East must, likewise, promulgate the principles of spiritual civilization in the western world. By this commingling and union the human race will attain the highest degree of prosperity and development. Material civilization alone is not sufficient and will not prove productive. . . . The honor of the human kingdom is the attainment of spiritual happiness in the human world, the acquisition of the knowledge and love of God. . . . This is his real happiness and felicity . . . if material happiness and spiritual felicity be conjoined, it will be "delight upon delight," as the Arabs say. We pray that God will unite the East and the West in order that these two civilizations may be exchanged and mutually enjoyed. I am sure it will come to

> pass, for this is the radiant century. This is an age for the outpouring of divine mercy upon the exigency of this new century—the unity of the East and the West. It will surely be accomplished.[7]

'Abdu'l-Bahá then answered a number of questions from the audience, something he did not usually do.

The next day 'Abdu'l-Bahá took the train to Milford, Pennsylvania, where he visited the estate of Gifford Pinchot, a prominent forestry expert, conservationist, and government official.[8] Pinchot, who was elected Governor of Pennsylvania in 1923 and 1931, assembled "prominent statesmen and dignitaries of the Republic" to meet 'Abdu'l-Bahá. They asked him numerous questions. According to Maḥmúd, in response to a question about a future war, 'Abdu'l-Bahá said "it will certainly come about." He also spoke about the great changes in Europe that would follow:

> Europe and most other areas will be forced to follow your system. Tremendous changes will take place in Europe. The great centralized powers will break up into smaller independent states. In reality it is not just that vast countries should be governed from a single center, for no matter how great the ability and wisdom of the statesmen of that center, or how developed their sense of justice, they will still not be fully informed of the needs of every town and village and cannot exert themselves justly for the betterment of their surrounding dependencies. For example, all parts of Germany concentrate their efforts to serve a single center, namely Berlin; and the whole of France is to serve Paris. Similarly, each of the colonial countries serves to adorn one great capital. But your government has a good system.[9]

The comment is prescient about the breakup of the Ottoman and Austro-Hungarian Empires, Europe's eventual application of the principles of federalism across the continent, and its acceptance of the partial autonomy of many regions within countries.

'Abdu'l-Bahá returned to New York City the next day. On June 5, he gave two public talks, to the Unity Club and the Women's Union, the last public events of this two-week period. 'Abdu'l-Bahá also gave at least nine talks in the homes of Bahá'ís or in his own rented residence. Many focused on general Bahá'í teachings and were suitable to a wide range of listeners. But on May 30, in a private talk, he said, "I am the interpreter of the Writings of the Blessed Beauty [Bahá'u'lláh], as explicitly designated by the Supreme Pen [Bahá'u'lláh]. All must obey. All matters pertaining to the Faith must be referred to the authorized interpreter. In the future all must turn to the divine House of Justice."[10]

Maḥmúd said 'Abdu'l-Bahá made this point "often." Since his arrival in the United States six weeks earlier, 'Abdu'l-Bahá had often spoken about obeying God's will and obeying Bahá'u'lláh's commands, but this appears to be the first time in a talk recorded in English that he called on the American Bahá'ís to recognize him as the authoritative interpreter of Bahá'u'lláh's writings and to obey him. For veteran Bahá'ís, this was not a new point; in 1900 'Abdu'l-Bahá had expelled from the Bahá'í Faith Ibrahim Kheiralla, the Arab who had introduced the Faith to North America, because Kheiralla had broken Bahá'u'lláh's explicit Covenant to turn to 'Abdu'l-Bahá and had instead sought to split the American Bahá'í community away from him.* But from 1900 to 1911, Bahá'ís had largely ignored Kheiralla, and many new Bahá'ís probably had heard little about him.

The talk was also the first time the term House of Justice appeared in Maḥmúd's Diary. The term does not appear in any talks recorded in *The*

* For the details of Kheiralla's disaffection, see Robert H. Stockman, *The Bahá'í Faith in America: Origins, 1892–1900, Volume 1,* 158–77.

Promulgation of Universal Peace until December 2, just days before 'Abdu'l-Bahá sailed from New York to Britain. His statement that "in the future all must turn" to the House of Justice was a disclosure of a provision of his Will and Testament, which delineated two institutions to guide the Bahá'í Faith after 'Abdu'l-Bahá's passing—the Guardianship and the Universal House of Justice—and which said that the Universal House of Justice would be elected by the national Bahá'í governing bodies, of which the Bahai Temple Unity Executive Board was a forerunner.

'Abdu'l-Bahá may have had one particular person in his audience in mind that day: Ameen Fareed, one of his interpreters and the son of his wife's sister. Fareed seems to have made much use of the relationship; newspaper articles refer to him as 'Abdu'l-Bahá's nephew. Maḥmúd writes on June 7 that "One of our companions showed such grave negligence and impudence that the heart of the beloved Master as well as our hearts were saddened. However, observing his connivance and the forbearance of 'Abdu'l-Bahá, we have not written about his actions, which were often the source of grief to the Master." Maḥmúd is not specific, except to note that the companion was "often" a source of grief. Zia Bagdadi is equally discrete in his memoir. But other sources indicate that Fareed approached individuals on several occasions with the promise that if they wanted to contribute money to 'Abdu'l-Bahá to defray his expenses, he could funnel the money to him. 'Abdu'l-Bahá consistently turned down all efforts to give him money; Fareed could not have intended to pass it on to 'Abdu'l-Bahá because he knew it would expose his own disobedience and greed.[11]

Fareed was a test not just for 'Abdu'l-Bahá, but ultimately for those who saw the Bahá'í teachings as the spirit of the age, destined to transform churches as well as nations, for such a view could not accommodate human egotism and ambition. The Bahá'í approach, already expounded by Bahá'u'lláh and 'Abdu'l-Bahá in their writings but now being gradually unfolded by 'Abdu'l-Bahá in his talks, included the teaching that divine revelation required divinely inspired interpretation to be preserved and applied rightly. As a result, the head of the Faith—in this case, 'Abdu'l-Bahá—was obligated to expel from the Faith any follower who opposed the authorized interpretation or disobeyed him. The Bahá'í Faith was not seeking the unity of humanity purely on the basis of love; it reserved the right to protect the community from its more selfish and power-seeking members.

Philadelphia, June 8–10, 1912

On Saturday, June 8, 'Abdu'l-Bahá took the train to Philadelphia for a long-awaited visit that lasted just forty-five hours. Maḥmúd says that exhaustion forced him to cancel some meetings—presumably scheduled that day—but he spoke four times on Sunday to audiences totaling more than three thousand and to another hundred people on Monday.[12] His talks fell into two types: private ones to the Bahá'í community designed to strengthen and consolidate it, and public ones designed to spread the Bahá'í principles and attract new people.

Sunday morning began early with a gathering of Bahá'ís in the hotel parlor. He asked them about their activities, and when they said they held the Bahá'í Feast every nineteen days, he spoke about gathering for it "in the utmost love"; "each one of you must think how to make the other members of your assembly happy and pleased." At 11am, he spoke to the Unitarian Church about how "the realm of Divinity" is "wholly sanctified above human comprehension" and therefore God's light was sent forth and reflected to humanity through the pure souls of the Manifestations of God. The latest divine Messenger was Bahá'u'lláh, Who proclaimed "the oneness of God and the unity of the world of humanity." One aspect of this oneness was "that men and women are equal in the sight of God and that there is no distinction to be made between them." Consequently, Bahá'u'lláh "promulgated the adoption of the same course of education for man and woman." He again stressed that "equality between men and women is conducive to the abolition of warfare" because "mothers will not give their sons as sacrifices upon the battlefield." 'Abdu'l-Bahá closed with an exposition about "harmony of science and religion"; "religion must stand the analysis of reason."[13]

'Abdu'l-Bahá returned to the Rittenhouse Hotel to a crowd awaiting him, where he spoke briefly, took questions, and met various people. Among the subjects he addressed was the unity of blacks and whites, perhaps because a black Bahá'í from Harrisburg, Pennsylvania, was present. After a walk in the park and a rest, he went to the Baptist Temple, where 2,500 people were in attendance. Its pastor, Russell Conwell (1843–1925) was one of America's most remarkable clergymen. A Civil War veteran, lawyer, author of ten books, and ordained American Baptist clergyman, he arrived in Philadelphia in 1882 with only two years of ministerial experience. Within four years, his new pastorate, Grace Baptist Church, had outgrown its brand-new building and needed an even larger facility, called Baptist Temple. Conwell began to tutor adults in university subjects and the resulting effort soon evolved into Temple University, one of Philadelphia's most distinguished institutions of higher education, of which Conwell was the first president. By 1912, Baptist Temple was also surrounded by three hospitals founded by the church. When Martha Root, a prominent Bahá'í speaker and journalist, visited in 1931, she commented how much Baptist Temple resembled the Bahá'í vision of the Mashriqu'l-Adhkár, the Bahá'í House of Worship and its numerous charitable dependencies. Conwell has acquired permanent recognition in books about American religion and culture because of a speech, *Acres of Diamonds,* that he gave some six thousand times around the world about the capacity of the average person to succeed in life and become prosperous. His optimism for the ability of the average person to succeed was also reflected in Temple, "the great people's university" he created. Toward the end of his life, Conwell told

Root that "The Baha'i Movement is the biggest Movement in the world today for world-wide Christianity, and 'Abdu'l-Bahá is the Peace Prophet of this age. I know because I spent seven months in the orient and I saw that millions of Muhammadans, Buddhists, Jews and other orientals have come up beautifully into Christianity through becoming Bahá'is. I cabled to Egypt, asking 'Abdu'l-Bahá to speak in my church (Baptist Temple)—and when He came to this country He did."[14]

Conwell's comment about "worldwide Christianity" seems to refer to a nonsectarian movement that accepts Jesus in a general sense and the highest spiritual and ethical principles for which He stood, though such principles no doubt would be defined differently by different persons. Late nineteenth-century Unitarians and liberal Protestants often spoke this way, sometimes envisioning a universal religion emerging out of the scaffolding of the love for Jesus and adherence to the Golden Rule provided by their versions of Christianity. The World's Parliament of Religions in 1893 was partially motivated by the belief that by bringing representatives of the religions together in Chicago, a "common religious discourse or a common community of sentiment for what was widely perceived as an emerging global society" could emerge.[15] While by 1912, clashes between religious representatives at interfaith gatherings and wildly different visions of how to implement a universal religion had dashed the hopes of many Christians, it appears that Conwell still held to part of the dream, and saw parts of it implemented in the inclusiveness of the Bahá'í Faith.

'Abdu'l-Bahá arrived at the church at 8pm. Even though the collection had already been taken, 'Abdu'l-Bahá had some money put in the plate for him. Conwell "greeted him most cordially, taking both his hands in his own, and seated him with evident pleasure and joy." After a brief introduction by Dr. Conwell, 'Abdu'l-Bahá gave a lengthy and comprehensive talk. He began by discussing the investigation of reality. Animals are "utterly lacking spiritual susceptibilities" whereas humans possess a capacity "beyond the range of the senses." Not all accept this; materialists "state that nothing is entitled to belief and acceptance except that which is sensible or tangible." In this sense "the animal is the greater philosopher because it is completely ignorant of the Kingdom of God, possesses no spiritual susceptibilities and is uninformed of the heavenly world." The comment anticipates 'Abdu'l-Bahá's description of cows being the greater philosophers, two months later.[16]

But the "pathway" of "religion, the road of the divine Kingdom" is available to people, thanks to the "the holy Manifestations of God; for They are, in reality, the foundation of the divine religion of oneness." They are the "source of human enlightenment, training and ethical improvement—the magnet which attracts the love of God because of the knowledge of God it bestows." Though Conwell no doubt would have wanted to hear more emphasis on Jesus—about whom 'Abdu'l-Bahá said little—in general, this was a reasonable description of the sort of divine religion many liberals sought.[17]

'Abdu'l-Bahá then fleshed out the sort of training and ethical improvement Bahá'u'lláh had in mind by describing ten principles: the investigation of reality, the unity of humankind, religion as a source of fellowship, the agreement of religion and science, the casting aside of prejudice, principles of economic adjustment, equal standards of human rights, universal education, a universal auxiliary language, and the equality of men and women. At Lake Mohonk, he had enumerated eight principles; 'Abdu'l-Bahá now chose to elaborate a longer list. He closed with a call to turn away from a material view of reality and toward the Holy Spirit:

> The body of man is in need of physical and mental energy, but his spirit requires the life and fortification of the Holy Spirit. Without its protection and quickening the human world would be extinguished.

> Jesus Christ declared, "Let the dead bury their dead." He also said, "That which is born of the flesh is flesh; and that which is born of the Spirit is spirit." It is evident, therefore, according to Christ that the human spirit which is not fortified by the presence of the Holy Spirit is dead and in need of resurrection by that divine power; otherwise, though materially advanced to high degrees, man cannot attain full and complete progress.[18]

Afterward, 'Abdu'l-Bahá met with some people in Conwell's private study. He concluded his visit to Philadelphia the next day with a talk at Mary J. Revell's house and a series of private meetings with Bahá'ís and inquirers. In his talk, he stressed devotion to Bahá'u'lláh:

> Be filled with the Spirit of Baha'o'llah. Your thoughts must be of Baha'o'llah. Your mention must be of Baha'o'llah. Your life must be devoted to Baha'o'llah. Your firmness must be evident in Baha'o'llah, for Baha'o'llah has endured for your sake infinite vicissitudes. All His life He was subject to persecutions. During the nights, He was not at rest. He did not sleep in peace for one night,—not one. Never did He find peace and composure. All His life He was subject to persecution. All His life He was exiled. All His life He was imprisoned. Therefore we must be loyal to Him; turn our faces to Him; praise His mention in this world; expound His teachings; quicken people with His Spirit, so that His Heavenly Image may descend and His Heavenly Power affect the hearts.[19]

'Abdu'l-Bahá called them to devotion, firmness, and service, but apparently did not yet call the Philadelphia Bahá'ís, who may not have heard about his declaration of himself as the Center of the Covenant, to obedience.

New York City, June 10–20, 1912

A crowd went to the train station to see him off on the 3pm train to New York City. He returned to a crowd at his Manhattan residence and gave an evening talk to them about his trip to Philadelphia and about "spiritual stations and the inner progress of the soul."[20]

The next ten days in New York City—June 11 through 20, at the end of which he went to Montclair, Newark, and West Englewood, New Jersey, for nine days—included two notable public addresses and a series of private talks that were very significant for the development of the Bahá'í community. The public discourses, to the Fourth Unitarian and the Central Congregational Churches in Brooklyn, occurred on Sunday, June 16. At the Unitarian church, playing on the term "unitarian" (which in Arabic means people who believe in unity) 'Abdu'l-Bahá spoke about five kinds of unity. The first—racial, linguistic, or national unity—is the most limited. The second—the unity of mankind—"is productive of unlimited results." Even greater is the third, "the spiritual unity which emanates from the breaths of the Holy Spirit." If the unity of mankind is like the body, spiritual unity is like "the spirit animating the body." This is the unity brought by Jesus Christ and Bahá'u'lláh. The fourth unity is the "oneness of the Manifestations of God, Abraham, Moses, Jesus Christ, Muhammad, the Báb and Bahá'u'lláh." Each represents the dawning of the same sun, but from different points on the horizon. Finally, there is "the divine unity or entity, which . . . cannot be comprehended nor conceived because it is infinite reality and cannot become finite."[21]

His talk to Central Congregational Church later that day represented a significant development of several themes he had mentioned in other church talks. He noted that "the Holy Manifestations . . . Abraham, Moses, Zoroaster, Buddha, Jesus, Muhammad, the Báb and Bahá'u'lláh are one in spirit and reality." It was his first published talk in English that mentioned Buddha as a Manifestation and one of his first references to Zoroaster. He continued, "Abraham foretold the coming of Moses. . . Moses prophesied the Messianic cycle [the cycle of Jesus], and Christ fulfilled the law of Moses." More specifically, "Moses and the prophets of Israel announced the advent of the Messiah [Christ] but expressed it in the language of symbols. When Christ appeared, the Jews rejected Him."[22]

'Abdu'l-Bahá then enumerated eight expectations that Jews had for the coming of the Messiah and showed how Jesus fulfilled every one—not literally, but metaphorically. Presumably the eight were current in the Middle East; his Congregationalist audience may not have known them. The first "sign of His appearance is . . . that He shall come from an unknown place," whereas Jesus came "from Nazareth." 'Abdu'l-Bahá said that this sign "did not refer to the birthplace of the physical body of Jesus. It has reference to the reality of the Christ—that is to say, the Christ reality was to appear from the invisible realm—for the divine reality of Christ is holy and sanctified above place."[23]

After explaining each of the eight proofs, 'Abdu'l-Bahá concluded that "because the Jews were captives of ancestral imitations and did not perceive the reality of the meanings of these words, they denied Christ." The same possibility applies today: "It is evident, then, that we must forsake all such imitations and beliefs so that we may not commit this error."[24]

'Abdu'l-Bahá next turned his argument to Islam. The Qur'án states that Christ "is the word of God" and the "Spirit of God"; that Mary was "holy and sanctified"; that Muhammad asked people "why have you not believed on Jesus Christ?" Muhammad exalted Moses and called on the Arabs to believe in Him as a Prophet as well. 'Abdu'l-Bahá exclaimed that

> therefore, it is evident that ignorance and misunderstanding have caused so much warfare and strife between Christians and Muslims. If both should investigate the underlying truth of their religious beliefs, the outcome would be unity and agreement; strife and bitterness

> would pass away forever and the world of humanity find peace and composure. Consider that there are two hundred and fifty million Christians and three hundred million Muslims. How much blood has flowed in their wars; how many nations have been destroyed; how many children have been made fatherless; how many fathers and mothers have mourned the loss of children and dear ones! All this has been due to prejudice, misunderstanding and imitations of ancestral beliefs without investigation of reality. If the Holy Books were rightly understood, none of this discord and distress would have existed, but love and fellowship would have prevailed instead. This is true with all the other religions as well.[25]

'Abdu'l-Bahá stopped short of calling on the Congregationalists to accept Muhammad as a divine Messenger, though the comparisons and the emphasis on freeing oneself from prejudices certainly implied such acceptance. Later, 'Abdu'l-Bahá said to Maḥmúd, "This is how we establish the truth of Islam in synagogues, churches, and great temples. And see what the Muslims say about us?"[26] Indeed, one focus in his later addresses in synagogues was exactly this: the proofs of the missions of Jesus and Muhammad, echoing arguments he made to the Congregationalists on June 16. But this Sunday, 'Abdu'l-Bahá sought to focus on Bahá'u'lláh, His principles, and His accomplishments:

> Bahá'u'lláh . . . removed all the imitations and prejudices which had caused separation and misunderstanding and laid the foundation of the one religion of God. When this was accomplished, Muslims, Christians, Jews, Zoroastrians, Buddhists all were united in actual fellowship and love. The souls who followed Bahá'u'lláh from every nation have become as one family living in agreement and accord, willing to sacrifice life for

> each other. The Muslim will give his life for the Christian, the Christian for the Jew and all of them for the Zoroastrian. . . . He upraised this standard of the oneness of humanity in prison. . . . He wrote to Victoria, Queen of Great Britain, the Czar of Russia, the Emperor of Germany, Napoleon III of France and others, inviting them to world unity and peace. . . . The King of Persia . . . killed twenty thousand Bahá'ís, martyrs who in absolute severance and complete willingness offered their lives joyfully for their faith. . . . Today in the East, only those who have not followed Bahá'u'lláh are in opposition and enmity. The people . . . who have accepted Him as the standard of divine guidance enjoy a condition of actual fellowship and love. If you should attend a meeting in the East, you could not distinguish between Christian and Muslim; you would not know which was Jew, Zoroastrian or Buddhist, so completely have they become fraternized and their religious differences been leveled. They associate in the utmost love and spiritual fragrance as if they belonged to one family, as if they were one people.[27]

The talk was well received; the pastor invited 'Abdu'l-Bahá to return and speak a second time, and the *Brooklyn Eagle* reprinted the entire talk the next day.[28]

The other meetings that occurred during this ten-day period were all held in homes. The crowds seeking to see him were so great that he became exhausted, so he limited private meetings to people who had never met him before and asked everyone else to attend general meetings.[29] Many of his talks focused on the development of the Bahá'í community.

The morning after 'Abdu'l-Bahá returned from Philadelphia, he was not feeling well, apparently because of disunity among the Bahá'ís. Maḥmúd-i-Zarqání and Zia Bagdadi both record this comment that he made "in the meeting with the friends":

> He spoke about differences that arise within religions after the ascension of their Founders, the Manifestations, to the heavenly abode. But the Blessed Beauty [Bahá'u'lláh] has shut the door on such differences and has referred all affairs to the House of Justice so that whatever the House of Justice commands, all must obey and submit to it. He said that if the Bahá'ís should become divided into two branches, each establishing a House of Justice of its own in opposition to the other, both would be false. Bahá'u'lláh wrote His Covenant with His own Pen and, prior to the establishment of the House of Justice, He appointed and confirmed the Center of the Covenant, 'Abdu'l-Bahá, directing that "whatever He does is correct."[30]

This is the first reference in a talk published in English to 'Abdu'l-Bahá calling himself the Center of the Covenant. The term may not have surprised the Bahá'ís; he had used it in letters to them for over a decade. By stating that Bahá'u'lláh had said that whatever 'Abdu'l-Bahá does "is correct," he offered a clear statement of the authority given to him. The passage cannot be found in the two other talks given at his residence that are recorded for that day, so it appears to represent a third address. In one of the other talks, he stated that he had "come for the purpose of admonition and voicing the teachings of Bahá'u'lláh. It is my hope that His will and guidance may influence your spirits, souls and hearts, causing them to become pure, holy, sanctified and illumined and making you lamps of heavenly illumination to the world."[31]

That evening the New York Bahá'í "Open Committee" invited him to meet with them. Probably this was the Spiritual Assembly (the coordinating council) of the New York Bahá'ís that he had commanded to be reorganized in the summer of 1911 and expanded to twenty-seven members in order for it to be inclusive of all the community's factions. 'Abdu'l-Bahá's brief comments focused on the investigation of reality and burnishing the mirror of one's heart so that it reflected "the radiance of the Sun of Reality." If they did this, then "opinions will coincide with Reality; day by day there will be the general development and each meeting become better, more radiant and more spiritual. This attainment is conditioned upon perfect unity and agreement. The more you realize of agreement and love, the more the confirmations of God and the help of the Blessed Perfection will descend." He warned that "no one" should "assert his own mere opinion." The goal was consultation "with the greatest love and agreement" so that concord and agreement would characterize the group. The goal was for the meetings of the Bahá'í Assembly of New York to "be as a meeting of the Supreme Concourse."[32]

The next day, June 12, 'Abdu'l-Bahá spoke at his residence to a gathering that apparently included many Bahá'ís. He focused on how blessed they were to have accepted Bahá'u'lláh:

> You have listened to the call of Bahá'u'lláh. Your nostrils are perfumed with the breezes of the paradise of Abhá. You have caught glimpses of the light from the horizon of the Orient. You were asleep; you are awakened. Your ears are attentive; your hearts are informed. You have acquired the love of God. You have attained to the knowledge of God. This is the most great bestowal of God. This is the breath of the Holy Spirit, and this consists of faith and assurance. This eternal life is the second birth; this is the baptism of the Holy Spirit. God has destined this station for you all. He has prepared this for you. You must appreciate the value of this bounty and engage your time in mentioning and thanking the True One. You must live in the utmost happiness. If any trouble or vicissitude comes into your lives, if your heart is depressed on account of health, livelihood or vocation, let not these things affect you. They should not cause unhappiness,

> for Bahá'u'lláh has brought you divine happiness. He has prepared heavenly food for you; He has destined eternal bounty for you; He has bestowed everlasting glory upon you. Therefore, these glad tidings should cause you to soar in the atmosphere of joy forever and ever. Render continual thanks unto God so that the confirmations of God may encircle you all.[33]

This does not seem like a talk for the public, but one aimed at strengthening the commitment of the Bahá'ís. On June 15, he offered a similar talk at his residence that urged Bahá'ís to achieve heights of service and love for humanity:

> I have made you wait awhile, but as I was tired, I slept. While I was sleeping, I was conversing with you as though speaking at the top of my voice. Then through the effect of my own voice I awoke. As I awoke, one word was upon my lips—the word imtíyáz ("distinction"). So I will speak to you upon that subject this morning. . . .
>
> I desire distinction for you. The Bahá'ís must be distinguished from others of humanity. But this distinction must not depend upon wealth—that they should become more affluent than other people. I do not desire for you financial distinction. It is not an ordinary distinction I desire; not scientific, commercial, industrial distinction. For you I desire spiritual distinction—that is, you must become eminent and distinguished in morals. In the love of God you must become distinguished from all else. You must become distinguished for loving humanity, for unity and accord, for love and justice. In brief, you must become distinguished in all the virtues of the human world—for faithfulness and sincerity, for justice and fidelity, for firmness and steadfastness, for philanthropic deeds and service to

> the human world, for love toward every human being, for unity and accord with all people, for removing prejudices and promoting international peace. Finally, you must become distinguished for heavenly illumination and for acquiring the bestowals of God. I desire this distinction for you. This must be the point of distinction among you.[34]

On Sunday, June 16—after his talk at the Unitarian Church and before his talk at the Congregational Church—'Abdu'l-Bahá spoke at Howard McNutt's home in Brooklyn, and again he called on the Bahá'ís to consecrate themselves. "You are not a large body of people," he said,

> but because the lamp of guidance has been lighted in your hearts, the effects will be wonderful in the years to come. It is evident and manifest that the world will be illumined by this light; therefore, you must thank God that—praise be to God!—through His grace and favor the lamp of the most great guidance has been ignited in your hearts, and He has summoned you to His Kingdom. . . . Although the bestowal is great and the grace is glorious, yet capacity and readiness are requisite. . . . Therefore, we must develop capacity in order that the signs of the mercy of the Lord may be revealed in us. . . . The doors of God are open, but we must be ready and fitted to enter. The ocean of divine providence is surging, but we must be able to swim. . . . Unless the soul hungers, the delicious foods of the heavenly table will not give sustenance. . . . Therefore, we must endeavor always, cry, supplicate and invoke the Kingdom of God to grant us full capacity in order that the bestowals of God may become revealed and manifest in us. . . . You must endeavor day and night to become worthy of a generous portion of these gifts and realize full capacity of attainment. . . . It is my hope that all of these degrees may

> be reached and these friends [Bahá'ís] attain a station which shall be an example and stimulus for all friends in the world. May the love of God spread from here onward and outward; may the knowledge of God be sent broadcast from this place; may spiritual forces become effective here; may the lights of the Kingdom shine; may intelligent souls be found here so that with all power they may be occupied in the service of God, furthering the oneness of the human world and the cause of the Most Great Peace. May these souls be lighted candles and fruitful trees; may they be pearls of the shells of providence; may they be stars of heaven. This is my supplication to God. This is my request from the Beauty of Abhá: that He may submerge all of you in the ocean of His grace.[35]

On Tuesday, June 18, 'Abdu'l-Bahá returned to the MacNutt residence in Brooklyn to make a moving picture. While living in the Middle East, he had not consented even to have his picture taken, but in Britain, he found that impossible to maintain; newspaper reporters always wanted to photograph him. By the time he had arrived in the United States, he had accepted the inevitable: "Some of the Bahai friends . . . were very much upset by the decision [to make a motion picture of 'Abdu'l-Bahá] and hastened to inform him that his photograph would be scattered all over the country in moving picture houses and theatres. He replied, 'Besyar Khub' 'Most good.'"[36] The cameraman took five different short movies of him.

He also consented to sit for a portrait by Juliet Thompson, who was an accomplished painter. Thompson quailed at the thought of painting the "Face of God," as she thought of him, but he instructed her to paint his "*Servitude* to God." She begged him to pray for her, and he agreed, adding that "as you are doing this only for the sake of God, you will be inspired." She found the inspiration, experienced a "clarity" of vision, "painted in ecstasy, free as I had never been before," and "at the end of the half hour the foundation of the head was perfect."[37]

On Wednesday, June 19, during the fourth sitting for the portrait, Lua Getsinger came and sat on a couch nearby to watch and talk to 'Abdu'l-Bahá in Persian. 'Abdu'l-Bahá grew sleepy, and Thompson said she could work on the painting while he slept, so he napped briefly. Then a look came over his face, "a God-like calm and grandeur":

> Suddenly, with a great flash like lightning He opened His eyes and the room seemed to rock like a ship in a storm with the Power released. The Master was *blazing*. "The veils of glory," "the thousand veils," had shriveled away in that Flame and we were exposed to the Glory itself.
>
> Lua and I sat shaking and sobbing.
>
> Then He spoke to Lua. I caught the words, *"Munádíy-i-'Ahd."* (Herald of the Covenant).
>
> Lua started forward, her hand to her breast.
>
> *"Man?"* (I) she exclaimed.
>
> "Call one of the Persians. You must understand this."
>
> Never shall I forget that moment, the flashing eyes of 'Abdu'l-Bahá, the reverberations of His voice, the Power that still rocked the room. God of Lightning and thunder! I thought.
>
> "I appoint you, Lua, the Herald of the Covenant. And I AM THE COVENANT, appointed by Bahá'u'lláh. And no one can refute His Word. This is the Testament of Bahá'u'lláh. You will find it in the Holy Book of Aqdas. Go forth and proclaim, 'This is THE COVENANT OF GOD in your midst.'"
>
> A great joy had lifted Lua up. Her eyes were full of light. She looked like a winged angel. "Oh, recreate me," she cried, "that I may do this work for Thee!"

By now I was sobbing uncontrollably.

"Julie too," said Lua, not even in such a moment forgetful of me, "wants to be recreated."[38]

'Abdu'l-Bahá then "shrouded Himself with His veils," perhaps because of the sobbing, urged Juliet not to cry and go back to painting—which she found impossible to do—laughed, and even offered to tell them a joke, which he then declined to do. "Perhaps He had just found it necessary, after that mighty Declaration, to bring us down to earth again," concludes Thompson.[39]

That afternoon he sent Lua Getsinger downstairs to the waiting audience of about 125 people to "proclaim the Covenant," and then he followed to give a talk. He started by explaining that previous religions had not had a covenant whereby the Founder had unambiguously appointed a successor to whom the followers had to turn:

> But in this Dispensation of the Blessed Beauty [Bahá'u'lláh] among its distinctions is that He did not leave people in perplexity. He entered into a Covenant and Testament with the people. He appointed a Center of the Covenant. He wrote with His own pen and revealed it in the Kitab-el-Akdas, the Book of Laws, the Book of the Covenant, appointing Him (Abdul-Baha) the Expounder of the Book. You must ask Him regarding the meanings of the texts of the verses. Whatsoever He says is correct. And outside of this, in numerous Tablets He (Baha'o'llah) has explicitly recorded it, with clear, sufficient, valid and forceful statements.
>
> In the Tablet of The Branch He [Bahá'u'lláh] explicitly states: "Whatsoever The Branch says is right, or correct; and every person must obey The Branch with his life, with his heart, with his tongue. Without His will, not a word shall any one utter." This is an explicit

> text of the Blessed Beauty. So there is no rescue left for anybody. No soul shall, of himself, speak anything. Whatsoever His (Abdul-Baha's) tongue utters, whatsoever his pen records, that is correct, according to the explicit text of Baha'o'llah in the Tablet of The Branch. . . . His Holiness the Bab, in all His books, in all His epistles, explicitly covenanted with regard to the Blessed Beauty, Baha'o'llah—that Baha'o'llah was the Promised One of His Holiness the Bab. His Holiness Baha'o'llah covenanted, not that I am the Promised One, but that Abdul-Baha is the Expounder of the Book and the Center of His Covenant, and the Promised One of Baha'o'llah will appear after one thousand or thousands of years. This is the Covenant which Baha'o'llah took. If a person shall deviate, he is not acceptable at the Threshold of Baha'o'llah. In case of difference, Abdul Baha must be consulted. They must revolve around His good pleasure. After Abdul Baha, whenever the Universal House of Justice is organized, it will ward off differences.[40]

'Abdu'l-Bahá generally referred to himself in the third person to remove personality from the talk. His point is clear: Bahá'u'lláh stated that the Bahá'ís should turn to 'Abdu'l-Bahá, accept his interpretations of Bahá'u'lláh's writings, and obey his directives. He again mentioned that the Universal House of Justice would be the head of the Faith in the future. He did not mention the institution of the Guardianship, probably because his chosen successor and the future Guardian, Shoghi Effendi Rabbani, was fifteen years old at the time and might be subjected to jealousy or harm if his future role were disclosed or suggested. 'Abdu'l-Bahá had the Tablet of the Branch read aloud in English so the audience would hear the words of Bahá'u'lláh themselves.

A month later in San Francisco, Lua Getsinger said that "those present shall never forget that day" and "He spoke the message very quietly and impressively . . . every person present . . . was touched with a spirit which in itself was creative."[41] To hear the announcement from his lips, to experience it in his presence, would have left a profound impression, especially after Lua Getsinger's preparatory comments, which likely reflected her experience of 'Abdu'l-Bahá's appointing her as Herald of the Covenant. Juliet Thompson's account of the spiritual power she experienced may have started to spread orally as well.

Recognizing the importance of his talk, 'Abdu'l-Bahá reviewed the Persian notes and revised them on June 25 so that Ameen Fareed could prepare an official English translation that Lua Getsinger and others could disseminate.[42] Presumably he also commanded it to be published. It appeared in a special "Center of the Covenant" edition of *Star of the West* on November 23, 1912, which appeared shortly before the Day of the Covenant (November 26), a Bahá'í holy day commemorating Bahá'u'lláh's Covenant. The talk was published along with the entire text of the Tablet of the Branch; all of Bahá'u'lláh's Book of the Covenant; an extract from Mírzá Abu'l-Fadl's *The Bahá'í Proofs,* published in English in 1902, about the "Center of the Covenant"; the text of a talk by 'Abdu'l-Karím-i-Tihrání, a Persian Bahá'í teacher who visited the United States in 1900, about how 'Abdu'l-Bahá was alluded to in the Bible, and about his appointment as the "Center of the Covenant" by Bahá'u'lláh; and a talk by Mírzá Abu'l-Fadl, delivered at Washington, D.C.'s Day of the Covenant commemoration in 1902, about the "Covenant" and the "Center of the Covenant." Clearly, the fact that 'Abdu'l-Bahá was the Center of Bahá'u'lláh's Covenant had been available for years, yet the editors of *The Star of the West* were worried about how the information would be received: "'To those who understand the claim and purpose of the Bahai Teaching the contents of this issue of the STAR OF THE WEST will be clearly apparent; to those who are but slightly familiar with the Movement or who know nothing of the Revelation, its contents may startle and shock. . . . we trust its contents will cause all seekers for knowledge to investigate thoroughly the precepts of the Bahai Revelation and what it is destined to accomplish throughout the world."[43]

Possibly 'Abdu'l-Bahá's announcement of his station as the Center of the Covenant was also connected with his decision to serve as host at "a large feast of unity." Speaking at his residence the next day, June 20, 'Abdu'l-Bahá explained the feast "must be outdoors under the trees, in some location away from city noise—like a Persian garden. The food will be Persian food. When the place is arranged, all will be informed, and we will have a general meeting in which hearts will be bound together, spirits blended and a new foundation for unity established. All the friends will come. They will be my guests."[44] This request set in motion planning for the unity feast in West Englewood, New Jersey, on June 29. The rest of 'Abdu'l-Bahá's talk on June 20 highlighted the profound unity of the Manifestations of God and of the believers. Perhaps the feast of unity was meant to demonstrate such love:

> The supreme love and unity is witnessed in the divine Manifestations. Among Them unity is indissoluble, changeless, eternal and everlasting. . . . If we deny One of the Manifestations of God, we deny all. To inflict persecution upon One is to persecute the Others. . . . Each of Them holds to the solidarity of mankind and promotes the unity of human hearts. Next to the divine Manifestations come the believers whose characteristics are agreement, fellowship and love. The Bahá'í friends in Persia attained such a brotherhood and love that it really became a hindrance in the conduct of material affairs. . . . There was no duality but complete mutuality of interests and love. . . . They wore each other's clothes as their own when necessary. . . . The owner of the clothing would be thankful and grateful that the garment had gone. When he returned home, he would perhaps be told, "So and so was here and took away your coat." He would reply, "Praise be

to God! I am so grateful to him. Praise be to God! I am so thankful I have been given this opportunity of showing my love for him." To such an extreme degree this love and fellowship expressed itself that Bahá'u'lláh commanded that no one should take possession of another's belongings unless presented with them. The intention is to show to what an extent unity and love prevailed among the Bahá'í friends in the East.[45]

Montclair, Newark, West Englewood, June 20–29, 1912

'Abdu'l-Bahá left for Montclair later that day to stay in a rented house for nine days. The heat and humidity of the New York summer and the crowds were impairing his health; as he noted at the beginning of the above talk, he was seeking a "few days of rest." The nine days were busy but included no talks in public places. On Sunday, June 23, in a talk at his residence—the only one recorded in *The Promulgation of Universal Peace*—he says, "I was not feeling very well this morning, or I would have gone to church," suggesting that a talk had been scheduled.[46]

Maḥmúd provides brief summaries of many of 'Abdu'l-Bahá's talks in Montclair and Newark. Many focused on consolidation of the faith of the Bahá'ís rather than attracting new people to the teachings, suggesting that Montclair gave him the opportunity to address smaller numbers of Bahá'ís from greater New York City. In that sense, the Montclair stay served similar purposes to 'Abdu'l-Bahá's later visit to Dublin, New Hampshire. On June 21, he counseled the Bahá'ís that it was "forbidden to interfere in political matters and that they should obey the laws of their country"; on the morning of June 22, he spoke about Bahá'u'lláh's half brother, Mírzá Yaḥyá, and his machinations against Bahá'u'lláh and the Bahá'í community; on the afternoon of that day, he eulogized the martyrs for the Faith, spontaneously dancing and repeating their cries of ecstasy to reenact the scenes of their martyrdom, which he compared to the early Christian martyrdoms; on June 23, he spoke about the happiness of the Bahá'ís in Baghdad, in spite of their poverty, because they were near Bahá'u'lláh; and on June 26, he described Bahá'u'lláh's withdrawal from Baghdad and the family's efforts to find him in Kurdistan. Other talks, often for inquirers, focused on the prohibition of self-mortification, the spiritual power of music, reincarnation, the teachings of Bahá'u'lláh, and the transitory nature of physical wealth.[47]

Even though his table was usually crowded at breakfast and dinner times, 'Abdu'l-Bahá had the time to go to the market to purchase groceries and to cook in the kitchen. He strolled in parks and visited stores. On several occasions, he entered the oriental art shop of Mr. Madris Bedekian, an Armenian, to see the merchandise and speak to the staff, including Mrs. Victoria Bedekian, the owner's wife. She became very attracted to 'Abdu'l-Bahá, began a correspondence with him, and became a devoted and active Bahá'í who served the Faith for decades.[48]

On Saturday, June 29, feeling rested, he left Montclair for West Englewood to attend the unity feast he had requested. Roy Wilhelm, a prominent New York Bahá'í and a coffee merchant, owned a large house there with an extensive lawn and a pine grove. Bahá'ís began to arrive in the early morning; 'Abdu'l-Bahá arrived by tram at noon. He explained the purpose of the gathering in these words:

> This is a delightful gathering; you have come here with sincere intentions. . . The motive is attraction to the divine Kingdom. Since the desire of all is unity and agreement, it is certain that this meeting will be productive of great results. . . . This is a new Day, and this hour is a new Hour in which we have come together. . . . The utmost love and unity will result; the favors of God will encompass us; the pathway of the Kingdom will be made easy. Like candles these souls

will become ignited and made radiant through the lights of supreme guidance. Such gatherings as this have no equal or likeness in the world of mankind, where people are drawn together by physical motives or in furtherance of material interests, for this meeting is a prototype of that inner and complete spiritual association in the eternal world of being.

True Bahá'í meetings are the mirrors of the Kingdom wherein images of the Supreme Concourse are reflected. In them the lights of the most great guidance are visible. They voice the summons of the heavenly Kingdom and echo the call of the angelic hosts to every listening ear. . . . Hundreds of thousands of meetings shall be held to commemorate this occasion, and the very words I speak to you today shall be repeated in them for ages to come. . . . Be happy and joyous because the bestowals of God are intended for you and the life of the Holy Spirit is breathing upon you. . . . You must become of one heart, one spirit and one susceptibility. May you become as the waves of one sea, stars of the same heaven, fruits adorning the same tree, roses of one garden in order that through you the oneness of humanity may establish its temple in the world of mankind, for you are the ones who are called to uplift the cause of unity among the nations of the earth. . . . You must be exceedingly kind and loving toward each other, willing to forfeit life in the pathway of another's happiness. . . . The rich among you must show compassion toward the poor, and the well-to-do must look after those in distress. . . . You should have neither will nor desire of your own but seek everything for the beloved of God and live together in complete love and fellowship. May the favors of Bahá'u'lláh surround you from all directions. This is the greatest bestowal and supreme bounty.[49]

'Abdu'l-Bahá went inside Wilhelm's house to speak to a clergyman while the food was prepared. When the Persian rice, sherbet, various sweets, and a Persian drink were ready, the almost two hundred fifty present sat at a large circle of tables under the pine trees; "Christians, Jews, Muhammadans and the white and black races were represented." Juliet Thompson (alone among the various sources) writes that just before the food was served, a storm blew in with thunder and lightning. Rain drops began to splash onto the tables. 'Abdu'l-Bahá rose, walked some distance from the pine grove, and lifted his face toward the sky; a wind then blew the storm away.[50]

After the dinner, 'Abdu'l-Bahá walked through the crowd and anointed everyone on the forehead with attar of rose, often lovingly rubbing it on the faces and hair. Ahmad Sohrab described the feast as a "wonderful event." Maḥmúd said that "the friends were ecstatic . . . since their Host was the Beloved of the Covenant, their meeting was an assembly of love and amity, and the surroundings were green and verdant, with trees in full bloom perfuming the air." The crowd lingered for hours. 'Abdu'l-Bahá spoke two more times, the last time to latecomers in the moonlight, including a carload that saw him speaking outside and spontaneously stopped to hear. True to 'Abdu'l-Bahá's word, the event has become an annual occurrence.[51]

New York City, June 30–July 23, 1912

'Abdu'l-Bahá spent the night at Roy Wilhelm's West Englewood residence. The next day, after a second visit to Consul Topakyan's residence in Morristown—the representative of Persia was impressed by 'Abdu'l-Bahá and saw him several other times as well—he returned to his apartment at 309 West Seventy-eighth Street, New York, for the first time in ten days. The word of his return spread quickly, and the next day, a crowd of people arrived to meet 'Abdu'l-Bahá or hear his daily talk. Ahmad Sohrab noted in a letter that "every night at 8 o'clock there is a large meeting in the Master's large home and hundreds of people attend every night. There is a great change in New York and although it is in the height of summer every night the three large rooms on the second floor are crowded with new people. The Master gives wonderful addresses on various subjects. It seems to us a wonderful panorama of God's spiritual wealth that He is showing to the people. People are very receptive. No one contradicts. Everyone marvels and is astonished."[52]

To meet the needs of the hundreds of visitors, 'Abdu'l-Bahá had two interpreters, Ameen Fareed and Ahmad Sohrab, who could also speak to the press, answer the spontaneous questions of visitors, handle business matters such as buying train tickets, translate English-language correspondence for him, and render his responses into written English. The two young Persians had lived in the United States for over a decade. Zia Bagdadi, an Arab Bahá'í physician living in Chicago, and Ali Kuli Khan, Persia's chargé d'affaires in Washington, sometimes helped. Mírzá Maḥmúd, the diarist, served as his Persian language secretary, for there was a heavy flow of correspondence from Iran and the Arab world. Valíyu'lláh Varqá and 'Alí-Akbar Nakhjavání arrived during his visit and also served as secretaries. Siyyid Asadu'lláh, an older gentleman, served as a cook, though many of the other Persians (including the interpreters and sometimes 'Abdu'l-Bahá himself) helped in the kitchen. Edward Getsinger, Lua's husband, often assisted with the guests. Grace and Ella Robarts, two devoted Bahá'ís and sisters cooked, cleaned, and served as hostess to the visitors, many of whom needed something to eat or a cup of tea to drink.

Because 'Abdu'l-Bahá was the head of the Bahá'í Faith, he was busy—especially in the early morning hours—reading and replying to reports about developments in the Bahá'í communities in Europe, the Ottoman Empire, Iran, India, and Burma. He reviewed Persian and Arabic manuscripts about the Faith and directed their translation into English, especially when they dealt with basic information or responded to attacks by missionaries.

'Abdu'l-Bahá remained in New York City another three and a half weeks, until July 23. In that time, he gave some thirty-one talks, though only one was in a public location: All Souls Unitarian Church, Fourth Avenue and Twentieth Street, on July 14. Before going to the church, he asked Howard MacNutt to be sure a stenographer was present to record every word because it "was to be a most important address" and "the daily papers should report every word" rather than the parts they thought were humorous or sensational. He spoke to a thousand people on that occasion for nearly fifty minutes. His theme, the oneness of humanity, focused on the barriers to unity: the disagreements of religion with science, the conflicts among religious communities, political and ethnic prejudices, diversity of languages, and lack of equality between men and women. In short, he took a talk he often gave about the basic principles of the Bahá'í Faith and turned it around to discuss the disunities the principles were meant to cure. As a solution to religious strife, he advocated the creation of an "interreligious body before which all disputes and difference of religious belief could be presented for investigation and discussion."[53]

Only six of the thirty talks he gave in homes that July were transcribed, though Maḥmúd describes others. On July 1, he spoke about economic problems and the reduction of the extremes of wealth and poverty. A second talk that day called on the Bahá'ís "to have infinite love for each another" and "be willing to sacrifice" themselves so that everyone will ask "why are these people so happy" and that 'Abdu'l-Bahá "will know the Cause of Bahá'u'lláh has been established" in America. Addresses on July 5 and July 15 described many of Bahá'u'lláh's important writings.* On July

* Many of these talks were published in Howard MacNutt, comp. ed., "Addresses Delivered by Abdul-Baha in New York City and Vicinity," *Star of the West* 3, no. 11 (Sept. 27, 1912): 6–7, 9–16.

12, he again spoke about Bahá'u'lláh's Covenant, Bahá'u'lláh's appointment of him as the "Expounder of the Book," and of the eventual establishment of the House of Justice as the "center of authority" in the Bahá'í Faith. The talks continued to alternate between themes for non-Bahá'í audiences eager to learn basics and themes to strengthen the devotion and commitment of Bahá'ís.[54]

The three-week period also saw many significant interactions with individuals. After appointing Lua Getsinger the Herald of the Covenant on June 19, 'Abdu'l-Bahá asked her to go to California and speak about the Covenant. She began to make plans but delayed because she didn't want to be separated from the Master. At the Unity Feast on June 29, she intentionally walked in a patch of poison ivy so she couldn't leave for California. Soon her feet were "terribly swollen"; Juliet Thompson visited her in her hotel room, and Lua asked her to go to 'Abdu'l-Bahá and say, "How can Lua travel now?" When Juliet spoke to 'Abdu'l-Bahá, he "laughed, then crossed the room to a table on which stood a bowl of fruit, and, selecting an apple and a pomegranate" gave them to Juliet and told her they would cure Lua's feet. Juliet took them back to Lua's hotel: "Oh precious Lua—strange mixture of disobedience and obedience—and all from love! I shall never forget her, seizing first the apple, then the pomegranate and gravely chewing them all the way through till not even a pomegranate seed was left: thoroughly eating her cure, which was certain to send her to California." 'Abdu'l-Bahá visited Lua that afternoon, "drew back the sheet and looked at Lua's feet, which by that time were beautifully slim." He burst out laughing. "See," he said, "I have cured Lua with an apple and a pomegranate." Perhaps her faith was the key to her cure, but Lua still did not leave for California. On July 7, 'Abdu'l-Bahá strongly admonished her:

> The Blessed Beauty entered into this Covenant for obedience and not for opposition. I say this merely for the protection of the Cause

> of God and for the purpose of safeguarding unity among the friends. Were it not for the removal of vain imaginings and the eradication of differences, I should not have asserted that I am "the Center of the Covenant." . . . If even a breath of egotism is found in us, we shall perish at once. The friends must be alert. Everyone who expresses a word not from the texts sows discord among the believers. . . . [Otherwise] everyone would open a way for himself . . . One would say, for instance, "As I have the power of the Holy Spirit, I have a greater capacity for understanding." . . . The power of the Holy Spirit is limited to the Blessed Beauty and the interpretation thereof to none but me. If it is so, then there will be no differences. We must occupy ourselves with thoughts of spreading the Cause. Know that whoever has any thought other than this will become the cause of discord among the friends.[56]

Lua left for California shortly thereafter.[57]

'Abdu'l-Bahá also gave a lot of time to Juliet Thompson, who visited him daily and often joined him and his party in their daily walk in Riverside Park. She was in love with Percy Stickney Grant, Rector of the Episcopal Church of the Ascension, Manhattan, but 'Abdu'l-Bahá cautioned her to be very careful to keep her relationship with Grant absolutely formal. He said nothing more about the suggestion he had given her several years earlier that she and Charles Mason Remey, a prominent Washington, D.C. Bahá'í, should marry. 'Abdu'l-Bahá ate several meals with Thompson and her mother, who was not a Bahá'í. He visited Thompson's home, where he had another meeting with Kahlil Gibran.[58]

He kept Howard MacNutt close to him as well; he was a frequent visitor at 'Abdu'l-Bahá's house. At one time, when MacNutt was leaving, 'Abdu'l-Bahá pinched him on the cheek "and told him he was only a youth as he had not any beard not even a mustache." He laughed and added MacNutt "was Ahmad [Sohrab's] son as Ahmad had at least a moustache." Another time he told MacNutt "I want to train you like a race horse so that you will be ready to go west at any moment"; he sent MacNutt to Chicago several weeks later and apparently had the mission in mind already. MacNutt replied, "It is impossible to train a donkey." 'Abdu'l-Bahá laughed and said, "No, no, you are a racehorse."[59]

'Abdu'l-Bahá showered affection on Grace Robarts, who served as hostess and kept his residence "immaculate."[60] Grace had asked specifically to serve 'Abdu'l-Bahá, and he had replied by asking her repeatedly if she was sure, for "'Abdu'l-Bahá" means "servant of Bahá," and to be a servant of the Servant was a high calling. She affirmed that she was sure. It would appear that he tested her, often leaving her at the house when everyone else accompanied him on a short trip and pouring his love and affection on others while ignoring her. Finally, one day, in an empty house, locked out of the room she wanted to clean and confronted by a totally empty pantry except for a tiny morsel of bread and a rotten egg that exploded on her when she tried to cook it, she broke down and cried out of a sense of abandonment and neglect. Afterward a "spirit of prayer" swept over her. As she later explained to Muriel Ives Barrow Newhall,

> that evening Lua came to Grace and said, "The Master has asked me to tell you that He knows you wept." And this was the first time it had occurred to Grace that all this dreadful experience might have a reason, a pattern. And—if this were true she must find out what the reason could be. So she went up to her room to pray about it. . . . as she prayed she heard a small voice saying 'Are you as happy scrubbing the garbage pails as you are arranging the roses?' And she suddenly realized what the spirit of true service was. It was to rise to selfless joy in offering the service, no matter what form that service might take.

> And as this truth swept over her, suffusing her, illuminating her, the door opened, and Abdu'l-Bahá walked into the room. His arms were outstretched; His dear face was glorified. "Welcome!" He cried to Grace, "Welcome to the Kingdom!" And he held her close, embracing her deeply. And never did He withdraw Himself from her again.[61]

'Abdu'l-Bahá also noticed something about Grace's personality and faith that seemed to harmonize well with that of Harlan Ober (1881–1962), a Harvard-educated Massachusetts lawyer and devoted Bahá'í who was in New York at the time. Perhaps the two of them were already attracted to each other, but on July 16, 'Abdu'l-Bahá suggested to the two of them that they should get married, and they immediately agreed. The marriage occurred the next day; 'Abdu'l-Bahá presided over a Bahá'í ceremony in the morning, and Howard Colby Ives, as a Unitarian minister, performed the legal ceremony at the regular evening meeting. The latter was attended by 150 guests; 'Abdu'l-Bahá revealed a prayer for the couple, one often said at Bahá'í marriages today.[62] It was one of the two marriage ceremonies that 'Abdu'l-Bahá attended during his North American tour, and one of two he suggested during this time.

While Grace was on her honeymoon, Corinne True served in his household in her place. She had assisted his household in Chicago, but presumably he had invited her to come to New York a few days before he encouraged the Ober marriage. He also wanted to talk to her about the Covenant, for the morning after her arrival, 'Abdu'l-Bahá summoned her and asked her about Dr. Frederick Nutt, a very active Chicago Bahá'í who had continued to associate with Ibrahim Kheiralla. 'Abdu'l-Bahá had told Bahá'ís to break off all contact with Kheiralla, for he had been using slander and misinformation to undermine the Bahá'ís' faith and pull them into his own separate organization.* True explained that she was aware that "there was something wrong" with Dr. Nutt but that she had been trying to look at the man's good side and overlook his faults. 'Abdu'l-Bahá replied that Dr. Nutt was a violator of the Covenant because of his continued association with Kheiralla in spite of 'Abdu'l-Bahá's commands, that "she should have known," and that she must take an "active part against the violation." Over the next five days, living in the household, True had many opportunities to see 'Abdu'l-Bahá in action and come to a deeper appreciation of his call for obedience in matters related to protection of the Bahá'í community. Before she left New York on July 22, 'Abdu'l-Bahá instructed her to be sure to be in Chicago in early August when MacNutt would arrive to speak to the Chicago Bahá'í community about its unity.[63]

'Abdu'l-Bahá's July days in New York City also included two important diplomatic meetings. On July 20, the Ottoman Consul General invited him to a large reception with "a number of prominent men and statesmen." On July 21, a number of Armenians and the Persian Consul General sponsored a memorial banquet in honor of the passing of a hero of Iran's Constitutional Revolution.† On July 22, he twice met the brother of the Khedive (viceroy) of Egypt, Muḥammad-'Alí Pá<u>sh</u>á, who was impressed by

* The account of Ibrahim Kheiralla's introducing the Bahá'í Faith into the United States in the 1890s and his rejection of 'Abdu'l-Bahá when 'Abdu'l-Bahá refused to give Kheiralla a secure, permanent leadership position in the Bahá'í community is given in Stockman, *The Bahá'í Faith in America,* volume 1.

† The dates of the meetings sponsored by the Ottoman and Persian Consul Generals are given in Ahmad Sohrab to Agnes Parsons, July 18, 1912, Agnes Parsons Papers. The names of the Consul Generals are not given; presumably the Persian Consul General is Topakyan. Maḥmúd puts both events on July 20. In this part of the diary, Maḥmúd usually is off by a day; for example, he puts the Ober wedding on July 16 when it actually occurred on July 17.

his "extraordinary sagacity and infinite intelligence" and called him "one of the exalted personages of the East."[64]

July, 1912, was fairly hot and humid; several times 'Abdu'l-Bahá fell ill. Apparently he was prone to *tab-i-'aṣabí,* "nervous fever," presumably a stress-related illness. The city's air pollution and 'Abdu'l-Bahá's childhood bout of tuberculosis may have been factors as well. "I cannot see him living through this heat," Ahmad Sohrab said in a letter to Agnes Parsons, "It melts iron." 'Abdu'l-Bahá himself commented on his eyes looking "sunken in the sockets" from the heat. He "endured all the discomfort of the hot weather," 'Abdu'l-Bahá explained, to strengthen the unity and amity of the New York Bahá'ís: "The condition is very different [now] . . . the friends invite each other and go to each other's meetings . . . unity + harmony are established . . . I am very happy."[65]

'Abdu'l-Bahá decided in his current state of health, that he could not continue across the United States to California, four or five days by train to the west. On July 5, he wrote a series of tablets to Bahá'ís in California informing them of his change of plans and consoling them. He sent a telegram to Helen Goodall and her daughter, Ella Cooper, two of the most active Bahá'ís in California, summoning them to New York to discuss the change of plans with them. They left San Francisco immediately and arrived in New York on July 9. "The distance is so great & the weather so warm," he explained. They were "heartbroken" at the thought that he wouldn't visit their state. He stressed to them the importance of firmness in the Covenant and obedience to the Center of the Covenant.[66]

Developments in the Middle East also influenced his decision to leave North America. Agnes Parsons had already invited 'Abdu'l-Bahá to come to her summer house in Dublin, New Hampshire, where it was cooler and the air fresher. Ahmad Sohrab wrote to her from New York on July 9, urging her to issue a second invitation. She did so, and 'Abdu'l-Bahá accepted on July 12. He made plans to visit Boston again, possibly Green

Acre and Montreal, then return to New York and sail for the Orient in mid-September.* He left New York City for New England on July 23.[67]

* These plans later changed.

8

A NEW ENGLAND SUMMER

'Abdu'l-Bahá spent the next thirty-nine days in New England, from July 23 through August 30. He visited Boston; Dublin, New Hampshire; Green Acre in Eliot, Maine; and Malden, Massachusetts, a northern suburb of Boston. He delivered at least fifty-eight talks to audiences totaling about ten thousand.

His second visit to Boston, three days in length, was packed with crowds of visitors and featured at least seven talks. During his first evening at the Hotel Victoria, as a result of questions asked by Helen Campbell, a Bahá'í who was a published social reformer, and Dr. Walter Bryant Guy, a Bahá'í physician, he spoke about "economic and social conditions," explaining that there are "ministers" and "Governor-Generals" in Iran who are Bahá'ís, but Bahá'ís cannot be engaged in "politics that lead to corruption." Rather, "the Bahai spirit is, that in order to establish a better economic and social condition you must abide by certain laws." This was an elucidation of the meaning of the Bahá'í principle of unity: the goal of unity requires law and order, hence actions that create disunity, such as strikes and resort to force, are to be eschewed. "Hearts must be so cemented together" that "the rich shall most willingly, out of the free will of their hearts, help and extend assistance to the poor" and take steps to establish "adjustments." 'Abdu'l-Bahá added that "you must strive as much as possible" to "show what love is, what kindness is, what severance is, what giving is." "Economic questions," he added in conclusion, "will not attract hearts."[1]

'Abdu'l-Bahá's comments paralleled some statements Helen Campbell had made about the Bahá'í approach to economics. They also echoed the assumptions of the Social Gospel movement, popular among many Protestants at the time, that the Christian principles of love, compassion, and assisting the poor were able to transform governmental and cultural institutions and social values, establishing the Kingdom of God on earth. A congregational minister, Charles Monroe Sheldon (1857–1946), published a popular version of the Social Gospel in his novel, *In His Steps,* in 1896. It described the impact on a small Wisconsin town when a local church congregation vowed always to ask themselves "What would Jesus Do?" before they carried out any major actions in their lives. As a result, wages of workers were raised, homeless people were housed, and honest leaders were elected to run the town. *In His Steps* had sold millions of copies—at least two million in the United States before World War I—and was probably known to many who heard 'Abdu'l-Bahá's addresses. Others, like Campbell, would have been familiar with more sophisticated works by Social Gospel theologians. Most likely, 'Abdu'l-Bahá's comments about social and economic reform were understood in the context of such ideas.[2]

The next day—Wednesday, July 24—was the most intense day of his brief visit. People arrived by 8am to meet him, and he was occupied for four hours with Bahá'ís and inquirers. He gave a public address at the hotel in the afternoon, then went to the Golden Circle Club—an organization for Middle Eastern immigrants—to visit and speak. Returning to his hotel, he was greeted by a crowd and addressed them as well. One visitor, the president of the Boston Theosophical Society, invited him to speak that night to the Theosophists, and because it was near the hotel, 'Abdu'l-Bahá agreed. Even though he was tired, he gave them a lengthy address about the human spirit, "the most noble of phenomena," "the meeting between man and God," "the cause of human life," "the collective center of all virtues," and "the cause of the illumination of this world." He offered proofs that it is "everlasting and permanent" and urged that "we must strive to learn of it." Maḥmúd notes that "when the meeting ended, the people ran to the door to shake hands with the Master and to express their joy and devotion." Before he left for Dublin on Thursday, he greeted more people at his hotel and spoke at least once, to a group of nineteen Bahá'ís, about release from self and desire and freedom from "satanic suggestions."[3]

Dublin, July 25–August 16, 1912

The eighty-mile train ride to Dublin, located in southwestern New Hampshire, took three hours. It was an idyllic setting to spend long, warm summer days; a "favored spot, a kind of Switzerland, with lines softened because of the wooded hills and the abundant verdure of the earth, which burgeons and blossoms in almost tropical luxuriance." Agnes Parsons turned over one of her houses to him: "the Parson farmhouse" also known as Day-Spring, which was "equipped with all the modern conveniences, including electric lights, telephones, and baths." She arranged for 'Abdu'l-Bahá's party to have an African American woman to cook and do housework as well.[4]

'Abdu'l-Bahá's retinue hoped that he would rest; Parsons tried to keep his arrival private for a few days. But 'Abdu'l-Bahá replied, "we have come for work and service and not for leisure." Still, a certain amount of rest was inevitable. Dublin's permanent population was less than five hundred, though its population quintupled in summer because of an important artists' colony and numerous private estates; the British embassy even moved there during the summer. Mr. Parsons had a carriage and took 'Abdu'l-Bahá for rides around beautiful Dublin Lake and through the countryside. He also took walks, usually every afternoon; the Parsons had an open, wooded area called the "Bird Cage" that he commonly visited.[5]

While the evening of July 25 and Saturday, July 26 proved to be quiet, on July 27 Mrs. Parsons invited 'Abdu'l-Bahá to her house for dinner with a group of her friends, and "from this day forward, visitors began to come in greater numbers." He began to speak at her house every day at 5:15 or 5:45pm. On August 1, she noted that seventy-five people came, probably a typical number, though half or less than the daily crowds he endured in New York and Washington. Many visited him at Day-Spring in the mornings, also, and he often gave informal talks there. It would have been easier for him to give time to everyone in town who wanted to meet him because the numbers were less than in the major cities. Bahá'ís who wanted to visit were told to ask permission to come to Dublin, which limited their numbers, as did the capacity of the two small inns, though most likely some people came without permission. 'Abdu'l-Bahá also systematically invited people to visit him in Dublin. The slower pace allowed him to try to "catch up with his enormous correspondence"; Ahmad Sohrab commented to a California Bahá'í, Ella Cooper, that he had been "doing so much writing and translating that my hands are very tired." Consequently, although 'Abdu'l-Bahá did not come for leisure, he was able, at least, to manage his work at a less frenetic pace.[6]

His first out-of-town visitor arrived two days after his sojourn began. W. W. Harmon was a "leader of the Theosophists" in Boston, who presumably had met 'Abdu'l-Bahá at one of his talks to the Boston Theosophical Society. 'Abdu'l-Bahá invited Harmon to stay with him and his party at Day-Spring, took him on a drive around Dublin Lake, and gave him time Saturday night, Sunday morning, Sunday evening, and Monday to ask his questions.[7] The meeting "was most delightful," Harmon later wrote, "especially so because the Master invited a discussion upon any subject I desired. Of course I realized later that He wished to draw me out, and as I look back upon that time, I guess He did, and most effectively":

> I can see Him now in that most majestic and sublime attitude with which those who are nearest to Him are so often impressed. His almost supernatural—for the want of a better word to express it—power. And one has to feel it and see it in order to understand the fullness and completeness of His majesty; for it is only under certain conditions that He drops the outer semblance of that all-loving man, Abdul Baha, and stands revealed for what He really is; fortunate are they who are permitted to see Him then. Fortunate, also, are they who have the eyes to see and the ears to hear Him in those rare moments when He lets fall the veil from the manifestation (or temple) of the Divine effulgence He so gloriously exemplifies revealing the One to whom all men must do homage in time to come. Fortunate too are those who can understand and realize in some degree the fullness and completeness of a Divine incarnation when it stands before them in all its radiance.[8]

Clearly, Harmon saw something deeper in 'Abdu'l-Bahá than just a kindly old gentleman. On Saturday evening, 'Abdu'l-Bahá spoke to him at length about the influence of the Word of God and the spread of civilization from East to West. On Sunday morning, he talked about "the sanctity of God . . . . the reflection of His attributes on the mirrors of the hearts of the Manifestations. . . . the meanings of the holy books and . . . the saying that 'everything is contained in everything.'" He specifically criticized the Theosophists in India for training a young man—Krishnamurti—to become a prophet, noting only God could select someone for such a role and station. On Sunday evening, 'Abdu'l-Bahá invited Harmon to expound on his ideas and show him the illustrations Harmon had created to represent them. According to Maḥmúd, Harmon was so impressed by 'Abdu'l-Bahá's suggestions and clarifications that he said, "Your explanations have opened the doors of understanding before me!" and "I feel that whatever you say comes from innate knowledge."[9]

Harmon added that 'Abdu'l-Bahá asked him to write a book about "divine illumination": "To say that I would, or would even try, was impossible; the subject was too vast, too incomprehensible, too utterly elusive for the mind to grasp or to put into words, even were it possible to see with the inner vision only the outer fringe of such glories, to witness that absolute perfection which the illumined eye must disclose, - so awe-inspiring that with one or two exceptions no living mortal has been able to endure more than the slightest glance, and then all but perish." Harmon left without making a commitment, knowing "that sooner or later I would make the attempt, because the Master wished it."[10]

In spite of Harmon's seeming sincerity, 'Abdu'l-Bahá spoke about him to his secretaries privately twice on Monday, July 29, once "for a considerable time," exclaiming in part, "What captives of superstition people are! What troubles they endure for the sake of name and fame! What fruit will these superstitions bear? All are transitory and perishable and no trace of them will remain."[11] Harmon did indeed write a book titled *Divine Illumination,* which mixed quotations from the Bahá'í writings with passages from the Bhagavad-Gita and the Bible to explore the inner illumination of the mind. Published in Boston by "the Bahai Movement" in 1915, the book raised Harmon's profile among American Bahá'ís and helped to popularize a series of esoteric lessons he created that diverged sharply from Bahá'í teachings.

The same day that Harmon left, a young Bahá'í from Portland, Oregon—George Latimer (1889–1948)—arrived in Dublin for three days. 'Abdu'l-Bahá met him within an hour of his arrival at Day-Spring and almost immediately asked him about the Portland Bahá'í community. The entire group at Day-Spring walked to Mrs. Parsons's house for the late afternoon meeting, which included in the audience the famous artist, George de Forest Brush (1855–1941), and an Episcopal minister.

After 'Abdu'l-Bahá's talk, Mrs. Parsons asked if he would like to go for a drive around Dublin Lake, and he took Edward Getsinger and George Latimer with him. George asked when he could see 'Abdu'l-Bahá again, and 'Abdu'l-Bahá replied that George would stay with them at Day-Spring—"such a blessing I had not expected!!!" George noted—so the car made a detour to the inn to get his baggage. As a result, George was with 'Abdu'l-Bahá almost continually for three days. On Wednesday, July 31, 'Abdu'l-Bahá spoke directly and at length to George Latimer about the importance of teaching the Faith; before Latimer left the next day, 'Abdu'l-Bahá spoke to him about steadfastness in the Covenant. These two themes were to dominate the Bahá'í community over the next few decades as a result of *The Tablets of the Divine Plan*, a series of epistles sent to the American Bahá'ís in 1916–17 directing them to spread the Faith over the entire world, and 'Abdu'l-Bahá's Will and Testament, which was made public after his passing in late 1921. They also increasingly dominated his North American sojourn.[12]

Most likely, 'Abdu'l-Bahá had seen some qualities in Latimer's character that he wished to cultivate, and the slower pace of life in Dublin made it possible to give Latimer the time. The effort paid off; George Latimer became a very active Bahá'í. He was a member of the American national Bahá'í governing body for fourteen years between 1922 and 1948 and frequently served as its chairman.[13]

In the middle of Latimer's visit, three Washington, D.C. Bahá'ís who had been vacationing in Maine arrived: Joseph Hannen, Pauline Hannen, and Fannie Knobloch. Joseph Hannen says they were "bidden" to come, suggesting that 'Abdu'l-Bahá had some matter he wished to discuss with them.[14] 'Abdu'l-Bahá went to the Harrisville train station to greet them, and while waiting gave away coins to some of the poorer looking boys there. Later that day 'Abdu'l-Bahá visited two San Francisco Bahá'ís who arrived and were staying at one of Dublin's inns; they were there partly to beg 'Abdu'l-Bahá to reconsider his decision not to travel to California. He offered them no commitment. His secretary, Ahmad Sohrab, without his permission, was writing repeatedly to Ella Cooper in Oakland and encouraging her to ask all the Bahá'ís to write and telegram 'Abdu'l-Bahá to beg him to come West.*

The Hannen-Knobloch party enjoyed several small gatherings with 'Abdu'l-Bahá and one private meeting where he spoke about Alma Knobloch's services teaching the Bahá'í Faith in Germany—she was the sister of Fannie Knobloch and Pauline Hannen—and revealed a tablet to her. Joseph Hannen left the next day after a touching private meeting with him.

Mary Hanford Ford (1856–1937), an early Boston Bahá'í, arrived on the same train as the Hannens and Fannie Knobloch but stayed until August 3. She accompanied him on Thursday, August 1, to a boy's summer camp, Marienfield Summer School, in the nearby village of Chesham. Dr. Charles Hanford Henderson, the owner and director, told 'Abdu'l-Bahá that his was the first summer camp in the United States. He gave 'Abdu'l-Bahá a tour of the facilities, and after 'Abdu'l-Bahá spoke to the boys, ages twelve through eighteen, they performed gymnastics for him. The visit echoed his May 10 visit to a children's settlement house in Washington and his August 19 visit to a girls' summer camp in Maine; together, they underline his interest in children's education.

---

* See, for example, Ahmad Sohrab to Ella Cooper, July 27, 1912, August 1, 1912, and August 8, 1912, Ella Cooper Papers. Sohrab engaged in a similar sort of campaign in April when he instructed Agnes Parsons how to ask 'Abdu'l-Bahá to stay in her house in Washington, and in July when he told her how to extend her invitation to 'Abdu'l-Bahá to come to Dublin.

Ford left on Saturday, August 3, the same day Alice Ives Breed and her husband, Francis, arrived to be his guests at Day-Spring; apparently 'Abdu'l-Bahá was regulating the timing of his guests. 'Abdu'l-Bahá had visited their house in Cambridge, Massachusetts, twice; their daughter was married to Ali Kuli Khan, the Persian chargé d'affairs in Washington. Alice attended the Saturday evening talk 'Abdu'l-Bahá gave at Mrs. Parsons's house. She wasn't impressed by "the cold blooded, unresponsive unspiritual persons" in attendance. Francis was disappointed to note that Charles MacVeagh (1860–1931), brother of the Secretary of the Treasury, had been drinking. But MacVeagh asked a question, and 'Abdu'l-Bahá "sat forward on the edge of the sofa and sent thundering forth with this mighty Spirit which seems to come at His bidding, and told of how people throughout the ages have worshipped the Dawning Points instead of the Sun which rises in different places and which is the Reality." MacVeagh apparently was impressed and returned frequently to the daily meetings. Almost two decades later, as United States ambassador to Japan, he was able to help Agnes Alexander to teach the Bahá'í Faith in that country, as she later explained: "When I offered to present him with a Bahá'í booklet, to my surprise he said that he did not need it for he already knew about the Teachings and had entertained 'Abdu'l-Bahá in his summer home in Dublin, New Hampshire. . . . He not only invited me to a tea party at his home to meet his wife, but offered to do anything he could to help me."[15]

On the next day, Sunday, August 4, Alice Ives Breed mentioned a 4pm meeting that 'Abdu'l-Bahá arranged for African American servants residing in Dublin. Mrs. Parsons arranged for a vehicle to transport her own servants to the gathering, which was held at her boat house. Maḥmúd reported that twenty-eight attended and that 'Abdu'l-Bahá addressed them about "unity and amity between blacks and whites": "He spoke of the approaching wedding of Miss [Louisa] Mathew, a white woman, and Mr. [Louis] Gregory, a black man, which is to take place shortly. . . The white people in the audience were astonished to see the influence of the Cause and the blacks were pleased. . . . This meeting was full of joy." 'Abdu'l-Bahá shook hands with all of them at the end. It was not his only meeting with African Americans; on Wednesday, August 14, when he lunched at the house of a Mrs. Caldwell, she mentioned that her cook wanted to meet and listen to 'Abdu'l-Bahá, so it was arranged for the cook to sit behind a tree and listen to a talk he gave out of doors. Subsequently he met all four of the house servants, gave them a talk, and shook their hands.[16]

Before the Breeds left on Monday, August 5, they had a long talk with 'Abdu'l-Bahá. He answered Alice's questions—"what particularly delights me is that I always find him so sane and normal and his answers satisfy me," she noted—and he emphasized the importance of firmness in the Covenant. She urged him to consider leaving the United States for Britain via Boston instead of New York because the latter Bahá'í community was so large and demanding of his attention, but he replied, "I must go to New York as I have work to do there." He did, however, ask her to find a house "quite near Boston and on high land" so that he could make one more visit to eastern Massachusetts.[17]

Later that same day, Howard MacNutt arrived to receive special instructions from 'Abdu'l-Bahá about his trip to Chicago. 'Abdu'l-Bahá wanted the House of Spirituality, the governing body of the Chicago Bahá'ís, reelected, primarily because the previous election in July 1911 had placed Dr. Frederick Nutt on the body. MacNutt's mission was to explain to the Chicago Bahá'ís the absolute importance of obeying 'Abdu'l-Bahá as the Center of the Covenant; ending all contact with people opposed to his authority, such as Kheiralla; and, in light of such principles, electing nine people to the House of Spirituality who were faithful to the Covenant. 'Abdu'l-Bahá had already explained this to MacNutt and Corinne True before he left New York, but apparently he wanted to be sure that MacNutt understood. A large portion of 'Abdu'l-Bahá's instructions involved what to do if Dr. Nutt "comes to you." The instructions were to "advise him [Dr. Nutt] in kindness and love" about how 'Abdu'l-Bahá ignores attacks and criticisms against him and focuses on advancing people "toward the Kingdom." He also told MacNutt that "if the women desire a separate organization, let them have it. If they want a distinct Board or Committee, let them have it." In the previous elections, women could vote for but not be elected to the House of Spirituality, but this time they could serve on the body as well. 'Abdu'l-Bahá gave MacNutt money to cover the costs of the trip.[18]

The purpose of MacNutt's visit to Dublin was private; Agnes Parsons stated in her diary in a margin note that MacNutt had been present for 'Abdu'l-Bahá's talks on Monday, Aug. 5, and had recorded them, but that she "wishes no record of his visit," so she did not include a summary of them in her diary. Her diary included only one sentence about the day, by far the shortest daily account she provided. MacNutt's record of 'Abdu'l-Bahá's August 5 talk and of a question-and-answer session on August 6 are the only Dublin talks published in *The Promulgation of Universal Peace.*[19]

To prepare for MacNutt's visit to Chicago, Corinne True spoke to as many people as she could. At the community's regular Sunday evening meeting on August 4, 'Abdu'l-Bahá's written instructions that an election should be held after a series of meetings with MacNutt were read. 'Abdu'l-Bahá could not attend in person; presumably, he wished to avoid too much of an imposition of his authority on the Chicago Bahá'ís.

MacNutt telegraphed from Dublin, probably on Monday, that 'Abdu'l-Bahá also commanded a "Feast" to be held "in the name of Abdul-Baha," to unite the community before the election. On Thursday, August 8, his first night in Chicago, MacNutt "gave the fundamentals leading up to the Center of the Covenant" to seventy people gathered at True's home and "all passed off harmoniously" even though "the opposers were there in abundance" and "were looking for trouble." On Friday, August 9, MacNutt "declared the Center of the Covenant most powerfully" at the home of Miss Mary Lesch, but none of "the other party" attended.[20]

On Saturday, August 10, "all came" to the home of George Lesch—about 150—and the "Feast was beautiful." On Sunday morning, August 11, the Bahá'ís gathered to watch the "moving picture of Abdul Baha" made at MacNutt's house in Brooklyn, which "had a very great effect" on everyone. Some traveled to Wilmette to pray at the temple site he had consecrated three and a half months earlier. The 5pm election meeting "was the most orderly peaceful & harmonious thing you can imagine." It elected six men and three women to the Chicago Bahá'í "Spiritual Meeting": Zia Bagdadi, Ida Brush, Charles Greenleaf, Charles Ioas, George Lesch, Mary Lesch, Carl Scheffler, Corinne True, and Albert Windust. The election had removed Dr. Nutt and had added female members. 'Abdu'l-Bahá cabled on August 13 "the news of the election of the members of the Spiritual Assembly gave much joy."[21]

Otherwise, the week had passed fairly quietly. Until Alice Buckton arrived on August 8, there were no new visiting Bahá'ís for him to nurture.* He discussed plans for the rest of his time in North America with his entourage and decided to leave Dublin for Green Acre in Maine on the 16th, go to Montreal and Buffalo, then back to New York City. However, he left open the option of continuing west, in which case he would get to California by late September and return to New York by late October.[22]

There were local people to nurture, too. The MacVeaghs continued to attend the daily meetings. The artist George de Forest Brush and his daughter, Nancy Bowdich, may have attended some; she became attracted to the Faith and eventually became a Bahá'í, as did her daughter, Polly Marlowe,

* 'Abdu'l-Bahá had invited both Harry Randall and Charles Mason Remey to Dublin, but neither was able to make it.

later. Together, they became the nuclei for the Bahá'í communities of southwestern New Hampshire. The Pumpelly family became attracted and invited 'Abdu'l-Bahá to lunch; their daughter, Daisy Pumpelly Smythe, eventually became a Bahá'í.

'Abdu'l-Bahá continued to spend considerable time with Agnes and Jeffrey Parsons, who devoted many hours of every day to assisting him. Agnes invited friends to the afternoon meetings, made sure there was tea and other provisions for the daily crowd, and handled other social details; Jeffrey drove 'Abdu'l-Bahá and his party around in his carriage and shuttled Bahá'ís to and from the train station three miles away. At one point, Jeffrey spent considerable time talking to 'Abdu'l-Bahá about his own religious opinions; he trusted and had immense respect for 'Abdu'l-Bahá, even though he never became a Bahá'í.[23]

On two occasions, 'Abdu'l-Bahá made comments relating to the Parsons' marriage. On July 31, at lunch with the Parsons and several others, Mrs. Parsons told 'Abdu'l-Bahá that many objected to the word "obey" in the traditional Protestant wedding vow taken by the bride. 'Abdu'l-Bahá replied "that it should not be there as God intended the man & the woman to be one and the use of the word 'obey' assumes <u>two</u>." But if Mrs. Parsons was pleased by that response, the other incident must have given her pause for reflection. On August 8, she was walking to Day-Spring with Jeffrey and a friend when they saw 'Abdu'l-Bahá approaching in a carriage. He stopped and Agnes, noticing her shoes were dusty, asked Jeffrey to clean them for her. He did, "looking up at Abdul Baha with a humorous expression which He enjoyed very much." Agnes says that 'Abdu'l-Bahá commented that "If that had been done to some Turks, the club would have been used." Maḥmúd records that 'Abdu'l-Bahá later recounted the incident and said that it did not reflect equality: "'You, too, must clean his shoes,' 'Abdu'l-Bahá explained. 'It would be better if you occasionally stand up for the rights of men.'"[24]

'Abdu'l-Bahá often spent time with their young son Jeffrey and exchanged letters with him when the boy was at camp nearby. The Parsons' older son, Royal, was handicapped and lived elsewhere, and 'Abdu'l-Bahá often spoke about the boy's pure soul and what the boy needed to progress, thereby encouraging and comforting his parents.[25]

On Saturday, August 10, Howard Colby Ives, the Unitarian minister, arrived in Dublin, having received an invitation to be a "guest" of 'Abdu'l-Bahá for the weekend. It arrived at an opportune time; his interest was wavering, partly because his ministerial colleagues were asking him, "Are you still Baha'ing around?" and partly because some members of his family were opposed. 'Abdu'l-Bahá was staying at the inn rather than Day-Spring because he was sleeping better there, so Ives had a room in the same building. Sunday morning 'Abdu'l-Bahá gave him over an hour in one of the inn's spacious private parlors before his talk at the First Congregational Church (Unitarian) of Dublin: "He came into the room where I awaited Him and embraced me, asking if I were well and happy. We must always be happy, He said, for it is impossible to live in the Spiritual World and be sad. God desires happiness for all His creatures. For man especially is this joy ordained for he has the capacity to understand Reality."[26]

After some preliminary exchange, Ives asked 'Abdu'l-Bahá, "why I should believe in Bahá'u'lláh as the latest and most universal of these Messengers." 'Abdu'l-Bahá's answer partially stressed the high station of being a true Christian clergyman instead:

> He looked at me long and searchingly. His smile broadened. Again He seemed to be enjoying a heavenly situation which was not without its humorous side. Then He was lovingly grave again. After a somewhat lengthy silence He said that it was not given to everyone to speak often of His Holiness Christ to men. He said that I must thank God daily for this great bounty, for men have entirely forgotten the

> pure teachings of this "Essence of Severance." He remarked that His Holiness Bahá'u'lláh speaks of this in the Book of Certitude and that I should study it carefully. In that book is explained how these stars of the Heaven of Christ's Revelation have fallen to the earth of worldly desires. On their tongues the mention of God has often become an empty Name; in their midst His Holy Word a dead letter. This condition is that to which Christ refers, He said, when He speaks of "the oppression or affliction of the Last Days." What greater affliction could be imagined than that under which the self-appointed spiritual leaders are themselves in darkness.
>
> Praise be to God that you are seeking Light. It behooves you to manifest Light; to express in word and deed the pure teachings of His Holiness the Christ. To the proud we must be humble; He said, to the humble, compassionate; to the ignorant ones be as a student before his master; to the sinful ones be as the greatest sinner of all. To the poor be a benefactor; to the orphan, a father; to the aged, a son. Take guidance, not from leaders of sectarian theology but from the Sermon on the Mount. Seek no earthly reward, nay, rather, accept calamities in His service as His first disciples did.
>
> He smiled at me with such heavenly radiance that I sat enthralled and overcome with an emotion indescribable. Then he fell silent and His eyes closed. I thought He was weary, as doubtless He was for His constant activity gave Him little rest. But it was plain to me later that He must have been praying for me.[27]

'Abdu'l-Bahá never said anything to Ives about Bahá'u'lláh being better or more recent; he never said Ives should abandon Christianity or that the Bahá'í Faith was its fulfillment; he also never came out and said Ives should become the best possible clergyman he could be. Instead, he called Ives to the highest calling, that of being a truly transformed human being, and to sacrifice for others and suffer in service to them. No doubt, many could have interpreted 'Abdu'l-Bahá to mean that Ives should be the best Christian minister he could be; but Ives understood that it was a summons to a higher calling.

Ives and 'Abdu'l-Bahá sat in silence for a while, then it came time for 'Abdu'l-Bahá to leave for the Unitarian church. It was 'Abdu'l-Bahá's only public talk in Dublin; otherwise he always spoke in someone's house or at the inn where he stayed. It was a special choice, because for a half century First Church had been Dublin's only church; its original building, owned by the town, had also served as the town meeting house. In 1912, First Church occupied a fairly modernized structure, built in 1852, with a furnace added in 1892, electricity in 1900, and running water in 1912. President Taft had attended services just two years earlier when visiting the MacVeagh family. Ives refers to "crowded pews" that August 11 at 11am, so presumably the church was filled to its capacity of three hundred.[28] 'Abdu'l-Bahá paced back and forth on the platform in front as he spoke:

> His cream-colored robe; His white hair and beard; His radiant smile and courteous demeanor. And His gestures! Never a dogmatic downward stroke of the hand; never an upraised warning finger; never the assumption of teacher to the taught. But always the encouraging upward swing of hands, as though He would actually lift us up with them. And His voice! Like a resonant bell of finest timbre; never loud but of such penetrating quality that the walls of the room seemed to vibrate with its music.[29]

Maḥmúd says 'Abdu'l-Bahá's lengthy, 50-minute address focused on "the necessity for true education and spiritual power," and "the coming of

Bahá'u'lláh and His teachings." He closed by chanting a prayer. "A wonderful spirit of humility seemed to permeate the building and the voice of acceptance seemed to issue from all sides," Maḥmúd reports. Agnes Parsons adds that "the people were motionless, so great was the power of His word" and "I have never seen Him look as He did nor have I ever been so impressed, except for that brief moment in Haifa." She asked Ameen Fareed about it and he confirmed that only once had he seen 'Abdu'l-Bahá appear as he had that day, which Fareed described as a state of "ecstasy." Even Agnes's little son was impressed: "The service was too long, but 'Abdu'l-Bahá was not too long." Many came to 'Abdu'l-Bahá afterward to speak with him, causing him to comment later that "the Call of God has been raised here and the work is finished."[30]

Howard Colby Ives was impressed as well: "What He said impressed me with the force of the impact of Divine Truth. There was not a question in my mind of the authority with which He spake. Truly, not as the scribes!" As he left the church he joined some of his friends from New York who were present, and said to one of them "At last I know. Never again will I doubt or question."[31]

But his spontaneous declaration of faith proved premature; his commitment to the Bahá'í community was still months into the future. Ives spent much of the day in turmoil, and he was unable to see 'Abdu'l-Bahá because 'Abdu'l-Bahá had a luncheon engagement at the Pumpelley's, then spoke at the Parsons residence and remained there late. Ives "watched for Him to come back to the inn after His day was ended." As a tired 'Abdu'l-Bahá was slowly ascending the stairs to his room, Ives followed:

> I can hardly believe now that I had the temerity to follow. He had entered the room when I reached it, and had closed the door. What gave me courage to knock I do not know; but knock I did, and He opened the door Himself. I did not know what to say. He beckoned

> me in and looked at me gravely. I stammered: "Will you please pray with me?"
>
> He motioned, and I knelt while He put His hands upon my head and chanted, in Persian, a brief prayer. It was all over within three minutes. But those moments brought to me a peace I had never known.[32]

Ives records two other observations about 'Abdu'l-Bahá's Dublin sojourn. He marveled at 'Abdu'l-Bahá's "unique power of adaptation to every environment"; that in spite of a lifetime of exile, imprisonment, and privation, he could impress and charm people of wealth, prominence, and sophistication. Ives attributed the ability to the fact that he "'saw the Face of His Heavenly Father in every face' and reverenced the soul behind it." The other observation related to 'Abdu'l-Bahá's deep concern for the poor, a theme that cropped up in nearly every city he visited. A woman visitor to the inn told Ives that one day when 'Abdu'l-Bahá was outside, pacing back and forth and dictating a tablet to one of his secretaries, a "very ragged and dirty" man walked past. 'Abdu'l-Bahá asked his secretary to call the man back:

> His trousers particularly were filthy and barely covered his limbs. 'Abdu'l-Bahá talked with him a few moments. His face a smiling benediction. He seemed to be trying to cheer the old man and finally there did appear the trace of a smile, but it was rather bleak. 'Abdu'l-Bahá's eyes swept the pitiable figure, and then He laughed gently: He said something to the effect that the old man's trousers were not very serviceable and that we must remedy that lack. It was very early in the morning and the street deserted. My friend, watching, saw 'Abdu'l-Bahá step into the shadow of the porch and He seemed to be

> fumbling under His Aba at the waist. Then He stooped. His trousers dropped to the ground. He gathered his robe about Him and turning handed the trousers to the old man. "May God go with you," He said, and turned to the secretary as if nothing unusual had happened.[33]

'Abdu'l-Bahá is known to give away his clothes, especially his coats, in Acre, where there were many poor people. [34]

Howard Colby Ives left Dublin on Monday. 'Abdu'l-Bahá's remaining five days in New Hampshire were packed with luncheon invitations from people who wished to spend time with him. He attended part of an afternoon theatrical performance in the yard of one person. On Thursday—the last full day of his stay—he called on various people to say good-bye to them. Mrs. Parsons sponsored a musical performance in her house, and the late afternoon meeting was standing room only. 'Abdu'l-Bahá summarized his daily talks as follows: "I have explained every question for you, delivered to you the message of God, expounded the mysteries of the divine Books for you, proved the immortality of the spirit and the oneness of truth and expounded for you economic questions and divine teachings." At the end of the gathering, everyone came to shake his hand and exchange parting words.[35]

He went to the house of the Pumpellys, where a large group had gathered, for a late dinner. They exchanged funny stories; 'Abdu'l-Bahá told several, adding, "It is good to laugh. Laughter is spiritual relaxation." He spoke about the humorous or ludicrous stories they told every evening when the family was in prison together during the years 1868–70 and the laughter that made the privations and difficulties much easier to bear. He did not speak directly about the Bahá'í Faith, but the stories made a deep impression on those present. Afterward, driving home, 'Abdu'l-Bahá said to Agnes Parsons, "with the simplicity of a child," "Now are you all pleased with Me?" She was overwhelmed by the remark; she noted in her diary that

"He was so unutterably kind, and made so happy these last moments at Dublin." Ives added that she "was never able to speak of this conclusion to the event without deep emotion."[36]

Green Acre, August 16–23, 1912

'Abdu'l-Bahá left for the Green Acre School in Eliot, Maine, the next morning at 10am. He traveled by automobile with three of his secretaries and Alfred Lunt; the rest of his entourage took the train. After lunch and a rest in Nashua, New Hampshire, they continued to Green Acre, arriving in mid-afternoon. 'Abdu'l-Bahá was already familiar with the place, having sent at least twenty-eight letters to Sarah J. Farmer (1847–1916), the founder. Farmer had been inspired to establish a summer school for religion and spirituality as a result of the World's Parliament of Religions in 1893. The first season—July 1 to August 30, 1894—involved some seventy-five speakers on Eastern religions, Theosophy, New Thought, Spiritualism, philosophy, the Bible, prophecy, poetry, esoteric subjects such as the soul and divine healing, and intellectual subjects such as evolution, sociology, and the function of art. Music also figured prominently and was planned by Mrs. Sara Chapman Thorp Bull, widow of a famous Norwegian violinist, one of Sarah Farmer's closest friends, and a leading Vedantist. Speakers ranged from college professors to clergymen, prominent but aging Transcendentalists, various religious practitioners, and the self-taught. Among the seventy-five prospective speakers that first season was Ibrahim Kheiralla, who introduced the Bahá'í Faith to the United States that very year, and two people—Margaret B. Peake and Josephine C. Locke—who later became Bahá'ís. Swami Vivekananda spent two weeks at Green Acre and may have given the first yoga classes in America there. Dharmapala was a speaker in August 1897.[37]

Green Acre soon emerged as a center—if not the very heart—of liberal religion in the United States. As the eminent religious historian, Leigh Schmidt, has observed,

> It was the last great bastion of Transcendentalism, a school of philosophy and art for Emersonians and Whitmanites; it was a New Thought proving ground for such leaders as Ralph Waldo Trine, Henry Wood, and Horatio Dresser; it was a hub for representatives of the Society of Ethical Culture, Theosophy, Buddhism, Reform Judaism, Vedanta, Zoroastrianism, Islam, and the Bahá'í Faith. It was the World's Parliament of Religions brought to its grandest fruition, attracting the curious and the questing . . . by the hundreds and even thousands in these years [1894–1916]. At Greenacre, the dream of a cosmopolitan spirituality found its flesh and blood.[38]

Presiding over the marketplace of religious ideas was Sarah Farmer, a saintly seeker after truth and tireless promoter of liberal ideas. In 1900 she encountered Bahá'í friends (one was Josephine Locke, who had spoken at Green Acre during its first season) while on a Mediterranean cruise. She accompanied them to Acre to meet 'Abdu'l-Bahá and became a Bahá'í. Subsequent Green Acre programs prominently included Bahá'í speakers. Her commitment to the Faith was seen by many of her friends as a betrayal of the questing spirit that Green Acre represented to them; they "preferred ongoing inquiry to actually finding one path to follow." 'Abdu'l-Bahá strongly encouraged her, in a stream of letters, to make Green Acre a center for teaching the Faith, rather than for the spread of ancient superstitions. He sent Mírzá Abu'l-Fadl and Ali-Kuli Khan to Green Acre to speak about the Bahá'í teachings. The resulting conflict between her Bahá'í interests and her non-Bahá'í colleagues brought Farmer to a state of mental exhaustion, and friends committed her to a series of asylums starting in 1909. When 'Abdu'l-Bahá arrived on August 16, 1912, she had not been to Green Acre for some three years.[39]

Because of Green Acre's reputation as a spiritual Mecca, 'Abdu'l-Bahá's visit there took on a character wholly different from his Dublin sojourn. The latter was a quiet resort town; the former, a magnet for seekers and an increasingly popular destination for Bahá'ís, many of whom had purchased summer homes in the area. Nearly eight hundred people were present for 'Abdu'l-Bahá's arrival; the twelve-hundred-foot driveway from Main Street to the Inn was lined on both sides by over a thousand Japanese lanterns, and the Eironion (a lecture hall) was decorated with flowers. After settling into his room on the third floor of the Eliot Hotel (now called the Sarah Farmer Inn), he went to the Eironion to speak briefly to a crowd so large that it filled the hall and the three verandas around it. Then he drove to the sanatorium where Sarah Farmer was resident. The doctor in charge had even denied family members the opportunity to visit, but he permitted 'Abdu'l-Bahá to see her.[40]

Later that evening, he gave what may be the longest talk he gave in America, focusing on the investigation of reality. He noted that the four means for investigating reality—the senses, reason, scriptural proof, and inspiration—were all faulty on their own but that together, all four were reasonably reliable for arriving at truth. He applied the four to the subject of love and expounded on its manifestation at the level of the mineral, vegetable, animal, and human kingdoms and in the lives and sacrifices of the Manifestations of God. He considered what God's love did for humanity. Turning to the rational powers with which humanity is endowed, he expatiated on our ability to understand and "break" the laws of nature. He concluded with a lengthy discourse on the powers of the human spirit and its continued existence after the death of the body. To close the gathering, he offered a prayer "on behalf of Miss Farmer," "the founder of this organization," for "quick recovery through Thy power and bounty." The prayer also included the following: "O God! The clouds of superstitions have covered the horizons of the hearts. O Lord! dispel these clouds so that the lights of the Sun of Reality may shine. O Lord! illumine our eyes so that we may behold Thy Light! O Lord! Cleanse our ears so that we may hear the call of the Supreme Concourse. . . . O Lord! sanctify and purify the hearts so that the effulgence of Thy Love may shine therein."[41]

'Abdu'l-Bahá mentioned Jesus Christ several times and quoted His words in the Gospels; he mentioned the Báb once; but he never mentioned Bahá'u'lláh or the Bahá'í principles. His presentation, by implication, rejected the claims of clairvoyants and oriental sages who professed to discern reality through only one of the four criteria, either rationality or inspiration. He emphasized monotheism and revelation through Manifestations of God rather than ancient truth discovered by sages or revealed by ascended masters. He praised human powers that related to science and rejected reincarnation in favor of an afterlife. The talk was a poetic statement of faith, a polite summary of how the Bahá'í Faith was different from these other beliefs. Maḥmúd stated in his diary that "everyone was deeply moved and their hearts were transformed."[42]

For the next six days, 'Abdu'l-Bahá spoke in the Eironion every evening at 7:30 to a crowd of between four hundred and six hundred persons. Including the talk described above, only the first two or three talks were recorded stenographically in English. On August 17, he spoke about the oneness of humanity, the need for world peace, and the role of love in bringing it about. He noted the long history of religions causing or exacerbating warfare through "religious prejudice, fanaticism and sectarian hatred." Bahá'u'lláh, however, by stating, "Ye are all the fruits of one tree, the leaves of one branch" had proclaimed the oneness of humanity and had abrogated "anathema and execration." Bahá'u'lláh has clearly said in His writings that "if you have an enemy, consider him not as an enemy. . . . You must behold him as a friend. You must treat him well. This is right."[43]

'Abdu'l-Bahá described how love was manifest throughout the universe: as attraction between atoms in the mineral kingdom, as growth in the plant kingdom, and in "emotions and sensibilities" made possible by the arrangements of atoms in the animal kingdom. Among human beings, "spiritual susceptibilities come into view, love exercises its superlative degree, and this is the cause of human life." Therefore, he concluded,

> we must exercise the utmost love toward each other. We must be loving to all the people of the world. We must not consider any people the people of Satan, but know and recognize all as the servants of the one God. At most it is this,—some do not know, they must be guided and trained. They must be taught humanitarianism and encouraged in the acquisition of virtues. Some are ignorant,—they must be informed. Some are as children, undeveloped,—they must be helped to reach maturity. Some are ailing,—their moral condition is bad,—they must be treated until their morals are purified. But the sick man is not to be hated because he is sick,—the child must not be shunned because he is a child,—the ignorant one is not to be despised because he lacks knowledge. They must all be treated, educated, trained and assisted in love. Everything must be done in order that humanity may live under the shadow of God in the utmost security,—in happiness of the highest type.[44]

On August 18, he chose to proclaim the Bahá'í concept of progressive revelation, thereby highlighting another key aspect of Bahá'í teaching. The audience that day was particularly large because it was Sunday, and many local people rode over in their horse-drawn carriages to hear him.* He

* This talk is listed for August 17 in *The Promulgation of Universal Peace* but is listed in Star of the West as being given in the Eironion on August 18; see *Star of the West* 3, no. 15 (Dec. 12, 1912): 47. It matches the description of an address he gave that afternoon "to a gathering of liberal minded visitors concerning the renewal of religious laws and the oneness of the Manifestations of God"; see Maḥmúd-i-Zarqání, *Mahmúd's Diary,* 212. Further background is provided in Remey, *Reminiscences of the Summer School,* 37.

began with an analogy he had used in Chicago: the various Manifestations of God were analogous to the physical sun. Jesus Christ was the "Sun of Reality which shone from the heavenly horizon of Christianity, training, protecting, confirming minds, souls and spirits until they came into harmony with the divine Kingdom." Just as the sun rises from different points along the horizon, the different Manifestations of God come at different times, yet manifest the same divine Sun. The problem is that people worship the point where the sun rose rather than the sun itself:

> The Jews adore the Mosaic point of dawning, the Zoroastrians that of Zoroaster. . . . When that Sun of Reality with its divine bestowal, its heavenly glow and effulgence transferred to the Messianic point of rising, the Jews denied its appearance in Jesus, for they were not worshipers of the Sun itself but adored its rising in Moses. Had they been worshipers of the Sun of Reality, they would have turned to Christ instead of denying Him as the Messiah. . . . Now, therefore, we must be admonished and realize that mere imitation of fathers and ancestors is fruitless. Nay, rather, we must exert ourselves to the utmost in investigating and turning toward the Sun of Reality, no matter from what dayspring or dawning point it may appear.[45]

The unspoken implication is that people should consider the claim of Bahá'u'lláh, the most recent Manifestation, although 'Abdu'l-Bahá tactfully did not mention Him. The talk was a counterpoint to the views of Theosophists, Hindus, and some others that ancient religions were truer and more spiritual than the later forms. 'Abdu'l-Bahá's eloquence produced "a wonderful impression . . . on the whole audience," noted Maḥmúd, "moving the chairman of the conference to tears. As the Master was offering a [closing] prayer, one lady stood up and then fainted. When she regained consciousness, she said that the power of the meeting overwhelmed her. It seemed to her that everyone in the audience was flying in Heaven."[46]

It was probably after this talk when a peculiar incident took place. After 'Abdu'l-Bahá finished speaking, he left the Eironion, walked to the fence where the horse-drawn carriages had been tethered, and sat down in a "one horse carriage of the Surrey type: two seats with a flat top with fringe hanging from it." The owner arrived with her three children shortly thereafter, was disturbed to find 'Abdu'l-Bahá seated in her carriage, and angrily ordered him to get out. He did not respond to her, so she began to scream at him. Grace Robarts Ober hurried over, grabbed the woman, and said in a stern voice, "Do you know to whom you are speaking in that way?" shaking the woman to emphasize her words. At that point, the woman broke down and began to weep. Ober embraced her, trying to comfort her. Then "without so much as looking at the woman," 'Abdu'l-Bahá got out of the carriage and walked to the inn. Charles Mason Remey, who witnessed the entire incident at "but arms length" away, reflected in 1949 that "to those of us who were at any length of time near the Master, it was borne in upon us that He was frequently functioning in a way we couldn't comprehend . . . Sometimes we saw the results . . . More often we didn't understand at all."[47]

'Abdu'l-Bahá also spoke to many small groups, often spontaneously; at least two such talks were recorded on August 17. The first focused on a materialist view of reality, starting with comments about the materialism of American city life, then turning to the materialist philosophers, whose ignorance of the spiritual world He compared to the worldview of the cow. He had made the same point in Philadelphia in June but referred to the worldview of animals instead; when he had used "cows" in an unrecorded talk in Dublin, it had struck a chord with his audience. 'Abdu'l-Bahá concluded that "The station of man is great, very great. God has created man after His own image and likeness. . . . Verily, God has created the animal in the image and likeness of man, for though man outwardly is human, yet in nature he possesses animal tendencies." The second small-group talk he gave that day reiterated similar points, stressing the weakness of the human body and the wondrous powers of the human spirit.[48]

'Abdu'l-Bahá charmed many of those present. "His majestic figure became a familiar object," noted Ahmad Sohrab, "greeting everyone, whether friend or stranger, young or old, in English, 'Good morning? How are you? Are you well? Are you happy? Very happy?' When the answer was given he said, in good English, as the first time, 'Very well? Very happy? *All right!*' And then the party addressed laughed because he laughed." Maḥmúd notes that 'Abdu'l-Bahá often joked with his audience. But his encounters were not without friction; at one point he "offered sweets to some visitors who, following the superstitious ideas of the ascetics, did not eat certain foods. He dispelled their belief by saying, 'Food has nothing to do with faith. Rather, you should eat things to gain strength and you should acquire spirituality.'" He also "encountered some women who were fortune tellers. Some read palms and others interpreted dreams. They all voiced their opinion that 'Abdu'l-Bahá possessed divine spirit and heavenly power. He showered kindness on all of them and then returned to the Inn and gave a talk about the superstitious beliefs and the severe discipline and asceticism of the Hindus." According to Maḥmúd, who viewed Green Acre's spiritual smorgasbord with disdain, the overall result was favorable: "Because Green Acre is known as a center for religious freedom and advanced liberal views, many fortune-tellers, spiritualists and ascetics came here every year to spread their superstitious views. The discourse of the Center of the Covenant completely swept away the cobwebs of superstitions. They were checked to such a degree that some of the impostors, who in previous years had delivered lectures contrary to the Cause of God, now came to see Him, bowing before Him and repenting." Ahmad Sohrab phrased it more positively; 'Abdu'l-Bahá "accomplished marvelous work at Green Acre. Those who were inimical have become most staunch friends."[49]

Green Acre also provided 'Abdu'l-Bahá with a chance to speak to many Bahá'ís. On Sunday morning, August 18, he met with a group of Bahá'ís, apparently at the summer residence of the Kinneys. He advised them "to devote their time to teaching the Cause of God" and counseled them "not to intervene in the affairs of the Green Acre Fellowship."[50]

Perhaps his best remembered encounter was with Fred Mortensen (1887–1946). Mortensen grew up poor in Minneapolis, and even though his mother "did everything in her power to make me a good boy," as a youth, he got involved in drinking, gangs, petty theft, and burglary. Escaping from jail, he was a fugitive for four years, and when he was recaptured by the police, a Bahá'í attorney, Albert Hall, became his public defender. Hall spent hours telling Mortensen of "love, God's love, Bahá'u'lláh's love, 'Abdu'l-Bahá's love, love for the Covenant, love for us, from us to God, to His Prophets, etc." At first, Fred "was bewildered," but soon it changed him; he became a law-abiding citizen, got a job in the printing business, and became a Bahá'í. When he heard 'Abdu'l-Bahá was in the United States, he yearned to meet him; when he heard 'Abdu'l-Bahá wouldn't travel west, he "immediately determined to go and see him." He had the money to travel as far east as Cleveland for a printers' convention. Rather than staying to the end of that event, he hopped onto freight trains without paying and rode to Portsmouth, New Hampshire, where he found his way to Green Acre on August 19. Mrs. Carrie Kinney invited him to stay in a spare bed in the former stable of the Kinney house and woke him early the next morning—Tuesday, August 20—to see 'Abdu'l-Bahá.[51]

There was a great crowd of people waiting to meet 'Abdu'l-Bahá that morning. When Mortensen was introduced to him, he didn't shake Fred's hand, which he understood to be a reflection of his dirty clothes and disheveled appearance. But 'Abdu'l-Bahá said, "sit down" and pointed to a chair, which Fred "didn't care to do, as elderly ladies were standing," but he "meekly obeyed" and sat. After a doctor went in to meet the Master, Ahmad Sohrab came out and announced, "'Abdu'l-Bahá wishes to see Mr. Mortensen."

> Why, I nearly wilted. I wasn't ready. I hadn't expected to be called until the very last thing. I had to go, and it was with a strange feeling in my heart and wondering, wondering what would happen next. He welcomed me with a smile and a warm hand-clasp, telling me to be seated, he sitting before me. His first words were, "Welcome! Welcome! You are very welcome,"—then, "Are you happy?"—which was repeated three times. I thought, why do you ask me that so many times? Of course I am happy; didn't I tell you so the first time?
>
> Then, "Where did you come from?"
> Answer: "From Minneapolis."
> Question: "Do you know Mr Hall?"
> Answer: "Yes. He told me about the Cause."
> Question: "Did you have a pleasant journey?"
>
> Of all the questions I wished to avoid this was the one! I dropped my gaze to the floor—and again he put the question. I lifted my eyes to his and his were as two black, sparkling jewels, which seemed to look into my very depths. I knew he knew and I must tell, and as I answered I wondered what Ahmad [Sohrab, the interpreter] thought—if I was a little unbalanced.
>
> I answered: "I did not come as people generally do, who come to see you."

> Question: "How did you come?"
> Answer: "Riding under and on top of the railway trains."
> Question: "Explain how."
>
> Now as I looked into the eyes of 'Abdu'l-Baha I saw they had changed and a wondrous light seemed to pour out. It was the light of love and I felt relieved and very much happier. I explained to him how I rode on the trains, after which he kissed both my cheeks, gave me much fruit, and kissed the dirty hat I wore, which had become soiled on my trip to see him.[52]

Maḥmúd adds that 'Abdu'l-Bahá said, "You are my guest" and "each day the Master bestowed kindness upon him." When 'Abdu'l-Bahá was invited to a dinner at the Magee residence on August 21, he sat Mortensen at his right hand at the dinner table, just as he had seated Louis Gregory in Washington. While Mortensen was white, he was also from a lower class background than the others present, hence possibly 'Abdu'l-Bahá was making a point about the mixing of social classes as well as encouraging Mortensen. Eventually, 'Abdu'l-Bahá gave Mortensen money to buy a train ticket home.[53]

It was the first memorable incident of a very busy day. After meeting with visitors, 'Abdu'l-Bahá drove to the Portsmouth sanatorium where Sarah Farmer was resident and took her for a ride around the area. They visited the Portsmouth Naval Shipyard, where she had witnessed the signing of the treaty that ended the Russo-Japanese War in 1905, then drove to Green Acre, a place she hadn't visited for three years. He later advised the Bahá'ís to get her out of the sanatorium by whatever legal means at their disposal. They also drove to "Monsalvat" or "Sunset Hill," a low, round hill about a mile from Green Acre, and walked around the top. 'Abdu'l-Bahá reportedly confirmed her vision of Green Acre and told her that the first Bahá'í university and the second American Bahá'í House of Worship would be built there.[54]

Later in the afternoon, 'Abdu'l-Bahá spoke to three hundred people under the "Persian Pine," where Mírzá Abu'l-Fadl and other Bahá'í speakers had delivered addresses. The grove also had a "Hindu pine" and pines devoted to the speakers of various other faiths. At 3pm, he hosted a unity feast at "Bahá'í House," now called Staples House, across the street from the main entrance to Green Acre, attended by five hundred people. When he addressed the gathering from the house's front porch, pacing back and forth and gesturing, his powerful but melodious voice prompted passers by on the street to stop and listen to him.[55]

The next day, Wednesday, August 21, 'Abdu'l-Bahá went to the top of Monsalvat again and addressed four hundred people there. He reiterated his remarks about the Bahá'í House of Worship and university to be erected on the hill.[56]

Thursday, August 22, was 'Abdu'l-Bahá's last full day at Green Acre. Following the pattern at Dublin, he spent the morning and afternoon meeting individuals who wished to speak to him, saying good-bye to acquaintances, and traveling about the area to make a last visit to several homes. He gave one last talk at the Eironion that evening about "the necessity for the oneness of the world of humanity in this enlightened age."[57]

Friday morning, the luggage was packed, and a crowd gathered to see 'Abdu'l-Bahá off. Fred Mortensen managed to stand close to the car, and as 'Abdu'l-Bahá prepared to step into it, he spotted Mortensen and "to my astonishment he ordered me to get into the automobile with him." Mortensen complied and found himself accompanying 'Abdu'l-Bahá for the next week in Malden, Massachusetts. On the way to Malden, 'Abdu'l-Bahá stopped for one last time to visit with Sarah Farmer, who "fell at His feet weeping."[58]

Malden, August 23–30, 1912

'Abdu'l-Bahá's week in the Boston area was the longest visit he made to eastern Massachusetts. Like his two earlier sojourns, he spoke in no churches, but he did speak again to the Theosophical Society, the New Thought Society, and at a major social service organization. This time he stayed at a small house owned by Maria P. Wilson, a close friend of Sarah Farmer who had accompanied her on the 1900 voyage when both had become Bahá'ís. How it was arranged for 'Abdu'l-Bahá to stay there is uncertain; most likely Alice Ives Breed set it up. It was on Belmont Hill, the "high land" he had requested. It may have had an apple orchard nearby. The house only had six rooms to accommodate the nine men in 'Abdu'l-Bahá's entourage; army cots were set up in the unfinished attic for some of them.[59] 'Abdu'l-Bahá's first talk at the Wilson house occurred within hours of his arrival. Much of Saturday was devoted to meetings with countless visitors and developing his itinerary.

One inquirer who was anxious to see 'Abdu'l-Bahá again was Harry Randall. He had had an unexpected private meeting with 'Abdu'l-Bahá during the May visit and ran into him by chance in the elevator of the Victoria Hotel during his July visit. On that occasion, when he saw Randall, 'Abdu'l-Bahá said, "We have not seen as much of you as We would have liked" and invited Randall to come to Dublin to visit him.[60] But Randall never followed up on the invitation.

Now 'Abdu'l-Bahá was staying one town over from Randall's house in Medford, less than half an hour away. Randall's wife, Ruth, who had been convalescing in California in May because of her severe tuberculosis, was now back home, essentially to die, as the doctors had given up on curing her. On Sunday morning, August 25, she asked Harry, "If 'Abdu'l-Bahá was all that the believers said he was why couldn't He heal me of tuberculosis?" Consequently, Randall went to Maria Wilson's house to invite him to come see his wife.

The house was crowded with visitors. Randall explained his request to one of the Persian secretaries, who replied that "'Abdu'l-Bahá had over a hundred invitations for the afternoon but never accepted one until the Spirit directed Him." Feeling hopeless, Randall turned to leave, but saw his friend Harlan Ober and lingered to chat with him. Much to his surprise, a few minutes later, "the kitchen door opened and a voice called out, "Abdu'l-Bahá will see Mr. Randall.'" Before Randall even had a chance to present his request to 'Abdu'l-Bahá, he said, "Yes, I will come and see your wife this afternoon."

Randall returned with an automobile and chauffeur at 4pm. 'Abdu'l-Bahá and his Persian entourage climbed in, filling all the seats; 'Abdu'l-Bahá pointed to a spot on the floor and motioned to Randall to sit there. "This did not please Harry but he did it. . . . Several times [during the trip] He looked at Harry and laughed heartily. Harry knew later in life that he was being taught humility."

When 'Abdu'l-Bahá arrived at the Randall house, he walked straight through the house, opened the rear screen door, and stepped onto the back porch, where Ruth was lying down and talking to a group of others. 'Abdu'l-Bahá was introduced to everyone, then turned to Ruth, saying, "I know her well!" Ruth later recalled, "He asked me why I thought I was sick and I made some senseless reply." 'Abdu'l-Bahá asked Dr. Fareed to take Ruth's pulse, then placed his hand on Ruth's forehead and looked deeply into her eyes; "At that moment I knew that my life was a book which He could read at will," she later wrote. "He told me to do the same things that my physician had told me, besides telling me to eat my noonday meal in the sun. This I never did because I did not like the heat of the sun."

'Abdu'l-Bahá walked around the Randall house a few minutes, drank part of a glass of grape juice and poured the rest onto the lawn, which he stamped into the grass with his feet, then he left. He placed Harry Randall on the floor of the car again for the return trip to Malden. 'Abdu'l-Bahá told Harry "not to mind if your wife does not like sweet things, that she will when she is better" and to keep her "always in the light."

Both comments puzzled Harry greatly, so when he returned home he told Ruth about them. "I wept," Ruth recounts. She told him that "the box of chocolates" he bought for her every Saturday "are so sweet they are cloying to me now and I struggle to eat even one to please you." As for the advice about keeping her in the light, Ruth confessed that darkness had always frightened her and that she associated it with dying. They "marveled at 'Abdu'l-Bahá's insight," and within a few hours Ruth "began to feel stronger." When she went to see her lung specialist two weeks later, he was amazed by her healing. "In a few months he dismissed me and said he was writing up my case for the medical journal because a person with my type of pulmonary tuberculosis had not been known to recover." She was to live another fifty-seven years; she died in South Africa, where she had moved to spread the Bahá'í Faith, in 1969, at age 82.[61]

From the Randall house, 'Abdu'l-Bahá went to the New Thought Forum in Boston, where, to his surprise, it was announced that he would speak on the subject of "Captivating the Souls." He spoke about the power of the Holy Spirit, manifested through Jesus Christ and Bahá'u'lláh, to resuscitate hearts and quicken spirits, and how all people must "strive with life and heart that the material and physical world may be reformed." He returned to the Wilson house in the evening to speak about twenty-one teachings of Bahá'u'lláh that the world needed.[62]

Among those who had patiently waited with Harry Randall to speak to 'Abdu'l-Bahá on Sunday morning had been the "superintendent" of Franklin Square House, a former world-class hotel that had been converted in 1902 into a facility to provide affordable housing and classes for Boston's working women. It is not known how the superintendent heard of 'Abdu'l-Bahá; the contact may have resulted from 'Abdu'l-Bahá's visit to nearby Denison House in May, or through the prompting of a Boston area Bahá'í,

Helen Stuart Campbell, who was a published author about women trapped in poverty.[63]

'Abdu'l-Bahá spoke to five hundred people—mostly resident women—on Monday evening, August 26. His discourse focused on the equality of women with men, their great historical achievements as queens and religious leaders, and the importance of educating women. He noted that "while this principle of equality [of the sexes] is true, it is likewise true that women must prove her capacity and aptitude, and must show forth the evidences of equality." Rather that using "demonstrations of force, such as are now taking place in England"—no doubt a reference to the violent campaign for suffrage being waged by some members of the Pankhurst family, some of whom 'Abdu'l-Bahá had met in London—"woman must especially devote her energies and abilities toward the industrial and agricultural sciences, seeking to assist mankind in that which is most needful."[64]

The meeting must have gone late; 'Abdu'l-Bahá stayed at a hotel in Boston that night and returned to Malden the next morning. But he drove back to Boston Tuesday evening to speak to five hundred at the Theosophical Society. After discoursing about the manifestation of divine virtues and powers in the mineral, plant, and animal kingdoms—"within it lies the true explanation of pantheism," 'Abdu'l-Bahá explained—he spoke about the Bahá'í teachings on the oneness of the religions, the purpose of religion, the harmony of science and religion, the destructiveness of prejudices of all kinds, the oneness of humankind, the need for world peace, and the need to balance material civilization with spiritual civilization.[65]

Wednesday was filled by private meetings with individuals. The Theosophists invited him to speak again, but he declined, promising to send another speaker. That evening he went to the house of Alice Ives Breed to attend the wedding of her daughter, Ruby; it was a small affair with only the members of the two families present. After the Episcopal rector concluded the service, 'Abdu'l-Bahá spoke about marriage and presented the bride with a diamond ring.[66]

The next day, Thursday, was 'Abdu'l-Bahá's last full day in Malden. Many wanted to see him, and the Wilson house was too small. Mrs. Wilson contacted local churches, and they were uninterested in providing space, so she asked her friend Madame Abbie Ellen Beale Morey (1850–1931), a Rosicrucian, who had a large, prominent house nearby. Madame Morey, who was a well-known local pianist, accepted. She began the program with music. 'Abdu'l-Bahá spoke about the religions of the world to the "nearly one hundred" present. Madame Morey accepted the Faith as a result of his visit.[67]

Early the next morning, 'Abdu'l-Bahá and two members of his party—Maḥmúd-i-Zarqání and Ahmad Sohrab, Persian and English secretaries respectively—went to the railroad station to catch the 9am train to Montreal. The other members of the entourage were to stay behind; 'Abdu'l-Bahá was traveling light. He had made the decision to go to California on or before August 16, when the California Bahá'ís were notified.* He later said in a tablet that "it is because the friends of California, and particularly those of San Francisco, have so frequently called and pleaded, expressed despair and wept, and sent incessant supplications, that I have determined to go to California." He even had a tentative itinerary planned involving stops in Montreal, Buffalo, Chicago, Minneapolis, Denver, and Salt Lake City over the next three to four weeks. While his health had improved considerably since the heat, humidity, and crowds of New York City had exhausted him, the continent-spanning trip was a daunting task for a sixty-eight-year-old with impaired health who spoke little English. Time would tell what challenges it would bring.[68]

---

* The postcard makes reference to a telegram sent earlier that day that probably constituted the official announcement of 'Abdu'l-Bahá's decision to proceed to California. The news that 'Abdu'l-Bahá was indeed traveling to California was published in the August 20, 1912 issue of *Star of the West* as well (vol. 3, no. 9, p. 8).

9

FROM BOSTON TO SAN FRANCISCO

The longest journey of 'Abdu'l-Bahá's visit took a month and four days, from his Boston departure on the morning of August 30 until his San Francisco arrival a bit after midnight October 3. In thirty-four days, he spanned a continent, traveling almost forty-five hundred miles, visiting fourteen towns and cities, and giving some forty-eight talks to Bahá'ís and their friends.

The opening day of his odyssey took him through Lowell in Massachusetts; Nashua, Manchester, Concord, and Lebanon in New Hampshire; White River Junction, Montpelier, and Burlington in Vermont; and Saint Jean in Quebec, delivering him to the Grant Trunk Railway station in Montreal, some twelve hours and 316 miles (509 kilometers) after his departure from Boston.

Montreal, August 30–September 9, 1912

The city he entered was similar to Boston in some ways; comparable in size (470,000 versus Boston's 670,000), majority Catholic (though in both he mostly spoke to the population of liberal Protestant background), and very sophisticated. Montreal was Canada's largest city and the hub of its commerce, banking, and culture. With fourteen Bahá'ís, the city had by far the largest Bahá'í group in the country.[1] Meeting him at the train station was William Sutherland Maxwell (1874–1952), a renowned Canadian architect. His wife, May Bolles Maxwell (1870–1940), had been one of the first Bahá'ís in Paris, a member of the first pilgrimage of Western Bahá'ís to meet 'Abdu'l-Bahá in 1898–99, one of Canada's first Bahá'ís after she married Maxwell in 1902, and the founder of the Montreal Bahá'í community. She had stayed at home with her infant daughter, Mary (1910–2000), who would marry 'Abdu'l-Bahá's eldest grandson, Shoghi Effendi Rabbani, in 1937.

Sutherland Maxwell, Ahmad Sohrab, Maḥmúd-i-Zarqání, and 'Abdu'l-Bahá went to the large and comfortable Maxwell residence on Pine Avenue West, where May and Mary awaited with a group of Bahá'ís and a newspaper owner. After greetings, 'Abdu'l-Bahá agreed to speak at the Unitarian Church of the Messiah on Sunday, the newspaperman said he would publicize it, and 'Abdu'l-Bahá consented to stay at the Maxwell residence.

The next day—Saturday, August 31—the Maxwell house was crowded with visitors, including newspaper reporters, to whom 'Abdu'l-Bahá spoke in the morning. In the afternoon, Sutherland Maxwell gave him a driving tour of the city that passed by McGill University and the Roman Catholic Cathedral of Notre Dame. He walked inside the latter and marveled at the sacrifice and devotion of the eleven disciples of Christ that made such a dissemination of the teachings of Christ possible. Returning to the Maxwell residence, he spoke to a large crowd about the manifestation of divine virtues in human beings and met with individuals privately until very late at night.

Sunday, September 1, after a warm introduction at the Church of the Messiah, 'Abdu'l-Bahá paced back and forth across the front of the church and delivered a talk about the oneness of humanity and religion. God created all human beings from the same dust and sent Messengers to teach them to love one another, he began, but "blind imitations" and "vain practices" crept into religion, allowing contention, bloodshed, and warfare to spread. Hence, the need for Bahá'u'lláh to come, both to reiterate the ancient truths and to apply them to the human situation in new ways. First, Bahá'u'lláh proclaimed that all of humanity was one family that needed love and unity for its development; second, that religion must be the cause of love and fellowship; third, that religion must be in accord with science and reason; fourth, that prejudices, especially those of race, nation, and religion, must be rooted out; fifth, that all people must have access to an education; sixth, that women and men are equal; seventh, that a universal language to supplement the various national and ethnic tongues is necessary; eighth, that a Supreme Tribunal must be formed by the nations in order to resolve their disputes and bring about world peace. He praised the "noble" people and "high-minded" government of America—apparently he was speaking of both the United States and Canada—and expressed the hope that they will be "instrumental in raising aloft the standard of universal peace" and that "the American nation and government will further the cause of international peace, and thus bring security to the whole world." He then closed by chanting a prayer.[2]

The audience responded with "great enthusiasm and attraction." The Maxwell house filled with visitors that afternoon and evening, and he spoke to crowds both times. 'Abdu'l-Bahá became so animated in his talk there that night that his taj fell off his head and his hair "tumbled down." Once again he was up late meeting with individuals and small groups. Afterward he told the Maxwells, over their objections, that he would move to a hotel.[3]

The next morning, after visiting a neighbor who had been opposed to the Bahá'í Faith until she had met 'Abdu'l-Bahá, he moved to a three-room suite at the luxurious Hotel Windsor for the remainder of his sojourn. He continued to speak at the Maxwell house, however; two rooms adjoining the main parlor were equipped with chairs to accommodate the overflow crowd. On Monday, he spoke there at least twice. At the second talk, he expressed concern that material civilization was advancing much faster than spiritual civilization and that as a result, "before international peace is established, a great war will in all certainty take place." On Tuesday, he spoke to various small groups of people during the day and to an audience of five hundred at the Socialist Club in the evening. The latter discourse focused on economics and went extremely late. That day was also memorable because 'Abdu'l-Bahá got lost; he went out for a walk on his own, took a tram out of the city and then another tram that went even farther into the countryside, and finally hailed a taxi to take him back to his hotel. Apparently he had forgotten the name of the hotel, because he gestured to the driver to go straight and "by chance" arrived at it.[4]

The talk at the Socialist Club was covered favorably by the press, and even more people came to hear him on Wednesday when he spoke at the Maxwell residence. Thursday he was visited by a bishop, a rabbi, and the editor of a Toronto magazine. That evening, he spoke at Saint James Methodist Church, where the illuminated sign outside announced him as a "Prophet of the East," and 1,200 people awaited him inside. He began by noting that some people have argued that God's bounty, once poured out on humanity in abundance, has now ceased; this presumably referred to the idea that revelation had occurred through Abraham, Moses, the Israelite prophets, and Jesus, then ended. This, he replied, was impossible; it would be like the sun ceasing to shine. He gave as a counter-example the progressive revelation of truth to humanity through the divine Messengers. God's truth was still pouring forth through the revelation received by Bahá'u'lláh: "His revelation of the Word embodies completely the teachings of all the Prophets, expressed in principles and precepts applicable to the needs and conditions of the modern world, amplified and adapted to present-day questions and critical human problems. That is to say, the words of Bahá'u'lláh are the essences of the words of the Prophets of the past. They are the very spirit of the age and the cause of the unity and illumination of the East and the West."[5]

'Abdu'l-Bahá offered eleven principles that Bahá'u'lláh had brought to humanity: that the investigation of reality is of paramount importance, that the oneness of humanity must be accepted, that religion must be the mainspring of love in the world, that religion must be in harmony with science and reason, that prejudice—religious, racial, patriotic, or political—is contrary to the religion of God, that humanity is in need of confirmations from the Holy Spirit, that education of all humanity is essential, that world peace will be established, that equality of rights between men and women must be achieved, that equality of human rights must be accomplished, and that a universal language must be selected. It was the first time 'Abdu'l-Bahá gave eleven principles; at the Church of the Messiah, he had given eight, and at Baptist Temple in Philadelphia, had given ten. Notably, when talking about the need for world peace, he added this ominous warning:

> Europe is a storehouse of explosives awaiting a spark. All the European nations are on edge, and a single flame will set on fire the whole of that continent. Implements of war and death are multiplied and increased to an inconceivable degree, and the burden of military maintenance is taxing the various countries beyond the point of endurance. Armies and navies devour the substance and possessions of the people; the toiling poor, the innocent and helpless are forced by taxation to provide munitions and armament for governments bent upon conquest of territory and defense against powerful rival nations. There is no greater or more woeful ordeal in the world of humanity today than impending war. Therefore, international peace is a crucial necessity.[6]

Possibly his warning about the inevitability of a major war reflected the news that Greece, Bulgaria, and Serbia were arming for a war with the Ottomans, which would be launched a month later. He closed his talk with a prayer. One member of the audience, a judge, rose to praise the address, and the clergy thanked him sincerely afterward.[7]

The talk produced another surge of press coverage about 'Abdu'l-Bahá. The next morning, his retinue showed him, to his surprise, a great pile of papers that had articles about him. One researcher, Will van den Hoonaard, counted a total of twenty-five English-language articles (including one editorial) and nine French-language articles about 'Abdu'l-Bahá in the Montreal press during his visit. The English-language articles tended to be sympathetic and emphasized his teachings about war and peace and about the nature of religion; the French press was more cynical and focused on 'Abdu'l-Bahá himself and his teachings about humanity and economics.[8]

'Abdu'l-Bahá had originally planned to remain in Montreal only three or four days—this was the standard for his later visits as he traveled west—but extended his stay because of the great receptiveness. He then planned to leave soon after his talk at Saint James Methodist Church, which occurred on the sixth full day of his sojourn. But the next morning he awoke with a cold, so he remained in Montreal three additional days. On Friday, September 6, apparently 'Abdu'l-Bahá did not speak at all, but he spoke at least twice at his hotel on Saturday and Sunday. His last full day in the city was occupied with farewells and exhortations to the Bahá'ís to continue their efforts to "educate the souls in divine morals, make them spiritual and lead them to the oneness of humanity and to universal peace."[9]

Monday morning, September 9, 'Abdu'l-Bahá departed for Buffalo at 9am, leaving a crowd of sad Bahá'ís at the train station. It was a long ride; the train car's doors and windows were closed to keep out the ashes and dust from the engine, but they got in anyway, making the car hot and dusty. The combination made 'Abdu'l-Bahá extremely tired—further evidence that his childhood tuberculosis may have weakened his lungs—and he wondered aloud how he'd ever make it to California. As the train passed through Belleville, Ontario, 'Abdu'l-Bahá apparently spotted a four-year-old Mohawk boy sitting on a fence watching the train and waved to him. The boy, Alfred James Loft, was so surprised that he fell off the fence; the event became one of his earliest childhood memories. In May 1948, the forty-year-old Loft became one of the first native Canadians to join the Bahá'í Faith.[10]

Buffalo, September 9–12, 1912

After walking a little on the train platform in Toronto, 'Abdu'l-Bahá got back on the train and continued to Buffalo, arriving there late at night for a visit of about fifty-six hours. The next morning, the Bahá'ís were informed that he was at the Hotel Iroquois, and soon a crowd assembled, including reporters. After a morning of private interviews and a public talk, 'Abdu'l-Bahá went for his customary afternoon walk and was persuaded to board a streetcar bound for Niagara Falls. He gazed at the falls for half an hour and said it was "unsurpassed in beauty and unique in awe inspiring charm."[11] Returning to his hotel, he gave a public talk to seventy in the "large parlor" about the message of love brought by the Prophets of God. Part of the talk again reiterated the danger of a war in Europe; indeed, the Buffalo *Courier,* in the headline of an article about his visit, said 'Abdu'l-Bahá "predicts a war in Europe" and "urges local Bahaists to Do All in Their Power to Avert Terrible Bloodshed Which He Says Is Pending in East":

> The continent of Europe is one vast arsenal, which only requires one spark at its foundations and the whole of Europe will become a wasted wilderness.

> And what flimsy, what impudent pretexts they use. Patriotism, say they; glory, say they; the upbuilding of the continent, say they. What a travesty of God's truth.[12]

Afterward, he met with more reporters—his visit resulted in at least nine local newspaper articles—and conducted more private meetings. When he went for a walk downtown late at night, he stopped to give money to some poor persons. Soon a crowd, recognizing him from the newspaper coverage, gathered around him, and he "showered kindness" on them.[13]

Wednesday, September 11 began with morning meetings with individuals, including the minister of the Universalist Church of the Messiah, where he was to speak that night. In the afternoon, he visited two local Bahá'ís who were ill and gave some coins to local children, then went to the home of a Bahá'í, J. Harrison Mills, to speak. His evening address at the Church of the Messiah had a "large audience." The minister, who was very sympathetic about the Bahá'í Faith and had prepared an account about it for his church newsletter, encouraged his flock to attend Bahá'í meetings. Even though 'Abdu'l-Bahá had wanted to leave the church early, they continued to ask him questions until very late; he got to bed about 2am. He awakened his entourage very early, too, because they had tickets for the 5:35am train for Chicago.[14]

Chicago and Kenosha, September 12–17, 1912

'Abdu'l-Bahá's second visit to the Chicago area began with his arrival at 8pm, September 12. His Chicago sojourn was unique, compared to the other stops of his western trip. He was not visiting a community for the first time, making new contacts for the Faith in churches and other organizations, and speaking to the newspapers for the first time; or as he put it in Minneapolis, "We come and in each city we create a stir, scatter some seeds, awaken the people, inform them of the Most Great Call and then leave."[15] He had already been in Chicago in May and had created a "stir" then. This time there were few newspaper articles and only one talk in a public place; instead, he concentrated on private meetings in the homes of Bahá'ís and strengthening the Bahá'í community. In particular, he was concerned about the issue of the Covenant of Bahá'u'lláh and helping the Chicago Bahá'ís understand what faithfulness to the Covenant meant.

'Abdu'l-Bahá was greeted by a large crowd of Bahá'ís at the train station, who "formed two lines and 'Abdu'l-Bahá walked majestically between them showering His blessings on each one." One of them was Saichiro Fujita, the second person of Japanese ancestry to accept the Bahá'í Faith. Fujita had climbed a lamp post to see 'Abdu'l-Bahá over the crowd; 'Abdu'l-Bahá spotted him, called him to come down, and invited him to ride in the automobile with him to Corinne True's house at 5338 Kenmore Avenue.[16] Later that evening, he seated Fujita at the dinner table near him. 'Abdu'l-Bahá kept Fujita close to him throughout his Chicago visit, just as he had earlier done with Louis Gregory, Louisa Mathews, Grace Robarts, George Latimer, Fred Mortensen, and others.

'Abdu'l-Bahá had consented to stay at the True home. After a brief rest, he gave a talk. The next day—Friday—her house thronged with a multitude all day, and he spoke three times. In the morning, "there was such a crowd that there was no way up or down the stairs"; in the evening "the three large rooms on the ground floor . . . were filled with so many visitors that people were standing in the hallways." A newspaper estimated the audience to be one hundred.[17] He spoke about divine civilization to the first gathering. The second gathering had African American Bahá'ís, and he focused on racial unity, noting that people are willing to associate with dogs because of their faithfulness but not with people of a different color:

> Some have protested to me, asking why I seek to cultivate love between the whites and the blacks. Yet what a great error they make.

> You see people who love their dogs because of their faithfulness and the protection they provide. If but one good trait endears a dog to a human, why shouldn't praiseworthy qualities cause a man to be loved and respected? Why should fellowship with an upright person be avoided? . . . My hope is that you will rid and purify yourselves of imitations so that your thoughts and minds will be broadened and elevated, that you will be seekers of the truth, the lovers of the servants of God and the cause of the oneness of humanity.[18]

The evening meeting focused on teaching the Faith and the divine confirmations that 'Abdu'l-Bahá's trip received. One visitor that day was Bernard Jacobsen, the chairman of the Kenosha, Wisconsin, Bahá'í community, who asked 'Abdu'l-Bahá to visit that city on Sunday, which 'Abdu'l-Bahá agreed to do.

Saturday morning the 14th saw another meeting at the True home. 'Abdu'l-Bahá spoke about the power of the Covenant to protect and unify the Bahá'í community and gave an account of Ibrahim Kheiralla, who had founded the Chicago Bahá'í community eighteen years earlier and had accomplished nothing since his break with the Bahá'í Faith in 1900. 'Abdu'l-Bahá had already sent Howard MacNutt to Chicago in August to speak about the Covenant and emphasize avoiding communication with Kheiralla; now he personally reiterated the same themes.

That afternoon, after a walk along Lake Michigan, 'Abdu'l-Bahá went to a meeting of the Theosophical Society and spoke about "the distinction between spiritual realities and the animal nature of man, and the appearance of the perfection of man in the image of God." He had given a similar talk to the Theosophists in Evanston, back in May.[19]

Before leaving for Kenosha on Sunday morning, 'Abdu'l-Bahá had a long talk with Dr. Frederick Nutt, the leading Bahá'í in Chicago who was continuing contact with Kheiralla. He spoke about Kheiralla "in such majestic and forcible tones that both the hearer and the translator trembled with fear."[20] He invited Nutt to accompany him to Kenosha, presumably to see how he served people and taught the Faith.

The first demonstration to Nutt of 'Abdu'l-Bahá's wisdom occurred before they reached Kenosha. The party arrived in the Chicago train station too late to catch the train to Kenosha that they were supposed to take. 'Abdu'l-Bahá said, "it matters not. There is a wisdom in this." As they were on the way to Kenosha on the second train, they passed the wreckage of the first, which had collided with another train, resulting in injuries to some passengers. 'Abdu'l-Bahá reflected that "some proposed that we leave [for America] via London by the S. S. *Titanic*, which sank on the same voyage. The Blessed Beauty [Bahá'u'lláh] guided us to come direct."[21]

The Kenosha Bahá'í community was overjoyed that 'Abdu'l-Bahá had come to visit them. The second Bahá'í community in America, it had been established in the fall of 1897. It was a community of blue-collar workers, many of Scandinavian and German background, few of whom had been interested in Theosophy or metaphysical groups; most had been Protestants. Entire families had become Bahá'ís in Kenosha. In contrast, the Bahá'í communities on the East Coast were mostly white-collar, middle- to upper-middle class, Anglo-Saxon in derivation, liberal Protestant, interested in metaphysical religious ideas, and mostly female. Chicago and Cincinnati partially resembled the East Coast communities and partially resembled Kenosha.* For the Kenosha Bahá'ís, Sunday was probably the only day they could easily host 'Abdu'l-Bahá; too many of them worked the other six days of the week.

* The sociological backgrounds of the various American Bahá'í communities are given in Stockman, *The Bahá'í Faith in America,* vol. 1, 100–104, 112–14, 126–30, 134–35.

The hall they rented was filled that day. 'Abdu'l-Bahá spoke briefly from the stage about the "victorious power and penetrating influence" of the Bahá'í Cause, and everyone ate lunch while the young Bahá'ís sang to piano accompaniment. Lunch was followed by another talk by 'Abdu'l-Bahá about Bahá'u'lláh's imprisonment and sufferings and the tumultuous events that led to 'Abdu'l-Bahá's freedom to travel to America and visit Kenosha. He spent time with the Bahá'í children, then went to the house of Henry Goodale, probably to rest and hold a few private meetings, and spoke to those gathered there about Bahá'u'lláh. The evening talk, in the city's Congregational Church, focused on the unity of the Manifestations of God. Old-time Bahá'ís may have been particularly pleased by the church's invitation, for the church was probably one of the churches that had sponsored anti-Bahá'í lectures in the autumn of 1899. After this talk, 'Abdu'l-Bahá returned to the Goodale home to sleep.[22]

'Abdu'l-Bahá returned to Chicago the next day to a packed house at Corinne True's and a musical program arranged by Louise Waite. He gave a very important talk about the Covenant that evening. He began by praising the Chicago Bahá'ís for their purity of heart and calling on them to become "the effulgence of God, replete with the efficacy of the Holy Spirit and the cause of unity and fellowship in the world of humanity, for today mankind has the greatest need of love and agreement." There are various sorts of unity in the world—family, patriotic, political—but none of them are the "source of perfect unity and love in the world of existence." Such a condition of perfect unity "can only come into being through the efficacy of the Holy Spirit." But for the power of the Holy Spirit to be effective, Bahá'u'lláh

> did not desire that among the Bahais there should occur any difference. Therefore, with His pen He wrote a Book of His Covenant, addressing all the Bahais, and all His relations saying: *"Verily, I have*

appointed a personage who is the CENTER OF MY COVENANT. All must obey him; all must turn to him; he is the expounder of My Book and he is informed of My purposes. All must turn to him. Whatsoever he says is correct, for, verily, he knoweth the texts of My Book. Other than him no one knows the Book." And this He said because among the Bahais there is not to take place any difference; that all were to be unified and agreed. . . . In all His Tablets, among which is the Tablet of The Branch, He has elucidated the various points or qualities of that personage; He has expounded the potency and power of that personage, so that no person with a new desire shall say, "I understand this from the writings of BAHA'O'LLAH," for He appointed the Center or Expounder of the Book. He said: *"Verily, he is the appointed one; other than him there is none"*—so that no sects or prejudices were to be formed; so that not every man with a new thought should create a thing. It is as though a king should appoint a governor general. Whosoever obeys that governor general has obeyed the king. Whosoever has violated the governor general has violated the king. Therefore, whosoever obeys the CENTER OF THE COVENANT, appointed by BAHA'O'LLAH, has obeyed BAHA'O'LLAH, and whosoever disobeys him has disobeyed BAHA'O'LLAH. It has nothing to do with him [Abdu'l Baha] at all.[23]

He closed with this warning:

Beware! Beware! if anyone should say anything out of his own thoughts or should create a new thing out of himself. Beware! Beware! you should care nothing at all for such a person, according to the explicit Covenant of BAHA'O'LLAH. His Holiness BAHA'O'LLAH shuns such souls, and for the conservation of the Teachings of BAHA'O'LLAH I have expounded for you, so that you

> may be informed lest any souls shall deceive you, lest any souls shall cause suspicion among you. You must love all people, though if any soul put you in doubt, you must know that BAHA'O'LLAH is quit with them. Anyone who works for unity, who works for amity, is a servant of BAHA'O'LLAH and BAHA'O'LLAH is his Helper and his Assistant. I ask God that He may cause you to be the very means of accord and unity, that He may make you radiant, merciful, heavenly, of the Kingdom Divine; that day by day you may advance; that you may become as bright as these lamps, thus shining throughout humanity and here I bid you farewell.[24]

It was the strongest and frankest talk 'Abdu'l-Bahá had given to date about the issue of Covenant-breaking. It was directed not only at Ibrahim Kheiralla and any Chicago Bahá'ís, like Frederick Nutt, who continued association with him, but also at the problem that associates of Kheiralla were attending the weekly Chicago Bahá'í public meetings. In places, the talk's tone and terms are reminiscent of 'Abdu'l-Bahá's Will and Testament. To those who thought the Bahá'í revelation was simply a call to reform the churches, the talk was a reminder that unity required more than love to be achieved; it also required discipline and adherence to values defined in Bahá'u'lláh's revelation and 'Abdu'l-Bahá's interpretations of it. If people claimed to believe in Bahá'u'lláh but opposed 'Abdu'l-Bahá, they were not to be associated with.

After the talk, 'Abdu'l-Bahá "seemed depressed." He spoke to his Persian assistants about "bearing the discomforts of this journey" in order to protect the Bahá'í Faith "from any breach"; "I fear that self-seeking persons may again disrupt the love and unity of the friends." He expressed worry about "what is going to happen after me" but was confident that "if the time were right and the House of Justice were established, the House of Justice would protect the friends." He noted that personal desires had broken the unity of Islam, a fate the Bahá'í Faith had to avoid. He didn't sleep well that night.[25] Clearly, the infection of Covenant-breaking in Chicago worried him in the extreme.

After the talk at Corinne True's, he moved to the Astor Hotel; this followed the pattern in Montreal, where he first acceded to a request to stay in someone's house, then moved out as soon as he felt he had discharged the obligation. The next morning, before he left Chicago for Minneapolis, he called Corinne True to his room at the Astor at 5:30am. He told True he had "prayed all night for her." Then "he told me the violation in Chicago was a malignant cancer, and would poison the entire Cause in America if it were not cut out. He instructed me to say to the violators who came to our meetings that they must not come; that as we do not go to their meetings they must not come to ours; they were working against us, and we did not want them to injure themselves by being hypocritical."[26]

It was a tremendous challenge to True; the Covenant-breakers had not been confronted publicly. Then 'Abdu'l-Bahá and his entourage went to the Chicago and Northwest Train Station, where a crowd of tearful Bahá'ís saw him off for his trip to Minneapolis.[27]*

---

* Maḥmúd says 'Abdu'l-Bahá left Chicago on Tuesday, September 17, arriving in Minneapolis that evening, and this agrees with the published talk by 'Abdu'l-Bahá on the night of September 16, saying he would leave for Minnesota the next morning. But a Minneapolis newspaper article provided to the author by Dr. Duane Troxel, dated September 19, says 'Abdu'l-Bahá arrived in Minneapolis "late last night." Other newspaper articles that mention events connected with 'Abdu'l-Bahá's visits to Minneapolis, Lincoln, Denver, and San Francisco all date the events to one day later than Maḥmúd. Either Maḥmúd's diary entries are off by a day (which appears to be true for the subsequent entries for Minnesota, Nebraska, and Colorado), or the train broke down and took two days to reach Minneapolis, or 'Abdu'l-Bahá stayed in Chicago an extra day.

Minneapolis and Saint Paul, September 18–21, 1912

'Abdu'l-Bahá's stay in Minneapolis followed the same pattern as his Buffalo sojourn: a late night arrival, two full days of activities, and an early morning departure. The community was of a similar size—perhaps a dozen active Bahá'ís and a few dozen sympathizers. He stayed in the Plaza Hotel with five assistants: Ahmad Sohrab, Maḥmúd-i-Zarqání, Ameen Fareed, Alí-Akbar Nakhjavání, and Saichiro Fujita. Fareed had joined 'Abdu'l-Bahá in Montreal; Nakhjavani had joined him in Chicago; and 'Abdu'l-Bahá had invited Fujita to go to Kenosha with him and had then asked Fujita to accompany him for the rest of his travels across the United States.[28] After a joyful morning meeting with Bahá'ís, their friends, a few newspaper reporters, and a rabbi who asked him to speak at his synagogue—which he agreed to do—'Abdu'l-Bahá went to the Commercial Club, where he spoke about the four criteria for investigating truth: the senses, the intellect, tradition, and inspiration.

The talk at Shaari Tov Temple at Fifth Avenue South and Tenth Street apparently occurred on September 20.* 'Abdu'l-Bahá's talk there "provided decisive proofs of the validity and truth of Christ and the Cause of Muhammad." No transcript of the talk is available, but most likely it was a development of the talk he gave at the Central Congregational Church in Brooklyn on June 16 (previously discussed) and similar to the talk he gave at Temple Emanu-El, San Francisco, on October 12. Maḥmúd records no controversy over the subject, noting instead that "it was so persuasive that men and women came to 'Abdu'l-Bahá with the utmost humility and admiration."[29]

---

* Maḥmúd-i-Zarqání, *Maḥmúd's Diary,* 273, says the synagogue talk occurred on September 18 (the first full day of 'Abdu'l-Bahá's visit), but a Minneapolis newspaper article dated September 19 says it will occur "tomorrow" (the second full day of his visit, Maḥmúd's dates being off by a day).

In addition to the two public talks and three talks at his hotel, 'Abdu'l-Bahá also spoke three times in the homes of Bahá'ís; twice in the home of Albert Hall, who was on the Bahai Temple Unity Board, and once in the home of Dr. Clement Woolson in St. Paul. Two of the latter talks are available in English; the talk at Hall's focused on material and "ideal" virtues, and the talk at Woolson's focused on education—especially spiritual education—through the Messengers of God. 'Abdu'l-Bahá does not appear to have spoken about the Covenant to the Minnesota Bahá'ís, who were not formally organized or in contact with Covenant-breakers. Altogether, about a thousand people heard him speak over two full days of events. 'Abdu'l-Bahá even found time to visit the Walker Art Gallery, where Mrs. Willis Walker escorted him around the exhibits. And, of course, he took a walk in a park (Loring Park).[30]

Omaha and Lincoln, September 21–23, 1912

'Abdu'l-Bahá left his hotel at 8am, September 21, and boarded a train to Omaha.* While his next major destination was Denver, on the way, he hoped to visit William Jennings Bryan (1860–1925) because Bryan had visited him in Acre in 1906.† Bryan was a statesman of considerable importance; he was a Congressman from Nebraska in 1890–92, the Democratic candidate for President of the United States in 1896, 1900,

* Maḥmúd-i-Zarqání, *Maḥmúd's Diary,* 276, says 'Abdu'l-Bahá left Minneapolis on September 20, but Ahmad Sohrab to Helen Goodall, Sept. 21, 1912, Goodall Papers, says 'Abdu'l-Bahá left Minneapolis for Omaha at 9am, September 21, 1912. This confirms that Maḥmúd's chronology is off by a day.

† Bryan wrote about his tour of Palestine and visit to 'Abdu'l-Bahá in an article published in the Chicago *Daily News,* Aug. 25, 1906 (copy in the National Bahá'í Archives, Wilmette, IL).

and 1908, and would be appointed Secretary of State in 1913. "The Great Commoner," as he was sometimes called, was a powerful advocate of Prohibition and a dedicated opponent of Darwinian evolution.

'Abdu'l-Bahá spent the day riding the train to Nebraska and, having missed the convenient connection to Lincoln, spent the twenty-second in Omaha. Even though there was no Bahá'í community in that city, newspaper reporters soon heard of his arrival and came to his hotel to interview him, which resulted in at least one newspaper article being written about him. The news about the impending Balkan war was ominous, and 'Abdu'l-Bahá spoke about ways a European war could be avoided: The American republics could pressure the European nations, financiers could refuse to give governments military loans, railroad companies could refuse to transport armaments, and national boundaries could be fixed.[31]

At midday 'Abdu'l-Bahá went to the station to take the train to Lincoln, but just missed it. While he waited in the station, a man spotted him and came to converse, for he had received a telegram from a friend telling him to look for 'Abdu'l-Bahá. He invited some friends of his over, and soon 'Abdu'l-Bahá was giving a talk to a small gathering.[32]

He didn't reach Lincoln until late at night. 'Abdu'l-Bahá's entourage telephoned the Bryan home the next morning and arranged to visit, even though Mr. Bryan was away campaigning for Woodrow Wilson, who was running for president. Meanwhile, reporters arrived and various people who saw him in the hotel wanted to meet him, so 'Abdu'l-Bahá gave a talk in his room. Afterward he drove to the Bryan home in a rented automobile, and Mrs. Bryan and her daughter entertained 'Abdu'l-Bahá and his party. Back at the hotel, a group of Arabs, who had read about him in the local newspaper, visited with him; at 8pm, he gave a talk in the hotel lobby to a small crowd. When he left Lincoln on the 11pm train for Denver, he had had a full day.

Denver and Glenwood Springs, September 24–28, 1912

The city he reached at 2pm, September 24, had over two hundred thousand people living in it; its twelve-year-old Bahá'í community had had seventeen members in 1907 and probably numbered closer to two dozen in 1912.[33] The approximately sixty-seven hours he spent in Denver constituted a stay that was only a little longer than his visits to Buffalo and Minneapolis. Since he arrived late at night, he was welcomed at the train station by a group of Bahá'ís and a few reporters; after resting at the Shirley Hotel, he offered Persian tea and an interview to three reporters at 5pm, then spoke at the home of Mrs. Sidney E. Roberts, 1751 Sherman Street, at 8pm about humanity's spiritual needs and capacities. So many people attended the talk that the crowd extended to the front door. The minister of the Divine Science Church, Nona L. Brooks (1861–1945), was present, and she asked 'Abdu'l-Bahá to speak at her church the next night, which he agreed to do. He also announced that he would entertain visitors at his hotel every morning from 9am to noon.

His hotel received a "rush of people" the next morning—"friends, seekers, professors, clergymen, and philosophers," said Maḥmúd. After a walk around the city, 'Abdu'l-Bahá took a train to the house of Mrs. Josephine Hall Clarke at 4141 Xavier Street. She had cleaned her house scrupulously for his visit except the kitchen sink, which she assumed he would never see, so she was horrified when 'Abdu'l-Bahá said, "I will go and get myself a glass of water" in English, entered the kitchen, selected a glass, and pumped a glass of water from the well. He returned to the living room, looked at her and laughed, as if to say, "You can't hide anything from 'Abdu'l-Bahá." He spoke in her living room and answered many questions. Before leaving, he reportedly blessed the house and said, "God willing it would always be a Mashrak el Adhkar."[34] The Bahá'ís of Denver were eventually able to buy it.

In the evening, he went to the Divine Science Church in an automobile put at his disposal by the editor of the *Denver Post*. The church, founded in 1899, was part of the New Thought Movement; it emphasized experiencing God, who was "pure Spirit, absolute, changeless, eternal, manifesting in and as all Creation, yet also transcending Creation"; the nonexistence of evil; affirmative prayer, contemplation, and meditation; and the importance of spiritual healing.[35] The Denver Church was the national center of the Divine Science movement.

'Abdu'l-Bahá's lengthy talk that night began with a discussion of investigation of reality. The barriers to such investigation are fanaticism and ignorant prejudice; as a result of them, "the nations of the world are on the verge of war." In contrast, the Messengers of God brought love, fellowship, and solidarity; "God has destined and intended religion to be the cause and means of cooperative effort and accomplishment." The religions have two kinds of teachings; essential ones that are eternal, and "accidental" ones that are "subject to change and supersedure according to exigencies of time, place and condition," such as polygamy and divorce. 'Abdu'l-Bahá recounted how Moses and Jesus educated and civilized Their followers, and he demonstrated that both of Them were heavenly Teachers and Educators. He then applied the same criteria to Bahá'u'lláh:

> When you enter their meetings [those of the Bahá'ís], you will find Christians, Muslims, Buddhists, Zoroastrians, Jews and representatives of other beliefs present, all conjoined in a wonderful unity without a trace of bigotry or fanaticism, and the light of the oneness of the world of humanity reflected in their faces. Day by day they are advancing, manifesting greater and still greater love for each other. Their faith is fixed upon the unification of mankind, and their highest purpose is the oneness of religious belief. They proclaim to all humanity the sheltering mercy and infinite grace of God. They

> teach the reconciliation of religion with science and reason. They show forth in words and deeds the reality of love for all mankind as the servants of one God and the recipients of His universal bounty. These are their thoughts, their beliefs, their guiding principles, their religion. No trace of religious, racial, patriotic or political prejudice can be found among them, for they are real servants of God and obedient to His will and command.[36]

'Abdu'l-Bahá's last full day in Denver, Thursday, September 26, included private meetings with visitors, a lengthy walk around downtown, an afternoon public meeting at Mrs. Roberts' house, and an evening public meeting in the large hall of the Shirley Hotel. Both meetings included words of farewell. Of the latter gathering, Maḥmúd writes, "The spacious room was filled to capacity. I will never forget the joy and excitement of the audience. At times the audience was plunged into a state of sadness and wonder and then into a state of such happiness and joy that peals of laughter could be heard outside the building. It is not possible to describe the excitement and attraction of the people. They all expressed their sadness that the Master was leaving the city."[37]

The morning of September 27 began with farewells to those who came to his hotel early. The visit had had many successes; he had spoken at least five times to perhaps a thousand people, and at least eight local newspaper articles had appeared.

'Abdu'l-Bahá left Denver at 9am, bound for Salt Lake City and San Francisco. Because there was no train line running due west—the Rockies at Denver were too steep and high for the trains of the day—the train first went south to Pueblo, then northwest around the Front Range, past the spectacular Royal Gorge, through the "Two Mile High" city of Leadville, then downhill and westward along the Colorado River. But 'Abdu'l-Bahá did not enjoy the scenery because he felt increasingly ill—possibly from the altitude; consequently, when the train reached Glenwood Springs at 2am—over two hours after its scheduled 11:45pm arrival—he and his entourage got off and took rooms in the Hotel Colorado, a famous resort with adjacent hot springs. The next morning they gazed at the spectacular scenery, strolled in the hotel's beautiful gardens, and bathed in the natural springs, which "relieved" 'Abdu'l-Bahá of his "fatigue." "Because of our work, we had no time to look at the scenery," he added. "Today, however, we have had a little respite."[38]

They lunched in the hotel's garden, which required the hotel to install a table where none normally rested; 'Abdu'l-Bahá tipped the waiters generously. They walked to some nearby shops and through more gardens. He spoke to many guests, who became curious about him. When he boarded the train at midnight, he felt much better.

Salt Lake City, September 29–October 1, 1912

The party reached Salt Lake City the next afternoon, September 29, at about 2pm. The city was thronging with crowds because the annual State Fair was occurring that week, along with the convention of the Mormon Church and a meeting of the National Irrigation Congress. Utah had no Bahá'ís, but much to their surprise, Feny E. Paulson, a Montana Bahá'í, met them at the train station. She had heard by telegram that 'Abdu'l-Bahá would be in the city and rode down to meet him. They all went to the Kenyon Hotel to take rooms, 'Abdu'l-Bahá having decided to stay in the city a day to visit the state fair and irrigation congress. A reporter soon interviewed him, resulting in an article in the September 30 issue of the Salt Lake City *Tribune*.[39]

The next day, September 30, 'Abdu'l-Bahá was invited to sit on the speakers' platform of the National Irrigation Congress, which was meeting in the Mormon Tabernacle. While touring the State Fair, he purchased some seeds to take back to the Holy Land. Apparently he planned to leave on the 2:50pm train for San Francisco, but didn't.* In the evening, he watched a parade of electrically lighted agricultural floats. The next morning, October 1, he invited Feney Paulson to tea and spoke with her. When the interview concluded, he gave her a Bahá'í ringstone and a locket-sized likeness of himself. He headed for the train station in the early afternoon. The ride to San Francisco proved longer than expected; leaving Salt Lake City about 2:50pm, they missed a connection in Montello, Nevada, were delayed several hours, and didn't reach San Francisco until about 2am on October 3.[40] In a little over a month, he had traveled from coast to coast.

* Ahmad Sohrab to Helen Goodall, Sept. 30, 1912, Goodall Papers, says 10,000 were present in the Mormon Tabernacle when 'Abdu'l-Bahá sat on the "platform." It also says he planned to leave for San Francisco that afternoon, but a postcard that Sohrab sent to Parsons from Ogden, Utah, on October 1 said they would reach San Francisco "tomorrow night."

10

THE GOLDEN STATE

'Abdu'l-Bahá's visit to California lasted just twenty-four days but resulted in forty-eight public talks to a cumulative audience exceeding ten thousand and at least thirty-seven newspaper articles. The Bahá'í community of greater San Francisco was among the nation's oldest—dating from 1898—and included some socially prominent and wealthy members, with Phoebe Hearst (1842–1919) being the best known among them. The community also had the distinction of sending the first pilgrimage of Occidental Bahá'ís to meet 'Abdu'l-Bahá, in 1898–99, led by Mrs. Hearst. In 1912, its membership probably exceeded one hundred. Los Angeles had a smaller and younger Bahá'í community, with perhaps one or two dozen members, but it was active and knowledgeable about the Faith. 'Abdu'l-Bahá found the California Bahá'ís to be of great capacity, collectively, and they were able to connect him to some prominent and important audiences. They planned his visit carefully and engaged Miss Bijou Straun, a young Bahá'í stenographer, to accompany him, with the result that all forty-eight addresses were captured in shorthand and turned into typescripts, along with forty-one informal talks by 'Abdu'l-Bahá to smaller groups and fifty-three interviews with individuals and small groups. The latter even included a conversation during an automobile ride. 'Abdu'l-Bahá delivered some of the most weighty talks of his North American sojourn in California, the record of which is richer and more complete than anywhere else.*

Anticipating his late arrival, 'Abdu'l-Bahá requested that only one person meet him at the station where the train passengers were ferried across the Bay. The planning committee chose Dr. Frederick D'Evelyn, chair of the San Francisco Bahá'í community. It was "in the weird moments between two and three in the morning" when "the white turban of Abdul-Baha at last issued from the long exit at the ferry, and his warm hand clasp, and the welcome of his eyes eliminated all the weary hours of hope delayed."† D'Evelyn, 'Abdu'l-Bahá, and his party took two taxis to the house rented for them at 1815 California Street, where Mr. and Mrs. Ralston, Mrs. Helen Goodall, Mrs. Ella Cooper, and others greeted them. A Persian supper prepared by a local Iranian Bahá'í, John Bozark, awaited the travelers.‡ 'Abdu'l-Bahá spoke briefly to the gathering, expressing his hope that great results would come from the meeting, adding, "I will meet you again soon" because "I . . . am a little fatigued."[1]

The house was perfect for his needs: the first floor had a kitchen, a dining room, and three large rooms "decorated with fine furniture" that

* Ella Cooper prepared a typescript of over five hundred pages about 'Abdu'l-Bahá's visit to California, which includes all the transcripts and considerable background information. Never published, it exists in multiple drafts in various degrees of editing in the Ella Cooper Papers.

† D'Evelyn was elected chair of the community on January 1, 1911; see *Star of the West* 2, no. 1 (March 21, 1911): 12.

‡ John Bozark, or Mírzá Buzurg as he was called in Bahá'í sources, arrived in the United States in November 1900 to serve as translator for Mírzá Asadu'lláh, and when the latter returned to the Middle East, Bozark remained in the United States, eventually settling in San Francisco, where he married a French woman in 1910 and joined the local Bahá'í community. See Stockman, *The Bahá'í Faith in America, vol. 2,* 36; Ella Cooper, "History of the Bahá'í Faith in California," typescript, Cooper Papers; D'Evelyn, "The Coming of Abdu'l Baha to California," 5; Jan Jasion, email to the author, May 5, 2011.

opened onto each other, allowing a very large crowd to gather; the second floor had 'Abdu'l-Bahá's bedroom, a room for other members of the party, and a tea room where 'Abdu'l-Bahá could entertain visitors; the third floor had bedrooms ample enough to accommodate the rest of the entourage. In addition to the Persians and Saichiro Fugita, George Latimer, who had spent time with 'Abdu'l-Bahá in Dublin, came down from Portland to serve in the house some of the time. John Bozark and his wife moved in to serve as cooks. Lydia Rainey greeted guests at the door and provided hospitality.[2]

Maḥmúd reports that the party soon settled into a daily routine: dawn prayers; tea, and a light breakfast with 'Abdu'l-Bahá when he spoke to his entourage informally about a spiritual subject; a morning talk about "great and lofty matters" in the three large rooms once a crowd had assembled; a walk, usually in Golden Gate Park (a short automobile ride away), sometimes accompanied by a small crowd; lunch; a talk or personal meetings; another walk, perhaps around the block; dinner; and an evening meeting. Helen Goodall and the Ralston family both had automobiles that they made available to 'Abdu'l-Bahá and his entourage every day.[3]

Presumably the routine did not start at dawn on the first day, because 'Abdu'l-Bahá may have just managed to get to sleep when the sky was brightening. But once he was awake, he had reporters to meet; the president of Stanford University, David Star Jordan (1851–1931), came to discuss the invitation, already extended to 'Abdu'l-Bahá, to speak at that institution; and other prominent people called.[4] Ramona Allen Brown (1889–1975), her mother Frances, father Woodson, and brother Warren, came to 'Abdu'l-Bahá's residence from Berkeley that day and were welcomed into his tea room for a short visit:

> For a moment we stood at the open door. I knew as I stood there that I expected to see an angel from Heaven. And I did! It was the Master! He came toward us, a wonderful smile on His saintly face, extending

His outstretched arms to us and saying in Persian, "Welcome! Welcome!"

That exhilarating, magic moment of seeing 'Abdu'l-Bahá for the first time was like seeing the sun burst forth through the soft, rosy glow of dawn. It brought nearness to God, and my heart was filled with praise and gratitude for the bounty of being with Him . . . . As we entered the presence of the Master, He appeared to be enveloped in a beautiful, ethereal, luminous light. The room seemed flooded with sunshine. . . . The Master took my mother's hands and said "Welcome, Mrs. Allen, welcome, very welcome! You have a very united family, and you will all be united through all the worlds of God." His words to my mother made us very happy. Then in His warm, gentle hands He took the hand of each of us and welcomed us. When I gave 'Abdu'l-Bahá some yellow roses I had gathered from our garden, He was very pleased. He smiled as He thanked me . . . . As He looked into my eyes, His gentle, smiling eyes touched my soul; they seemed to tell me that He knew what was in my heart and everything about me. I felt as though I were in another world. At that moment I silently gave my heart and dedicated my life to Him.

He invited us to be seated, and continued speaking, telling us how happy He was to meet the California believers and that He hoped His Father's Message would reach the hearts of the people. He conversed with us as though we were old friends, and to each one of us He spoke some special words. Then 'Abdu'l-Bahá arose from His chair and, stepping lightly, but like a king, served us with His own hands, in small crystal glasses, the most delicious tea I had ever tasted. . . . To this day I can remember its fragrance and taste its sweetness.

> The happiness of that first meeting has remained with me all of my life. . . . We were full of deep joy as we basked in His love. Soon it was time to take His leave. For other people were waiting to greet Him.[5]

When the crowd downstairs grew large, 'Abdu'l-Bahá gave a short talk about the spiritual life. Later that day he crossed the Bay to the Oakland house of Helen Goodall for a grand meeting with the area Bahá'ís. Located at 1537 Jackson Street, it was large, with a spacious entry hall, a drawing room, a library, and a dining room; the first floor "is so connected by great sliding doors, that it seems one vast salon."[6] That Thursday afternoon there was plenty of room for the hundred or so Bahá'ís and their friends.

They had been waiting for 'Abdu'l-Bahá in anticipation for days. Juanita Storch (1895–1987), then seventeen, recorded in her diary on October 1 that "we have expected Abdul Baha for so long that it is hard to realize he will really be with us soon." They had hoped he'd be there on that day; on October 2 she reports that "the train didn't arrive so we cannot have a meeting." But on October 3 a Bahá'í friend, Mrs. Berdette Matteson, stopped by to tell them "Abdul Baha arrived last night and would be at Mrs. Goodalls this afternoon to meet us all. I was so happy I could hardly get ready." The Mattesons took Juanita with them in their automobile.[7]

When they reached the Goodall house, 'Abdu'l-Bahá was upstairs meeting with individuals while the crowd gathered. Juanita described the meeting in great detail:

> I was sitting on the floor, my favorite place, and happened to be in an excellent position, for as the rooms were filled it was much better to be up front and below the people. Besides, I could see the whole front room out of the drawing room into the hall and up the stairs.

> When all the people were settled Mrs. Cooper went up to tell Abdul Baha.
>
> He came down the stairs quickly, yet giving the impression of walking slowly and in a stately manner. . . . the light from a window above happened to fall so tenderly and suitably on his head and shoulders. Then I heard him speaking in the hall. His voice coming into the rooms was like spoken magic.
>
> Then he appeared in the doorway. He looked just as I have imagined and dreamed him. I was so happy!
>
> We all arose and he said "Allah'o'Abha" several times and we answered as he walked to his seat.
>
> With a motion of his hand he bade us be seated. He sat in the archway only a few seats from me. . . . I saw his profile the whole time he talked and once towards the last . . . I saw his eyes . . . I shall never forget it. He seemed as if I had known him always and I know I really have. . . .
>
> Occasionally he would draw his white turban over his forehead or push it back a little and the expressions on his face changed so beautifully as he emphasized his words—sometimes using his hands and feet. He sat there so peacefully and at ease . . .[8]

'Abdu'l-Bahá began his talk by saying "I am going to say 'Welcome' to you, instead of you welcoming me." He thanked Bahá'u'lláh for bringing about such a meeting, "for the hearts are connected and the souls are attracted and the spirits are exhilarated" and expressed the hope that it "may be a heavenly meeting" with "everlasting" traces and "eternal results." This will be possible "by your acting in accordance with the teachings of BAHA'O'LLAH."[9]

The talk that followed was well-suited both for a Bahá'í audience that had already heard the Bahá'í principles and non-Bahá'ís who knew little about them. He explained that the revelation of Bahá'u'lláh "in relation to the soil of the hearts" is like a "quickening shower"; it is "love among all mankind . . . a bond which unites all religions . . . the unity which welds together all the races . . . the connection between all the countries . . . universal peace among all the peoples." He offered some spiritual principles from the revelation as examples, beginning with the problem of overcoming "superstitions" and "blind imitations," which lead to "prejudice, hatred, and rancor." He emphasized "good conduct" as the "greatest effulgence of the All-Glorious" and spoke about the improvement of ethics and adoption of "divine morals." He expatiated about the oneness of humanity: "It is self-evident that this teaching is the very spirit of the age. It is life-giving, because through love it animates the people, and it casts alienation utterly aside." He stressed the requirement "under all conditions and circumstances, to be forgiving." He explained the importance of sacrifice, even one's "*life* must be sacrificed for humanity." People have been created "to yield some fruit," hence each individual "must be a blessed tree bearing eternal fruits." The "real fruit" of the human tree is "*love for God,* that is the *knowledge of God,* that is *service to the world of humanity,* that is *kindness to all mankind,* and that is endeavoring and striving for the *material and spiritual—or ideal—development*" of humanity. He closed with a prayer.[10]

Maḥmúd says that the Bahá'ís "rejoiced at meeting Him and the seekers were grateful and appreciative of His guidance." Storch says 'Abdu'l-Bahá "passed around the room shaking hands with everyone." She recalls: "I can never forget the wonderful soul-look I received as he grasped my hand. It seemed as if he held my hand and looked at me for ten minutes but it was only a second and even as he turned away he still had my hand. . . . He kissed the babies and his voice seemed to vibrate through the room when he spoke."[11]

Juanita even met Maḥmúd, "the one whom I had the pleasure of speaking with most." Her recollection of him is one of the few that exist, and shows that Maḥmúd knew some English. He asked her whether she was happy, and when she said "Yes," he said, "you are happy because you have seen Abdul Baha." Then Maḥmúd kissed a little baby and said, "I want to kiss you because Abdul Baha has kissed you!"[12]

When 'Abdu'l-Bahá finished shaking hands with everyone, he moved to the dining room, where the Bahá'í children of Oakland had gathered to meet him. Juanita was not invited, but because of the thick crowd in the main rooms, she decided to move into the dining room:

> I felt attracted to go there. I stepped in. The sight I saw was so beautiful and unexpected to me, yet it was as I had often read about. Abdu'l Baha was there. He was sitting in a chair by the window and the little children were all around him. The setting was wonderful . . . . Dr. Fareed was introducing the people to Abdul Baha . . . and interpreting the things he said to them in English. To the little children he spoke in English. I could not stand at a distance and just look . . . so I . . . sat on the floor at his feet with the others. I feasted on the way he patted and kissed the little children and the simple loving words he said to them. The spirit showed itself most beautifully as he held them and loved them. As he was holding one little blond girl I slipped a little jasmine flower into her hand for it seemed symbolic of her soul which showed itself on her face and in the way she wanted to stay with Abdul Baha. As he sat there the Master motioned to one man to sit in front of him

in a rocking chair. This man was brimming over and could not say a word. Abdul Baha said to him "Do not cry, be happy!"

The man could only shake the tears from his eyes and his whole face was quivering with joy.[13]

Frances Orr Allen adds that one girl of four years asked whether she could "pet the God-man." 'Abdu'l-Bahá remained at the Goodall house until late; his automobile was ferried across the Bay at night when "the splendid buildings and towers adorned with brilliant lights seemed to be golden palaces set with colored jewels" and "lights from the homes crowning the high hills appeared like a string of pearls." It was a glorious end to a glorious day.[14]

The next day—Friday, October 4—'Abdu'l-Bahá stayed at his house, entertained guests all day except when he went for a drive and walk in Golden Gate Park. He gave two talks. All three big rooms downstairs were full for the evening talk. Ernest A. Rogers, a Bahá'í who was the headmaster of a private school, was present and described the house as "crowded with doctors, professors, Jews, Gentiles, Hindus, Chinese, Japanese—men, women, and children." Juanita Storch, who was again fortunate to be seated on the floor near 'Abdu'l-Bahá, said that he "walked back and forth as he spoke. The hem of his garment nearly touched me when he turned around. I saw his beautiful hands as he delicately, yet firmly passed them over his rosary, usually holding them in back of him but once he held them in front and slipped a finger at either end so that they were suspended in the air." The talk was about the animal and spiritual natures of humans. "It was wonderful!" she exclaimed to her diary. Rogers added perceptively that "everyone seemed so pleased, so thrilled, *although they had heard no new truths*. . . it was not the Message in itself, but the spirit, the wonderful love of the man. Not the man himself but his life as seen and felt when he talked." 'Abdu'l-Bahá was extremely pleased by how well his visit was going; that night he sent telegrams to the Bahá'í communities in the Middle East, and one read, "Rejoicing among friends of God in San Francisco. Truly confirmations are overwhelming and happiness is complete."[15]

The success of his trip may have prompted some comments about the spiritual capacity of Americans, "greater capacity than the Europeans," as he said at a meeting the next morning. "I have pondered over the condition of the masses of the people of Europe," he observed. "They are like machines that work day and night unconscious of their motive power. They seem to be divided into two classes. The religionists are submerged in superstitions and prejudices, and those who are not religionists are materialists. The people of America are noble, energetic, spiritually susceptible and keen. That is why the Bahai cause has spread here."[16]

The San Francisco Bahá'ís normally met every Saturday evening, and 'Abdu'l-Bahá was their featured guest and speaker on October 5. Some Japanese Bahá'ís—possibly Kanichi Yamamoto and his wife—came to meet 'Abdu'l-Bahá, and he highly praised the qualities of the Japanese people. He also spoke to two more reporters.

Important Talks and Meetings, October 7–18, 1912

Sunday, in a sense, was 'Abdu'l-Bahá's public debut in California, for on that day, he spoke at two churches: the First Unitarian Church in San Francisco on Sunday morning, and the First Congregational Church in Oakland on Sunday evening. 'Abdu'l-Bahá addressed the problem of warfare, the need for religion to be a cause of peace, the role of the Manifestations of God in offering teachings of love and unity, the truth of Islam, and the advent of Bahá'u'lláh. Many people wrote down the address of his house so they could visit him later. Much to his amazement, the congregational minister, in his introduction, referred to 'Abdu'l-Bahá as a "messenger of God." "No one will believe it unless they see it themselves," he later remarked. "No matter to whom you may write these words, they will think it is an exaggeration and will not believe it."[17]

Juanita Storch was in the Congregational Church that evening and noted that a group of hostile but polite Persian Christians attended; it was common for Middle Eastern immigrants, seeing 'Abdu'l-Bahá's name and country of origin in the newspapers, to attend his talks. When the collection plate was passed around, 'Abdu'l-Bahá made a contribution; he usually gave generously. 'Abdu'l-Bahá paced as he spoke, which was also common; he turned occasionally toward the choir so they could see his face as well. Juanita notes that a "most beautiful silence reigned" while he spoke. Afterward, 'Abdu'l-Bahá gave his rosary as a gift to Mr. Takeshi Kanno (1877–1938), a renowned Japanese poet and philosopher, which made Mr. Kanno "a mighty happy man."[18]

In between the two addresses, 'Abdu'l-Bahá spoke at his residence. One result of the two public talks was eight new articles in local newspapers over the next three days and a great increase in the flow of visitors to his residence.[19]

On Monday he had a prominent visitor: Jackson Stitt Wilson (1868–1942), Mayor of Berkeley, a former Methodist Minister, former candidate for Governor of California, and a leading Christian Socialist. Wilson saw Jesus's the Sermon of Mount as a "code of social duties" and a "revelation of the fundamental principles of Social Justice and human fellowship for this our everyday world." Lua Getsinger had introduced him to the Bahá'í Faith. He and 'Abdu'l-Bahá discussed economic issues. 'Abdu'l-Bahá noted that society needed an order where there were "differences of rank" but where everyone, even the servants, needed to live in "comfort"; otherwise, "if these ills are allowed to become chronic, their cure will be difficult and they will precipitate a great revolution." He advocated a "storehouse" where all contributed based on their wealth and all drew from it based on their needs. Wilson, impressed, invited 'Abdu'l-Bahá to speak to the city at Berkeley High School, and he accepted.[20]

That evening, 'Abdu'l-Bahá went to the Japanese Y.M.C.A. of Oakland to speak to the Japanese Independent Church, formerly a branch of the local Congregational Church.* Prejudice against Chinese and Japanese Americans was strong among California's whites; it was a race issue almost as serious as the prejudice against African Americans. Hence 'Abdu'l-Bahá wished to meet the Japanese. After he arrived, the Japanese congregation sang "Nearer My God to Thee" in Japanese; a prayer in Japanese was offered by Mr. Togo, President of the Japanese Y.M.C.A.; and Mr. Kanno, who had received the rosary from 'Abdu'l-Bahá the day before, recited a poem he had composed in honor of the Master. Then 'Abdu'l-Bahá spoke. He began by stressing his happiness to meet them:

> For some time I have had a special desire to meet the friends from Japan, for, as I have often mentioned, the Japanese nation has achieved extraordinary progress in a short space of time—such progress, such achievements, as have astonished the world. Just as they advance along material lines, assuredly they must possess the capacity to advance along spiritual lines also. . . . Judging by the accounts which have reached my ears, the Japanese as a nation are not prejudiced. They investigate reality—truth. . . . Therefore I entertain the greatest desire to speak to them, in order that through these remarks there

* Maḥmúd erroneously dates the talk at the Japanese Independent Church to October 9, two days too late. The only other event mentioned for that day was 'Abdu'l-Bahá's return from Palo Alto. The talk occurred the day before the Palo Alto trip. Most likely, Maḥmúd had written the entry on an undated piece of paper, and possibly wrote down the Palo Alto trip on a separate piece of paper, and arranged them incorrectly when he organized the diary for publication in 1913.

> will result more of a blending together, more of a unity between the eastern nations and the western peoples.[21]

'Abdu'l-Bahá gave many examples of the warfare and bloodshed that resulted from religious, racial, and national prejudices. The purpose of the religions, however, was to foster love and justice. The Manifestations of God come to serve the world of humanity and summon "souls to peace and accord." 'Abdu'l-Bahá spoke at length about Moses and Christ, adding that "the light of Christ is evident. The candle of Buddha is shining. The star of Moses is sparkling. The flame ignited by Zoroaster is still burning. To deny this light would be an injustice."[22]

He turned to Muhammad and spoke of the transformation that His teachings made in barbarous desert tribesmen, who eventually erected a great, brilliant civilization. "Then why should we deny Muhammad?" 'Abdu'l-Bahá described the praise of Jesus and Mary in the Qur'án.[23]

He then turned to Bahá'u'lláh, Who "hoisted the banner of the oneness of the world of humanity" and "proclaimed international peace." He described the unified community of Bahá'ís that was being built around the world, among whom "rancor and hatred, opposition and molestation, are no longer evident." He called on the Japanese people to "shine as stars . . . radiate the light of love to all humanity. Thus may you be the establishers of love among all mankind. . . . Make peace with all the world. Love every one and serve every one."[24]

'Abdu'l-Bahá spoke in Persian, was translated into English by Ameen Fareed, and then into Japanese by Reverend Kunio Kodahira. Maḥmúd says the audience "was awed and excited to hear His powerful reasoning." 'Abdu'l-Bahá had accomplished three things in his address: he spoke against prejudice and in favor of the Japanese people; he called the audience to a kind of interfaith dialogue where the Messengers of God were all respected and appreciated rather than deprecated; and he proclaimed the

Messengership of the latest Manifestation, his father, Bahá'u'lláh. The talk was eventually published in a local Japanese newspaper.[25]

Tuesday, October 8 was one of the most momentous days in 'Abdu'l-Bahá's journey. It was packed with talks and meetings with prominent individuals from early morning to late at night. Accompanied by a party of twenty-nine people, he left for Palo Alto, thirty-four miles south of San Francisco, fairly early, and was met by President Jordan of Leland Stanford Jr. University at the train station. Jordan escorted 'Abdu'l-Bahá to the Assembly Hall for the 10:15am special meeting. The entire campus was there: 1,800 students and 175 faculty, plus many visitors. President Jordan's introduction was warm and welcoming: "He is said sometimes to be the founder of a new religion. . . . It is not exactly a new religion, however. The religion of brotherhood, of good will, of friendship between men and nations—*that* is as old as good thinking and good living may be. It may be said in some sense to be the oldest of religions."[26] Jordan set the tone: to appreciate 'Abdu'l-Bahá's words as a reiteration of the eternal ethics of liberal religion, rather than the setting forth of something profoundly new.

'Abdu'l-Bahá began with science rather than morality. "The greatest attainment in the world of humanity has ever been scientific in nature," he began. "It is the discovery of the reality of things." Because Bahá'u'lláh's "greatest and most fundamental teaching" is the oneness of humanity, 'Abdu'l-Bahá started with an explanation of the "oneness of phenomena." He reminded his audience of the cycling of atoms from minerals to plants, animals, and humans, in every case acquiring new powers and capacities through their combinations. This shows that "phenomena, fundamentally, are one; that is to say, existence is fundamentally one."[27]

'Abdu'l-Bahá noted that the world of humanity, also, is fundamentally one. It possesses the elemental cohesion exhibited in the mineral kingdom, the growth capacity of plants, the power of perception of the animals, plus the "sound mind" of humanity. Normally, the elements are at peace with each other; when they are not one gets disasters such as the San Francisco earthquake and fire of six short years earlier. 'Abdu'l-Bahá said, "Then consider what will be the result of discord, sedition and war in the human kingdom, a superior kingdom of creation. How great will be the attendant catastrophes!"[28]

'Abdu'l-Bahá discoursed briefly on human rational capacity to control electricity, fly through the air, cruise in submarines, and to record sound. Having such great capacity, he asked, "is it becoming of us to remain still like the ferocious animals, like the wolves fighting each other, killing each other?" Animals are ferocious in order to meet their physical needs, but humans are ferocious "for greed." "Is it becoming that such a noble creature . . . with such a sound mind, with such lofty thoughts, with all his scientific achievements . . . to go on to the battle-field, to spill the blood of his fellow men?" Humans are a temple of God, and when they destroy a divine temple they "deserve the wrath of God."[29]

He then asked, "When we are *not* captives of Nature, when we *can* control ourselves, shall we allow ourselves to be captives of Nature?" If we leave a plot of ground alone, it goes from a fertile field to a patch of brush and weeds; similarly, "the world of humanity should not be left to its naturalism," but should be trained and educated. And the best educators are the "Holy, Divine Manifestations of God." He did not offer a list of them, but noted that Bahá'u'lláh "declared the necessity of peace among the nations" fifty years ago. He proclaimed that "the fundamental basis of all religions is one" that religion was aimed to unite in fellowship all humans, but blind imitations and dogmas "have caused differences." "If a religion should prove to be the cause of dissention and discord," 'Abdu'l-Bahá added, "it is better to do without religion entirely."[30]

Instead, he explained, "religion was destined to be a remedy"; "a salve for the wounds of man." Bahá'u'lláh declared the oneness of humanity; "all are the progeny of Adam." "If we had two Adams for our father, then we might say we had some difference," but we are "one progeny," we are not "various and divergent"; to say "this is Italian, this is German, this is French, the other Russian—this is nonsense." Consequently, warfare makes no sense; "boundary lines have been created by people who were despotic. Their aim was fame, their aim was conquest of land." To an audience of young men, many of whom would soon be drafted to fight in the bloodiest war in human history, he used the prescient examples of Germany and France: "To the poor people—the farmers, the laborers, the soldiers—they said: Go to the battle-field while we are enjoying ourselves. We are captains and officers; you are the soldiers. . . . The others said 'You are destroying our homes. Why?' They answered: 'Because they are Germans; we are French.' . . . The blood of the innocent poor was shed. For what? For a superstition such as 'this is German, the other is French' when both are human; both belong to Adam, one family, one people."[31]

The senseless slaughter of World War One, less than two years away, could not have been more eloquently envisioned.

'Abdu'l-Bahá concluded that

> God created one earth, one globe, and one mankind. . . . But we have come forth and have imagined certain superstitional boundary lines. . . . [A] claim for territory is a claim just for dust—the love of, or attachment to, dust. Did you ever stop to think that we live on this earth of dust for a few days, and then we remain beneath it forever? So it is our *graveyard* eternally. Is it becoming of man to fight for his graveyard, which devours him, an eternal cemetery? For man to fight over his *grave,* to kill one another for his *grave*; what an ignorance! What an inadvertence! What a thoughtlessness on the part of man!

> I hope that you people are reasonable enough not to fight over your graves, and that you will enjoy the utmost of fellowship, like one family—brothers, sisters, mothers, fathers—enjoying peace.[32]

Maḥmúd reports that "the entire audience was overcome with admiration" and that "the applause shook the building to its very foundation." Marion Carpenter Yazdi, a student at Stanford eleven years later who researched the visit, says "thunderous applause" followed. The *Daily Palo Altan* wrote approvingly that 'Abdu'l-Bahá had "demonstrated the utter senselessness of war and its waste. . . . Speaking quietly in Persian, his expressive features and gestures made the services of his interpreter seem at times almost superfluous." Professor Samuel Swayze Seward, Jr., was present that day and said the students reacted to 'Abdu'l-Bahá "with great respect and interest"; "'Abdu'l-Bahá won them!" Albert Léon Guérard, a French and English professor at Stanford, told several generations of Bahá'í students about his positive impression of 'Abdu'l-Bahá; "I have the greatest respect and sympathy for their [the Bahá'ís'] ideals." While the talk contains elements 'Abdu'l-Bahá had used in many other talks, the combination of the elements was new, as were some of the points he made.[33]

From Assembly Hall, President Jordan gave 'Abdu'l-Bahá a tour of the campus. There, Ernest A. Rogers caught up with 'Abdu'l-Bahá and introduced him to the boys of the Montezuma School, who had walked five miles from their school in the mountains above Los Gatos to the nearest street car line and ridden thirty miles to hear him speak.* Jordan took

* Correspondence and other information from Prof. E. A. Rogers about his visits with 'Abdu'l-Bahá, 1912, typescript, Ella Cooper Papers; historical information about the Montezuma School for Boys is available at http://www.mariposaresearch.net/santaclararesearch/montezuma.html (accessed April 17, 2011).

'Abdu'l-Bahá to Xasmin House—the president's residence—for a rest and lunch. At 4:30pm, Jordan drove him to the house of Mrs. Frederick Marriott, where Isabella C. Merriman, a prominent resident and humanitarian, offered him tea. At 8pm he spoke at the First Unitarian Church of Palo Alto. Inspired by the name of the church, he discoursed on unity.

He began with a common theme—the mineral, plant, animal, and human kingdoms—and how each is progressively superior over the previous and unable to comprehend the capacities of the kingdoms that are higher up. For humans, the Incomprehensible that is higher than they are is God, even though "the qualities of Divinity are evident and can be seen." Such qualities are reflected in the "divine prophets" who "are like mirrors" reflecting the attributes of God perfectly to humanity. 'Abdu'l-Bahá used the analogy of the sun reflecting in perfect mirrors, from which one can feel the sun's heat and see its light perfectly. He added that this was the meaning of the words of Jesus, "Verily, the Father is in the Son."[34]

'Abdu'l-Bahá said that all of humanity receives a portion of the heat and light of the divine Sun; none are Satanic, and all are God's creation. Hence, we must be kind to all. He said, "Some are sick; they must be treated. Some are childlike; they must be helped to reach maturity. Some are asleep; they must be gently awakened. But everyone must be loved. That is it!" Since God is kind to all of us, 'Abdu'l-Bahá reasoned, "then why should we not be kind to one another, instead of saying 'This is a Jew, this is a Christian, the other is a Musselman or Mohammedan, this is a Buddhist.' This is none of our business. God has created us all and it is our duty to be kind to everybody. That is our duty. But as to their respective beliefs, that is between them and their God, and at the last day He will look out for their account. He has not appointed us as their expert accountants."[35]

The mission and purpose of the Prophets has always been to establish unity among the people. Blind imitations and dogmas, always the cause of strife and disunity, must be cast aside. Bahá'u'lláh came at a time when "the Orient was enveloped in the gloom of prejudice and fanaticism" and established "teachings which united all the nations, which caused fellowship among the various religions, which dispelled religious prejudice, which dispelled the political prejudice, which dispelled the patriotic prejudice, and which dispelled the racial prejudice." 'Abdu'l-Bahá quoted Bahá'u'lláh about the oneness of humankind and closed with the exhortation, "Let no sedition tarry. Let no hatred or rancor prevail. All must live in the utmost kindness, in the utmost love, the utmost fellowship. . . . this is our wish in its entirety."[36]

His talk made quite an impression on the audience. Mrs. Percy Martin, wife of a Stanford History professor, said, "He was the most venerable man I ever remember hearing."[37]

After the Unitarian church talk, 'Abdu'l-Bahá returned to the home of Mrs. Marriott for what Mr. H. W. Simkins, editor of the *Palo Altan,* called "an evening of profitable and delightful discussion of the Bahai movement" followed by "a sumptuous dinner at which all the appointments of refinement and good taste pervaded." Professor Samuel Swayze Seward, Jr., found himself seated at 'Abdu'l-Bahá's right hand at dinner and asked him several questions. One was about whether his reception in the United States "was more encouraging than he met with elsewhere":

> I felt in my heart that our reception meant very little, rather an easy curiosity than an eagerness for light, and I wondered whether he would set a higher value on it. To my delight I found that he had anticipated my attitude, and did not set an undue importance upon our good-natured welcome. The only other question escapes me in detail, but I remember that I had a wicked intention of testing his alertness. There was, therefore, a meaning behind a rather innocent remark that I made. When the interpreter passed the question to him

> he paused for a moment thoughtfully, and then looked at me with a shrewd twinkle which I reciprocated; and then he interpreted his twinkle with an understanding comment that showed alertness and humor and grasp. I was delighted, and felt more and more that the restriction of free intercourse prevented what might have been a most interesting give and take, and we established in the shortest time a friendly sense of understanding.[38]

Professor H. D. Gray was also present that evening and was impressed by 'Abdu'l-Bahá; though he did not become a Bahá'í, he told many people about the Faith, including an entire English class that a Bahá'í student was attending. Yazdi notes that eleven years after the event, Gray and Seward "were still enthralled by His charm and humor."[39] David Starr Jordan remained favorably disposed toward the Bahá'í Faith for the rest of his life.

The late dinner was not the end of 'Abdu'l-Bahá's day, however, because after most people left, H. W. Simkins, editor of the *Palo Altan,* remained to talk with 'Abdu'l-Bahá for a long time. Finally it was time for bed, quite a challenge for Mrs. Merriman, who had agreed to put up 'Abdu'l-Bahá and all twenty-nine of his party in Mrs. Marriott's house. As large as it was, she had "to make beds on the tops of tables, put a mattress on the bath tub, and finally had everyone stowed away except herself. Then she found a lean-back chair which she put in a clothes closet, closed the door, and went to 'bed.'"[40] Thus ended what may have been the most extraordinary day in 'Abdu'l-Bahá's North American tour.

The next morning, after some further discussion with inquirers, 'Abdu'l-Bahá returned to San Francisco. That evening he crossed the Bay to speak at the Berkeley High School. His host was the city itself; the mayor being unable to attend, he was warmly introduced by a member of the Board of Education. 'Abdu'l-Bahá's talk focused on the Manifestations of God—Abraham, Moses, Christ, and Muhammad—the eternal problem of people falling in love with one to the exclusion of others, and the need of the "people of truth" to see the light regardless of its dawning-point. He spoke of God's sovereignty, the reality of divinity manifest in all things, and the noblest of humans.

On the morning of October 10, after entertaining visitors at his house, 'Abdu'l-Bahá went to visit Mr. Charles Tinsley, an African American Bahá'í and employee of Phoebe Hearst, who had been unable to visit him because of a broken leg. 'Abdu'l-Bahá assured him that he "will soon recover and be spiritually stronger than ever before."[41]

That evening, even though he was not feeling well, he went to the Open Forum in San Francisco, an organization for the discussion of economic and related subjects. The talk began with a discussion of ways to determine truth. Western philosophers emphasize "the five senses"; Eastern philosophers "such as those of Greece and Persia" focus on "the intellect." 'Abdu'l-Bahá noted that sense perception is not always reliable; he cited mirages and other instances when our senses can fool us. 'Abdu'l-Bahá was indeed noting an important difference between the two philosophies of the day, for philosophy in the Islamic world—extensively utilized in the Bahá'í scriptures—was heavily dependent on metaphysical notions such as the realm of ideas, whereas Western philosophy was increasingly based on science and observation.[42]

Much of 'Abdu'l-Bahá's talk was a critique of the latter approach. The Western approach, as he saw it, had much in common with the worldview of animals, which similarly was based on perception. The animal kingdom "is incapable of discovering a latent mystery of nature, such as electricity, and bringing it from its invisible state to the plane of visibility."[43] The sentence expresses 'Abdu'l-Bahá's notion that electricity already exists in the realm of ideas. Astronomical discoveries and inventions were not based solely on perception but on rational interpretation of sensory information.

'Abdu'l-Bahá then turned to the example of human evolution. He often brought up subjects that people asked him about or that had appeared in the press, so one wonders what prompted the subject. A major paleontological controversy broke out in December 1912, and hints of it appeared in the press a month or so before, though perhaps not as early as October 10. During the summer of 1912, the paleontologist and antiquarian Charles Dawson (1864–1916), assisted by a team that included a young French Jesuit priest and geologist named Teilhard de Chardin (1881–1955), conducted an excavation at Piltdown in southern England, where they found some old bones; they were later exposed as being two fragments of a medieval human skull, an orangutan jawbone, an elephant molar, a hippopotamus tooth, and a fossilized chimpanzee canine tooth. In December, 1912, Dawson announced that he had found the "Piltdown man," a human ancestor half way between humans and apes. The announcement was electrifying because in 1912, no transitional species had been discovered; the only "primitive human" known was the Neanderthal, skeletons of which had been found in Europe. But the Neanderthals were tens of thousands of years old, not hundreds of thousands or millions of years old. There was a palpable gap between modern humans and modern apes, and no "missing links" connecting the species were known.[44]

The Piltdown man was immediately controversial because of its theological implications, the suspicious nature of the fossils, and the dubious geology of the site where they were found. Within a decade, it was exposed as a hoax, and modern tests have determined the origin of the fragments. Subsequently, the story of human evolution has been filled in with dozens of fossils spanning the entire range of time during which the hominid line separated from the various ape lines. Even the term "missing link," popular in the nineteenth and early twentieth centuries, has been replaced by more specific scientific language such as "transitional fossil."[45]

On that evening at the Open Forum, 'Abdu'l-Bahá spoke about human evolution and missing links. He noted that vestigial organs in the human body, such as the coccyx bone that is the remnant of a tail, show that the human body has changed over time. But this does not mean that humans once were animals; "we acknowledge the fact that at one time man was an invertebrate [,] was an inmate of the sea, that at another time he was a four-limbed being, later assuming an upright position, nevertheless we must also believe that in each of those stages there were peculiarities of his human specie [*sic*]." The proof of this is that "animals are captives of nature. All phenomena are captives of nature. They can not deviate one hair's breadth from the laws of nature." Only humans, through their reason, can seize control over nature, discover its mysteries, and harness its powers. "Man" in his marine and invertebrate forms obviously did not have such capabilities, but nevertheless possessed human potential: "the fact that the foetus presented many forms, even that of a worm, is not proof than man was ever animal in specie. The transformation from the form resembling a worm to the comely form of man shows the conservation of the human specie."[46]

In the midst of this argument, 'Abdu'l-Bahá noted, almost as an aside, "the missing link of the Darwinian theory is an evidence that man is not an animal in origin, otherwise the most important link could not be missing, and this link has not yet been found[,] never will be found."[47] Was this meant to be a denial of physical human evolution from the animals, even though 'Abdu'l-Bahá stated humans might have once been a member of the group of creatures called invertebrates? Was it an allusion to the Piltdown man, soon to be announced in the popular press? This is a possibility. Or was it meant to be an assertion that no "missing link" between humans and animals was possible? The latter seems plausible because, according to 'Abdu'l-Bahá, the archetype of humanity (which in Persian is the same word as "specie") is distinct and unique from the archetypes of the animal species.

'Abdu'l-Bahá closed by returning to the issue of sense perception versus rationality. He gave other examples of the power of reason, such as the ability to record sound. Notwithstanding this,

> some of the sagacious men who have attained to a great degree of knowledge in the human world assert that only the tangible is real. In the laboratory of nature they have investigated facts as they are, and have studied sciences and arts, yet they have arrived at the conclusion that only the tangible is a reality worthy of credence and that all else is nonsense and superstition.
>
> How strange it is that men study twenty years in school and college only to reach a point where they accept naught but the tangible and deny the existence of ideal realities! Have you ever stopped to think that the animal has already attained to such a degree of wisdom? Have you ever stopped to think that the cow is already a professor emeritus in such a school of philosophy? Have you ever stopped to think that the cow, without any hard labor or study, is already a philosopher of the superlative degree in the school of nature. Then why should we go to the college? Let us go to cowlege![48]

Maḥmúd says that "everyone burst into laughter" at the conclusion and made jokes about each other being cows afterward. An argument that 'Abdu'l-Bahá had previously delivered in Philadelphia, Dublin, and Green Acre had reached its culmination.

On Friday, October 11, 'Abdu'l-Bahá received a letter from the Middle East mentioning the sadness of the Persian Bahá'í pilgrims who were traveling all the way from Iran to 'Akká to visit to the Shrines of the Báb and Bahá'u'lláh but who weren't able to meet him. The sad news triggered a consultation with Helen Goodall about his West Coast plans and when he should return to the Middle East. 'Abdu'l-Bahá had never ruled out a trip northward to Portland and Seattle, but if he made the trip, his Atlantic crossing would occur in winter when it was cold and stormy, and that might impair his health. As a result of the consultation, he asked Mrs. Goodall to write the Bahá'ís in Washington and Oregon and invite them to come see him in San Francisco, as he did not have the time to travel north.[49] He would travel to Los Angeles, however, to visit the grave of Thornton Chase, the first American Bahá'í, who had died less than two weeks earlier.

In addition to morning interviews in his residence, 'Abdu'l-Bahá strolled Golden Gate Park across the lake from the "Portals of the Past" arch with Dr. Woodson Allen, discussing eternal life and healing. Ten days later at the Allen residence, he talked to three physicians extensively about health. In the evening, he spoke to the Theosophical Society. His introduction began with the unusual assertion of the chairman that "some sixty thousand years ago, when our Aryan race was in its infancy, a great teacher came to the world—a teacher known as the Lord Vyasa." He then noted that Vyasa had been followed by Thoth, Zoroaster, Buddha, Jesus, various lesser teachers, and Bahá'u'lláh. 'Abdu'l-Bahá spoke about progressive revelation—without mentioning Vyasa or Thoth—stressed the immortality of the spirit, and "the universality of the new Revelation." In the question and answer session that followed, he discretely avoided a direct response to a question about his view of reincarnation.[50]

Saturday, October 12 saw yet another of 'Abdu'l-Bahá's most memorable discourses, at Temple Emanu-El at 450 Sutter St.* It appears to be the

---

* Bahá'í sources consistently spell the name of the synagogue as "Emmanu-el" but contemporary newspapers and the synagogue's current website spell it "Emanu-el." I will adopt the latter.

longest talk he delivered in North America. Two thousand were present, mostly Jews, including some Bahá'ís. Ramona Brown recalls that 'Abdu'l-Bahá "stood in the Temple between two lovely palm trees while a shaft of light from a window fell across Him and bathed Him in the morning sunshine." Dr. Martin A. Meyer (1879–1923), the chief rabbi, welcomed 'Abdu'l-Bahá to the synagogue in Arabic—the rabbi had a Ph.D. in Semitic languages and had lived in Jerusalem—led him into the worship space, and warmly welcomed him. His address on the "Fundamental Unity of Religious Thought" began with the observation that "the first bestowal of God to the world of humanity is religion"; that it "confers on man life everlasting" and "has ever helped humanity toward progress." How do we know this? 'Abdu'l-Bahá said, "Let us investigate in search of truth, without being bound by blind imitations or dogmas."[51] This can be accomplished by reviewing the lives of the Prophets.*

'Abdu'l-Bahá started with Abraham and listed the very long line of distinguished descendants that sprang from Him, from Ishmael to Solomon, and their accomplishments. He noted, "All of this was due to the religion which was founded." From such results, we learn that religion is the cause of honor, advancement, civilization, and happiness. Moses appeared when the children of Israel were in the "utmost state of degradation and slavery" and rescued them from bondage. He led them to the land of Israel, where they built a great civilization and "advanced in culture, in the arts and sciences, in philosophy and in craftsmanship." Their progress was so great

* There are at least three or four different versions of this talk. The oldest published form is found in "Message to the Jews" in the November 1, 1912 issue of the *Palo Altan*. Bijou Straun was the stenographer. Various typescripts exist in the Ella Cooper Papers and some of them may preserve older phrasing. An edited version appears in 'Abdu'l-Bahá, *The Promulgation of Universal Peace,* 510–23. A new translation of the Persian transcript of the talk, authorized by the Universal House of Justice, appears in Maḥmúd-i-Zarqání, *Maḥmúd's Diary,* 316–24.

that they attracted the attention of even the Greek philosophers. When the "foundation of the law of God was ignored" by the Jews, they were conquered by the Babylonians and, later, by the Romans.[52]

What do we learn from this? That "the mission of the Prophets is no other than the advancement and education of the world of humanity." 'Abdu'l-Bahá elaborated on the point by noting that some religious teachings provide eternal morality (presumably he had such virtues as kindness, mercy, justice in mind) or metaphysics ("knowledge of God"), while other teachings are temporal social laws, such as those relating to polygamy and divorce. He provided examples of changes in marriage laws from the Book of Genesis and, knowing the Reform nature of his Jewish audience, asked how the traditional enforcements of Jewish laws ("an eye for an eye and a tooth for a tooth") could be carried out in the modern day. "Wise men [even] maintain that capital punishment should be abolished," he noted.[53] His Reform audience would have largely agreed.

Then he asked his audience to "be fair in your judgment," and enumerated similar proofs that Jesus Christ was a divine Messenger. Jesus came when the Jews were at the depths of abasement, just as Moses did; He accepted the revelation of Moses and the Hebrew Bible; and He spread the fame of Moses, and of His teachings, across the world. 'Abdu'l-Bahá said, "Hence Christ promulgated Judaism." He ushered into the community of His followers members of "most of the nations of the East and the West," educated them, and blended them together into a "heavenly civilization."[54]

At this point, one Bahá'í observer noted that "the Rabbi wiped perspiration from his forehead, although the autumn day was not warm." 'Abdu'l-Bahá turned to the story of Muhammad, repeating the same proofs about His mission. He proclaimed the Prophethood of Moses and the truths of the Torah, transformed the barbaric Arabian tribes, and created a religion that built a civilization stretching westward as far as Spain. Then came the challenge: "Has any harm come to Christians and Muslims because they have admitted the validity of Moses? No, on the contrary, their acceptance of Moses and confirmation of the Torah prove that they have been fair-minded. . . . What harm is there if the Jews would say that Christ was the Spirit of God and Muhammad was the Messenger of God?" He noted that as a result "there will be no hatred, no disputation, no warfare and no bloodshed."[55]

'Abdu'l-Bahá, however, was not calling on the Jews to become Christians or, more specifically, Muslims. Religion in the Middle East particularly emphasized the essential role of the Prophet-Founders, and even among early twentieth century liberal Protestants, Jesus had a centrality and importance that made ignoring Him evidence of rational inconsistency. We have already seen how Russell Conwell, the minister at Baptist Temple in Philadelphia, saw "the Baha'i Movement" as "the biggest Movement in the world today for world-wide Christianity" and "saw that millions of Muhammadans, Buddhists, Jews and other orientals have come up beautifully into Christianity through becoming Bahá'ís." This was partly because the Bahá'ís, by accepting Christ, were seen as Christians in some sense. For 'Abdu'l-Bahá, good relations between religious communities—what today we call interfaith dialogue—required recognition of the historical truths of the Prophet-Founders. As he said, "What harm comes from it [accepting Christ and Muhammad]? None at all. Nay rather you are contributing to the welfare of mankind. . . . Nay rather the eternal honor of man depends on this modern liberalism." Rather than tarrying "in our prejudice" and "shunning one another," he said, "is it not better for us to be most loving to one another . . . enjoy fellowship together, unite and sing anthems towards God, and praise all the Prophets in a good and praiseworthy spirit?"[56]

'Abdu'l-Bahá did not elaborate on the possible theological implications of recognizing the historical truths of Jesus and Muhammad and, by implication (because 'Abdu'l-Bahá did not mention Him, except in passing), Bahá'u'lláh. He concluded by referring to Isaiah 65:25, "The wolf and the lamb shall feed together." This, he said, is a prophecy that "is symbolic of the state of affairs when nations and races, symbolized by wolves and sheep, among whom there is a bond of fellowship and association, will be unified and will treat each other kindly and liberally in that promised day":

> In a word, the century is upon us when fellowship is to be established!
>
> The century has come when all the religions are to be at peace with each other!
>
> The century has come when all the nations shall become one nation!
>
> The century has come when all mankind shall live under the tabernacle of the oneness of mankind.[57]

Maḥmúd admits that not everyone was pleased; "after His talk, many humbly came to see Him to express their gratitude, except for a few narrow-minded ones who turned their heads away and left in scorn." 'Abdu'l-Bahá's talk was not the sort of interfaith dialogue that some members of the Jewish community expected. But overall, the reaction was much milder than a month later, when 'Abdu'l-Bahá gave a similar talk to the Washington Hebrew Congregation. Possibly Dr. Meyer's training in Semitics and his time in the Holy Land were a factor. It is also possible that Rabbi Meyer had already preached a Jewish view of Jesus. American reform rabbis had been revising their approach to Jesus for decades; the founder of American Reform Judaism, Isaac Mayer Wise (1819–1900), had published articles about Jesus as a great Pharisaic teacher as early as 1869. By the 1890s, several books about Jesus had been published by Reform Jews. By 1899, many Reform rabbis were praising Jesus as "the gentlest and noblest rabbi of all." In 1900, Stephen Wise (1874–1949; no relation to Isaac Mayer Wise) supported a campaign to introduce classes about Jesus the Jew into Sabbath schools. Perhaps the most prominent early twentieth century Reform rabbi in the United States, Stephen Wise often preached about Jesus from a Jewish perspective in liberal Protestant churches. Such sermons, however, emphasized Jesus's Jewishness, stripped away Christian dogmatism, and used Jesus's high ethics to condemn anti-Semitism.[58] Rabbis rarely preached about Jesus in their synagogues.

It is possible Rabbi Meyer already had a liberal, accommodating view of Jesus when 'Abdu'l-Bahá spoke at his synagogue. Five years younger than Stephen Wise, Meyer had been strongly influenced by Wise when both had been rabbis in New York City, and they remained in close correspondence. Wise in turn "greatly liked and admired" Meyer.[59] Like Wise, Meyer preached in churches; in 1910, Meyer had delivered the Sunday sermon at First Congregational church, located diagonally across the street from Temple Emanu-El. The synagogue started a joint Thanksgiving service with them in November, 1911 (which was actually the outgrowth of an earlier joint Thanksgiving service with the other synagogues in the city). When the Congregational Church needed a larger building and resolved to tear down its existing building to rebuild on the spot, Rabbi Meyer invited them to worship in the synagogue on Sundays, and for a period of nine months, they did so. The two congregations continued to alternate Thanksgiving services; the synagogue has continued to participate in such a service up to the present day. Many Bahá'ís have stated that 'Abdu'l-Bahá's talk initiated interfaith cooperation in San Francisco, but the talk represented a chapter in such efforts, which probably can be traced back in rudimentary form to the founding of Temple Emanu-El in the gold rush days of 1850.*

---

* Temple Emanu-el's archivist, Paula Freedman, supplied the author with a pdf of the program of the eighth annual joint Thanksgiving Service of the First Congregational Church and the Congregation Temple Emanu-El, held at Temple Emanu-

On Saturday afternoon, 'Abdu'l-Bahá returned to Helen Goodall's Oakland residence and said how pleased he was by the results of the synagogue talk. "From the beginning of Christianity and Islam up to the present day, no one has spoken thus, proving the validity of Christ and Muhammad in a Jewish temple and in a manner to which no one took exception," he said to the people present. "Rather, most were appreciative and content. This is none other than the power of Bahá'u'lláh." He went upstairs for a rest, then came back downstairs to greet Bahá'í children, almost thirty in number, who sang for him the hymn "Softly His Voice is Calling Now." 'Abdu'l-Bahá spoke to them, gave them candy and flowers, and showered them with his love. A group photograph was taken. Then he went for a walk, where he encountered some Indian students, who walked and talked with him.[60]

'Abdu'l-Bahá had not yet visited a settlement house or school, as he had done in London, Paris, New York, Chicago, Washington, and Boston. On Sunday afternoon, October 13, he went to the Reading Room of the Blind, 1665 Jackson St., San Francisco, which was a vocational training and braille literacy center. Children and youth from the State Educational Institution in Berkeley and the blind at the Adult Home in Oakland came to hear him. 'Abdu'l-Bahá spoke about how, in receiving education, the blind were endued with sight and contrasted the eternal advantages of spiritual insight with the temporal advantages of physical sight.[61]

El on November 28, 1918; this indicates that the first service was November 1911. Hatch, "'Abdu'l-Bahá and the Rabbi," 110, describes the Congregationalists' use of the synagogue while replacing their building and 'Abdu'l-Bahá's pleasure to hear about the interfaith cooperation it indicated. Information about other Thanksgiving services and the rabbi's sermon in the Congregational church is contained in an e-mail from Paula Freeman to the author, April 13, 2011.

Ramona Brown was at 'Abdu'l-Bahá's residence on Monday, October 14, when Phoebe Hearst arrived in a black limousine to escort 'Abdu'l-Bahá to her 1400-acre estate, the Hacienda del Pozo de Verona in Pleasanton. He remained two nights and returned to San Francisco on the morning of Wednesday, October 16. It was a quiet, intimate visit that included members of the Hearst family, a few family friends, and several members of 'Abdu'l-Bahá's entourage. They took pleasant walks among the estate's many gardens and automobile rides through the countryside. 'Abdu'l-Bahá gave short talks and told amusing stories that were "brief but full of wisdom," and the Americans sang around the piano. At one meal, 'Abdu'l-Bahá chanted a prayer. The guests asked each other about the Bahá'í Faith, but 'Abdu'l-Bahá did not discuss it directly until Phoebe Hearst asked him to do so on the last evening. She then described her experience going on pilgrimage in 1898 to meet him and visit the Bahá'í shrines. William Randolph Hearst, the famous newspaper publisher and son of Phoebe Hearst, apparently was present—his children were there—and possibly because of Randolph's political ambitions, one evening 'Abdu'l-Bahá spoke about the humility and selflessness that ideally should characterize the President of the United States.[62]

On his last day at the Hacienda, 'Abdu'l-Bahá requested to meet the estate's servants. He spoke to them briefly and gave all of them a generous tip for their services, to the astonishment of the other guests. On the ride back to San Francisco, 'Abdu'l-Bahá had a conversation with Phoebe Hearst about the difficulties she had previously had with Bahá'ís who had asked her for money. He told her that "if you should see a man coveting property and evincing greed toward the wealth of others, know that he is not of the people of Baha."[63]

The comment, meant to assure her that greedy Bahá'ís were rare exceptions, also proved to be a prescient warning. The next day, 'Abdu'l-Bahá discovered that his seal was missing. He had used the seal on all his letters; subsequently, he began to sign them "abdul Baha abbas" in the Roman alphabet, the only capital letter being in the name of his father, to denote his servitude to Bahá'u'lláh. Shortly thereafter, Phoebe Hearst received a letter purportedly from 'Abdu'l-Bahá, asking her to give him a sum of money. She saw through the fake letter—he had repeatedly said during the trip that he would not accept any money from anyone—and did not give anything. The forger was 'Abdu'l-Bahá's wife's nephew, Ameen Fareed, who had committed a similar indiscretion earlier on the East Coast. It was the second strike against him. Fareed's conduct brought so much sadness to 'Abdu'l-Bahá that at times he visibly trembled with rage. When 'Abdu'l-Bahá left Europe for Egypt in 1913, Fareed committed a third act of disobedience, and 'Abdu'l-Bahá expelled him from the Bahá'í Faith.[64]

Hours after returning from the Hearst residence, 'Abdu'l-Bahá spoke at the Century Club on equality of men and women. It was his last talk in a public venue in the Bay area, even though he spent six more days there. It is not known whether he turned down any additional invitations, but he often did toward the end of his stay so that he could spend more time with the Bahá'ís. The rest of his visit was devoted to consolidation. The Portland Bahá'ís having arrived, he spent some time with them. That evening he went to the Goodall house in Oakland for the Bahá'í Nineteen-day Feast, which was attended by 125 people. 'Abdu'l-Bahá spoke, and everyone ate a meal. All the rooms of the first floor had been filled with tables that were adorned with yellow chrysanthemums and pyramids of fruit. 'Abdu'l-Bahá walked among the gathered people, speaking to them as they ate, then pronounced a benediction on all.[65]

The next day—Thursday, October 17—he remained at his residence and met many individuals, including the Bahá'ís who had arrived from Portland, Seattle, Tacoma, and Spokane. They were heartbroken he couldn't visit, but he apologized: "I am very much ashamed because it was my part to go there and see them. But what could I have done? I did not have the time." He still planned, however, to make a very short trip to Los Angeles to visit the grave of Thornton Chase.[66]

In the afternoon, 'Abdu'l-Bahá met with Ella Cooper's "Peaches," a group of young women, most of whom were Bahá'ís, who met regularly to discuss spiritual subjects. The Bay area was one of the few places in North America with a Bahá'í youth group. 'Abdu'l-Bahá instructed them how to teach the Faith, offering them six "implements" that the gardeners of God needed to sow seeds and reap harvests: severance and detachment from the things of this world; love of God; knowledge of God; endeavor; praiseworthy attributes; and eloquence. Ramona Brown was moved and prayed that her friends present who were not confirmed Bahá'ís would dedicate their lives to the Bahá'í teachings. She was also moved to speak to other friends about 'Abdu'l-Bahá. One of them was Joseph Grandin Bray, who expressed acceptance of 'Abdu'l-Bahá and his teachings, to her astonishment. He became an active Bahá'í and, in 1916, her husband.[67]

Los Angeles, October 18–20, 1912

Before leaving for Los Angeles on Friday, 'Abdu'l-Bahá met with the Portland and Seattle Bahá'ís once again. A Los Angeles Bahá'í, Alec Frankland, was telegraphed and asked to reserve hotel rooms for the entire party. Mrs. Goodall arrived with her car to drive him and his party to the train station for the ride to Los Angeles, and he insisted that she come along, which she did "most happily," though "without even a comb or brush by way of preparation."[68] The long train ride culminated with his arrival at Los Angeles' Lankershim Hotel in the early evening. After consultation about the next day, every Bahá'í from Bakersfield to San Diego was telephoned to come and meet him. Clergy asked him to speak from their pulpits, but he turned down all invitations because he could stay only two days.

Saturday morning, October 19, after speaking to the Bahá'ís, 'Abdu'l-Bahá boarded a street car with his entourage and twenty-five local Bahá'ís and rode to Thornton Chase's grave in Inglewood, a city in the South Bay area of greater Los Angeles, eleven miles from downtown. 'Abdu'l-Bahá had eulogized Thornton Chase (1847–1912) on October 4, not long after arriving in San Francisco: "This revered personage was the first Bahai in America. He served the Cause faithfully and his services will ever be remembered throughout future ages and cycles. . . . Praise be to God! The tree of Mr. Chase's life brought forth fruit. It gave complete fruit, therefore he is free. He attained to eternal rest."[69]

Chase's significance was also underlined by the fact 'Abdu'l-Bahá traveled hundreds of miles to visit his grave. When the streetcar reached the cemetery, 'Abdu'l-Bahá led the Bahá'ís directly to the grave, where he took the flowers everyone had brought and placed them on the grave with great love and affection. He stood at the head of the grave, raised his hands to heaven, and chanted a prayer for Chase, then gave a short talk about his significance. At various times in San Francisco and Los Angeles, he told the Bahá'ís to visit the grave annually "to pray and have a meeting there" and to give "a feast to the poor" and give charity annually in his name.* Thus 'Abdu'l-Bahá gave the West Coast Bahá'ís an annual observance in Inglewood, California, just as he had given the East Coast Bahá'ís an annual Unity Feast in Englewood, New Jersey.[70]

He returned to a hotel filled with a "multitude" of people waiting to see him. He met with reporters—at least three newspaper articles resulted—and spoke briefly to the Bahá'ís at 4pm. "I came especially to see you," he began, "that I might know how you are, that I might inquire about your health and your faith, and ascertain whether you are engaged in the service of the kingdom of God." He hoped that great results would come out of

* For a lengthier description of 'Abdu'l-Bahá's visit to Chase's grave, see Stockman, *Thornton Chase: First American Bahá'í*, 261–62.

his meetings with them. He said that "the believers must be confirmed in the covenant" and there was "no greater necessity"; "that which issues from the Center of the Covenant is the truth, which is unchangeable; and that which issues from his pen is true and everlasting." It was his first exposition in California about his station as the Center of the Covenant. It may have been prompted by efforts by Shua Ullah Behai, His nephew and the leading Covenant-breaker in the United States, who lived in Pasadena. Articles had recently appeared about him in two San Francisco newspapers.[71]

'Abdu'l-Bahá spoke at a public meeting at the hotel that night, at the conclusion of which he was "so exhausted He could not even take supper." The next morning he went on an excursion to the Busch Gardens in Pasadena, then returned to the hotel to speak at least four times to the crowd that came to hear him. The first talk was about "the purpose of being a Bahai" and he spoke at length about firmness in the Covenant. He warned that "unless the Bahais remain firm great injury will befall the Cause, even as the other religions have become divided into numerous sects and denominations" and noted that Bahá'u'lláh had "provided against such a possibility by appointing a center of the covenant." Later in the afternoon he again spoke about Thornton Chase. 'Abdu'l-Bahá and party left the hotel at 5pm and took an overnight train back to San Francisco.[72]

Consolidation in San Francisco, October 21–25, 1912

With his return on Monday morning, October 21, 'Abdu'l-Bahá had only four full days left in the Bay area; he departed Friday morning, October 25. The four days were focused on the Bahá'ís and further strengthening their devotion and faith; 'Abdu'l-Bahá gave no talks in public places. On the evening of October 22, according to Frances Allen, 'Abdu'l-Bahá spoke about Bahá'u'lláh's two years in solitude in Kurdistan, then at the end of the account "Abdul-Baha arose and, in no uncertain terms, declared himself to be the CENTER OF THE COVENANT; and exhorted all believers to firmness, calling upon them to spread the message of the Kingdom both by deed and word." The transcript of his talk that evening includes 'Abdu'l-Bahá's words about Bahá'u'lláh's Book of the Covenant where "he appoints a center of the covenant, who is to be the expounder of the books and the judge between the false and the true." 'Abdu'l-Bahá also mentioned that Bahá'u'lláh "has commanded the organization of a universal house of justice, which shall have the power to legislate regarding all questions not elucidated in the books, and the decisions of this body are to be accepted as the law. Hence there should be no excuse for dissentions among you." This is quite an exact summary of the legislative authority of the Universal House of Justice as described in His Will and Testament. The talk does not mention the appointment of a Guardian who would interpret the sacred Bahá'í writings. This follows the pattern in 'Abdu'l-Bahá's earlier talks, where he is silent about the Guardianship, probably to protect his future successor, then fifteen years old, from scrutiny.[73]

Frances Allen's daughter, Ramona Brown, reports a similar incident two nights later, on October 24, when 'Abdu'l-Bahá talked about Bahá'u'lláh's life, His declaration of His mission in the garden of Riḍván in April 1863, His exposition of principles of His revelation, and His establishment of a Covenant to safeguard the unity of His Faith. "Suddenly, the atmosphere of the room became electrified," Brown recalls,

> 'Abdu'l-Bahá rose majestically from His chair and in a powerful voice declared "I am the Center of that Covenant! I am the Center of the Covenant!" The friends stood up. They seemed stunned by this great announcement and filled with indescribable emotion. Wonder, joy, and happiness showed on their faces. . . . Several moments passed before 'Abdu'l-Bahá spoke again. Then, looking at each one, almost pleading, He asked those who believed to spread the Teachings, to be firm and steadfast, to teach not by words alone but by deeds. He said

"These wonderful days are passing swiftly; and once gone, they will never come again."[74]

Brown recalls many other incidents that occurred in the last four days of 'Abdu'l-Bahá's visit to the Bay area: a private interview her mother had with 'Abdu'l-Bahá on October 21; another meeting of Ella Cooper's "Peaches"—including Ramona's friend, the new Bahá'í Joseph Bray—with 'Abdu'l-Bahá; a dinner 'Abdu'l-Bahá had at the Allen residence on October 21; a meeting 'Abdu'l-Bahá had with Ramona and two friends, where he talked to them about teaching the Faith; and another meeting of 'Abdu'l-Bahá with the Bahá'ís of Seattle. 'Abdu'l-Bahá also met privately again with the Japanese poet Takeshi Kanno. He encouraged the Bahá'ís to be very kind to his wife, Gertrude Boyle, because "she has been persecuted for marrying a Japanese. It is well to become the wife of a Japanese. This is a bond, uniting the East and the West."[75]

'Abdu'l-Bahá arranged meetings as well; he telegrammed Ernest A. Rogers to come from Los Gatos on October 22 and bring his mother to meet 'Abdu'l-Bahá, which Rogers did. Allen notes that Wednesday and Thursday "went all too quickly . . . the friends spent as much time as possible at the house of Abdul-Baha, realizing that the days of great privilege were swiftly passing."[76]

The sad departure came 8am Friday morning at 'Abdu'l-Bahá's house. "I do not know how to express my sadness at parting," 'Abdu'l-Bahá said. "It grieves me excessively to leave you and I have sensed the fragrance of the love of Baha'o'llah from you . . . Although I am going away from you and a separation seemingly takes place, nevertheless you are in my heart. . . . When I reach the Holy Tomb, there I shall lay my head at His Threshold, supplicating, invoking, seeking for each and all of you confirmation and assistance."[77]

A crowd of Bahá'ís awaited at the Oakland railroad station to say goodbye. 'Abdu'l-Bahá and his party arrived by ferry and got on board the train. Helen Goodall, Ella Cooper, Bijou Straun, and a few others had requested to accompany him as far as Sacramento, prompting Ramona Brown and a few others spontaneously to do the same.

Sacramento, October 25–26, 1912

Sacramento was on the train route back to Colorado and Chicago, but it is not clear how 'Abdu'l-Bahá received an invitation to speak there. Christine Fraser, the forty-eight-year-old operator of a "Home of Truth," the local branch of a chain of New Thought healing centers, invited him to her "home" for a luncheon. Ella Cooper accepted the invitation on 'Abdu'l-Bahá's behalf and failed to inform him, which caused him considerable distress. Fraser was prominent in the "Home of Truth" movement, which was very open to other religions and philosophies; Swami Vivekananda had stayed and spoken at the Los Angeles, San Francisco, and Alameda Homes of Truth in 1899–1900. She met the party at the Central Pacific Arcade Station about noon and took 'Abdu'l-Bahá, his interpreter, and Bijou Straun to her home; most of the rest of the party went to the Hotel Sacramento, presumably to register and finalize plans for a series of meetings there. 'Abdu'l-Bahá was the guest of honor and spoke at a luncheon with dozens of local New Thought sympathizers. When Ella Cooper arrived, he asked her advice, as Mrs. Fraser was urging him to spend the night there. He declined and invited Fraser to come to the hotel that evening to share the stage with him. Later he admonished Cooper for failing to tell him about the luncheon. She wept and said that she had failed in her service to him.[78]

That evening, at 8:30pm, 'Abdu'l-Bahá gave a public address at the Assembly Hall of the Hotel Sacramento about the basics of the Bahá'í Faith, with Christine Fraser introducing him. He began by briefly describing the mission and early followers of Christ and their impact on the world, then turned to the lives of the Báb and Bahá'u'lláh. His review of the "teachings of Bahá'u'lláh" covered seven principles: the investigation of reality; the oneness of humanity; the elimination of prejudice in order to establish world peace; the purpose of religion as a cause of love, fellowship, and unity rather than enmity and strife; the conformity of religion with science and reason; the equality of men and women; and the incompleteness of material civilization without divine civilization. The talk was followed by a smaller, more informal talk at 9:15pm about the development of humanity and the need for divine education from the Manifestations of God.[79]

On Saturday morning, October 26, 'Abdu'l-Bahá met with various individuals, took a drive around the city, walked the beautiful parklike grounds of the Capitol, and gave a final talk in the hotel's assembly hall. The talk was on "the issue of paramount importance in the world today": international peace. He again reiterated that "the European continent is like an arsenal, a storehouse of explosives ready for ignition, and one spark will set the whole of Europe aflame, particularly at this time when the Balkan question is before the world." He added, "Inasmuch as the Californians seem to be so peace-loving and possessed of great worth and capacity, I hope that peace advocates among them will daily increase in numbers, until the whole population stands for peace. May the men of affairs in this democracy uphold the standard of peace. Then may altruistic thoughts radiate from this center towards all other regions of the earth, and may this glory exist forever for this country. May the first flag of international peace be upraised in this state." Several generations of California Bahá'ís have meditated on this passage. As Ramona Brown notes, "I heard 'Abdu'l-Bahá utter these words in Sacramento in 1912. Imagine my great happiness when I had the special good fortune to be present in the audience at the Conference of the United Nations on June 26, 1945, in San Francisco! . . . After addresses were made by several important statesmen, the time came for the signing of the Charter. Then, in the most thrilling moment of the conference, a flag was brought onto the stage: the flag of the United Nations. To my great astonishment I saw the fulfillment of prophecy."[80]

When the talk ended, the time to leave the hotel and board trains—'Abdu'l-Bahá to the east, the American Bahá'ís to the west—had come. There was one last round of tearful farewells as many wondered whether they would ever see their Master again on this earthly plane. Many of the Americans must have wondered, also, what endeavors lay ahead of them, because 'Abdu'l-Bahá had issued a challenge to them on October 22: "Praise be to God, the call of the kingdom has been raised in America through the grace and favor of Baha'o'llah. . . . Many souls have heard the blessed name. In short, by the grace and favor of the Blessed Perfection [Bahá'u'lláh], and the confirmations of His Kingdom, seeds have been sown. If they are now watered and cared for by the friends of God and the maid-servants of the Merciful, they will without doubt yield a tremendous harvest."[81]

'Abdu'l-Bahá had helped thousands of members of the public to become aware of the Bahá'í Faith, had stimulated hundreds of those who were aware to become interested, had moved dozens of the interested to investigate, had brought a handful of investigators into the circle of believers, and had inspired many of the believers to dedicate their lives to the Faith of Bahá'u'lláh. Furthermore, many of those who had become interested were in influential positions to implement, in small ways, aspects of the Bahá'í teachings in California society. It fell on the shoulders of the small band of California Bahá'ís to bring everyone to the next step.

11

FROM SACRAMENTO TO THE *CELTIC*

When 'Abdu'l-Bahá left Sacramento on the afternoon of October 26, 1912, he had just forty days remaining in his North American sojourn. In a little over two weeks, he rode three thousand miles east by train, stopping in five cities (Denver, Chicago, Cincinnati, Washington, and Baltimore). Two—Cincinnati and Baltimore—were new destinations, with Bahá'í communities who yearned to meet him. His final three-and-a-half weeks were spent wrapping up matters in New York and booking his voyage on the *Celtic* to Liverpool.

The two-and-a-half day train ride to Denver was nearly as busy as the days in San Francisco. Some of the train crew recognized 'Abdu'l-Bahá from his previous trip out of Salt Lake City. There were a large number of Turks on board, heading home to join the war against the Greeks, Serbs, and Bulgarians; 'Abdu'l-Bahá spoke to them in Turkish and ordered them tea and soup. He bought trinkets for some children. Many passengers recognized him, and soon he was speaking to small groups about spiritual matters; one lady apparently became a Bahá'í. Because Mrs. Goodall insisted on purchasing Pullman berths for the entire party, they rested well the first night; on the second night, they slept in their seats. As the clock on Tuesday, October 29 passed midnight, the train approached Denver. They had already informed the Bahá'ís of that city that they would visit for twenty-four hours. They spent the night in the Oxford Hotel, which was very close to the train station.[1]

Bahá'ís, inquirers, and reporters arrived the next morning. At least three newspaper articles resulted from the visit. In the afternoon, 'Abdu'l-Bahá went to Mrs. Sidney E. Roberts' house to give a talk; in the evening, he spoke at the Universalist Church of the Messiah. As he left the church, people pleaded with him to stay longer, but he apologized that he could not. 'Abdu'l-Bahá and his entourage returned to the hotel, packed, and caught the midnight train for Chicago. They slept in their seats that night, had many conversations with passengers the next day, and took Pullman accommodations the night after.[2]

Chicago, October 31–November 4, 1912

The train reached Chicago about dawn on Thursday, October 31, where he remained five days. The length of his last stay in the Windy City underlines the importance of the Bahá'í community there and his concern to solidify their faith.

'Abdu'l-Bahá made three public appearances. On Saturday, November 2, he spoke at the Frederick Douglass Center, 3032 South Wabash, a settlement house patterned after Hull House that served the city's African American population. Fannie Barrier Williams (1855–1944) played a central role in its development; she was a member of the N.A.A.C.P., a friend of Jane Addams, and a member of Jenkin Lloyd Jones' All Souls Unitarian Church. She could have met 'Abdu'l-Bahá or heard of him through any of the three. He gave an "impressive talk" about "love and brotherhood among the different races and nationalities," adding that "if a believer in God prays for piety, it does not matter whether he is robed in black or white."[3]

On Sunday, November 3, 'Abdu'l-Bahá spoke at two churches. In the morning, he addressed Pilgrim Congregational Church about "the appearance of the Manifestation of God, the veils and opposition of the people, the Tablets of Bahá'u'lláh to the kings, and the influence of the Cause of God among the people." He addressed Plymouth Congregational Church at 4pm. He had spoken at the church in May. His address, titled "Universal Peace," focused on "the greatness of this age, the necessity of achieving the oneness of humanity, universal peace," and "the oneness of creation." It concluded with "explanations of the teachings of Bahá'u'lláh." The talk was well-received; he was surrounded by a crowd as he left the church, and many came to Reverend Joseph A. Milburn's house afterward to meet him.[4]

At least one prominent person met 'Abdu'l-Bahá during his last stay in Chicago: Rabindranath Tagore, a prominent Indian author who would win the 1913 Nobel Prize in Literature, the first non-European to do so. Tagore arrived in New York City on October 28, 1912 and went to Champaign-Urbana, Illinois, with his son Rathindranath, who was studying at the University of Illinois for a Ph.D. in agriculture. Apparently they were in Chicago either October 30, 31, or November 1. In May, 'Abdu'l-Bahá had met a group of Indian students studying at the University of Chicago, so possibly the Tagores made contact with them and heard of 'Abdu'l-Bahá; or possibly Tagore coincidentally was staying in the Hotel Plaza and met 'Abdu'l-Bahá accidentally. In 1937 or 1938, Tagore explained to Martha Root, an American Bahá'í visiting India, that "He was staying in an hotel; He was talking to His followers who gathered around Him and I, too, spoke with Him." He expressed "deep love and appreciation of 'Abdu'l-Bahá," who invited Tagore to visit him in Palestine. It is reported that Tagore changed his manner of dress in order to copy 'Abdu'l-Bahá's clothing.[5]

The principal reason for 'Abdu'l-Bahá's visit, however, was to deepen the Chicago Bahá'í community in the Covenant and strengthen them against

Covenant-breaking. He spent much of his time with the Bahá'ís, speaking with many individuals and families and enjoying informal occasions, such as a stroll through the Lincoln Park Zoo near his hotel. But he was frank and direct in his talks to the Bahá'ís. His first talk to them, on October 31 at the Plaza Hotel, confronted the issue directly:

> The friends in Los Angeles and San Francisco are very firm in the Covenant. If they sense the least violation on the part of anyone, they shun him entirely; for they know that such a person is engaged in extinguishing the lamps of faith . . . For instance, the firm ones teach a person. Then the violators go to him and instill suspicion until he becomes lukewarm. There have been violators here in Chicago for twenty years. What have they done? Nothing. Have they been able to teach anybody? Have they been able to speak in churches or address audiences elsewhere? Have they been able to make anybody firm in the Cause? They are doing nothing except extinguishing the lamps we ignite. The friends in San Francisco are exceedingly firm. They do not receive violators in their homes. Recently a violator went to that city. The Bahá'í friends turned him away, saying, "You are not with us; why do you try to come among us?" Today the most important principle of faith is firmness in the Covenant, because firmness in the Covenant wards off differences.[6]

The numbers of Covenant-breakers had indeed dwindled. Ibrahim Kheiralla's movement had shrunk from about three hundred in 1900 to perhaps a handful in 1912. Shua Ullah Behai was not working with Kheiralla but competing with him for attention and is not known to have had any followers. The Kenosha "Behaists," numbering perhaps twenty or thirty, were the only functioning community and was independent of both men, though in touch with both. Their main efforts focused on recruiting new followers from among the Bahá'ís because the non-Bahá'í public was not particularly attracted by discussions about disputes with 'Abdu'l-Bahá. For this reason, telling the Bahá'ís not to associate with the Covenant-breakers was a highly effective strategy.[7]

'Abdu'l-Bahá offered a historical comparison with Christianity, noting the many sects and divisions in that religion: "If Christ had revealed a Covenant with some soul, commanding all to cling to his word and interpretation as correct, it would have been evident which belief and statement was valid and true."[8] Bahá'u'lláh had done exactly that:

> To ward off such dissensions as these and prevent any person from creating a division or sect the Blessed Perfection, Bahá'u'lláh, appointed a central authoritative Personage, declaring Him to be the expounder of the Book. . . . Bahá'u'lláh said, "He is the explainer of My Book and the Center of My Testament." In the last verses of the Book instructions are revealed, declaring that, "After Me," you must turn toward a special Personage and "whatsoever He says is correct." In the Book of the Covenant Bahá'u'lláh declares that by these two verses this Personage ['Abdu'l-Bahá] is meant. In all His Books and Tablets He has praised those who are firm in the Covenant and rebuked those who are not. . . . Bahá'u'lláh has not left any possible room for dissension. . . . Notwithstanding this safeguard and provision against disagreement, there are certain souls here in America and a few in Akká who have violated this explicit command. For twenty years these violators have accomplished nothing. Have they accomplished anything in Chicago? The friends here must be like the friends in San Francisco. Whenever they sense the least violation from anyone, they should say, "Begone! You shall not associate with us."[9]

The next night, 'Abdu'l-Bahá gave a similar talk at Corinne True's house. He began by talking about Bahá'u'lláh's imprisonment and sufferings for His teachings. 'Abdu'l-Bahá expressed his happiness because "your hearts are filled with the love of God, you are thinking of service in the Cause of God." He spoke about the "attracted friends" he had met in San Francisco and Los Angeles and hoped "that the fire of the love of God may be so enkindled in Chicago that all the cities of America shall be ignited." This was the reason for his visit: "This is my third visit to you here and this in itself expresses the degree of my longing to see you and the extent of my love for you. It was thought that I should go from San Francisco to the Orient going directly to New York, but out of excessive love for you all here, during my second visit I passed through here and in my third journey I have sojourned in Chicago in order to visit with you and to associate with you in good fellowship. I hope that these three visits of mine may be most productive in the future."[10]

'Abdu'l-Bahá spoke about the devotion of the Bahá'ís in Iran and how many of them had been martyred for the Faith, sometimes horribly, and how they never responded to their persecution with violence. They were thrilled to hear of the spread of the Faith in the West; they "look forward to hearing that the friends of the West are in the utmost state of firmness and steadfastness; that the friends of the West are distinguished in founding the oneness of the world of humanity; the friends of the West are even offering their lives for the establishment of International Peace." "There are no waverers in the East," he added, "there are none who oppose the Covenant of God." He suggested they ask Dr. Susan Moody, a Chicago Bahá'í physician residing in Tehran about this; Covenant-breaking in Iran "is confined to three persons." Whenever anyone claimed to speak in Iran with any authority about something, the Persian Bahá'ís knew to ask whether 'Abdu'l-Bahá endorsed the ideas or gave him permission to travel and teach.[11]

'Abdu'l-Bahá reiterated the history of Christianity. Jesus had not appointed a "Center"; He had called Peter a "rock," but this was a sanction of Peter's faith and did not give Peter any authority to command obedience or expel anyone from Christianity who created disunity. As a result, Christianity acquired sects and denominations, "each one claiming to be the right one, and none of them had any written document from Christ." But Bahá'u'lláh "with His own pen, has written a Covenant and Testament in which He declares Himself, covenanting that the one who is the Center of the Covenant is the one to be turned to."[12] 'Abdu'l-Bahá continued:

> The purpose of the Covenant was simply to ward off differences, so no one can say, "My opinion is the valid one." Any opinion expressed by the Center of the Covenant is correct, and there is no way for disobedience for anyone. You must be very careful, perchance amongst you may be those who will be nakazeen, the violators of the Covenant. Do not listen to them. Read the Book of the Covenant. All have been commanded to obey the Covenant, each and all . . . You must turn to the Center—He is the Expounder of the Book. Should any soul so clearly disobey the Command, can he even say he is a Bahai? If anyone should have disobeyed the explicit Command of Christ, could he truthfully have said that he was a Christian? Impossible![13]

He closed by commending the Chicago Bahá'ís and reminding them they should be grateful for having been "chosen" for "endless graces and favors." "I am hopeful that after I leave here I shall ever hear good news from you," he said, "showing that the friends in Chicago are occupied with the services of the Cause, are occupied with the joy of promoting the Word of God . . . are kind to all people and they exhibit the utmost love impartially to all humanity. This is the one hope that I have."[14]

His talk both inspired the Chicago Bahá'ís and soberly warned them. The next evening—Saturday—after his talk at the Frederick Douglass Center, he met with the members of the Chicago "Spiritual Meeting," the city's Bahá'í governing body, also known as the House of Spirituality. He spoke to them about the "duties of a board of consultation":

> The first duty of the members is to be in harmony and unity among themselves, for this will bear good results. . . . If Assemblies of consultation or the general meetings of the friends become the cause of ill feelings, they must be abandoned. . . . when the unity of the members has been achieved, their second duty is to recite verses and prayers in a state of contriteness and spiritual awareness . . . Third, their thoughts and discussions must be directed to the teaching of the Cause of God in all areas and regions. They must arise with all their strength for this great matter and make the necessary arrangements and prepare for the teaching of the Cause.
>
> Fourth, they must be occupied and concerned with rendering help to the poor, the needy and the sick.
>
> Fifth, they must improve and administer the affairs of the believers and other matters.[15]

'Abdu'l-Bahá's reference to "general meetings" prompted the question whether the Chicago Bahá'ís should give up their Sunday evening meeting, because the Covenant-breakers always attended, sat in a corner, and observed who came. 'Abdu'l-Bahá said the Assembly could write a letter to them saying, "You are not with us. Why do you come? Do we come to your place? Do you see us coming to your houses? So, if you are not with us, why do you trouble yourselves and trouble us?" But if that didn't work, he advised that it would be better to give up the Sunday evening worship.[16] Such an action, however, created another risk: if the Covenant-breaking group organized regular meetings of their own, their meetings would fill a vacuum.

On Sunday evening, after speaking in the two churches, 'Abdu'l-Bahá attended the Nineteen-day Feast at the house of Mrs. Davies. It was his opportunity to say good-bye to the Chicago Bahá'í community for the last time; he was departing the city the next morning. To a small group, he spoke about the Universal House of Justice to be formed in the future and the unity it would bring. In his farewell address, he warned about superstitions and imitations destroying "the edifice of human prosperity" and conflicting "with the religion of God." "It is not possible to describe the impact on the minds, the exhilaration of the spirits and the delight of the souls," noted Maḥmúd. "When His automobile left, everyone wept and expressed their sorrow at their separation from their beloved." The weeping was repeated the next morning at the train station when 'Abdu'l-Bahá left Chicago for the last time, bound for Cincinnati.[17]

Cincinnati, October 4–5, 1912

Before leaving Chicago, 'Abdu'l-Bahá sent a telegram saying he could stay in Cincinnati only one night. He arrived that evening—Monday, November 4—two or three hours before an 8pm public meeting at the Grand Hotel, attended by five hundred people.* He spoke about "the sovereignty and endless bounties of God" and concluded with "explanations of the teachings of Bahá'u'lláh from the holy writings." From the meeting, 'Abdu'l-Bahá went to a banquet for him, his entourage, and the Cincinnati

* He probably took the Pennsylvania Railroad, leaving Chicago at 9:15am and passing through Logansport, Kokomo, Anderson, and Richmond, arriving in Cincinnati at 5:15pm.

Bahá'ís, a party of fifty altogether. He spoke to them and had informal conversations with individuals and groups late into the night. Not wanting to lose any time with their Master, forty local Bahá'ís stayed overnight at the hotel.[18]

The next morning, 'Abdu'l-Bahá spoke about various subjects, including the Universal House of Justice. This suggests that he discussed matters related to the Covenant, even though he was in the city a short time. He gave one talk aimed at the public that was recorded in *The Promulgation of Universal Peace*. Noting that Cincinnati was the home of President Taft, he offered a "statement for the people of Cincinnati and America generally" about the "cause of peace." He noted that "having traveled from coast to coast," America had proved to be "vast and progressive; the government just; the nation noble." He spoke about Bahá'u'lláh's teachings of international unity and the reconciliation of religions, and noted that in the Persian Bahá'í community, people of many religious backgrounds were living in harmony. He closed by calling America "the standard bearer of peace throughout the world" and specifically mentioned Bahá'u'lláh's teaching that "the parliaments of the world [should] . . . send their wisest and best men to an international world parliament, that should decide all questions between the peoples and establish universal peace."[19]

Washington, D.C., November 6–11, 1912

Maḥmúd says 'Abdu'l-Bahá prolonged his stay in Cincinnati "until noon" because of the "crowd of seekers and the attraction of the friends." His Baltimore and Ohio train traveled through Athens, Ohio, across Pennsylvania, and reached Washington at 8:45am, about two hours late.*

---

* Maḥmúd says 'Abdu'l-Bahá arrived in Washington the same afternoon as he left Cincinnati (p. 375), but this is impossible. Parsons, *'Abdu'l-Bahá in America: Agnes Parsons' Diary*, 127, says he arrived at "nearly nine" a.m. on a train scheduled to arrive

Wednesday, November 6 was 'Abdu'l-Bahá's first day of five in Washington, D.C.; one day longer than his Chicago sojourn. Joseph Hannen and Agnes Parsons met him and his entourage at the train station and went with them to the house rented for his stay, 1901 Eighteenth Street Northwest, where they reviewed plans for his visit. 'Abdu'l-Bahá accepted two speaking invitations, at the Universalist Church at Thirteenth and L Streets and the Eighth Street Temple, and agreed to speak at Mrs. Parsons's every afternoon at 4pm, as he had previously. He also spoke at his house every morning.[20]

'Abdu'l-Bahá's plans in Washington were distinctly different from those in Chicago. The community had not had contacts with Covenant-breakers, so the Covenant was not a major concern, as it had been in Illinois; furthermore, Charles Mason Remey, a local Bahá'í, had published a booklet about the Covenant and Ali Kuli Khan was very familiar with the subject, so the local Bahá'ís may already have been familiar with some of its provisions. Community members had significant contacts with the city's elite, with the diplomatic corps, and with the capital's African American community. As a result, 'Abdu'l-Bahá's visit focused on solidifying contacts with those who were interested and interesting new members of the public in the Bahá'í teachings. 'Abdu'l-Bahá gave at least thirteen talks in his five days in Washington, not counting the luncheons Mrs. Parsons organized and the small groups who came to meet him. Joseph Hannen took notes of ten of the talks.[21]

His first day in the city, crowded with visitors, culminated with a public talk at the Universalist Church of Our Father, Thirteenth and L Streets, at 8:15pm. He had previously spoken at the church on April 21. This time,

---

at 6:30. This matches the schedule of the Baltimore and Ohio railroad listed in *The Official Guide of the Railways and Steam Navigation Lines of the United States, Puerto Rico, Canada, Mexico, and Cuba, Also Time Tables of Railroads in Central America, January 1910,* 504.

his lengthy address focused on the four kinds of brotherhood: with members of one's family, with citizens of the same nation, with members of the same race, and with all human beings. All four, however, had limitations, hence God sent Manifestations to establish spiritual brotherhood. He gave examples of the spiritual unity exhibited by the early Christians and described the brotherhood of the Persian Bahá'ís, as a result of the teachings of Bahá'u'lláh. He noted that religious teachings could be divided into two types: eternal and unchanging truths, and social teachings suited for a certain time and place. He enumerated four principles brought by Bahá'u'lláh: that the foundations of all the religions are one, that religion must be the cause of love and unity, that religion must be in conformity with reason and science, and that men and women are equal. He closed with high praise of the American nation, which possesses "the capacity and capability of holding aloft the banner of international peace. May this nation, this noble people, be the cause of unifying humanity! May this noble people spread broadcast the heavenly civilization and illumination!"[22] Just as he did on April 21, Reverend van Schaick asked everyone to come shake 'Abdu'l-Bahá's hand, closing the meeting on a friendly note.*

The next morning, 'Abdu'l-Bahá paid a long visit to the Ottoman ambassador, Yusuf Zia, who had met with 'Abdu'l-Bahá several times on his previous visits to Washington. The day was packed with visitors, a luncheon at Mrs. Parsons's for various guests—including the Dutch minister (one rank below ambassador) and Abram Simon (1872–1938), rabbi of the Reform Jewish synagogue where 'Abdu'l-Bahá spoke the next night—and

* This version of the talk, representing the original typescript of the spontaneous English interpretation, has 'Abdu'l-Bahá mentioning the third, fourth, and fifth principles of Bahá'u'lláh, but he does not enumerate the first and second principles, and it is not clear what the first principle was (one can infer a principle before the "third" one). The edited version of the talk, in 'Abdu'l-Bahá, *The Promulgation of Universal Peace*, 549–59, drops all numbering of principles.

a 4pm talk in her large function room. Friday, November 8 was a repeat of the same. As was common in other cities, 'Abdu'l-Bahá went for a walk in the afternoon. He praised Washington, D.C., as "better planned" than most American cities because of the wide boulevards, beautiful landscaping, and the scale of its buildings, which were not too tall or congested. He contrasted this with the "narrow gorges" of New York and Chicago, "their tall buildings looming like steep mountain peaks.[23]

That evening 'Abdu'l-Bahá spoke at the Eighth Street Temple, home of the Washington Hebrew Congregation, the capital's oldest Jewish congregation. The talk resembled the one he had given at Temple Emanu-El a month earlier. He began by stressing the oneness of God and God's creation of humanity "from the same progeny in order that His creatures may associate one with the other in good fellowship." Humans, however, "have acted contrary to the good pleasure of God"; they fought bloody wars and used religion as a source of alienation and separation. This was not as it was meant to be: "In reality, let it be known that the foundations of the Divine Religions are one, and the differences which have occurred are due to the blind imitations. His holiness Abraham was the founder of reality. His holiness Moses was the founder of reality. His holiness Christ was the founder of reality. His holiness Mohammed was the founder of reality. His holiness Baha'o'llah was the founder of reality. And this is to be proved; it is not simply an assertion."[24]

'Abdu'l-Bahá had summarized his argument; people knew where he planned to go with it. He described the two divisions into which the teachings of each religion fall: "essential or spiritual: to wit, faith in God, the acquisition of virtues . . . praiseworthy morals, the acquisition of the bestowals that result from divine effulgences" and "non-essential" which have to do with the workings of society, such as what foods are lawful or how to punish thieves. These were the aspects of Judaism his Reform Jewish audience had also come to see as outdated.[25]

'Abdu'l-Bahá then reviewed the civilizing impact of Moses on the people of Israel, concluding that he "founded the law of God and readjusted the morals of the people of Israel" but after the era of Solomon, "morality suffered a change," Israel suffered a "state of corruption," and they were conquered by powerful neighbors—first the Babylonians, then the Romans. "These were the conditions amongst the people of Israel, when, lo and behold,—his holiness Jesus Christ appeared amongst them." The reaction in Eighth Street Temple to the mention of Jesus was immediately much stronger than it has been in Temple Emanu-El a month earlier. "This produced a stir among the people," noted Agnes Parsons, "and an effort was made by the Rabbi through Dr. F[areed] to stop the address." Maḥmúd added, "some of the Jews sitting near the pulpit actually made signs to the interpreter that the time was over. But the Master ignored this and went on."[26]

'Abdu'l-Bahá spoke about the civilizing and moralizing impact of Jesus and Muhammad on the world, focusing especially on Their praise of Moses as a Prophet of God and Their insistence that Christians and Muslims accept His revelation. "Have the Christians suffered from their investigation of Moses? . . . Have they suffered any loss in their religious enthusiasm, any defect in their religious belief? . . . It is self-evident that no loss comes from that. And now it is time for the Jews to declare that Christ was the Word of God, and then this enmity between two great religions will pass away."[27] He closed with a call for interfaith understanding:

> In conclusion, since the prophets themselves, the founders, have been loving, and testified of each other, they have praised each one the other, why are we to disagree? Why should we be alienated? They have been kind to one another and God is One. He is the Shepherd of all, and we all constitute His sheep, hence we should be in the state of love and amity. . . . Praise be to God, you are living in a land of freedom.

> You are blessed with men of learning, men who are well informed, and are well versed in the study of comparative religions. You realize the need of unity, and you know the great harm which comes from prejudice or superstition . . . is not good fellowship preferable for a state of society rather than hatred and enmity? The answer is self-evident. Love and fellowship are the things needed . . . We must ever give commendation to all the people, thus removing discord and hatred, which has suffered alienation amongst men. Otherwise the same state of affairs will continue, each praising his own people and condemning the others; religious wars will continue, and religions prejudice is the cause of this havoc. This must be done away with, and the way to do it is to investigate the reality which underlies all the religions, and which reality is love of humanity. For God is One and humanity is one, and the prophets have brought the creed of amity.[28]

Parsons says that in the latter part of ʻAbduʼl-Bahá's talk, "many people left the Church [sic]" and that after he finished, the rabbi rose and said that "we are not accustomed here to the mention of other prophets than our own, but people of culture all over the world listen to others with ideas different from their own." Maḥmúd offered a similar summary and stated that "the firmness and courage of ʻAbduʼl-Bahá and the force of His argument were noted by everyone both inside and outside the synagogue."[29]

One wonders why the talk was not as well received as the Temple Emanu-El discourse. It may have to do with Rabbi Simon's approach to interfaith relations or the history of Jews in Washington. At any rate, Agnes Parsons telephoned Rabbi Simon the next day and invited him to come see ʻAbduʼl-Bahá at 4pm. Later that evening, ʻAbduʼl-Bahá offered a lengthy summary of their conversation. Among the points he made to the rabbi, he noted that the French acknowledge the greatness of Voltaire, an atheist, or Rousseau, an irreligious man, or Napoleon, a military genius, who "in comparison with Jesus Christ" are "as nothing." The Jews should be proud of Jesus as "a great man" and "mighty personage" they had given to the world. As previously noted, many Reform rabbis had been saying this for decades, though they had been advocating a Jewish Jesus to Christian audiences for their own purposes, not Jesus as a Manifestation of God. 'Abdu'l-Bahá, in contrast, envisioned a world where everyone could back away from their prejudices and extreme positions and embrace each other and their Manifestations in fellowship:

> When you express your glory and honor in the recollection of Christ, rest assured that the Christians will shake your hands in fellowship. There will be no trouble therein . . . what persecutions have been heaped upon you in Russia. And you must not think that this is all ended! This humiliation will continue forever! The times may come when in Europe itself they will arise against the Jews. But if you should declare Christ to be the Word of God, then you will rid yourself of all the trouble. . . . At last, he [Rabbi Simon] said: "I guess that is so. I believe that it is perfectly so! But I ask one thing me of you. Cannot you tell the Christians to love us a little bit more?"
>
> I said: Very well. I have done so, and I will continue to do so.[30]

There is a striking parallel between 'Abdu'l-Bahá's comment and that of a Christian professor, Edwin Knox Mitchell, in 1925. Writing in *The New York Times* about a sermon by Rabbi Stephen Wise titled "A Jew's View of Jesus," which presented a positive and appreciative view of the Man from Galilee, Mitchell said by "accepting the moral and spiritual leadership of Jesus" Wise had taken "a first step toward religious toleration and racial reconciliation."[31]

Some may wonder whether 'Abdu'l-Bahá was predicting the Holocaust. Simple recognition of Jesus as a divine personage would not have prevented Nazi persecution, but an entire religious community cannot transform itself and its religious views to the extent 'Abdu'l-Bahá advocated unless the world around it changes as well. A different international religious and social context—a two-way street—is implied, where the Christians, as 'Abdu'l-Bahá and the rabbi agreed, love the Jews more as well.

After the 8:30 talk at Mrs. Parsons's house was over—it was already 'Abdu'l-Bahá's second talk of the day—the Bahá'ís went to Rauscher's Hall for a banquet, starting at 10pm. The Rauschers, as recent Swiss immigrants, were willing to permit racially mixed groups to rent their catering facility, while the city hotels would not. Three hundred attended the "Feast of the Covenant," a commemoration of the Bahá'í holy day of the Day of the Covenant, but they celebrated seventeen days early in order to take advantage of 'Abdu'l-Bahá's presence. It began with Charles Mason Remey, a local Bahá'í, reading a paper that assured 'Abdu'l-Bahá of the obedience of the Washington Bahá'ís. 'Abdu'l-Bahá gave a short talk that included a prayer; afterward, he walked around the room, giving people sweets and flowers and anointing them with attar of rose. After dinner, the Bahá'ís sang songs to piano accompaniment, and 'Abdu'l-Bahá spoke again. The long evening program was followed by private meetings with 'Abdu'l-Bahá. The Ottoman Consul General was present and met briefly with 'Abdu'l-Bahá, who spoke to him about the future Universal House of Justice.[32]

A large crowd assembled at 'Abdu'l-Bahá's house early the next morning, Sunday, November 10, which was his last full day in Washington. Among other subjects, he spoke about firmness in the Faith and teaching the Faith. He spoke twice at Mrs. Parsons's house that afternoon, entertaining a steady stream of visitors in between. The second talk, about the oneness of God, he closed with words of farewell and inspiration:

> This is our last evening, and I ask God that His confirmations may encompass you; that your hearts may become radiant; that your eyes become illumined through witnessing the signs of God; that your ears hearken to the anthems of heaven; that your faces be set aglow with the radiant light of the word of God. May you all be united; may you be agreed, may you serve the solidarity of mankind. May you be well wishers of all humanity. May you be assistants of every poor one. May you be nurses for the sick. May you be sources of comfort to the broken in heart. May you be a refuge for the refugee. May you be a source of courage to the affrighted one. Thus through the favor and assistance of God may the standard of the happiness of humanity in the center of the world be held aloft, and may this flag be unfurled.
>
> Adieu to each and all of you![33]

From Mrs. Parsons's house, 'Abdu'l-Bahá went to the house of Joseph and Pauline Hannen for an interracial meeting. The Hannens had pioneered racial integration in the Washington, D.C., Bahá'í community, teaching the Faith to their family's African American seamstress and cook, who had in turn taught the Faith to Louis Gregory, who had studied the Faith partly at the Hannen residence. By the time 'Abdu'l-Bahá reached the Hannen residence, he was so exhausted that he had to rest. He called people upstairs to meet with him quickly in small groups, then came down to speak to everyone about interracial unity, giving the example of Bahá'u'lláh's black servant, Isfandíyár. When the meeting ended, he had dinner with the Hannens.[34]

Baltimore, November 11, 1912

He must have gotten home very late, but there was a crowd at his residence very early the next morning, and he gave a short talk to them, assuring them that even if people arose in opposition to the Bahá'í Faith, the Faith would be victorious. Then he was off to the train station for a 9am departure to Baltimore. The Bahá'í community there dated back to 1897; by 1912, they numbered perhaps two dozen. They greeted 'Abdu'l-Bahá at the train station at 11am and escorted him to the Hotel Rennert, where he rested before going to the Unitarian Chapel at noon. It had filled an hour earlier. He referred to his talk to the Washington Hebrew Congregation and repeated many of the same points; he spoke about proofs of prophethood, referred to Moses and Jesus, and distinguished between each Revelation's eternal spiritual teachings and temporal social laws.[35]

From the Unitarian Chapel, 'Abdu'l-Bahá went to the house of Howard and Hebe Struven for lunch with the Bahá'ís and their friends, some fifty-five in number; "a grand chicken dinner, with rice and celery, peas, ice cream and cake." It was a quick but joyous occasion, for 'Abdu'l-Bahá was back on the train at 3pm, bound for New York City. The Philadelphia Bahá'ís asked him to visit with them for a few hours, but the Baltimore stop took too long; 'Abdu'l-Bahá telegraphed them to see him at the station during the stop, and thirty did so. Some paid to ride the train several stops so they had more time with him. When 'Abdu'l-Bahá finally arrived at his rented house in New York City—he was able to get the same one he had occupied in July—it was 1am.[36]

New York City, November 12–December 5, 1912

When 'Abdu'l-Bahá reached New York, he did not know how long he would stay. Two considerations determined his departure date: the availability of berths on ships sailing to Britain and the tasks he judged he needed to complete in New York City. The *New York Tribune* reported on Sunday, November 24 that "the Oriental Savant is to leave the country this week, presumably on the steam ship Mauretania"; his actual departure on the *Celtic* was on December 5. Parsons notes that he stayed "longer in

New York than was at first expected," suggesting he might have decided to tarry because of tasks he perceived to be urgent. Maḥmúd states the desired task as follows: "a spirit of steadfastness in the Covenant of God, unity and faithfulness"; "this was the Master's purpose in staying so long in New York." To accomplish his purpose, 'Abdu'l-Bahá gave nearly forty talks in the homes of Bahá'ís over the next three and a half weeks, but spoke in public venues only three times.[37]

The Covenant came up in 'Abdu'l-Bahá's talks and conversations as early as November 13, his second full day in New York. 'Abdu'l-Bahá invited Juliet Thompson to walk with him in the park nearby. He closely questioned her whether the Bahá'ís in New York were firm in the Covenant. She replied that she didn't know of any troubles. "I know you don't know. . ." he replied. "I was only testing you. . . . With those who are against the Center of the Covenant you must not associate at all. When you find that a soul has turned away from the Covenant you must cut yourself off completely from him." When Juliet said she felt she had failed him and had not been strictly obedient to him, he replied, "Obedience is firmness in the Covenant." She asked, "am I not firm in the Covenant?" and he replied, "you could be more firm." This prompted deep introspection on her part.[38]

That day, 'Abdu'l-Bahá spoke twice about firmness in the Covenant at the Kinney residence in Manhattan, if Maḥmúd's chronology is correct. The second talk was "a lengthy discourse on firmness in the covenant of God, obedience to the Center of His covenant, the unity of the believers, the afflictions and tribulations of the Abhá Beauty and the martyrdom of the Manifestations in order that unity and harmony might be brought to the nations of the world." In a third talk that day, 'Abdu'l-Bahá encouraged the Bahá'ís "to arise, teach and spread the fragrances of God" and "inspired them to render service to the world of humanity so that others might arise from among the friends, girding their loins to bring about unity and harmony among the nations." The talks foreshadowed themes from both of 'Abdu'l-Bahá's most important works: his Will and Testament and the Tablets of the Divine Plan. Juliet Thompson records a conversation she had with 'Abdu'l-Bahá the next day where he talked to her about being a teacher of the Cause.[39]

One reason for the emphasis on the Covenant may have been the mission 'Abdu'l-Bahá gave to Howard MacNutt shortly after he reached New York City. Thompson says that "last week"—apparently relative to Monday, November 18—'Abdu'l-Bahá sent MacNutt to Chicago to meet with Dr. Nutt and his associates in that city and warn them either to cease their contact with Ibrahim Kheiralla or be permanently expelled from the Faith. He even authorized MacNutt to "cut them off from the faithful believers" if they refused. MacNutt met with Nutt and his associates but found them to be "angels" and wrote Zia Bagdadi, a Chicago Bahá'í visiting New York at the time, to that effect. Bagdadi, upset, gave the letter to 'Abdu'l-Bahá. Maḥmúd says 'Abdu'l-Bahá visited MacNutt on November 15 to ask him about the letter he had written to Bagdadi and admonish him about the content, and on November 19, Maḥmúd describes a meeting where MacNutt publically repented of his action. Thompson has both events on November 18 and would probably put MacNutt in Chicago on the 15th.[40]

Most likely, Maḥmúd's chronology is unreliable, as it has proven to be in other cases. A train ride from New York to Chicago in 1912 took a bit more than a day, and if MacNutt spent two days in Chicago and returned on the 18th, he would have left for Chicago on the 14th or 15th.* That may explain 'Abdu'l-Bahá's heavy emphasis on the Covenant on November 13. Most likely, MacNutt was in the audience.

---

* For example, one could leave New York City on the New York Central at 2pm one day and reach Chicago at 5:31pm the next day; see *The Office Guide of the Railways and Steam Navigation Lines,* 266.

According to Thompson, on the evening of November 18, 'Abdu'l-Bahá was at the Kinney residence to deliver a talk to the crowd. MacNutt arrived, and 'Abdu'l-Bahá asked Hooper Harris to talk instead, probably so that he could immediately meet with MacNutt. Maḥmúd, on the other hand, says MacNutt asked to speak to 'Abdu'l-Bahá because his "apparent equivocation and lack of firmness seemed to be causing his degradation in the eyes of the friends"; hence, he came to implore 'Abdu'l-Bahá to "recommend him" to the Bahá'ís. But it is not clear why the Bahá'ís would have already viewed MacNutt that way. Thompson says MacNutt had just arrived from Chicago and that 'Abdu'l-Bahá wanted to meet with him to hear his report and ask him about the letter he wrote to Bagdadi (which 'Abdu'l-Bahá apparently already had). Juliet Thompson says she "was in the second-floor hall with the Master and Carrie Kinney" when MacNutt arrived:

> The Master took him to His own room. After some time they came out together into the hall.
>
> An immense crowd had gathered by then on the first floor, which is open the whole length of the house.
>
> I heard the Master say to Mr MacNutt: "Go down and tell the people: 'I was like Saul. Now I am Paul, for I see.'"
>
> "But I *don't* see," said poor Howard.
>
> "Go down and say: 'I was like Saul.'"
>
> I pulled his coattail. "For God's sake," I said, "go down."
>
> "Let me alone," he replied in his misery.
>
> "GO DOWN," commanded the Master.
>
> Mr. MacNutt turned and went down, and his back looked *shrunken*. The Master leaned over the stair rail, His head thrown far back, His eyes closed, in anguished prayer. I sat with Carrie on the top step, watching Him. This is like Christ in Gethsemane, I thought.

> We could hear the voice of Howard MacNutt stumbling through his confession: "I was like Saul." But he seemed to be saying it by rote, dragging through it still unconvinced. Nevertheless when he came upstairs again, the Master *deluged* him with love.
>
> By that time the Master was back in His room and as Mr. MacNutt appeared at the door, He *ran* forward to meet him. Our Lord was all in white that night and as He ran with His arms wide open He looked like a great flying bird. He enfolded Howard in a close embrace, kissed his face and neck, welcomed with ecstasy this broken man who, even though bewildered, had obeyed Him.[41]

Lest one think the "immense crowd" on the first floor had no context for his confession, Maḥmúd provides different details: that 'Abdu'l-Bahá told MacNutt in the private meeting upstairs that his rehabilitation "depends upon your sincere repentance and your open denouncement of the violators in the meetings of the friends." Hence, when MacNutt went downstairs, he "gave an account of his journey to Chicago." Maḥmúd says nothing about Paul and Saul, possibly because as a Bahá'í of Muslim background, he was unaware of its significance. MacNutt's words seemed ambiguous, so 'Abdu'l-Bahá asked him to repeat them more clearly. Maḥmúd says that 'Abdu'l-Bahá then "went to the podium and expressed His pleasure at Mr Harris's talk and for Mr MacNutt's words of repentance. The Master then went upstairs and called Mr Hoar, Mr Harris, Mr Dodge and other friends to Him and asked them to embrace Mr MacNutt and exhorted them to have the utmost love and unity among themselves." As 'Abdu'l-Bahá later commented to Thompson, "I immersed Mr. MacNutt in the *fountain of Job* last night. The next day, 'Abdu'l-Bahá asked a group of Bahá'ís to show kindness and love to McNutt.[42]

The matter wasn't completely resolved, however, because doubt lingered over MacNutt's understanding of the Covenant and Covenant-breaking.

Ibrahim Kheiralla and Shua Ullah Behai continued to seek opportunities to recruit Bahá'ís to their cause; 'Abdu'l-Bahá's visit had, if anything, made them more active, and they had gotten perhaps a dozen articles in Kenosha, Chicago, San Francisco, and Los Angeles newspapers over the last six months questioning 'Abdu'l-Bahá's authority and character. Kheiralla later admitted that 'Abdu'l-Bahá's visit had been a "death blow" to his own efforts, but 'Abdu'l-Bahá couldn't take any chances; the Covenant-breakers in Acre had even accused 'Abdu'l-Bahá of acquiring a store of arms and plotting to raise an army to overthrow the Ottoman rule of Palestine. They had almost succeeded in getting him exiled to the Sahara of southern Libya.[43] Had Kheiralla and Shua Ullah become bolder and stronger, they could have created all sorts of troubles.

MacNutt had repeatedly demonstrated an inability to understand the divine source of 'Abdu'l-Bahá's authority, whom he had often explained was like the Apostle Peter, who had had no authority in Christianity at all. MacNutt also believed in the basic goodness of all humans and thus did not understand that Covenant-breaking was a spiritual condition of the ego that was, in fact, something that could be spread to others by flattery, sowing doubt, and undermining faith. He had remained in contact with Kheiralla and his associates; 'Abdu'l-Bahá had written to MacNutt in 1909 about it. This was one reason 'Abdu'l-Bahá remained in New York as long as he did; he wanted to do everything he could to save MacNutt. As it was, on April 16, 1913, 'Abdu'l-Bahá sent a cable to Ali Kuli Khan from Europe, "MACNUTT REPENTED FROM VIOLATION OF THE COVENANT BUT WAS NOT AWAKENED AWAKEN THE BAHAIS." By this cable, he expelled MacNutt from the Bahá'í community. It would be four months before 'Abdu'l-Bahá, satisfied that MacNutt was finally awakened, readmitted him.[44]

The Covenant remained an important theme throughout 'Abdu'l-Bahá's sojourn in New York. On Saturday evening, November 23, the New York

Bahá'ís celebrated the Day of the Covenant. 'Abdu'l-Bahá had established it as a holy day a decade earlier so that Bahá'ís wouldn't celebrate his birthday (which fell on the Declaration of thc Báb, another holy day). Three hundred attended the sumptuous banquet, which featured a talk by William Hoar, one of the first Bahá'ís on the area, about the Covenant, and a talk by 'Abdu'l-Bahá (which was on the oneness of humanity rather than on the Covenant). On November 26—the actual Day of the Covenant—'Abdu'l-Bahá spoke about the Covenant at an afternoon meeting at the residence of Grace and Florian Krug. On December 2, at the Kinney residence, he spoke about the Covenant, the Center of the Covenant, obedience to the Center of the Covenant, and the Universal House of Justice.[45]

The Covenant was not the only subject 'Abdu'l-Bahá addressed, however. The first night after his arrival—November 12—he spoke to a gathering primarily of African Americans at the Kinney residence. An even more important gathering was held on November 24, the day after the Day of the Covenant Banquet, because when the black Bahá'ís arrived at the Great Northern Hotel to attend the banquet, the hotel turned them away. Consequently 'Abdu'l-Bahá held a separate banquet for them at the Kinney residence, where the whites served them. 'Abdu'l-Bahá was very pleased and said: "Today you have carried out the laws of the Blessed Beauty and have truly acted according to the teachings of the Supreme Pen. Behold what an influence and effect the words of Bahá'u'lláh have had upon the hearts, that hating and shunning have been forgotten and that prejudices have been obliterated to such an extent that you arose to serve one another with great sincerity." Maḥmúd added that "the meeting embodied the grandeur of the Covenant and demonstrated the power and influence of the Cause in uniting, in sincerity and love, two races of humanity."[46]

Other subjects addressed during his last twenty-three day sojourn in New York City included the reality of God; the Manifestations of God; the need for divine revelation; the suffering of the followers of the Manifestations; the suffering and martyrdom of the Iranian Bahá'ís; the life of Bahá'u'lláh; the maturation and future perfection of the world; the problem of world peace and the role of the United States in bringing it about; the influence of the Bahá'í Cause in the world and its progress; love and unity; prejudice, alienation, and disunity; the problem of superstition and blind imitation; the equality of women and their education; material and spiritual civilization; the "special" teachings of Bahá'u'lláh; teaching the Faith; the nature and meaning of sacrifice; and the eternity of God's kingdom. Twice, Bahá'ís came to his household at dawn to watch him pray and thereby learn how to pray.[47]

Twice during his last week in New York, Bahá'ís sought to give him money. On November 29, some Bahá'ís offered to cover some of his travel expenses. He asked them to give the money to the poor, adding, "The most acceptable gift to me is the unity of the believers, service to the Cause of God, diffusion of the divine fragrances, and adherence to the counsels of the Abhá Beauty." Not satisfied, on November 30 "some believers agreed among themselves to go to 'Abdu'l-Bahá and cling to His robe until He accepted their gifts," reports Maḥmúd. Some of the gifts were jewelry for the members of his family back in Palestine. 'Abdu'l-Bahá expressed considerable gratitude and praised them for their hospitality and service to the Faith, but explained that no one in his household wore diamond rings and rubies. "I . . . have accepted your gifts," he concluded, "but I entrust them to you for you to sell and send the proceeds to the fund for the Mas͟hriqu'l-Ad͟hkár [Bahá'í House of Worship] in Chicago." He had to repeat himself twice because the Bahá'ís at first did not accept his reply.[48]

'Abdu'l-Bahá met with groups of clergymen on November 22, 25, and December 1, and he renewed his acquaintance with Haozoun Hohannes Topakyan, the Persian Consul-General for the New York area, on two occasions—November 15 and 23. His public talks were only three: to the Minerva Club, a women's club of which Mrs. Mary McNutt was a member, on November 25, where he spoke about the rights and education of women; to Mr. Kinney's Bible study class at the Kinney residence on December 3, where he spoke about the symbolic meanings of biblical texts; and to the Theosophical Society on December 4, the night before he sailed, where he spoke about the nature and purpose of the Manifestations of God.

The bulk of his meetings were directed at the Bahá'ís and their friends, and they flocked to meet him. May Maxwell came down from Montreal; Agnes Parsons, Pauline Hannen, and Mariam Haney came up from Washington. The New York Bahá'ís came night after night so that "the first to third floors" of the Kinney residence "were filled with people, some even standing on the stairs." "*Those last meetings in the Kinneys' house,*" reminisced Juliet Thompson, "those divine talks of the Good Shepherd leaving His flock for a while: too tender, too sad for the heart to bear." "I fear that the first five days of December, 1912, my home and church people saw little of me," Howard Colby Ives wrote later. "Wherever He was there was I if by any juggling of hours and duties it could possibly be managed. . . . [D]ay and night, I haunted the home at 780 West End Ave. where 'Abdu'l-Bahá spent those last days." "As the multitude grew," added Maḥmúd, "and the Master could not easily see everyone individually, He went downstairs to apologize for not being able to see them owing to the volume of His work, His preoccupation with other matters and His fatigue and frailty."[49]

Some days 'Abdu'l-Bahá spoke three or four times to crowds. The meetings were decisive for some. Juliet Thompson says Ives, who "would sit with streaming eyes in the meetings," accepted the Faith during the last few days of 'Abdu'l-Bahá's visit; he himself says that he accepted 'Abdu'l-Bahá's station but did not accept Bahá'u'lláh until a few months later. Thompson mentions a Mrs. Moore, who became a Bahá'í during this period. Maḥmúd says 'Abdu'l-Bahá's landlady, Mrs. Champney, and her family became believers. Dr. Florian Krug, who had been so violently opposed to his wife’s religion that he had even had her examined by “alienists” (doctors specializing in mental illness), and who threatened physically to prevent ‘Abdu’l-Bahá from speaking at his house, warmed to ‘Abdu’l-Bahá considerably, and later became a Bahá’í. Ironically, he and his wife Grace were on pilgrimage in 1921 when ‘Abdu’l-Bahá passed away; he was called to ‘Abdu’l-Bahá’s bedside on that terrible night, pronounced him dead, and closed his eyes.[50]

As the day of departure grew near, it was time for farewells. ‘Abdu’l-Bahá spent the afternoon of November 20 at Hooper Harris’s house in Newark and much of Saturday, November 23, in Montclair, New Jersey, visiting the Bahá’ís of that suburb for one last time.[51] On Tuesday morning, December 3, ‘Abdu’l-Bahá gave a tender and inspiring farewell address at the Kinney residence:

> I have to go away day after tomorrow. I therefore look upon this gathering of ours today as the farewell gathering.
>
> I am pleased with you all. I am very much rejoiced because of you all, because you have all shown the utmost kindness towards me; the utmost affection have you demonstrated towards me. I desire that his holiness, BAHA’O’LLAH, be pleased with you . . . your hearts must be illumined, your souls must be rejoiced with the glad tidings of God, your morals must be spiritual morals, your conduct must be an evidence of faith and assurance, you must be in the utmost of sanctity and purity and in the high degree of love and attraction toward the Kingdom of Abha. You must become the lamps of BAHA’O’LLAH so that you may give eternal light . . . so that all men may say, “Verily, ye are the proofs of BAHA’O’LLAH. Verily, BAHA’O’LLAH is the true One . . . .” Ye must so live that they may say to others, “Come and see the conduct of these souls, come and listen to their words,

come and witness the illumination of their hearts, come and see the traces of the love of God within them, come and see praiseworthy morals in them, come and find the foundation of the oneness of humanity within them. What greater proof can there be than these persons as to the truth of BAHA'O'LLAH?"

His holiness, BAHA'O'LLAH endured great hardship . . . . for our sakes. Therefore, we must be faithful towards him, we must not follow the selfish desires of our fancies. We must arise to accomplish that which is required by the Lord.

It is my hope that you will arise to live in accord with all these teachings and exhortations . . . so that we may reach the paradise of the spiritual kingdom, and diffuse the lights of the Sun of Truth and cause the waves of the Most Great Ocean to reach all the souls, so that this world of earth may be converted into the world of heaven, this devastated ground be converted into a delectable paradise, and this jungle of confusion be converted into a paradise of Abha.[52]

At the last meeting at the Kinney residence on the evening of December 3, "the rush of friends and seekers was greater than ever before and all hearts were aflame," reported Maḥmúd. "After the meeting the believers gathered around Him. He bade farewell to each, bestowed His favor upon all."[53]

Wednesday, December 4 was busy with last-minute visitors and a final talk to the Theosophical Society; the choice was indicative of the warmth and receptiveness of the Theosophists to 'Abdu'l-Bahá's message. Thursday, December 5, 'Abdu'l-Bahá called a few believers to the Emery house (where he had stayed for a few nights), including Juliet Thompson, the Kinneys, Agnes Parsons, Ali Kuli Khan, Florence Khan, and Pauline Hannen, and they accompanied him to the *Celtic.* After 'Abdu'l-Bahá settled into his room, they went to the first class lounge, where he delivered a final talk to about one hundred Bahá'ís, whose tears "bespoke their great sorrow," noted Maḥmúd. Some passengers and officers of the steamer happened to be present. The room was packed to the doors, with some standing outside. "In a few minutes our steamer will leave these shores and this is my last exhortation to you," he began:

> I have repeatedly spoken to you and invited you to realize the oneness of humanity. I have impressed upon you that all human beings are the servants of the same God . . . His bounties are equally distributed among all. We must also be kind to the people of the world and forget all religious, racial, patriotic and political prejudices. The whole earth is one globe. . . . he who causes grief to another's heart has sinned against the Lord. . . . He wishes that every individual may pass his life in utmost happiness and felicity and should abandon religious, racial, patriotic and political prejudices. . . . You must be friends to all and regard all as your own kith and kin. Your supreme object must always be to bring pleasure to a heart, to give food to the hungry, clothes to the naked, honor to the degraded, help to the helpless and comfort to the distressed. This is the way to win the good pleasure of God. This is that which is conducive to eternal happiness. This is the light of the world of man. . . .
>
> Behold what is happening in the Balkans! . . . God has created them to love one another but they are shedding one another's blood. . . . Make your motives lofty and exert with heart and soul every effort; perchance, the light of universal peace may shine forth and this gloom of estrangement be dispelled. May all human beings become one family and every individual seek the welfare of all. May the East

help the West and the West assist the East, for the whole earth is one country and all its people are under the favor and protection of one Shepherd.

Behold! What persecutions have the Prophets of God suffered so that human beings may love one another and cling to the cord of love and unity. These sanctified souls ever sacrificed themselves for this aim. But behold! How ignorant is man! In spite of all these sufferings, people are warring against one another. . . . How heedless they are! Your duties are different because you have been informed of the divine mysteries and your eyes and ears are opened. You are to deal kindly with all the people of the world. You have no excuse before God. . . . You must love all, even your enemies. . . . To those who oppose you be a faithful friend. . . . Perchance, the abysmal gloom of war and bloodshed may vanish; the light of God may shine forth; the East may be enlightened; the West may be filled with fragrance; the North and the South may embrace each other; and the nations of the world may associate with one another in utmost love and amity! . . . if men act according to these holy teachings, the world of dust shall reflect the lights of the Kingdom and the earth shall become the Abhá paradise, a garden of blissful joy. I hope that each one of you will be assisted to act according to these teachings so that, like a brilliant star, you may give light to humanity and like a spirit move the body of the contingent world. This is eternal glory! This is everlasting happiness! This is the image and likeness of God and unto this I call you! I pray God that you may attain it.[54]

One by one, the Bahá'ís went to 'Abdu'l-Bahá to shake his hand, then left. "It was death to leave that ship," said Thompson. Maḥmúd added from the deck, "They stood on the wharf, weeping and overcome with emotion, their heads bowed in grief and their hands lifted towards the heavens in prayer as they gazed their last at the Center of the Covenant. The throng of believers . . . waved farewell to the Master." On the pier, Thompson stood with May Maxwell, "tears blurring my sight. Through them I could see the Master in the midst of a group of Persians waving a patient hand to us. It waved and waved, that beautiful patient hand, till the Figure was lost to sight."[55]

12

"THE CALL OF GOD HAS BEEN RAISED IN ALL THE CITIES OF AMERICA"

Shoghi Effendi, head of the Bahá'í Faith from 1921 to 1957, has called 'Abdu'l-Bahá's trip to the Western world the "culmination" of his ministry and its "greatest exploit." When 'Abdu'l-Bahá left North America on December 5, 1912, he had laid the cornerstone of the Bahá'í House of Worship in Wilmette; had designated New York the "City of the Covenant" and affirmed the implications of Bahá'u'lláh's Covenant to his assembled followers there; had made a pilgrimage to the grave of the first American Bahá'í; had established the annual Souvenir Picnic in Inglewood, New Jersey; had visited Green Acre School and blessed its mission; had spoken before the Bahai Temple Unity convention; and "last but not least" had encouraged the first interracial marriage among American Bahá'ís. Shoghi Effendi's characterization of the voyage as an "astonishing manifestation of the boundless vitality of 'Abdu'l-Bahá" is amply justified by his remarkable accomplishments. The results are even more remarkable when one considers 'Abdu'l-Bahá's age, the impairment of his health from four decades of imprisonment, and his unfamiliarity with western customs and languages. 'Abdu'l-Bahá himself said that "all the doors" had been "opened" and "the ideal power of the Kingdom of God" had removed "every obstacle and obstruction."[1]

While Bahá'ís have written much about 'Abdu'l-Bahá's visit, to date religion scholars have paid little attention to it. They have focused much more attention on the visits of Protap Chunder Mozoomdar, Swami Vivekananda, and Anagarika Dharmapala. But a few comparisons make the importance of 'Abdu'l-Bahá's eight-month sojourn clear.

While in the United States and Canada, 'Abdu'l-Bahá gave approximately 401 addresses in eight months, not counting short talks to small groups or interviews. If California is any measure—the very thorough stenographic record by Bijou Straun includes forty-eight addresses, forty-one informal talks, fifty-three interviews—the latter two were similar in number to the former. In addition to the approximately ninety-three thousand people who attended his addresses, possibly millions read about him in the at least 358 newspaper articles that appeared in U.S. newspapers during his visit.[2]

The range of venues where 'Abdu'l-Bahá spoke included thirty-one liberal and moderate white Protestant churches (including thirteen Unitarian churches), fourteen Theosophical and New Thought gatherings, Hull House and six other settlement houses, five universities, five women's groups, three synagogues, one African American church, the Lake Mohonk Peace Conference and three other peace groups, and the fourth annual NAACP conference. By way of comparison, Mozoomdar spoke primarily to Unitarian churches and at a few universities. Vivekananda spoke to Unitarian, Universalist, and Congregational churches and to various metaphysical groups. His tour of opera houses took him to Memphis, Tennessee, farther south than any of the others. Dharmapala's audience included Unitarians, Universalists, Theosophists, Spiritualists, a Jewish club in San Francisco, "German liberals" in Minnesota, and a "Lady's Club" in Fargo.

None of the three spoke to African Americans, Japanese Americans, Greek and Syrian Americans, or to audiences at settlement houses. Their audiences were primarily white, well educated, and prosperous. In contrast, the Bahá'í community and the audiences for 'Abdu'l-Bahá's talks included significant numbers of middle- and working-class members, including African Americans.

Race, Religion, and Progress

A central characteristic of American religious discourse in the late nineteenth and early twentieth centuries has been described as the "conflation of race, religion, and progress"; in other words, that the superior white race, equipped with the superior form of religion (Christianity in its Protestant form) was producing the superior form of capitalist, industrialized, democratic civilization.[3] Indeed, it is fair to say that race, religion, and progress and two related aspects of progress—the advancement of women and the problem of war—were central themes of the dialogues that went on between civilizations in the late nineteenth and early twentieth centuries. They are central themes in the Bahá'í teachings as well.

It is illustrative to look at how the Asian religious visitors of the day responded to these themes. Mozoomdar expounded on them by emphasizing the progress India was achieving under the Brahmo Somaj, the organization he represented. He described it as a form of modern liberal religion, similar to Unitarianism, and highlighted its strenuous efforts to bring about social reform and development. Mozoomdar envisioned a universal theism based on enlightened liberal forms of Hinduism, Christianity, and other faiths. It was appreciative of Jesus; he had published an important book about Jesus Christ from a Brahmo perspective, which expressed great love and respect for the Nazarene.[4]

Swami Vivekananda addressed the issues of race, religion, and progress by stressing the organic unity of human beings with each other and with all living things. He saw an ultimate unity of religions based on direct perception of the Reality behind each faith and stressed the need for religions to tolerate each other and not try to convert each other's adherents. Many of his talks focused on India, its conditions, and progress in alleviating its poverty. He spoke about the importance of improving the lives of women through education. He commented on the expensive arms race occurring in Europe. He focused a considerable fraction of his comments on ridiculing the ugly cultural stereotypes promulgated by Christian missionaries, criticizing aggressive Christian missionizing of India, detailing the abuses caused by the British colonial system, and exposing the social evils of "Christian civilization."[5]

Dharmapala summarized his approach to race, religion, and progress at the World's Parliament of Religions. He described Buddhism's universal love and sympathy for all mankind and for all animal life and emphasized that it created a "brotherhood without distinction of caste and race." He described Buddhism as a rational philosophical religious system based on unbiased investigation of the truth, in accordance with science, that rejected the notion of a supreme God. Wherever it spread, it brought civilization and progress. It stressed moral purity and purity of the mind and gave women the "same rights" as men. The Buddha provided the "wisdom of the ages," Dharmapala pointed out, six centuries before Jesus was born.[6]

'Abdu'l-Bahá's response to the conflation of race, religion, and progress focused on the oneness of humanity, the civilizing forces of religion in general and the Bahá'í Faith specifically, and the urgent need to establish world peace in order to avoid an impending war and build a world civilization. Generally, it avoided overt criticism and focused on building bridges with others. 'Abdu'l-Bahá's message emphasized reverence and love for the founders of all the religions; as he explained to Rabbi Meyer in Washington: "Whenever these people mention each other's leaders with due reverence then . . . instead of hatred there will be love and instead of enmity and disunity there will be harmony and affection. This is my purpose."[7]

'Abdu'l-Bahá's message stressed equal education and full citizen rights for women, including the vote, a controversial position at the time. His proclamation of the oneness of humanity utilized both modern science and venerable philosophical arguments, was delivered frequently to racially and socially diverse audiences, and was usually related to the need to eliminate racial prejudice and provide equal treatment and fraternal love to America's African Americans and other minorities. He provided a vision of a future world united in love and justice, a world he sought to exemplify in his contagious love for those around him.

His talk at the Kinney residence on December 2, 1912—three days before his departure—perhaps summarized the Bahá'í approach to race, religion, and the progress of humanity most fully. That day, he offered "certain new teachings which are not found in any of the religious books of the past." The list of twelve distinctive Bahá'í teachings began with the oneness of humanity, followed by independent investigation of truth, the oneness of the religions of the world, the need for religion to be a cause of unity and harmony, the principle that religion must be in accord with science and reason, the equality of men and women, the principle that human beings must free themselves from religious and patriotic prejudices, the need to establish universal peace, the importance of universal education, the solution to economic questions, the need for the organization of the Universal House of Justice to explain and implement the commands of Bahá'u'lláh, and Bahá'u'lláh's establishment of a Covenant. All this will be possible, he asserted, through obedience to the Center of the Covenant. The talk blended together the themes he often presented to the public with those he emphasized to the Bahá'í audience.[8] It made clear an important Bahá'í teaching: that the principles of social reform could accomplish only so much without the spiritual impetus provided by Bahá'u'lláh's establishment of a system to embody the principles and direct their implementation in the world.

The paradigmatic example of 'Abdu'l-Bahá's approach to the oneness of humanity was his gentle encouragement of Louis Gregory, an African American lawyer, and Louisa Mathew, a white English woman, to marry. Not only did the marriage demonstrate the oneness of humanity, it also showed obedience to 'Abdu'l-Bahá and firmness in the Covenant, because the Gregorys never would have considered marriage or fostered a growing love for each other without his counsel.

'Abdu'l-Bahá often included in his discourses about world peace a condemnation of the horrible bloodshed and destruction wrought by the Italians in their unprovoked and unjustified campaign to wrest modern Libya from the Ottomans. When that war helped to spawn the first Balkan War—during which Serbia, Bulgaria, and Greece, emboldened by Ottoman weakness in Libya, sought to enlarge their domains at the expense of the Turks—he condemned the bloodshed there, warned it would continue, and praised efforts to end the war. At least six times in his North American travels—in New York City; Milford, Pennsylvania; Montreal; Buffalo; Omaha; and Sacramento—he warned that Europe was a powder keg and that a much greater and more destructive war there was coming soon. In 1919 he noted that he had predicted the war repeatedly, "but the appeal was not heeded and therefore this great carnage has come to pass."[9]

Influence on American Culture

Mozoomdar, Dharmapala, and Vivekananda arrived in North America earlier than 'Abdu'l-Bahá, at a time when appreciation for non-Christian religions was confined to a few Transcendentalists and Theosophists and when ignorance about, and prejudice against, the "heathen" faiths was strong. The three men attended a pivotal event in American religious history, the World's Parliament of Religions, held in Chicago in September, 1893, where the Bahá'í Faith received its first public mention in the West. Their presence on the stage as equals to the Christians implied an equality between Christianity and other religions, an idea either flatly rejected or beyond the imagination of most American Christians of the time. By puncturing stereotypes about "pagans"—sometimes in dramatic and controversial ways—they inaugurated a revolution in thinking for many liberals that moved Christianity from "the truth" to a "religion" like the others.

Thus, for example, the twenty-year-old Ernest Hocking (1873–1966)—decades later a prominent idealist philosopher at Harvard University and an important lay Protestant thinker—attended a talk by Vivekananda at the World's Parliament of Religions and came away with the realization that secular thinkers like Herbert Spencer did not have the last word about the biological and psychological origins of religion; rather, that transcendent religious experience was real, whether experienced by a Hindu such as Vivekananda or a Methodist such as himself. Hocking went on to pen a Preface to the Bhagavad-Gita, write a book titled *The Meaning of God in Human Experience,* teach comparative religion at Andover Theological Seminary, and chair a major mainstream Protestant commission that critically examined the nature and purpose of international Protestant missionary work in the 1930s and recommend that it focus on education and welfare rather than evangelization.[10] Hocking did not become a Hindu or a Vedantist, but his Methodism was broadened and nuanced by them.

The nearest equivalent to Hocking, in the Bahá'í context, was Albert Léon Guérard (1880–1959), a professor of French at Stanford University, who attended 'Abdu'l-Bahá's talk there in October 1912. Guérard, a French Protestant who became an Episcopalian, maintained a lifelong respect and sympathy for Bahá'í ideas about race unity, world peace, a world government, and an international language. He published four articles in the Bahá'í periodicals *World Unity, The Bahá'í Magazine,* and *World Order* between 1927 and 1938, one of which reviewed attempts to create and disseminate an international language. In 1945–48, he was a member of a University of Chicago-sponsored "Committee to Frame a World Constitution," whose proposed document received international attention. He published twenty-eight books and numerous essays, some of which were on "the hope of an international government and of an international language." But the extent 'Abdu'l-Bahá's talk influenced his thinking, or whether it simply reinforced interests he already had, cannot be determined.[11]

Ironically, the main impact of Mozoomdar, Vivekananda, and Dharmapala on American religion was in fostering a change in the way many Christians viewed their own faith. This had not been their main purpose for coming to America; rather, they had come to proclaim the teachings of their religions and obtain resources for their projects. Even the establishment of Hindu or Buddhist communities was not their purpose. Mozoomdar made no attempt to convert Americans to Hinduism; his goal was an alliance with the Unitarians, who had a small missionary presence in India. Vivekananda discovered to his surprise that he had acquired a following of a few dozen people and reluctantly organized them before he left America in 1899. Dharmapala held meditation classes for up to several hundred people and formally inducted two Americans into a lay Buddhist order. Their lack of followers proved to be a major limitation to their efforts, because there was no one to organize their travel and follow up on contacts. It has made a reconstruction of their tours, talks, and results very difficult for later scholars.

Building a Community

In contrast, 'Abdu'l-Bahá built a community. His efforts began in the 1890s in his extensive correspondence with American Bahá'ís and continued through the guidance provided via the Persian Bahá'í teachers he sent in 1900–01 and in his advice to Americans when they visited him in Acre. After he proclaimed the implications of the Covenant to the assembled Bahá'ís in New York City in June 1912, his talks to Bahá'í audiences usually emphasized three things: first, the supreme importance of Bahá'ís loving each other and all of humanity, demonstrated through acts of service; second, teaching the Faith through word and deed; and third, the Bahá'í Covenant and obedience to 'Abdu'l-Bahá as its Center. 'Abdu'l-Bahá warned against association with Covenant-breakers, gave examples of communities that were politely avoiding them effectively, and noted that communities with enduring connections to them tended to be stagnant. He warned specific Bahá'ís about their connections with Covenant-breakers and, in 1913, even temporarily expelled Howard MacNutt from the community for his failure to understand and obey. His efforts prevented the splitting of the American Bahá'í community into sects and kept it unified in its vision.

'Abdu'l-Bahá's effort to build a unified community included the establishment of annual gatherings such as the souvenir picnic in West Englewood, New Jersey, and the gathering at the grave of Thornton Chase in Inglewood, California. Significantly, it did not include an emphasis on distinctive aspects of Bahá'í practice. There are no talks preserved in English that discuss fasting or the obligatory prayers, even though some Bahá'ís were already following these practices. He did not tell the Bahá'ís that they should stop consuming alcohol, although a few had already done so. He did not ask them to leave the churches. The time had not yet come to close the liminal space, not quite in the community nor fully outside it, occupied by Alice Buckton and others who were "young in the Kingdom."[12] The call to conform to those Bahá'í practices occurred in the 1920s and 30s.

'Abdu'l-Bahá's great care to establish and maintain the unity of the Bahá'ís and give them an outward orientation produced a community that, historically, has steadily grown. While religion scholars often note that the American Bahá'í community is much smaller that the communities of American Hindus, Buddhists, and Muslims, the vast majority of those communities are recent immigrants; conversions from the white, Christian majority of the country are still relatively few. Today there are more Euro-American Bahá'ís than Euro-American Hindus. The number of Euro-American Muslims is roughly comparable, and among the Buddhist groups, only Soka Gakkai reports more Euro-American members. African American Bahá'ís probably outnumber blacks who have become Hindus, Buddhists, or Jews.*

The relative size of the American Bahá'í community is even more remarkable when one considers that Buddhism and Hinduism are ancient and vast religious-cultural traditions. Colonialism, commercial ties with Asia, military involvement in the Asiatic region, tourism, musical and dance programs, yoga and meditation classes, films, museum wings filled

* Melton and Jones, "Reflections on Hindu Demographics in America: An Initial Report on the First American Hindu Census," estimate 1.2 million Hindus in the United States, but the vast majority are Americans of Indian background. Indian Americans usually belong to "traditional temples" and "temple associations"; Euro-Americans primarily belong to the "Renaissance" and "Post-Renaissance" groups, which total 20,000 and 35,000 members respectively. Melton, "Report on a Census of Buddhist Groups in the United States," estimates two million Buddhists in the United States, the vast majority being Americans of Asian heritage (Tibetans, Thais, Japanese, etc.). Soka Gakkai, with 286,000 members, is the only one with significant numbers of Euro-Americans; it is mostly Euro-American. There is also a significant number of sympathizers who are not affiliated with a Buddhist group but attend Buddhist meditation classes and read Buddhist literature. A few African Americans belong to Hindu and Buddhist groups as well, but their presence is so small that no one has studied them. According to the Pew Forum's 2007 survey "Muslim Americans: Middle Class and Mostly Mainstream," 10, 22, there are approximately 2.35 million American Muslims, of whom 23% are converts; of them, 34% are white, for a total of 184,000 white Muslim converts. Of the 170,000 Bahá'ís in the United States, the very rough ethnicity estimates are 25,000 African Americans, 25,000 Persian Americans, 2,000 American Indians, 2,500 Southeast Asians, and 4,000 Hispanics, leaving 110,000, the vast majority of whom are Euro-Americans.

with paintings and sculpture, university chairs, abundant translations, and large immigrant communities have continually exposed Americans to the Hindu and Buddhist traditions. In contrast, the Bahá'í Faith is a religious community of modest size (about five million worldwide), a minority in every land where it is found, with relatively undeveloped secondary literature and artistic expressions. No cultural, commercial, and political forces were available to continue the momentum started by 'Abdu'l-Bahá's visit. The Bahá'ís had to do it themselves.

Setting a New Future in Motion

'Abdu'l-Bahá's visit had a profound influence on the development of the Bahá'í Faith, and not just in North America. Much of what he said and did can be seen as preparation for the implementation of his two most important texts: his Will and Testament and The Tablets of the Divine Plan, 'Abdu'l-Bahá's fourteen epistles to the North American Bahá'ís, composed in 1916–17, mandating them to take the Bahá'í Faith to the entire world.

In his talks, he often mentioned that in the future, the Universal House of Justice would be formed, thus alluding to a central provision of his Will and Testament and preparing the Bahá'ís for building the Administrative Order in the 1920s and 1930s. By laying the cornerstone of the House of Worship in Wilmette and addressing the convention of the Bahai Temple Unity (BTU), he blessed "the beginnings of that Administrative Order which they [the American Bahá'ís] were soon to initiate and champion." Inevitably, the BTU took on continent-wide functions as it grew in capacity and prestige. In 1916, 'Abdu'l-Bahá gave the responsibility to review all publications by American Bahá'ís about their Faith to the BTU. In 1919, the BTU established a National Teaching Committee to carry out the provisions of the Tablets of the Divine Plan in the United States and Canada. In 1920–22, the Bahai Publishing Society, which today is called the Bahá'í Publishing Trust, became an agency of the BTU.[13] When the provisions of 'Abdu'l-Bahá's Will and Testament became known after his passing in 1921 and Shoghi Effendi (1897–1957), the Guardian* of the Bahá'í Faith, called for the establishment of National Spiritual Assemblies as described in the Will, it was inevitable that the Bahai Temple Unity would evolve into the National Spiritual Assembly of the Bahá'ís of the United States and Canada. Many National Spiritual Assemblies were later patterned after its organization and policies.

'Abdu'l-Bahá met with the Chicago and New York Bahá'í consultative bodies and had the former reelected to ensure that all its members understood the importance of the Covenant. His guidance about how they should function helped to remove some of the confusion that had developed about the creation of local Bahá'í organization and set the stage for the election of local spiritual assemblies—also called for in the Will and Testament—all across the United States.

'Abdu'l-Bahá had begun to lay the foundations for the Tablets of the Divine Plan at least eight years before he arrived in North America. Between 1904 and 1912, he encouraged and coordinated five teaching trips to India, Iran, Central Asia, Burma, and Japan by seven North American Bahá'ís.† In dozens of tablets and many of his North American talks he encouraged countless local and regional teaching trips as well. His writings and talks emphasized that teaching the Bahá'í Faith should be a natural

* 'Abdu'l-Bahá's Will and Testament established a new institution, Guardian of the Bahá'í Faith, gave it authority to interpret the Bahá'í authoritative texts and maintain the Faith's unity, and appointed his eldest grandson, Shoghi Effendi Rabbani, to the position.

† The travels of Sydney Sprague, Harlan Ober, Hooper Harris, Laura Barney, Charles Mason Remey, Aurelia Bethlen, and Howard Struven have been summarized or mentioned in Robert H. Stockman, *The Bahá'í Faith in America, vol. 2: Early Expansion, 1900–1912* (Oxford: George Ronald, 1995).

consequence of one's love of humanity and one's desire to serve others, which will lead to questions about the Bahá'í teachings and attraction to Bahá'u'lláh and His community of followers. He exhorted the Bahá'í communities to strengthen their love and unity to such a degree that they became magnets for others. Watching 'Abdu'l-Bahá in action teaching the Faith was a profound encouragement and inspiration for the Bahá'ís, and caused hundreds to devote their lives to spreading the word. He said that his "long voyage" would "prove how great is My love for you" and his visit became an example of love for Bahá'ís, causing them to fall in love with him and, to an increasing extent, with their fellow human beings.[14]

Many Bahá'ís eventually relocated to other states or countries to fulfill the ambitious expansion goals delineated in the Tablets of the Divine Plan, especially after Shoghi Effendi created plans to diffuse the Faith worldwide and gave the American National Spiritual Assembly the responsibility to coordinate their accomplishment. May Maxwell left Montreal for Argentina in 1940 and died there; Shoghi Effendi named her a Hand of the Cause of God* for her sacrificial devotion to the Faith. Juliet Thompson settled for a time in Mexico in the 1940s. Ruth Randall and Harlan Ober moved permanently to South Africa in the 1950s and are buried there. Louis and Louisa Gregory were unable to travel together to teach the Faith, except for three months they spent in Haiti in 1936; otherwise, Louis spent many months every year traveling across the American South while Louisa lectured about the Faith in Europe. For his devoted services, Shoghi Effendi named Louis Gregory a Hand of the Cause of God as well.[16]

'Abdu'l-Bahá's presentations of the "basic and distinguishing principles" of the Bahá'í Faith to the Western public profoundly affected the talks that

* A Hand of the Cause of God is a person appointed to a position of high rank in the Bahá'í Faith, who possesses no administrative authority but exercises moral influence in the community by consulting with and advising Bahá'ís and Bahá'í institutions about the expansion and protection of the Bahá'í Faith.

Bahá'ís gave about their Faith for over half a century. His points were soon converted into a list of twelve social principles, summarized in pamphlet form, elaborated in books, and repeated in hundreds of speeches. They became a standard synopsis offered in scholarly works about the Bahá'í Faith. They still influence the way Bahá'ís think about, and describe, their beliefs.[16]

The Bahá'í emphasis on the oneness of humanity is one reason the American Bahá'í community in 1912 included one or two dozen African American members. As we have seen, 'Abdu'l-Bahá's words and deeds greatly impressed W. E. B. Du Bois. The partial transformation of the attitudes of white Bahá'ís about black people and the interracial marriage of the Gregorys helped to create an interracial culture in the American Bahá'í community and made it possible for prominent African Americans, such as Alain Locke—one of the founders of the Harlem Renaissance—and Robert Abbott to be attracted to the Bahá'í Faith. The continued progress of the American Bahá'í community made it possible for such prominent African Americans as Robert Hayden and Dizzie Gillespie to become Bahá'ís in 1943 and 1968, respectively; set the stage for over ten thousand African Americans to become Bahá'ís in the 1970s; and made possible the prominent roles African Americans and American Indians have played on the National Spiritual Assembly of the United States throughout the last century. African Americans have served as Secretary (chief executive officer) of the Assembly for thirty-seven of its eighty-seven years.[17]

'Abdu'l-Bahá's talks and private interviews helped to bring scores into the Bahá'í Faith.* Robert Abbott, publisher of the *Chicago Defender,* was

---

* We can roughly estimate how many people became Bahá'ís in North America as an immediate result of meeting 'Abdu'l-Bahá as follows: Zia Bagdadi says four people became active Bahá'ís in Chicago as a result of 'Abdu'l-Bahá's three visits (Zia Bagdadi, "'Abdu'l-Bahá in America, Chapter III—Chicago, Ill," *Star of the West: The Bahá'í Magazine,* 19, no. 4 [July, 1928], 115). To this number we can add two more who

impressed by 'Abdu'l-Bahá, but waited until 1934 to join the community. Nevertheless, from his position of prominence, he was able to mention the Bahá'í Faith to many and promote its ideals. Howard Colby Ives resigned from the Unitarian pulpit and traveled from city to city, residing in each long enough to start a Bahá'í community, then moving on. Ruth Moffett, a Wisconsin housewife who heard of 'Abdu'l-Bahá when she and he were both in Chicago, became one of the most active traveling teachers in the 1930s and 40s and established Bahá'í communities in dozens of places that had previously had no Bahá'ís at all. Harry Randall became a Bahá'í as a result of 'Abdu'l-Bahá's visit and became active in reorganizing Green Acre as a Bahá'í retreat and conference center. He was also elected to the Bahai Temple Unity Executive Committee. Albert Vail became a Bahá'í as a result of 'Abdu'l-Bahá's visit, resigned from his Unitarian position in Champaign-Urbana in 1918, and became a full-time traveling Bahá'í lecturer in the 1920s and 30s.[18]

---

are known to the author, raising the total to six. A similar number is known to the author from New York. Washington and the San Francisco Bay area had communities of comparable size. If we assume that six new Bahá'ís resulted in both of those areas, that raises the total to twenty-four. We know that two people became Bahá'ís in Dublin, two in Boston, and one in Montclair, New Jersey. If we assume that all the smaller places 'Abdu'l-Bahá visited (Dublin, Boston, Green Acre, Montclair, Philadelphia, Montreal, Buffalo, Pittsburgh, Cincinnati, Cleveland, Minneapolis-Saint Paul, Denver, Los Angeles) each saw two new Bahá'ís, that adds twenty-six more, giving a total of fifty. In 1935 the National Spiritual Assembly asked the American Bahá'ís to complete historical record cards, and 1,813, or about half, did so. Of that number, fifty-one indicated that they had become Bahá'ís in 1912. The number includes some children of Bahá'ís who put down 1912 because they met 'Abdu'l-Bahá that year, and by 1935 some of the people who became Bahá'ís in 1912 had died or ceased to be Bahá'ís. Both sources of information therefore suggest that the number of people who became Bahá'ís as an immediate result of 'Abdu'l-Bahá's visit was in the fifty to one hundred range. There is no easy way to estimate how many became sympathetic or interested in aspects of the Bahá'í teachings.

'Abdu'l-Bahá's face-to-face meetings transformed some veteran Bahá'ís. He kept Howard MacNutt close to him and nurtured his acceptance of African Americans, against whom he had previously harbored strong prejudices. After being readmitted to the Bahá'í community in 1913, MacNutt became the editor of *The Promulgation of Universal Peace,* the premier collection of 'Abdu'l-Bahá's North American talks. He resumed his role as a prominent Bahá'í speaker. He was killed in a street accident in 1926 on his way to a Bahá'í meeting he had organized in an African American neighborhood of Miami, Florida. Agnes Parsons also had to overcome her racial biases and accept black people into her house as guests. 'Abdu'l-Bahá asked her to spearhead the planning of a series of racial amity conferences starting in 1920, a task she accomplished ably.[19]

'Abdu'l-Bahá strengthened the faith and devotion of some younger or newer Bahá'ís, often by keeping them close to him for a period of time, so they could see him at work and he could direct their service. In modern terms, he was mentoring them; or to use terminology current in the Bahá'í community today, by having them accompany him on his journeys, he was "accompanying" them in their service. Saichiro Fujita, the young Japanese-American Bahá'í who watched 'Abdu'l-Bahá's arrival in Chicago from a lamppost, traveled with 'Abdu'l-Bahá to California and back to the East Coast, serving him the entire time. He devoted his life to the Bahá'í Faith, serving 'Abdu'l-Bahá, Shoghi Effendi, and the Universal House of Justice in Haifa and settling for seventeen years as a Bahá'í teacher in Japan. Grace Robarts Ober, who served in his New York household and married Harlan Ober at his suggestion, went on to serve as chair of the National Teaching Committee. It was in that role on May 1, 1938, exactly twenty-six years after she helped excavate the hole to lay the cornerstone of the Bahá'í House of Worship, while giving an inspiring report at the National Convention in the Temple's Foundation Hall, when she was stricken by a heart attack and suddenly passed away. She was also instrumental in teaching the Faith to her nephew, John Robarts, who later was elevated to the rank of Hand of the Cause by Shoghi Effendi.[20]

George Latimer, who spent a week with 'Abdu'l-Bahá in Dublin and assisted in his house in San Francisco, went on to serve on the National Spiritual Assembly, for a time as its chair. Fred Mortensen, the juvenile delinquent who rode the rods between the wheels of the trains to Green Acre and spent a week with 'Abdu'l-Bahá in Malden, traveled to Montana to teach the Bahá'í Faith, published several essays on Bahá'í subjects, and was preparing to move to Austria to help establish the Faith there when he died in 1946.

Even people who had only brief encounters with 'Abdu'l-Bahá found their lives profoundly changed. John Henry Hyde Dunn and Clara Davis, both residents of Washington state, went to San Francisco to hear 'Abdu'l-Bahá—Hyde for a week, Clara for just a day. Both were immensely impressed by him and dedicated themselves to spreading the Faith. After they married in 1917, they devoted most of their resources to hosting Bahá'í meetings in their house or to Hyde's travels in the western states to speak about the Faith. When they read the Tablets of the Divine Plan in early 1919, Clara saw 'Abdu'l-Bahá's comment that he longed to travel to promote the Bahá'í teachings, "even though on foot and in the utmost poverty." Clara said to Hyde, "Let us go where 'Abdu'l-Bahá wished to go," adding, "We are almost in poverty." Hyde replied unhesitatingly, "Yes, we will go." They set out for Australia in a few months. By getting a job as a traveling salesman, Hyde was able to visit nearly the entire country and attract people to the Faith in all of Australia's states. For vacation, they went to New Zealand to teach the Faith there. Their decades of patient work built Bahá'í communities in both countries. Shoghi Effendi elevated both of them to the rank of Hand of the Cause of God.[21]

'Abdu'l-Bahá's loving presence solidified the Bahá'í identity of many children of Bahá'ís, who often considered 1912 to be the year they accepted the Faith. Monroe Charles Ioas (born 1899) considered 1912 to be the year he "possibly" became a Bahá'í because 'Abdu'l-Bahá "kissed me on the forehead. I shall never forget the occasion."[22] 'Abdu'l-Bahá's humor and his profound rapport with people remain important examples for all Bahá'ís. His "home visits" to the sick, his engagement in public discourse, and his social action in caring for the poor and needy have been sources of inspiration for generations of Bahá'ís. They have acquired added importance with the increasingly systematic emphasis on those activities in the Bahá'í community in recent years.

'Abdu'l-Bahá had repeatedly told the American Bahá'ís that their unity was the key to their success. In a tablet to them in 1911, he wrote, "verily, verily, I say unto you, were it not for this difference [disunity] amongst you, the inhabitants of America in all those regions would have, by now, been attracted to the Kingdom of God, and would have constituted themselves your helpers and assisters." Some felt overwhelmed by the extent of the personal transformation he called on them to achieve. Juliet Thompson thought that she saw "profound agony" on 'Abdu'l-Bahá's face as the *Celtic* steamed away from New York City, "as He bade His immature children farewell, foreseeing for us so many sorrows, so many failures, and a world gone to pieces because of our failures."[23]

Some months later, however, when 'Abdu'l-Bahá was in Paris, he expressed confidence in the future. He told a group of American Bahá'ís, "I have planted . . . Seeds in America. You must nurture them and care for them. If you do this, they will yield an abundant harvest."[24] For generations, the American Bahá'ís have harvested some of those seeds, increasing their community's size and strength a hundredfold. Their growing strength allowed them to spearhead efforts to spread Bahá'u'lláh's teachings to the entire globe, express them in diverse art forms and literature, and embody them in an organizational system that would preserve their integrity. 'Abdu'l-Bahá's addresses and actions continue to provide seeds: to

Bahá'ís seeking to demonstrate their teachings through words and deeds, to religious seekers pursuing their quest, to civil rights workers struggling to break down racial barriers, to human rights groups striving to establish human decency and justice around the world, to activists searching for peaceful ways to bring about world peace, to advocates of the advancement of women seeking principles and examples to further their work. The abundant harvest awaits anyone who seeks the seeds and nurtures them.

NOTES

1 / The First Day

1. Wendell Phillips Dodge, "Abdul-Baha's Arrival in America," *Star of the West,* 3, no. 3 (Apr. 26, 1912): 3. Much of this account of his arrival comes from the article.
2. Ibid., 4.
3. Ibid., 4; *Star of the West,* 3, no. 10 (Sept. 8, 1912): 4; see also 'Abdu'l-Bahá, *The Promulgation of Universal Peace,* 3.
4. Maḥmúd-i-Zarqání, *Maḥmúd's Diary,* 38. Maḥmúd's discussion of 'Abdu'l-Bahá's meeting with journalists seems to occur at the Hotel Ansonia, and possibly two meetings with journalists occurred that day; the subjects covered appear to be the same as the ones described by Wendell Phillips Dodge on board the *Cedric.*
5. Dodge, "Abdul-Baha's Arrival in America," 4.
6. Ibid., 4.
7. Ibid.
8. Thompson, *Diary of Juliet Thompson,* 233–34.
9. Maḥmúd-i-Zarqání, *Maḥmúd's Diary,* 37; Ives, *Portals to Freedom,* 28–29.
10. Thompson, *Diary of Juliet Thompson,* 235–36.
11. 'Abdu'l-Bahá, *The Promulgation of Universal Peace,* 3–4. The older text is in *Star of the West,* 3, no. 10 (Sept. 8, 1912): 4–5 and has no major differences, but is not as eloquent.
12. Ives, *Portals to Freedom,* 29.

2 / "My Invitation to America will be the Unity of the Believers"

The words of the chapter title are attributed to 'Abdu'l-Bahá in Thompson, *Diary of Juliet Thompson,* 177.

1. Statistics for Bahá'u'lláh's writings come from a memorandum of the Research Department of the Universal House of Justice, October 1, 2010.
2. For details about the founding of the Persian American Educational Society, see Stockman, *The Bahá'í Faith in America,* vol. 2, 354–58.
3. Supplication to 'Abdu'l-Bahá and attached list of signatories, Thornton Chase Papers; 'Abdu'l-Bahá to Ahmad Yazdi, translated by Ameen Fareed on October 20, 1902, *Tablets of Abdul Baha Abbas,* vol. II, 352.
4. *Star of the West* 2, no. 3 (April 28, 1911): 5.
5. Agnes Parsons, "The Story of the Parsons House in Washington Having to do with the History of the Divine Cause in our Land," second page, Agnes Parsons Papers.
6. 'Abdu'l-Bahá to the "members of the Assembly of Bahais of America," through Lua Getsinger, trans. Ameen Fareed Dec. 8, 1912, author's personal papers.
7. *Star of the West* 2, no. 3 (April 28, 1911): 8.
8. *Star of the West* 2, no. 14 (Dec. 12, 1911): 3–4. The tablet (letter) 'Abdu'l-Bahá sent, which was much longer, was translated August 9, 1911, two days before he departed Egypt for Europe.
9. *Star of the West* 2, no. 4 (May 17, 1911): 6–7. The tablet was translated by Ahmad Sohrab on April 28, 1911.
10. *Star of the West* 2, no. 6 (June 24, 1911): 6. No translation information is available.
11. Smith, "The American Bahá'í Community, 1894–1917: A Preliminary Survey," 155–94.
12. Blomfield, *The Chosen Highway,* 147–48; Lil Abdo, *Religion and Relevance: The Bahá'ís in Britain, 1899–1930,* PhD dissertation, University of London School of Oriental and African Studies, 2004. Chapter 1 traces the connection between the British Bahá'ís and several specific Anglican churches in London.
13. Thompson, *The Diary of Juliet Thompson,* 173.
14. 'Abdu'l-Bahá's visit to City Temple is described in *Star of the West* 2, no. 11 (Sept. 27, 1911): 3–4.
15. Blomfield, *The Chosen Highway,* 157.
16. Ibid., 150. Blomfield may have included in this list people 'Abdu'l-Bahá met during his second trip to Britain in 1913 as well.

17. Blomfield, *The Chosen Highway,* 154.
18. Thompson, *The Diary of Juliet Thompson,* 184.
19. Ahmad Sohrab to Agnes Parsons, December 16, 1911, pp. 2–4, Agnes Parsons Papers. Ultimately 'Abdu'l-Bahá did not accept all the invitations, including the one from the Ethical Culture Society.
20. Protap Chunder Mozoomdar, *The Oriental Christ* (Boston: George H. Ellis, 1883); Mullick, *The First Hindu Mission to America: The Pioneering Visits of Protap Chunder Mozoomdar* provides separate chapters on all three of his visits to the United States.
21. Seager, *The Parliament of the World's Religions,* 150–51.
22. Bartholomeusz, *Women Under the Bo Tree,* 48.
23. Seager, *Buddhism in America,* 37; Bartholomeusz, *Women Under the Bo Tree,* 56.
24. http://www2.census.gov/prod2/decennial/documents/00190404p1ch2.pdf. All the numbers were self-reported to the Census Department.
25. *Star of the West* 7, no. 11 (Nov. 4, 1916): 122.

3 / "His wisdom is surely not His own"

The words of the chapter title are taken from Randall-Winckler, *William Henry Randall,* 41.

1. "Table of Talks," author's personal papers; Thompson, *Diary of Juliet Thompson,* 267; Amín Egea, personal electronic communication, December 16, 2010; *The Evening World,* April 12, 1912; *New York Herald,* April 15, 1912; *New York Herald,* April 13, 1912; clippings in National Bahá'í Archives.
2. Shoghi Effendi, *God Passes By,* xv; Weber, *From Max Weber: Essays in Sociology,* 245–47, introduction by the editors, 52–53.
3. Weber, *From Max Weber: Essays in Sociology,* 53.
4. James Fowler, *Stages of Faith,* 200–201.
5. Dorothée Soelle, quoted in Bass, *Practicing Our Faith,* 67.
6. Ives, *Portals to Freedom,* 27–28.
7. Ibid., 30–31.
8. Ibid., 31–33.
9. Ibid., 35.
10. Stanwood Cobb, *Memories of 'Abdu'l-Bahá,* 17–18, 19.

11. Ives, *Portals to Freedom,* 116; Thompson, *Diary of Juliet Thompson,* 239.
12. "Science: Death of Maxim." *Time* magazine, May 16, 1927, http://www.time.com/time/magazine/article/0,9171,736695,00.html; "Hudson Maxim," http://en.wikipedia.org/wiki/Hudson_Maxim; Zia Bagdadi, "'Abdu'l-Bahá in America," in *The Bahá'í Magazine: Star of the West* 19, no. 2 (May 1928): 55; "Interview of W. H. Short, Secy N.Y. Peace Society and Hudson Maxim with Abdul-Baha at the Hotel Ansonia, New York City, April 15th, 1912," *Star of the West* 3, no. 7 (July 13, 1912): 10–11.
13. Ives, *Portals to Freedom,* 36.
14. *New York Tribune,* May 5, 1912, section 2, p. 1.
15. Ibid.
16. Ibid. I have cut out more than half of the interview for reasons of space.
17. Ibid.
18. *The Sacramento Bee,* Oct. 26, 1912, p. 1.
19. Thornton Chase to George Buchanan, June 12, 1912, Thornton Chase Papers. The entire letter has been published in Thornton Chase, "Impressions of 'Abdu'l-Bahá and His Station," comp. Robert H. Stockman, *World Order* 25, no. 1 (Fall, 1993): 20.
20. Bahiyyih Randall-Winckler and Mabel Garis, *William Henry Randall,* 26.
21. Bahiyyih Randall Ford, "Experiences with 'Abdu'l-Bahá of the Randall Family," typescript by Kay Zinky of a recorded talk Ford gave in Colorado, June 11, 1953, Kay Zinky papers, Bahá'í National Archives; Randall-Winckler, *William Henry Randall,* 40–41; Randall Ford, "Experiences with 'Abdu'l-Bahá of the Randall Family," 4; Randall-Winckler, *William Henry Randall,* 40–41.
22. Randall-Winckler, *William Henry Randall,* 41.
23. 'Abdu'l-Bahá, *The Promulgation of Universal Peace,* 4–5.
24. Ibid., 6.
25. Ibid., 8–9.
26. Ibid., 9–10.
27. Ibid., 10–12; cf. *Star of the West* 3, no. 8 (Aug. 1, 1912): 3–4.
28. 'Abdu'l-Bahá, *The Promulgation of Universal Peace,* 14. The version in *Star of the West* 3, no. 8 (Aug. 1, 1912): 4–5, was edited by Howard MacNutt, and the only changes he made when producing *The Promulgation of Universal Peace* was to regularize spelling and punctuation, so I have used the latter version.
29. Thompson, *Diary of Juliet Thompson,* 241–42.
30. The service is described in various sources; the starting time is mentioned in Zia Bagdadi, "'Abdu'l-Bahá in America," *The Bahá'í Magazine: Star of the West* 19, no. 2 (May 1928): 54.

31. The description of Grant's introduction comes from Alice Ives Breed (Ali Kuli Khan's mother in law) to Thornton Chase, May 1, 1912, Thornton Chase Papers; "Address by Abdul Baha at the Church of the Ascension, Fifth Avenue and Tenth Street, New York City, Rev. Percy Stickney Grant, Rector, April 14, 1912," in *Star of the West* 4, no. 7 (July 13, 1913): 7.
32. 'Abdu'l-Bahá, *The Promulgation of Universal Peace,* 14–17. The *Promulgation* text is based on a Persian notes by Ahmad Sohrab; see *Star of the West* 4, no. 1 (March 21, 1913): 7–8, particularly the footnote on page 7. The changes made subsequently involved spelling and punctuation.
33. Thompson, *Diary of Juliet Thompson,* 247.
34. Ibid., 247–48.
35. Maḥmúd-i-Zarqání, *Maḥmúd's Diary,* 43.
36. Ibid., 44.
37. "Bahaism in the Pulpit," editorial in *The Churchmen, A National Church Weekly,* Saturday, April 27, 1912, 550.
38. "Episcopalian Ban on Persian Speaker," Baltimore *News,* April 27, 1912.
39. "Abdul Baha Prays in Ascension Church: His Appearance Striking: Congregation Lingers After Service to See Him, in Oriental Robes, Enter a Modern Limousine," The New York Times, April 15, 1912, clipping in National Bahá'í Archives.
40. 'Abdu'l-Bahá, *The Promulgation of Universal Peace,* 18–21. An earlier version, also edited by MacNutt, appeared in *Star of the West* 3, no. 10 (Sept. 8, 1912): 5–6.
41. Wilson, *Bahaism and its Claims,* 281; GhaneaBassiri, *A History of Islam in America,* 99; Weber, *From Max Weber: Essays in Sociology,* 53.
42. *Star of the West* 3, no. 10 (Sept. 8, 1912): 10–11; *The Promulgation of Universal Peace,* 27–30. He gave a similar talk at Green Acre on August 16; see *Star of the West* 3, no. 16 (Dec. 31, 1912): 5–9; *The Promulgation of Universal Peace,* 353–55.
43. Maḥmúd-i-Zarqání, *Maḥmúd's Diary,* 46.
44. Bagdadi, "'Abdu'l-Bahá in America," 55. The talk recorded in *The Promulgation of Universal Peace* for that night (31–33) does not include this text. Possibly it was a remark separate from the talk. Bagdadi's account was partially based on notes by 'Abdu'l-Bahá and others and thus contains some original material.
45. Marzieh Gail, "Juliet Remembers Gibran As Told To Marzieh Gail," *World Order,* 12, no. 4 (summer 1978): 30; Bushrui and Jenkins, *Kahlil Gibran: Man and Poet,* 125, 9.

46. 'Abdu'l-Bahá, *The Promulgation of Universal Peace,* 39–40. An earlier version of the Columbia University address, also edited by Howard MacNutt, was printed in *Star of the West* 3, no. 8 (Aug. 1, 1912): 8–10.
47. 'Abdu'l-Bahá, *The Promulgation of Universal Peace,* 42–44.
48. Thompson, *Diary of Juliet Thompson,* 251–52, 256. Our sources for the Bowery visit are fivefold; *Maḥmúd's Diary,* which incorrectly places the visit on Thursday evening, April 18; *Diary of Juliet Thompson*; *Star of the West* 3, no. 7 (July 13, 1912): 11–12, which records his talk; *The Promulgation of Universal Peace,* which has a slightly edited version of the talk; and Kate Carew's interview in the *New York Tribune.*
49. 'Abdu'l-Bahá, *The Promulgation of Universal Peace,* 44–46.
50. Maḥmúd-i-Zarqání, *Maḥmúd's Diary,* 47.
51. Thompson, *Diary of Juliet Thompson,* 259–61.
52. *New York Tribune,* May 5, 1912, section 2, p. 7.
52. Thompson, *Diary of Juliet Thompson,* 266; Dorothée Soelle, quoted in Bass, ed., *Practicing Our Faith,* 67.

4 / The Oneness of Humankind

1. Table of talks, author's personal papers; Nellie S. French, "A Portrait of 'Abdu'l-Bahá," *Star of the West* 14 (1923): 117–19. The painting is in the National Bahá'í Archives, Wilmette, IL.
2. Mariam Haney, "Mrs. Agnes Parsons," 410; Agnes Parsons, "The Story of the Parsons House in Washington Having to Do with the History of the Divine Cause in our Land," MS, Agnes Parsons Papers; Joseph Hannen, "'Abdu'l-Bahá in Washington, D.C.," 7; Thompson, *Diary of Juliet Thompson,* 273.
3. Marzieh Gail, "Ali-Kuli Khan," 351–53; Stockman, *The Bahá'í Faith in America, vol. 2,* 48–49. The invitations to the White House and to the United States Congress are mentioned in Alice Ives Breed (Ali Kuli Khan's mother in law) to Thornton Chase, May 1, 1912, Thornton Chase Papers.
4. Morrison, Gayle, "Gregory, Louis George," in *The Bahá'í Encyclopedia Project,* http://www.bahai-encyclopedia-project.org (accessed Dec. 9, 2010); Morrison, *To Move the World,* 36.
5. Morrison, "Gregory, Louis George."
6. Marzieh Gail, *Arches of the Years,* 79–80.
7. Joseph Hannen, "Abdul-Baha in Washington, D.C." p. 7; Parsons, *Agnes Parsons' Diary,* 11; Maḥmúd-i-Zarandí, *Maḥmúd's Diary,* 49.
8. *Star of the West* 3, no. 3 (Apr. 28, 1912): 8–9; cf. 'Abdu'l-Bahá, *The Promulgation of Universal Peace,* 47.
9. *Star of the West* 3, no. 3 (Apr. 28, 1912): 8–9; cf. 'Abdu'l-Bahá, *The Promulgation of Universal Peace,* 48.

10. *Star of the West* 3, no. 3 (Apr. 28, 1912): 8–9; cf. 'Abdu'l-Bahá, *The Promulgation of Universal Peace,* 49.
11. Hannen, "Abdul-Baha in Washington," p. 7.
12. 'Abdu'l-Bahá, *The Promulgation of Universal Peace,* 50–51. Also see a slightly rougher version in *Star of the West* 3, no. 3 (Apr. 28, 1912): 9–10.
13. Parsons, *Agnes Parsons' Diary,* 17.
14. "John van Schaick," http://www25.uua.org/uuhs/duub/articles johnvanschaick.html (accessed April 28, 2011); Maḥmúd-i-Zarqání, *Maḥmúd's Diary,* 50.
15. Maḥmúd-i-Zarqání, *Maḥmúd's Diary,* 50–54. This authorized translation also varies from the published Persian text. An early version of the talk, with remarks by Rev. van Schaick, appear in *Star of the West* 3, no. 3 (Apr. 28, 1912): 10–12; it can also be found in 'Abdu'l-Bahá, *The Promulgation of Universal Peace,* 53–54.
16. Maḥmúd-i-Zarqání, *Maḥmúd's Diary,* 50–54. This authorized translation also varies from the published Persian text. An early version of the talk, with remarks by Rev. van Schaick, appear in *Star of the West,* vol. 3. no. 3 (Apr. 28, 1912): 10–12; it can also be found in *Promulgation of Universal Peace,* 50–58.
17. Parsons, *Agnes Parsons' Diary,* 17–18; Maḥmúd-i-Zarandí, *Maḥmúd's Diary,* 54.
18. Parsons, *Agnes Parsons' Diary,* 19.
19. 'Abdu'l-Bahá, *The Promulgation of Universal Peace,* 60–63. This is a new translation from the Persian notes by Amin Banani made for the second edition of *Promulgation.* An earlier version of the talk was published in *Star of the West* 3, no. 3 (Apr. 28, 1912): 14–15.
20. Hannen, "Abdul-Baha in Washington, D.C.," 7; Shoghi Effendi, *The Advent of Divine Justice,* 40.
21. Morrison, *To Move the World,* 52; Harlan Ober, "Louis G. Gregory," *The Bahá'í World: A Biennial International Record, vol. XII, 1950–54* (Wilmette, IL: Bahá'í Publishing Trust, 1981): 668.
22. Morrison, *To Move the World,* 53.
23. "Duke Lita," *New York Times,* April 27, 1907. Jan Jasion gave the author the Duke's correct full name in an email dated December 13, 2010; Thompson, *The Diary of Juliet Thompson,* 272–73; Alice Ives Breed to Thornton Chase, May 1, 1912, Thornton Chase Papers.
24. Thompson, *The Diary of Juliet Thompson,* 273; 'Abdu'l-Bahá, *The Promulgation of Universal Peace,* 46; cf. *Star of the West* 3, no. 3 (Apr. 28, 1912): 15–16; Hannen, "Abdul-Baha in Washington, D.C.," 7; "Metropolitan African Methodist Episcopal Church," http://www.metropolitanamec.org/aboutus.asp (accessed Dec. 12, 2010).
25. Hannen, "Abdul-Baha in Washington, D.C.," 7.
26. 'Abdu'l-Bahá, *The Promulgation of Universal Peace,* 66–71. An earlier version was published in *Star of the West* 3, no. 3 (Apr. 28, 1912): 16–18.

27. *The Washington Herald,* Apr. 25, 1912, Bahá'í National Archives.
28. Maḥmúd-i-Zarandí, *Maḥmúd's Diary,* p. 57 and note 52; 'Abdu'l-Bahá, *The Promulgation of Universal Peace,* 77–79. An earlier version was published in *Star of the West* 3, no. 3 (Apr. 28, 1912): 21–22.
29. Spicer-Simson, *A Collector of Characters: Reminiscences of Theodore Spicer-Simson,* 60–61, quoted by Joseph Roy Sheppherd at http://master-in-america.blogspot.com/2011_05_01_archive.html; Lee McClung, quoted in Thompson, *Diary of Juliet Thompson,* 280.
30. Thompson, *The Diary of Juliet Thompson,* 276; Alkan, *Dissent and Heterodoxy in the Late Ottoman Empire,* 171–72.
31. *Star of the West* 3, no. 5 (June 5, 1912): 7–8; cf. 'Abdu'l-Bahá, *The Promulgation of Universal Peace,* 84–88.
32. Maḥmúd-i-Zarandí, *Maḥmúd's Diary,* 63; Hannen, "Abdul-Baha in Washington, D.C.," 7.
33. *The Washington Herald,* April 27, 1912, Bahá'í National Archives. 'Abdu'l-Bahá commented about the incident in instructions "Dictated to Howard MacNutt by Abdul-Baha at Dublin N. H. 7 a.m. August 6th, 1912," Albert Windust Papers.
34. "Pray for Abdul Baha," Washington, D.C. *Post,* April 29, 1912, Bahá'í National Archives.
35. Instructions "Dictated to Howard MacNutt by Abdul-Baha at Dublin N. H. 7 a.m. August 6th, 1912," Albert Windust Papers.
36. Maḥmúd-i-Zarqání, *Maḥmúd's Diary,* 64; Alice Ives Breed to Thornton Chase, May 1, 1912, p. 3, Thornton Chase Papers. According to Remey, "Reminiscences of My Visit to the Master in England the Summer of 1911," 8, 'Abdu'l-Bahá was driven to the White House to meet President Taft but was turned away because the President couldn't see him. This information cannot be corroborated by another source at this time.
37. Maḥmúd-i-Zarqání says 'Abdu'l-Bahá left Washington at 5:30pm (*Maḥmúd's Diary,* 66) but Alice Ives Breed (Breed to Thornton Chase, May 1, 1912, Chase Papers) says his train left at 1:25pm.
38. *Chicago Defender,* May 5, 1912, National Bahá'í Archives, Wilmette, IL.
39. Maḥmúd-i-Zarandí, *Maḥmúd's Diary,* 68–70. The principles were published in "Baha Is Peace Herald," *Chicago Daily News,* April 30, 1912, clipping in National Bahá'í Archives.
40. Rutstein, *Corinne True,* 99–100.
41. "Wisdom-Talks of Abdul-Baha (Abbas Effendi) at Chicago, Illinois, April 30th to May 5th, 1912," 5–6, published with *Star of the West* 3, no. 3 (Apr. 28, 1912); cf. 'Abdu'l-Bahá, *The Promulgation of Universal Peace,* 92–94.

42. Zia Bagdadi, "'Abdu'l-Bahá in America, Chapter III-Chicago, Ill.," in *Star of the West: The Bahá'í Magazine* 19, no. 4 (July 1928): 111.
43. W. E. B. Du Bois, "The Fourth Annual Conference of the National Association for the Advancement of Colored People," *The Crisis,* June 1912, 80, available at http://books.google.com/ (accessed December 13, 2010); "The National Association for the Advancement of Colored People Program of the Fourth Annual Conference at Chicago, April 28, 29, and 30, 1912," pdf copy in author's personal papers; "Wisdom-Talks of Abdul-Baha (Abbas Effendi) at Chicago, Illinois, April 30th to May 5th, 1912," 6–7, cf. 'Abdu'l-Bahá, *The Promulgation of Universal Peace,* 95–97.
44. Mildred Miller, "Echoes of the N. A. A. C. P.'s Fourth Annual Conference," *Chicago Defender,* May 4, 1912.
45. "Wisdom-Talks of Abdul-Baha (Abbas Effendi) at Chicago, Illinois, April 30th to May 5th, 1912, 3–4; cf. 'Abdu'l-Bahá, *The Promulgation of Universal Peace,* 90–91.
46. Mark Perry, "Pioneering Race Unity: The Chicago Bahá'ís, 1919–39," 51, 45; Buck, *Alain Locke: Faith and Philosophy* reviews Locke's conversion and many contributions to the Bahá'í Faith.
47. Gayle Morrison, citing a column in *The Crisis,* says Du Bois met 'Abdu'l-Bahá in New York and Chicago; see Gayle Morrison to the author, email dated Nov. 7, 2010, author's personal papers; *The Crisis,* vol. 4, no. 1 (May 1912), 14-15, available at http://books.google.com/ (accessed December 14, 2010); *The Crisis* 4, no. 2 (June 1912): 80, 88, available at http://books.google.com/ (accessed December 14, 2010); Nina Gomer Du Bois's Bahá'í membership is mentioned in Morrison, *To Move the World,* 27–28, 262–63. *The Crisis* 23, no. 4 (Feb. 1922): 151, http://books.google.com/ available at (accessed December 14, 2010). Note that this was published one month after Eugene Debs was released from prison (on December 25, 1921) and two months after 'Abdu'l-Bahá's passing (on November 28, 1921), hence the sentence pairing the two.
48. "Record of the Fourth Annual Convention of the Bahai Temple Unity, Chicago, April 27–May 1, 1912," *Star of the West* 3, no. 5 (June 5, 1912): 6.
49. Morrison, *To Move the World,* 67.
50. "Ghodsiyeh Ashraf's Memoirs," 352. I am indebted to Bijan Ma'sumian for pointing out this text to me and translating it into English from Persian.
51. "Ghodsiyeh Ashraf's Memoirs," 352.
52. Shoghi Effendi, *God Passes By,* 288.

5 / "The Temple is already built"

The chapter title is taken from Louise Waite, "My Visits with and Instructions from Abdul Baha while He was in Chicago from April 30th to May 6th 1912," manuscript, Louise Waite Papers, p. 7.

1. Other sources, notably Maḥmúd, say the audience numbered two thousand that evening; see *Maḥmúd's Diary,* 71.
2. Maḥmúd-i-Zarqání, *Maḥmúd's Diary,* 38. Maḥmúd says 'Abdu'l-Bahá's meeting with journalists occurred at the Hotel Ansonia, and possibly two meetings with journalists occurred that day; the subjects appear to be the same as the ones described by Wendell Phillips Dodge when journalists interviewed 'Abdu'l-Bahá on board the *Cedric.*
3. GhaneaBassiri, *A History of Islam in America,* 84.
4. "Wisdom-Talks of Abdul-Baha (Abbas Effendi) at Chicago, Illinois, April 30th to May 5th, 1912," 3, also see 'Abdu'l-Bahá, *The Promulgation of Universal Peace,* 89.
5. "Wisdom-Talks of Abdul-Baha (Abbas Effendi) at Chicago, Illinois, April 30th to May 5th, 1912," 3; also see 'Abdu'l-Bahá, *The Promulgation of Universal Peace,* 89–90.
6. Isaiah 2:3–4.
7. *Star of the West* 3, no. 10 (Sept. 8, 1912): 7; 'Abdu'l-Bahá, *The Promulgation of Universal Peace,* 25–26. 'Abdu'l-Bahá made similar statements about Bahá'u'lláh establishing unity among the sects and communities of Iran or the Orient; see 'Abdu'l-Bahá, *The Promulgation of Universal Peace,* 20, 404, and 491.
8. "Wisdom-Talks of Abdul-Baha (Abbas Effendi) at Chicago, Illinois, April 30th to May 5th, 1912," 3; cf. 'Abdu'l-Bahá, *The Promulgation of Universal Peace,* 65–66.
9. "Wisdom-Talks of Abdul-Baha (Abbas Effendi) at Chicago, Illinois, April 30th to May 5th, 1912," 4; cf. 'Abdu'l-Bahá, *The Promulgation of Universal Peace,* 91.
10. Hannen, "The Public Meeting of the Fourth Annual Convention of Bahai Temple Unity," 32.
11. "Bahaist Site Dedicated," *Chicago Evening Post,* May 1, 1912, clipping in Bahá'í National Archives. Much of this account is a summary of Honore J. Jaxon, "Dedication of the Mashrak-El-Azkar Site," 5–7.
12. Rutstein, *Corinne True,* 101; Bruce Whitmore, *The Dawning Place,* 61.

13. "Wisdom-Talks of Abdul-Baha (Abbas Effendi) at Chicago, Illinois, April 30th to May 5th, 1912," 4–5, cf. 'Abdu'l-Bahá, *The Promulgation of Universal Peace,* 97–98. The "many" Maskrak-el-Azkars of Persia refers to places devoted to Bahá'í worship; today, Bahá'ís would call them *Bahá'í Centers.*
14. Louise Waite, "My Visits with and Instructions from Abdul Baha while He was in Chicago from April 30th to May 6th 1912."
15. Louise Waite, "My Visits with and Instructions from Abdul Baha while He was in Chicago from April 30th to May 6th 1912."

6 / Enunciating the Bahá'í Principles

1. Table of Talks by 'Abdu'l-Bahá, author's personal papers.
2. Rutstein, *Corinne True,* 102–3. 'Abdu'l-Bahá did not attend the funeral, possibly because if he did, the event would have been about him rather than about Davis True.
3. Maḥmúd-i-Zarqání, *Maḥmúd's Diary,* 74.
4. "Wisdom-Talks of Abdul Baha Given at Chicago, Ill., April 30th to May 5th, 1912," 7, also see 'Abdu'l-Bahá, *The Promulgation of Universal Peace,* 99.
5. "Wisdom-Talks of Abdul Baha Given at Chicago, Ill., April 30th to May 5th, 1912," 7–8.
6. For more information about the early American Bahá'í use of consultation, see Stockman, *The Bahá'í Faith in America,* vol. 2, 19.
7. "Wisdom-Talks of Abdul Baha Given at Chicago, Ill., April 30th to May 5th, 1912," 11, also see 'Abdu'l-Bahá, *The Promulgation of Universal Peace,* 108–9. This talk is also given in *Star of the West* 3, no. 4 (May 12, 1912): 15, where it is stated as having been given in the morning.
8. Louise Waite, "My Visits with and Instructions from Abdul Baha while He was in Chicago from April 30th to May 6th 1912," 9–10; "Wisdom-Talks of Abdul Baha Given at Chicago, Ill., April 30th to May 5th, 1912," 8, also see 'Abdu'l-Bahá, *The Promulgation of Universal Peace,* 102.
9. "Wisdom-Talks of Abdul Baha Given at Chicago, Ill., April 30th to May 5th, 1912," 9, also see 'Abdu'l-Bahá, *The Promulgation of Universal Peace,* 103–4.
10. "Wisdom-Talks of Abdul Baha Given at Chicago, Ill., April 30th to May 5th, 1912," 9, also see 'Abdu'l-Bahá, *The Promulgation of Universal Peace,* 104–5.
11. "Wisdom-Talks of Abdul Baha Given at Chicago, Ill., April 30th to May 5th, 1912," 9, also see 'Abdu'l-Bahá, *The Promulgation of Universal Peace,* 105.
12. "Wisdom-Talks of Abdul Baha Given at Chicago, Ill., April 30th to May 5th, 1912," 10, also see 'Abdu'l-Bahá, *The Promulgation of Universal Peace,* 106.

13. Rothman, *Woman's Proper Place,* 21–23, 82.
14. 'Abdu'l-Bahá called for women to be elected to the House of Spirituality later in 1912.
15. "Wisdom-Talks of Abdul Baha Given at Chicago, Ill., April 30th to May 5th, 1912," 10, also see 'Abdu'l-Bahá, *The Promulgation of Universal Peace,* 107.
16. "Wisdom-Talks of Abdul Baha Given at Chicago, Ill., April 30th to May 5th, 1912," 11–13, also see 'Abdu'l-Bahá, *The Promulgation of Universal Peace,* 109–14.
17. *Chicago Daily Tribune,* May 1, 1912, clipping in Bahá'í National Archives.
18. "Ruth J. Moffett," *The Bahá'í World: An International Record, vol. XVII, 1976–79,* 463, 464; Zia Bagdadi, "'Abdu'l-Bahá in America, Chapter III—Chicago, Ill," *Star of the West: The Bahá'í Magazine* 19, no. 4 (July, 1928): 115; Maḥmúd-i-Zarandí, *Maḥmúd's Diary,* 74–76; *Star of the West* 14, no. 8 (Nov. 1923): 247–48.
19. "Wisdom-Talks of Abdul Baha Given at Chicago, Ill., April 30th to May 5th, 1912," 17–18, also see 'Abdu'l-Bahá, *The Promulgation of Universal Peace,* 115.
20. "Wisdom-Talks of Abdul Baha Given at Chicago, Ill., April 30th to May 5th, 1912," 19, also see 'Abdu'l-Bahá, *The Promulgation of Universal Peace,* 119.
21. "Dictated to Howard MacNutt by Abdul-Baha at Dublin, N.H. 7 a.m. August 6th, 1912," Windust Papers.
22. Honoré J. Jaxon, "A Stroll with Abdul Baha," *Star of the West* 3, no. 4 (May 17, 1912): 27–29; "Wisdom-Talks of Abdul Baha Given at Chicago, Ill., April 30th to May 5th, 1912," 15–18, also see 'Abdu'l-Bahá, *The Promulgation of Universal Peace,* 120–26.
23. "Abdul-Baha with the Children of the Friends in Chicago. From Notes Taken By Ella Goodall Cooper and Ella M. Bailey," *Star of the West* 3, no. 7 (July 13, 1912): 6–7. A very similar account of the meeting can be found in Louise Waite, "My Visits with and Instructions from Abdul Baha while He was in Chicago from April 30th to May 6th 1912," 23–24.
24. Words of 'Abdu'l-Bahá quoted in Maḥmúd-i-Zarqání, *Maḥmúd's Diary,* 80–81; also see 'Abdu'l-Bahá, *The Promulgation of Universal Peace,* 127–29. The nature of Chicago's problems will be discussed in chapter eleven.
25. "Abdul-Baha with the Children of the Friends in Chicago. From Notes Taken By Ella Goodall Cooper and Ella M. Bailey," *Star of the West* 3, no. 7 (July 13, 1912): 7.
26. Mullick, *The First Hindu Mission to America,* 72; Maḥmúd-i-Zarandí, *Maḥmúd's Diary,* 77.
27. "Wisdom-Talks of Abdul Baha Given at Chicago, Ill., April 30th to May 5th, 1912," 22–23, also see 'Abdu'l-Bahá, *The Promulgation of Universal Peace,* 129–33.

28. "Wisdom-Talks of Abdul Baha Given at Chicago, Ill., April 30th to May 5th, 1912," 23–24, also see 'Abdu'l-Bahá, *The Promulgation of Universal Peace,* 132–33.
29. Maḥmúd-i-Zarandí, *Maḥmúd's Diary,* 77.
30. "Jenkin Lloyd Jones," at http://www25.uua.org/uuhs/duub/articles/jenkinlloyd jones.html (accessed December 28, 2010). Regarding Mozoomdar and Dharmapala, see Mullick, *The First Hindu Mission to America,* 115, and Schmidt, *Restless Souls,* 167.
31. Louise Waite, "My Visits with and Instructions from Abdul Baha while He was in Chicago from April 30th to May 6th 1912," 24; "Wisdom-Talks of Abdul Baha Given at Chicago, Ill., April 30th to May 5th, 1912," 18–20, also see 'Abdu'l-Bahá, *The Promulgation of Universal Peace,* 134–35.
32. "Wisdom-Talks of Abdul Baha Given at Chicago, Ill., April 30th to May 5th, 1912," 20–22, also see 'Abdu'l-Bahá, *The Promulgation of Universal Peace,* 137–38.
33. *Star of the West* 3, no. 4 (May 17, 1912): 26–27; also see 'Abdu'l-Bahá, *The Promulgation of Universal Peace,* 138. The prayer is a popular one and found in many Bahá'í prayer books. Interestingly, the Lincoln Center talk is also published in "Wisdom-Talks of Abdul Baha Given at Chicago, Ill., April 30th to May 5th, 1912," 22, the closing prayer is a different one; Maḥmúd-i-Zarandí, *Maḥmúd's Diary,* 79; Shahnaz [Louise] Waite, "The Changed Man," 108.
34. Louise Waite, "My Visits with and Instructions from Abdul Baha while He was in Chicago from April 30th to May 6th 1912," 31–32.
35. "Abdul Baha Ready To Face Malcontents," Chicago *Examiner,* May 6, 1912, clipping in National Bahá'í Archives.
36. Louise Waite, "My Visits with and Instructions from Abdul Baha while He was in Chicago from April 30th to May 6th 1912," 28; "A Brief History of the Early Development of the Bahá'í Community of Cleveland, Ohio, through 1932," typescript, National Bahá'í Archives; "Table-Talk by Abdul-Baha at Cleveland, O," *Star of the West* 3, no. 6 (June 24, 1912): 5; also see 'Abdu'l-Bahá, *The Promulgation of Universal Peace,* 143. "Bahaist Approves Union of Races," *Cleveland Plain Dealer,* May 7, 1912, mentioned in Ward, *239 Days,* 60–61; *Star of the West* 3, no. 4 (May 17, 1912): 32; also see 'Abdu'l-Bahá, *The Promulgation of Universal Peace,* 143.
37. Garis, *Martha Root,* 51–52; "Address by Abdul-Baha at Hotel Schenley, Pittsburgh, PA., May 7, 1912," *Star of the West* 3, no. 6 (June 24, 1912): 2–4, 8; also see 'Abdu'l-Bahá, *The Promulgation of Universal Peace,* 145–52.
38. Garis, *Martha Root,* 52; Maḥmúd-i-Zarandí, *Maḥmúd's Diary,* 86–87.
39. "Talk Given by Abdul-Baha at 227 Riverside Drive, New York City, May 11, 1912," in *Star of the West* 3, no. 10 (Sept. 8, 1912): 11–13; also see 'Abdu'l-Bahá, *The Promulgation of Universal Peace,* 153–56.

40. Thompson, *The Diary of Juliet Thompson,* 284.
41. Maḥmúd-i-Zarandí, *Maḥmúd's Diary,* 89; "Baha Likes 'All Right': Persian Prophet Thinks It Is Our Most Characteristic Expression," *The New York Times,* May 13, 1912.
42. *Star of the West* 3, no. 9 (Aug. 20, 1912): 12–13; also see 'Abdu'l-Bahá, *The Promulgation of Universal Peace,* 161–64.
43. Ibid., 15–16; also see 'Abdu'l-Bahá, *The Promulgation of Universal Peace,* 167–69.
44. *Star of the West* 3, no. 9 (Aug. 20, 1912): 16; also see 'Abdu'l-Bahá, *The Promulgation of Universal Peace,* 169; Ahmad Sohrab to Agnes Parsons, May 13, 1912, Agnes Parsons Papers.
45. Thompson, *Diary of Juliet Thompson,* 285; "Reception to Abdul-Baha by the New York Peace Society at Hotel Astor, May 13, 1912 (afternoon), *Star of the West* 3, no. 8 (Aug. 1, 1912), 10–13.
46. "Reception to Abdul-Baha by the New York Peace Society at Hotel Astor, May 13, 1912 (afternoon), *Star of the West* 3, no. 8 (Aug. 1, 1912): 15; also see 'Abdu'l-Bahá, *The Promulgation of Universal Peace,* 170–73.
47. Ahmad Sohrab to Agnes Parsons, night letter [a kind of telegram] May 14, 1912, Agnes Parsons Papers, Bahá'í National Archives; Maḥmúd-i-Zarandí, *Maḥmúd's Diary,* 100.
48. http://www.hopefarm.com/ulster2.htm (accessed May 19, 2011); "Lake Mohonk Conference on International Arbitration" at http://en.wikipedia.org/wiki/Lake_Mohonk_Conference_on_International_Arbitration (accessed May 19, 2011); Ahmad Sohrab to Agnes Parsons, May 15, 1912, Agnes Parsons Papers.
49. "Report of the Eighteenth Annual Lake Mohonk Conference on International Arbitration, May 15th, 16th, and 17th, 1912," 42–44.
50. Ahmad Sohrab to Agnes Parsons, night letter [a kind of telegram] May 15, 1912, Agnes Parsons Papers.
51. Maḥmúd-i-Zarandí, *Maḥmúd's Diary,* 101.
52. "Address at Metropolitan Temple Reception," *Star of the West* 3, no. 7 (July 13, 1912): 15.
53. Zia Bagdadi, "'Abdu'l-Bahá in America," *The Bahá'í Magazine: Star of the West* 19, no. 6 (September 1928): 180–81.
54. Bagdadi, "'Abdu'l-Bahá in America," 181.
55. Ibid., 182.
56. Telegram from 'Abdu'l-Bahá to the Allen family, Berkeley, California, May 1, 1912, quoted in Brown, *Memories of 'Abdu'l-Bahá,* 33; Ahmad Sohrab to Agnes Parsons, May 22, 1912, Parsons Papers.
57. Bagdadi, "'Abdu'l-Bahá in America," 182.
58. 'Abdu'l-Bahá, *The Promulgation of Universal Peace,* 174–78; also see MacNutt, "Addresses Delivered by Abdul-Baha in New York City and Vicinity," *Star of*

the West 3, no. 9 (Aug. 20, 1912): 10. I have used the *Promulgation* text here because it is clearer.

59. Ives, *Portals to Freedom,* 87.
60. Ibid., 82.
61. 'Abdu'l-Bahá, *The Promulgation of Universal Peace,* 179; also see MacNutt, "Addresses Delivered by Abdul-Baha in New York City and Vicinity," *Star of the West* 3, no. 9 (Aug. 20, 1912): 6.
62. 'Abdu'l-Bahá, *The Promulgation of Universal Peace,* 180–81.
63. Ibid., 182.
64. Maḥmúd-i-Zarandí, *Maḥmúd's Diary,* 109.
65. Ives, *Portals to Freedom,* 86.
66. Maḥmúd-i-Zarandí, *Maḥmúd's Diary,* 105.
67. MacNutt, "Addresses Delivered by Abdul-Baha in New York City and Vicinity," *Star of the West* 3, no. 8 (Aug. 1, 1912): 19; also see 'Abdu'l-Bahá, *The Promulgation of Universal Peace,* 184–85. Regarding the link between the education of women and social and economic development, see Geeta Gandhi Kingdon's article, "Education of Women and socio-economic development" at http://bahai-library.com/kingdom_education_women_development.
68. MacNutt, "Addresses Delivered by Abdul-Baha in New York City and Vicinity," *Star of the West* 3, no. 8 (Aug. 1, 1912): 19; also see 'Abdu'l-Bahá, *The Promulgation of Universal Peace,* 186.
69. MacNutt, "Addresses Delivered by Abdul-Baha in New York City and Vicinity," *Star of the West* 3, no. 8 (Aug. 1, 1912): 20; also see 'Abdu'l-Bahá, *The Promulgation of Universal Peace,* 189.
70. Maḥmúd-i-Zarandí, *Maḥmúd's Diary,* 106.
71. "Unitarians begin Anniversary Week: Nearly 1000 Delegates From all Over Country Here for Meetings—Persian Prophet Among Speakers," *Boston Post,* May 20, 1912, clipping in Bahá'í National Archives; Mullick, *The First Hindu Mission to America,* 159; Maḥmúd-i-Zarandí, *Maḥmúd's Diary,* 107.
72. 'Abdu'l-Bahá, *The Promulgation of Universal Peace,* 195–98. This talk is listed as given to the "Free Religious Association, or Unitarian Conference" on May 24, 1912, but the published Persian text is listed as the talk he gave on May 22, 1912 at Tremont Temple. Furthermore, the Free Religious Association, to whom he spoke on May 24, published his talk to them, and it is identical to the published Persian text for the May 24 address. Consequently it appears *The Promulgation of Universal Peace* is in error in the dating of the talk. The title of the organization is also incorrect; the Free Religious Association and the American Unitarian Association were two separate organizations, and the FRA membership included many people who were not Unitarians. The only English-language text I have found is the one in *Promulgation.*

73. Maḥmúd-i-Zarandí, *Maḥmúd's Diary,* 107; Edwin Mead, remarks introducing 'Abdu'l-Bahá, in *The Free Religions Association: Proceedings at the Forty-fifth Annual Meeting,, Held in Boston, Mass., Thursday and Friday, May 23 and 24, 1912,* 85.
74. Ives, *Portals to Freedom,* 88, 90.
75. Ibid., 80.

7 / The Center of the Covenant

1. Maḥmúd-i-Zarandí, Maḥmúd's Diary, 109; Zia Bagdadi, "'Abdu'l-Bahá in America," *The Bahá'í Magazine: Star of the West* 19, no. 6 (Sept. 1928): 183; Burke, *Swami Vivekananda in America: New Discoveries, His Prophetic Mission, Part Two,* 74–76; Mullit, *The First Hindu Mission to America,* 58; "Bab Religion's Leader Talks to Clark Students," *Worcester Evening Gazette,* May 24, 1912, copy in author's personal papers; Gail, *Arches of the Years,* 89; Maḥmúd-i-Zarandí, *Maḥmúd's Diary,* 111.
2. 'Abdu'l-Bahá, *The Promulgation of Universal Peace,* 193–98; Maḥmúd-i-Zarandí, *Maḥmúd's Diary,* 113.
3. 'Abdu'l-Bahá, *The Promulgation of Universal Peace,* 203–7.
4. "Abdul-Baha's Address to Theosophists of New York City," *Star of the West* 4, no. 3 (Apr. 28, 1913): 55–56; also see 'Abdu'l-Bahá, *The Promulgation of Universal Peace,* 216–22. The short description of the talk in Maḥmúd-i-Zarandí, *Maḥmúd's Diary,* 117, is totally different, suggesting either that the transcript or the description are misdated, or that he gave two talks.
5. Thompson, *The Diary of Juliet Thompson,* 293; "Address of Abdul Baha at Protestant Episcopal Church of the Ascension, Fifth Ave. and 10th St., New York City, Sunday, June 2, 1912, 8pm, Rev. Dr. Percy Stickney Grant, Rector," *Star of the West* 3, no. 10 (Sept. 8, 1912): 25.
6. 'Abdu'l-Bahá, *The Promulgation of Universal Peace,* 226–28; also see "Address of Abdul Baha at Protestant Episcopal Church of the Ascension, Fifth Ave. and 10th St., New York City, Sunday, June 2, 1912, 8 P.M., Rev. Dr. Percy Stickney Grant, Rector," *Star of the West* 3, no. 10 (Sept. 8, 1912): 25
7. 'Abdu'l-Bahá, *The Promulgation of Universal Peace,* 229–30; also see "Address of Abdul Baha at Protestant Episcopal Church of the Ascension, Fifth Ave. and 10th St., New York City, Sunday, June 2, 1912, 8 P.M., Rev. Dr. Percy Stickney Grant, Rector," *Star of the West* 3, no. 10 (Sept. 8, 1912): 25.
8. Baghdadi, "'Abdu'l-Bahá in America," 184. Information on the life of Pinchot comes from "Pinchot, Gifford," *Funk & Wagnalls New Encyclopedia,* vol. 21, 15–16.
9. Maḥmúd-i-Zarqání, *Maḥmúd's Diary,* 121.

10. Ibid., 119.
11. Ibid., 125; Baghdadi, "'Abdu'l-Bahá in America," 218; Gail, *Arches of the Years,* 96.
12. Maḥmúd-i-Zarqání, *Maḥmúd's Diary,* 125.
13. McKinney, "Abdul-Baha in Philadelphia," 83; 'Abdu'l-Bahá, *The Promulgation of Universal Peace,* 239–45; also see *Star of the West* 5, no. 7 (Jul. 13, 1914), 99–102.
14. Hutchison, *Religious Pluralism in America,* 93–96; Martha Root, "My Visit to Temple University," *Star of the West* 22, no. 9 (Dec. 1922): 265, 266; "Russell Conwell," http://en.wikipedia.org/wiki/Russell_Conwell (accessed January 15, 2011).
15. Seager, *The World's Parliament of Religions,* 44.
16. Edna McKinney, "Abdul-Baha's Visit to Philadelphia," 89; 'Abdu'l-Bahá, *The Promulgation of Universal Peace,* 246, 248; Maḥmúd-i-Zarqání, *Maḥmúd's Diary,* 193; also see *Star of the West* 5, no. 7 (July 13, 1914), 102–103, 105–106.
17. 'Abdu'l-Bahá, *The Promulgation of Universal Peace,* 248–49.
18. Ibid., 253–54.
19. McKinney, "Abdul-Baha in Philadelphia," 90.
20. Maḥmúd-i-Zarqání, *Maḥmúd's Diary,* 126. This entry is identified as Sunday, June 9, 1912, and illustrates well some of the difficulties in interpreting Maḥmúd's chronology. The entry for Saturday, June 8 describes 'Abdu'l-Bahá's talks at the Unitarian Church and the Baptist Temple in Philadelphia, which we know from other sources occurred on Sunday, June 9. The entry for Sunday, June 9 (which should be labeled Monday, June 10) has a paragraph describing 'Abdu'l-Bahá's hours in Philadelphia, followed by a paragraph describing his evening talk in New York City. These are then followed by a paragraph about 'Abdu'l-Bahá revealing a tablet to Hippolyte Dreyfus (something 'Abdu'l-Bahá often did in the quiet of the early morning before a crowd arrived), a description of what he did "day and night," and a summary of his evening talk, which is different from the previous summary of an evening talk. It appears that Maḥmúd has placed two day entries together, labeled "Sunday." But it is not clear that we have Monday and Tuesday in this entry because the "Monday" entry describes 'Abdu'l-Bahá's talk that *The Promulgation of Universal Peace* lists as occurring on Tuesday and because Bagdadi, in his memoir, places the tablet to Dreyfus as being revealed on the first day back to New York City (which he also misidentifies as June 9 rather than June 10; see Bagdadi, "'Abdu'l-Bahá in America," 218). Subsequent entries apparently remain off by one day, because Maḥmúd has 'Abdu'l-Bahá speaking at two churches on Saturday, June 15, and no talks at all on Sunday, June 16. Maḥmúd must have inserted dates into his "diary" later. When he did so, he

used the Western convention of starting with the morning rather than the Middle Eastern convention of starting the day at sunset. It is also possible that not all the pages were composed in a book; some may have been composed on loose pieces of paper and inserted later, which may be true of the second half of the "Sunday" entry.

21. 'Abdu'l-Bahá, *The Promulgation of Universal Peace,* 266–69. Also see *Star of the West* 3, no. 10 (Sept. 8, 1912): 30–32.
22. 'Abdu'l-Bahá, *The Promulgation of Universal Peace,* 276–77; also see *Star of the West* 3, no. 10 (Sept. 8, 1912): 19–23.
23. 'Abdu'l-Bahá, *The Promulgation of Universal Peace,* 277–79.
24. Ibid., 280.
25. Ibid., 280–82.
26. Maḥmúd-i-Zarqání, *Maḥmúd's Diary,* 134–35.
27. 'Abdu'l-Bahá, *The Promulgation of Universal Peace,* 282–84.
28. Maḥmúd-i-Zarqání, *Maḥmúd's Diary,* 135.
29. Ibid., 130.
30. Maḥmúd-i-Zarqání, *Maḥmúd's Diary,* 127–28. Bagdadi, "'Abdu'l-Bahá in America," 219, phrases the comment in almost exactly the same way. Both men date this comment as June 10 but say 'Abdu'l-Bahá returned to New York City from Philadelphia on June 9, which is one day early, so presumably it happened on June 11. It may be that Bagdadi's account is dependent on Maḥmúd and is not an independent source.
31. 'Abdu'l-Bahá, *The Promulgation of Universal Peace,* 261; also see *Star of the West* 3, no. 10 (Sept. 8, 1912): 14–15.
32. Stockman, *The Bahá'í Faith in America,* vol. 2, 338–39; *Star of the West* 3, no. 10 (Sept. 8, 1912): 14–15; also see 'Abdu'l-Bahá, *The Promulgation of Universal Peace,* 255–56.
33. 'Abdu'l-Bahá, *The Promulgation of Universal Peace,* 263. See also *Star of the West* 3, no. 10 (Sept. 8, 1912): 15.
34. Ibid., 264–66. See also *Star of the West* 3, no. 10 (Sept. 8, 1912): 17.
35. Ibid., 272–74. See also *Star of the West* 3, no. 10 (Sept. 8, 1912): 17–19.
36. J. G. Grundy and H. MacNutt, "Taking of the Moving Picture of Abdul-Baha, The Centre of the Covenant," *Star of the West,* vol. 3, No. 10 (Sept. 8, 1912): 3.
37. Thompson, *The Diary of Juliet Thompson,* 299.
38. Ibid., 313–14.
39. Ibid., 315.
40. Address about the Covenant by 'Abdu'l-Bahá, June 19, 1912, trans. Ameen U. Fareed, revised by 'Abdu'l-Bahá on June 25, 1912, quoted in a talk by Lua Getsinger, San Francisco, July 19, 1912, pp. 5–6, transcript in Leroy Ioas Papers. Also see *Star of the West* 3, no. 14 (Nov. 23, 1912): 9–10.

41. Talk by Lua Getsinger, San Francisco, July 19, 1912, p. 3, transcript in Leroy Ioas Papers.
42. "Address upon the Covenant by Abdul-Baha," June 19, 1912, trans. Ameen U. Fareed.
43. *Star of the West* 3, no. 14 (Nov. 23, 1912): 8.
44. 'Abdu'l-Bahá, *The Promulgation of Universal Peace,* 289; also see *Star of the West* 3, no. 10 (Sept. 8, 1912): 23–24.
45. Ibid., 291–92; also see *Star of the West* 3, no. 10 (Sept. 8, 1912): 24.
46. Ibid., 293.
47. Maḥmúd-i-Zarqání, *Maḥmúd's Diary,* 140–49.
48. Ibid., 142; Doris Ebbert and Olga Finke, "Victoria Bedekian," 884.
49. 'Abdu'l-Bahá, *The Promulgation of Universal Peace,* 298–300. Also see "A Memorable Feast: Abdul-Baha the Host," *Star of the West* 3, no. 8 (Aug. 1, 1912): 16–18.
50. Thompson, *The Diary of Juliet Thompson,* 323.
51. Ahmad Sohrab to Agnes Parsons, July 9, 1912, Agnes Parsons Papers; Maḥmúd-i-Zarqání, *Maḥmúd's Diary,* 151.
52. Ahmad Sohrab to Agnes Parsons, July 13, 1912, Parsons Papers, Bahá'í National Archives.
53. Ella Cooper's New York Diary, entry for July 14, 1912, National Bahá'í Archives, Wilmette, IL; Ahmad Sohrab to Agnes Parsons, July 15, 1912, Parsons Papers; *Star of the West* 3, no. 11 (Sept. 27, 1912): 15–16; also see 'Abdu'l-Bahá, *The Promulgation of Universal Peace,* 326.
54. 'Abdu'l-Bahá, *The Promulgation of Universal Peace,* 304, 311–14, 331; Maḥmúd-i-Zarqání, *Maḥmúd's Diary,* 166–67. No English version of this talk exists.
55. Thompson, *The Diary of Juliet Thompson,* 325.
56. Maḥmúd-i-Zarqání, *Maḥmúd's Diary,* 160–61.
57. Metalmann, *Lua Getsinger: Herald of the Covenant,* 161, says, "July 11, 1912 is the probable date that Lua left for California" but gives no reasoning. George Latimer, "Abdu'l-Baha in America," typescript, George Latimer Papers, says, "On July 7th Lua Getsinger was sent back to California" but doesn't say how he knows (though he may have been there when she arrived).
58. Thompson, *The Diary of Juliet Thompson,* 345.
59. Ella Cooper's New York diary, entries for July 14 and 15, 1912, manuscript, Ella Cooper Papers. The words of 'Abdu'l-Bahá are quoted by her from memory.
60. Ives, "Grace Robarts Ober," 658.
61. Muriel Ives Barrow Newhall, "Stories of Muriel Ives Newhall Barrow: Grace Robarts Ober," at http://bahai-library.com/ives_stories_grace_ober (accessed January 28, 2011).

62. Ives, "Grace Robarts Ober," 658; "Matrimony in the Bahai Spirit: Mr. and Mrs. Ober," *Star of the West* 3, no, 12 (Oct. 16, 1912): 14-15; Ahmad Sohrab to Agnes Parsons, July 18, 1912, Parsons Papers. Ella Cooper says the ceremony was held "at the meeting" in her New York diary entry for July 16, 1912. The prayer 'Abdu'l-Bahá revealed at the Obers' wedding begins, "Glory be to Thee, O my God! Verily, this Thy servant and this Thy maidservant have gathered under the shadow of Thy mercy. . ." ('Abdu'l-Bahá, in *Bahá'í Prayers,* 107).
63. Report of the Baha'i Committee of Investigation, 1917-1918, 20; Corinne True to Helen Goodall, August 16, 1912, Helen Goodall Papers.
64. Muḥammad-'Alí Pásḫá, quoted in Maḥmúd-i-Zarqání, *Maḥmúd's Diary,* 177. Note that Maḥmúd is quoting from page 414 of a book Muḥammad-'Alí Pásḫá subsequently published, which shows that Maḥmúd edited and fleshed out his account, probably in Egypt after returning from the trip.
65. Ali Nakhjavani to the author, email, April 25, 2011, author's personal papers; Balyuzi, *'Abdu'l-Bahá: Center of the Covenant,* 13; Ahmad Sohrab to Agnes Parsons, July 9 and July 13, 1912, Agnes Parsons Papers; Ella Cooper's "New York" Diary, entry of July 20, 1912, manuscript, Ella Cooper Papers.
66. "A Pioneer at the Golden Gate," *Star of the West* 13, no. 8 (Nov. 1922): 205; Ella Cooper's "New York" Diary, entries of July 10, 19 and 20, 1912, manuscript, Ella Cooper Papers; Ahmad Sohrab to Agnes Parsons, July 13, 1912, Parsons Papers; Maḥmúd-i-Zarqání, *Maḥmúd's Diary,* 158.
67. Ahmad Sohrab to Agnes Parsons, July 9 and 12, 1912, Parsons Papers, Bahá'í National Archives; "Special Notice," *Star of the West* 3, no. 8 (Aug. 1, 1912): 22; Ahmad Sohrab to Agnes Parsons, July 13, 1912, Parsons Papers, Bahá'í National Archives.

8 / A New England Summer

1. "Addresses by Abdul-Baha Delivered in Boston," in *Star of the West,* vol. 4, no. 7 (July 13, 1912): 122. The talk itself is labeled as "extracts." Also see 'Abdu'l-Bahá, *The Promulgation of Universal Peace,* 333-35.
2. See Helen Campbell, *Bahaism in its Social-Economic Aspect* (Chicago: Bahai Publishing Society, 1910); Stockman, *The Bahá'í Faith in America,* vol. 2, 369–71; Hutchison, *Religious Pluralism in America,* 97.
3. "Addresses by Abdul-Baha Delivered in Boston," in *Star of the West* 4, no. 7 (July 13, 1912): 115-17; cf. 'Abdu'l-Bahá, *The Promulgation of Universal Peace,* 335-41;Maḥmúd-i-Zarqání, *Maḥmúd's Diary,* 179-80; "When the Mirror is Free from Dust," *Star of the West* 7, no. 12 (Oct. 16, 1916): 116; cf. 'Abdu'l-Bahá, *The Promulgation of Universal Peace,* 341.

4. Hannen, "With Abdul-Baha in Dublin, New Hampshire," 3; George Latimer's account of meeting 'Abdu'l-Bahá in Dublin, New Hampshire, p. 3, George Latimer Papers; Alice Ives Breed to Thornton Chase, August 6, 1912, Thornton Chase Papers.
5. Maḥmúd-i-Zarqání, *Maḥmúd's Diary,* 181; Town of Dublin, New Hampshire, "About the Town of Dublin," http://www.townofdublin.org/pages/DublinNH_WebDocs/about (last accessed February 12, 2011); Hannen, "With Abdul-Baha in Dublin, New Hampshire," 3.
6. Maḥmúd-i-Zarqání, *Maḥmúd's Diary,* 183; Alice Ives Breed to Thornton Chase, August 6, 1912, Thornton Chase Papers; Parsons, *Agnes Parsons' Diary,* 88; Ahmad Sohrab to Ella Copper, August 8, 1912, Ella Cooper Papers.
7. Maḥmúd-i-Zarqání, *Maḥmúd's Diary,* 183; Parsons, *Agnes Parsons' Diary,* 79 (entry for July 29, 1912).
8. Harmon, *Divine Illumination,* 7-8.
9. Maḥmúd-i-Zarqání, *Maḥmúd's Diary,* 184, 185.
10. Harmon, *Divine Illumination,* 8.
11. Maḥmúd-i-Zarqání, *Maḥmúd's Diary,* 185-86.
12. George Latimer, diary for Dublin, New Hampshire, Albert Windust Papers, Bahá'í National Archives, Wilmette, IL; Hannen, "With Abdul-Baha in Dublin, New Hampshire," 5. A nearly identical version of the talk exists in George Latimer's unpublished notes about his visit to Dublin.
13. Holley, "George Orr Latimer," 512.
14. Hannen, "With Abdul-Baha in Dublin, New Hampshire," 3.
15. Alice Ives Breed to Thornton Chase, August 6, 1912, Thornton Chase Papers; Alexander, Agnes. [Unknown published source], p. 71, quoted in Tussing, "FINISHING THE WORK, 1912," unpublished typescript.
16. Alice Ives Breed to Thornton Chase, August 6, 1912, Thornton Chase Papers; Maḥmúd-i-Zarqání, *Maḥmúd's Diary,* 189-90; Parsons, *Agnes Parsons' Diary,* 107.
17. Alice Ives Breed to Thornton Chase, August 6, 1912, Thornton Chase Papers.
18. Instructions "Dictated to Howard MacNutt by Abdul-Baha at Dublin N. H. 7 A.M. August 6th, 1912," Albert Windust Papers. Maḥmúd notes that "Twice He ['Abdu'l-Bahá] sent a speaker from New York to Chicago and adjacent cities and on each occasion, although the person was rich, 'Abdu'l-Bahá gave him more than enough money to defray the expenses of his journey" (Maḥmúd-i-Zarqání, *Maḥmúd's Diary,* 214). The only person 'Abdu'l-Bahá is known to have sent from New York to Chicago is MacNutt, and he sent him twice.
19. 'Abdu'l-Bahá, *The Promulgation of Universal Peace,* 343-52; also see *Star of the West* 3, no. 18 (Feb. 7, 1913): 4, 6.

20. Instructions "Dictated to Howard MacNutt by Abdul-Baha at Dublin N. H. 7 a.m. August 6th, 1912," Albert Windust Papers; Corinne True to Helen Goodall, August 16, 1912, Helen Goodall Papers. The term "Spiritual Meeting" was an old translation of *mahfil-i-rawhání,* the term currently translated as "Spiritual Assembly." See "Chicago News Notes," *Star of the West* 3, no. 9 (Aug. 20, 1912): 16.
21. Corinne True to Helen Goodall, August 16, 1912, Helen Goodall Papers; *Report of the Baha'i Committee of Investigation, 1917–1918,* 18.
22. Ahmad Sohrab to Ella Cooper, August 8, 1912, Cooper Papers. The actual schedule was very close; after Green Acre, 'Abdu'l-Bahá went to Boston, reached San Francisco on October 1, and returned to New York on November 12.
23. Parsons, *Agnes Parsons' Diary,* 109.
24. Ibid., 86, 97–98; Maḥmúd-i-Zarqání, *Maḥmúd's Diary,* 365.
25. Parsons, *Agnes Parsons' Diary,* 84–85, 88, 93, 75.
26. Ives, *Portals to Freedom,* 122, 124.
27. Ibid., 125–26.
28. Leonard and Seward, *The History of Dublin, N.H.,* 260–62, 264, 303; Rev. Mike Scott to Robert Stockman, email, May 12, 2011.
29. Ives, *Portals to Freedom,* 127.
30. Maḥmúd-i-Zarqání, *Maḥmúd's Diary,* 202–3; Parsons, *Agnes Parsons' Diary,* 103.
31. Ives, *Portals to Freedom,* 127.
32. Ibid.
33. Ives, *Portals to Freedom,* 115–16, 195, 128.
34. Tussing, *FINISHING THE WORK,* 16. Tussing interviewed someone in Dublin in the 1980s who made the tentative identification of the recipient as Mr. John A. Upton.
35. Maḥmúd-i-Zarqání, *Maḥmúd's Diary,* 208.
36. Parsons, *Agnes Parsons' Diary,* 114–15; Ives, *Portals to Freedom,* 119–20. The evening is also mentioned in passing in Maḥmúd-i-Zarqání, *Maḥmúd's Diary,* 153.
37. Burke, *Swami Vivekananda in America: New Discoveries, His Prophetic Mission, Part Two,* 135–60, 147, 395–99; Schmidt, *Restless Souls,* 167–68.
38. Schmidt, *Restless Souls,* 185.
39. Ibid., 186; Perry, *Green Acre on the Piscataqua,* 51.
40. Ahmad Sohrab to Agnes Parsons, Aug. 18, 1912, Parsons Papers; Sohrab, "A Glimpse of Abdul Baha at Green Acre, Maine," 3; Randall-Winckler, *William Henry Randall,* 56, 59.

41. *Star of the West* 3, no. 16 (Dec. 31, 1912): 9; cf. 'Abdu'l-Bahá, *The Promulgation of Universal Peace,* 364.
42. Maḥmúd-i-Zarqání, *Maḥmúd's Diary,* 210.
43. *Star of the West* 8, no. 7 (July 13, 1917): 77–78; cf. 'Abdu'l-Bahá, *The Promulgation of Universal Peace,* 371–73.
44. *Star of the West* 8, no. 7 (July 13, 1917): 80; cf. 'Abdu'l-Bahá, *The Promulgation of Universal Peace,* 374–77.
45. 'Abdu'l-Bahá, *The Promulgation of Universal Peace,* 378–81. The older text in *Star of the West* 3, no. 15 (Dec. 12, 1912): 6 is identical except for clumsier use of capitalization and punctuation.
46. Maḥmúd-i-Zarqání, *Maḥmúd's Diary,* 212.
47. Remey, *Reminiscences of a Summer School,* 37–39.
48. 'Abdu'l-Bahá, *The Promulgation of Universal Peace,* 365–77; Maḥmúd-i-Zarqání, *Maḥmúd's Diary,* 193; 'Abdu'l-Bahá, *The Promulgation of Universal Peace,* 366–67.
49. Sohrab, "A Glimpse of Abdul Baha at Green Acre, Maine," 3; Maḥmúd-i-Zarqání, *Maḥmúd's Diary,* 209–10, 213; Aḥmad Sohrab to Agnes Parsons, August 22, 1912, Parsons Papers.
50. Maḥmúd-i-Zarqání, *Maḥmúd's Diary,* 211–12.
51. The details of this account are taken from Mortensen, "When a Soul Meets the Master," 365–67.
52. Mortensen, "When a Soul Meets the Master," 367.
53. Maḥmúd-i-Zarqání, *Maḥmúd's Diary,* 214; Edith Magee Inglis, "Abdul Baha Dines with Mrs. Magee and the Inglises," typescript, Sarah Farmer Papers.
54. Perry, *Green Acre on the Piscataqua,* 53. According to Maḥmúd-i-Zarqání, *Maḥmúd's Diary,* 215, 'Abdu'l-Bahá drove to Portsmouth to get Sarah Farmer, but according to Edward Kinney (quoted in Randall-Winckler, *William Henry Randall,* 61) Kinney arranged for a car to bring Sarah Farmer and her physician to Green Acre, where 'Abdu'l-Bahá met them.
55. Maḥmúd-i-Zarqání, *Maḥmúd's Diary,* 215. According to Ella Robarts, the feast 'Abdu'l-Bahá hosted occurred on August 21, not August 20; see Randall-Winckler, *William Henry Randall,* 59.
56. Perry, *Green Acre on the Piscataqua,* 57.
57. Maḥmúd-i-Zarqání, *Maḥmúd's Diary,* 219.
58. Mortensen, "When a Soul Meets the Master," 367; Maḥmúd-i-Zarqání, *Maḥmúd's Diary,* 220.
59. David Weigert, email communication, March 16, 2011; Anise Rideout, "Early History of Baha'i Community, Boston, Mass," typescript, National Bahá'í Archives, Wilmette, IL.

60. Randall-Winckler, *William Henry Randall,* 43.
61. Ibid., 43–47, 260. It should also be noted that 'Abdu'l-Bahá did not cure Corinne True's son of tuberculosis; he died the day 'Abdu'l-Bahá visited him.
62. 'Abdu'l-Bahá, *The Promulgation of Universal Peace,* 389. *Star of the West* 4, no. 7 (July 13, 1913): 119, is identical except for punctuation. Maḥmúd-i-Zarqání, *Maḥmúd's Diary,* 222.
63. http://www.franklinsquarehousefoundation.org/foundation/history (accessed March 10, 2011); Stockman, *The Bahá'í Faith in America,* vol. 2, 369–72; Paulson, "Campbell, Helen Stuart," 281.
64. 'Abdu'l-Bahá, *The Promulgation of Universal Peace,* 395. No earlier copy of this talk has been found.
65. Ibid., 396–403. No earlier copy of this talk has been found.
66. Gail, *Arches of the Years,* 90.
67. Maḥmúd-i-Zarqání, *Maḥmúd's Diary,* 225, where Maḥmúd's has the talk at Madame Morey's on Wednesday instead; 'Abdu'l-Bahá, *The Promulgation of Universal Peace,* 403-12; Anise Rideout, "Early History of Baha'i Community, Boston, Mass.," typescript, National Bahá'í Archives. Information on Madame Morey and her house, which was a stop on the underground railroad and frequented by leading Transcendentalists, can be found at http://kinnexions.com/branches/beal/index.htm#Morey (accessed April 20, 2011). I have not located a copy of the talk at Madam Morey's in *Star of the West.*
68. Ahmad Sohrab to Ella Cooper, August 16, 1912, Ella Cooper Papers; Maḥmúd-i-Zarqání, *Maḥmúd's Diary,* 247–48.

9 / From Boston to San Francisco

1. Van den Hoonaard, *The Origins of the Bahá'í Community of Canada, 1898–1948,* 61.
2. Maḥmúd-i-Zarqání, *Maḥmúd's Diary,* 232, 235. Maḥmúd provides the entire talk by 'Abdu'l-Bahá in the Church of the Messiah in Persian, and it has been retranslated into English by the Bahá'í World Center. Hence I have preferred it over the version in 'Abdu'l-Bahá, *The Promulgation of Universal Peace,* 413–20, which appears to be based on the text published in the September 2, 1912 issue of the *Montreal Gazette.* See *Star of the West* 13, no. 11 (Feb. 1923): 291–92. There, 'Abdu'l-Bahá refers to "western peoples," not to "America"; possibly the interpreter, in the context, understood 'Abdu'l-Bahá's closing remarks to be referring to both the United States and Canada.
3. The talks are published in 'Abdu'l-Bahá, *The Promulgation of Universal Peace,* 429–34 (no earlier copies of them have been found); Maḥmúd-i-Zarqání, *Maḥmúd's Diary,* 236–37.

4. Maḥmúd-i-Zarqání, *Maḥmúd's Diary,* 239, 241–42.
5. 'Abdu'l-Bahá, *The Promulgation of Universal Peace,* 446. Parts of this text were published in the Sept. 6, 1912, issue of the Montreal Daily Star; see Star of the West 13, no. 11 (February, 1923): 292–93. The excerpts there show that the Promulgation text has been heavily edited.
6. 'Abdu'l-Bahá, *The Promulgation of Universal Peace,* 451.
7. Maḥmúd-i-Zarqání, *Maḥmúd's Diary,* 246.
8. Van den Hoonaard, *The Origins of the Bahá'í Community of Canada,* 1898–1948, 55-60.
9. Maḥmúd-i-Zarqání, *Maḥmúd's Diary,* 247, 249.
10. Evelyn Loft Watts and Charles Jardine, "Alfred James Loft," 514.
11. Ahmad Sohrab to Agnes Parsons, postcard, Sept. 12, 1912, Parsons Papers.
12. Buffalo, N.Y., *Courier,* Sept. 11, 1912, clipping in U.S. Bahá'í Archives, Wilmette, IL. 'Abdu'l-Bahá's prediction of a war was also reported by the *Buffalo Commercial,* Sept. 11, 1912, and the *Buffalo Times,* date unknown; both clippings are in the U.S. Bahá'í Archives. The language is very similar in each.
13. Ahmad Sohrab to Albert Windust, telegram, September 10, 1912, Windust Papers; Maḥmúd-i-Zarqání, *Maḥmúd's Diary,* 253–54.
14. Ahmad Sohrab to Albert Windust, telegram, September 11, 1912, Windust Papers; *Maḥmúd's Diary,* 256–57.
15. Maḥmúd-i-Zarqání, *Maḥmúd's Diary,* 271.
16. True, "Saichiro Fujita," 406.
17. Maḥmúd-i-Zarqání, *Maḥmúd's Diary,* 261; *Chicago Examiner,* Sept. 14, 1912, clipping in National Bahá'í Archives, Wilmette, IL.
18. Maḥmúd-i-Zarqání, *Maḥmúd's Diary,* 261.
19. Ibid., 262–63.
20. Maḥmúd-i-Zarqání, *Maḥmúd's Diary,* 264.
21. Ibid., 265.
22. Maḥmúd-i-Zarqání, *Maḥmúd's Diary,* 265–66; Collins, "Kenosha," 4–5; Dahl, "A History of the Kenosha Bahá'í Community, 1897-1980," 24.
23. *Star of the West* 3, no. 15 (Dec. 12, 1912): 10; cf. 'Abdu'l-Bahá, *The Promulgation of Universal Peace,* 459.
24. *Star of the West* 3, no. 15 (Dec. 12, 1912): 10; cf. 'Abdu'l-Bahá, *The Promulgation of Universal Peace,* 460.
25. Maḥmúd-i-Zarqání, *Maḥmúd's Diary,* 268, 271.
26. *Report of the Bahai Committee of Investigation, 1917–1918,* at http://www.h-net.org/~bahai/docs/vol5/RCI/RCI.html (accessed April 19, 2011).
27. Bartlett, "'Abdu'l-Bahá in Chicago," 6; Maḥmúd-i-Zarqání, *Maḥmúd's Diary,* 269–70.
28. Maḥmúd-i-Zarqání, *Maḥmúd's Diary,* 240, 270; True, "Saichiro Fujita," 407.

29. Maḥmúd-i-Zarqání, *Maḥmúd's Diary,* 273.
30. "Mrs. Willis J. Walker 840 Powell St., San Francisco," biographical notes, Ella Cooper Papers. The art gallery was the property of her father-in-law, Thomas B. Walker, and was built as an extension of his home.
31. Maḥmúd-i-Zarqání, *Maḥmúd's Diary,* 278–79.
32. Ibid., 280.
33. Stockman, *The Bahá'í Faith in America,* vol. 2, 333; Tablet to the Bahá'ís of Denver [twenty-six names in all], August 3, 1914, attached to Elizabeth Clark, "Account of 'Abdu'l-Bahá's Two Stays, Denver Colorado in 1912, When En Route to and Returning From California to New York," typescript, National Bahá'í Archives, Wilmette, IL.
34. Elizabeth Clark [daughter in law of Josephine Clark], "Account of 'Abdu'l-Bahá's Two Stays, Denver, Colorado, in 1912, While En Route to and Returning From California to New York," typescript, National Bahá'í Archives, Wilmette, IL, pp. 1–2.
35. "Church of Divine Science," http://en.wikipedia.org/wiki/Church_of_Divine_Science (accessed April 3, 2011); "Nona Lovell Brooks," http://en.wikipedia.org/wiki/Nona_L._Brooks (accessed April 3, 2011).
36. 'Abdu'l-Bahá, *The Promulgation of Universal Peace,* 478–84. I have not found an earlier form of the talk to date.
37. Maḥmúd-i-Zarqání, *Maḥmúd's Diary,* 290.
38. Ibid., 292–93.
39. Feny E. Paulson's account of meeting 'Abdu'l-Bahá is given in Ward, *239 Days,* 159–63.
40. Ahmad Sohrab to Helen Goodall, Montello, Nevada, 2:52am, October 1, 1912, Goodall Papers.

10 / The Golden State

1. "The Feast of Rizwan," 36; transcript of part of 'Abdu'l-Bahá's talk is published in Brown, *Memories of 'Abdu'l-Bahá,* 34–35.
2. Maḥmúd-i-Zarqání, *Maḥmúd's Diary,* 299–300; Storch, "You Are Happy Because You Have Seen 'Abdu'l-Bahá," 39; "Notes dictated by Mrs. Lorrol Luther in January 1929, to Miss Fay Swain," typescript, 3, 7, author's personal papers.
3. Maḥmúd-i-Zarqání, *Maḥmúd's Diary,* 300.
4. Ibid., 301.
5. Brown, *Memories of 'Abdu'l-Bahá,* 36–37.
6. Ibid., 54; "The Feast of Ridwan," 35. In 1912, Helen Goodall no longer lived in the house; when her husband died a few years earlier, she had moved into the house of her daughter, Ella Cooper, in San Francisco. Kanichi Yamamoto,

a Japanese Bahá'í, and his family lived in the Oakland house and served as caretakers. It seems to have been used primarily for large Bahá'í meetings.

7. Storch, "You Are Happy Because You Have Seen 'Abdu'l-Bahá," 33.
8. Ibid., 34.
9. "Abdul-Baha's 'Welcome' to California," 190.
10. Ibid.
11. Maḥmúd-i-Zarqání, *Maḥmúd's Diary,* 302; Storch, "You Are Happy Because You Have Seen 'Abdu'l-Bahá," 34.
12. Storch, "You Are Happy Because You Have Seen 'Abdu'l-Bahá," 34.
13. E. A. Rogers to his mother, October 4, 1912, typescript, Ella Cooper Papers; Storch, "You Are Happy Because You Have Seen 'Abdu'l-Bahá," 34–35.
14. Allen, "Abdul-Baha in California," 9; Maḥmúd-i-Zarqání, *Maḥmúd's Diary,* 302.
15. Storch, "You Are Happy Because You Have Seen 'Abdu'l-Bahá," 37; E. A. Rogers to his mother, Oct. 4, 1912, typescript, Ella Cooper Papers; Maḥmúd-i-Zarqání, *Maḥmúd's Diary,* 304.
16. "San Francisco, Saturday Morning, October 5, 1912, Mirza Ahmad Sohrab, Interpreter," pp. 152–53, Ella Cooper Papers.
17. Maḥmúd-i-Zarqání, *Maḥmúd's Diary,* 308–9. Bijou Straun's transcript of the evening has the Rev. Herbert Jump referring to 'Abdu'l-Bahá as a "prophet of God." Newspapers and even signs in front of churches sometimes called him a "prophet" or a "prophet from the East" but not a "prophet of God."
18. Storch, "You Are Happy Because You Have Seen 'Abdu'l-Bahá," 38. Storch spells his name "Kano," but Brown (*Memories of 'Abdu'l-Bahá,* 64) says that Takeshi Kanno, a well known Japanese poet, visited 'Abdu'l-Bahá in San Francisco some time after his talk in the Japanese church. A Google search reveals that Kanno was married to a well-known sculptor, Gertrude Boyle, which may explain why Brown misidentified him as a sculptor.
19. Excel Spreadsheet of Newspaper Articles about 'Abdu'l-Bahá's North American Trip by Duane Troxel; Maḥmúd-i-Zarqání, *Maḥmúd's Diary,* 312.
20. "Jackson Stitt Wilson," http://en.wikipedia.org/wiki/Jackson_Stitt_Wilson (accessed April 10, 2011); Yazdi, *Youth in the Vanguard,* 17; Maḥmúd-i-Zarqání, *Maḥmúd's Diary,* 309; typescript of conversation between 'Abdu'l-Bahá and Jackson Stitt Wilson, Ella Cooper Papers.
21. "Japanese Independent Church," Oakland, 8pm, October 7, 1912, 35–36, Ella Cooper Papers; cf. 'Abdu'l-Bahá, *The Promulgation of Universal Peace,* 485.
22. "Japanese Independent Church," Oakland, 8pm, October 7, 1912, 37, 40, Ella Cooper Papers; cf. 'Abdu'l-Bahá, *The Promulgation of Universal Peace,* 487–89.

23. "Japanese Independent Church," Oakland, 8pm, October 7, 1912, 41, Ella Cooper Papers; cf. 'Abdu'l-Bahá, *The Promulgation of Universal Peace,* 490.
24. "Japanese Independent Church," Oakland, 8pm, October 7, 1912, 42–43, Ella Cooper Papers; cf. 'Abdu'l-Bahá, *The Promulgation of Universal Peace,* 491–92.
25. Maḥmúd-i-Zarqání, *Maḥmúd's Diary,* 312; Ella Cooper to Mr. Y. Ishimura, July 16, 1922, Ella Cooper Papers.
26. "Address by Abdul Baha at Leland Stanford Junior University, Palo Alto, California," 10. The version in the *Palo Altan* was corrected by 'Abdu'l-Bahá. Also see 'Abdu'l-Bahá, *The Promulgation of Universal Peace,* 492–502.
27. "Address by Abdul Baha at Leland Stanford Junior University, Palo Alto, California," 11.
28. Ibid.
29. Ibid, 12.
30. Ibid., 13.
31. Ibid., 13–14.
32. Ibid., 14.
33. Maḥmúd-i-Zarqání, *Maḥmúd's Diary,* 311; Yazdi, *Youth in the Vanguard,* 114–15, 137, 125. The author also heard about Albert Leon Guérard from Firuz Kazemzadeh and Amin Banani, who were undergraduates at Stanford in the mid-1940s.
34. "Message to the Church," *The Palo Altan,* 4.
35. Ibid.
36. Ibid.
37. Yazdi, *Youth in the Vanguard,* 124.
38. Samuel S. Seward, Jr., to Ella Cooper, Dec. 7, 1931, Ella Cooper Papers.
39. Yazdi, *Youth in the Vanguard,* 119.
40. Ibid., 119, 167.
41. "The Visit of Abdul-Baha to Mr. Charles Tinsley," 205.
42. "The Open Forum, San Francisco, 8 P.M., October 10, 1912," p. 74, Cooper Papers. For another version of the talk, see 'Abdu'l-Bahá, *The Promulgation of Universal Peace,* 503.
43. "The Open Forum, San Francisco, 8 P.M., October 10, 1912," p. 76, Cooper Papers.
44. "Piltdown Man," http://en.wikipedia.org/wiki/Piltdown_Man (accessed April 12, 2011); Richard Harter, "Piltdown Man," http://www.tiac.net/~cri_a/piltdown/piltdown.html (accessed April 12, 1912).
45. "Transitional Fossil," http://en.wikipedia.org/wiki/Transitional_fossil (accessed April 12, 1912).

46. "The Open Forum, San Francisco, 8 P.M., October 10, 1912," pp. 77–78, Cooper Papers.
47. Ibid., pp. 80–81.
48. Ibid.
49. Typescript of conversations between 'Abdu'l-Bahá and Mrs. Goodall, Oct. 11, 1912, Ella Cooper Papers.
50. Brown, *Memories of 'Abdu'l-Bahá,* 48–49, 69–75; typescript of the introductory remarks by Mr. W. J. Walters, October 11, 1912, Ella Cooper Papers; Maḥmúd-i-Zarqání, *Maḥmúd's Diary,* 315.
51. Brown, *Memories of 'Abdu'l-Bahá,* 49; "Dr. Martin Abraham Meyer," typescript, Ella Cooper papers; Maḥmúd-i-Zarqání, *Maḥmúd's Diary,* 316.
52. Maḥmúd-i-Zarqání, *Maḥmúd's Diary,* 318–19.
53. Ibid., 320.
54. Ibid., 321.
55. Hatch, "'Abdu'l-Bahá and the Rabbi," 110; Maḥmúd-i-Zarqání, *Maḥmúd's Diary,* 322–23.
56. Root, "My Visit to Temple University," 265; "Message to the Jews," 10.
57. Maḥmúd-i-Zarqáni, *Maḥmúd's Diary,* 324.
58. Prothero, *American Jesus,* 238, 240, 244, 247. As already noted, Rabbi Stephen Wise met 'Abdu'l-Bahá on May 13, 1912, in New York City.
59. Rosenbaum, *Visions of Reform,* 117–18.
60. Maḥmúd-i-Zarqaní, *Maḥmúd's Diary,* 325; Storch, "You Are Happy Because You Have Seen 'Abdu'l-Bahá," 39–41; Brown, *Memories of 'Abdu'l-Bahá,* 50–51; Allen, "'Abdu'l-Bahá in San Francisco, California," 11.
61. Allen, "'Abdu'l-Bahá in San Francisco, California," 12.
62. Brown, *Memories of 'Abdu'l-Bahá,* 53; Maḥmúd-i-Zarqaní, *Maḥmúd's Diary,* 327.
63. Maḥmúd-i-Zarqaní, *Maḥmúd's Diary,* 331.
64. Ibid., 334; Hogenson, *Lighting the Western Sky,* 261; Taherzadeh, *The Covenant of Bahá'u'lláh,* 341.
65. Brown, *Memories of 'Abdu'l-Bahá,* 53–56; transcripts of 'Abdu'l-Bahá's talks at the Century Club and at the Feast on October 16, Ella Cooper Papers.
66. Brown, *Memories of 'Abdu'l-Bahá,* 57.
67. Ibid., 59–61, 66, 68.
68. "From Kathryn Frankland, October 1912," typescript, Ella Cooper Papers; "A Pioneer at the Golden Gate," *Star of the West* 13, no. 8 (Nov. 1922): 205.
69. Sohrab, "Abdul-Baha at the Grave of Thornton Chase," 14.
70. Maḥmúd-i-Zarqání, *Maḥmúd's Diary,* 337–38; "First Anniversary of the Passing of Thornton Chase," *Star of the West* 4, no. 13 (Nov. 4, 1913): 225.

71. Maḥmúd-i-Zarqání, *Maḥmúd's Diary,* 338–41; "Los Angeles, 4 P.M., October 19, 1912, Mirza Ahmad Sohrab, Interpreter," typescript, Ella Cooper Papers.
72. "Los Angeles, Sunday Morning, October 20, 1912, _______, [*sic*] Interpreter," typescript, Ella Cooper Papers (the lack of initial capital letters on "Covenant" and "Center of the Covenant" are in the original); "Los Angeles, Sunday Afternoon, October 20, 1912, _______, [*sic*] Interpreter," typescript, Ella Cooper Papers. Maḥmúd-i-Zarqáni, in Maḥmúd's Diary, 341–43, says 'Abdu'l-Bahá left Los Angeles the next day, but one of the Sunday afternoon talks makes mention of a Sunday, 5pm departure, and Ella Cooper in her "Foreword, California Book," 2, typescript, Cooper Papers, says the party left on Sunday, October 20, at 5pm.
73. Allen, "Abdul-Baha in San Francisco, California. Continued from last issue of the Star of the West," 12; "Oakland, 8 P.M., October 22, 1912, Dr. Ameen U. Fareed, Interpreter," typescript, Ella Cooper Papers (the lack of initial capital letters on "Center of the Covenant" and "Universal House of Justice" are in the original).
74. Brown, *Memories of 'Abdu'l-Bahá,* 84–85. There is no transcript of 'Abdu'l-Bahá's talk that night; it is possible Brown has misremembered the date and is recalling the talk of October 22.
75. Brown, *Memories of 'Abdu'l-Bahá,* 63–83; "Notes of a 'Consultation,'—'Abdu'l-Baha, Mrs. Helen Goodall, Dr. Fareed, present," Ella Cooper Papers.
76. Correspondence and other information from Prof. E. A. Rogers about his visits with 'Abdu'l-Bahá, 1912, typescript, Ella Cooper Papers; Allen, "Abdul-Baha in San Francisco, California. Continued from last issue of the Star of the West," 12.
77. "Abdul Baha's farewell words to the friends gathered around Him, October 25, 1912, 8 A.m. [*sic*], 1814 California Street, San Francisco. Interpreted by Dr. Fareed; stenographic notes by Mss [*sic*] Straun," typescript, Cooper Papers.
78. Burke, *Swami Vivekananda in the West: New Discoveries, A New Gospel, Part Two,* 111, 407, 411; Brown, *Memories of 'Abdu'l-Bahá,* 85–86; Caton, "A History of the Sacramento Bahá'í Community, 1912–1991," 242–46.
79. "Assembly Hall, Hotel Sacramento, Sacramento, 8:30 P. M., October 25, 1912," typescript, Ella Cooper Papers; "Sacramento, 9.15 P. M., October 25, 1912, Dr. Ameen U. Fareed, Interpreter," typescript, Ella Cooper Papers; 'Abdu'l-Bahá, *The Promulgation of Universal Peace,* 523–31.
80. "Assembly Hall, Hotel Sacramento, Sacramento, 9:30 A.M., October 26, 1912," 136, Ella Cooper Papers; cf. 'Abdu'l-Bahá, *The Promulgation of Universal Peace,* 532; Brown, *Memories of 'Abdu'l-Bahá,* 88.
81. "Oakland, 8 P. M., October 22, 1912, Dr. Ameen U. Fareed, Interpreter," typescript, Ella Cooper Papers.

11 / From Sacramento to the *Celtic*

1. Maḥmúd-i-Zarqání, *Maḥmúd's Diary,* 352–56; "Seventieth Anniversary Commemoration," Kay Zinke Papers.
2. Maḥmúd-i-Zarqání, *Maḥmúd's Diary,* 356–57.
3. http://www25.uua.org/uuhs/duub/articles/fanniebarrierwilliams.html (accessed April 18, 2011); Maḥmúd-i-Zarqání, *Maḥmúd's Diary,* 369.
4. Maḥmúd-i-Zarqání, *Maḥmúd's Diary,* 368–69; "Peace Advocate in Chicago, Abdul Baha Abbas Arrives Here to Make Several Addresses," Chicago *Inter-Ocean,* November 1, 1912, National Bahá'í Archives.
5. Terry, "Rabindranath Tagore: Some Encounters with Bahá'ís"; Root, "The Bahá'í Faith and Eastern Scholars," 687; "Martha Root's Travels in India, Burma and Australia—Her Death in Honolulu," 63; Ong, *Vignettes from the Life of Shirin Fozdar,* 20. I am indebted to Peter Terry and John A. Milne for information about Tagore's meeting with 'Abdu'l-Bahá.
6. 'Abdu'l-Bahá, *The Promulgation of Universal Peace,* 537–38. No earlier version of this talk has been been found in *Star of the West.*
7. For more about the various Covenant-breaker groups, see Stockman, *The Bahá'í Faith in America,* vol. 1, 177–83.
8. 'Abdu'l-Bahá, *The Promulgation of Universal Peace,* 538.
9. Ibid, 538–39.
10. "'The Purpose of the Covenant Was Simply to Ward off Differences,' Address delivered by Abdul-Baha at the home of Corinne True, Chicago, November 1, 1912," 230. The talk appears in edited form in 'Abdu'l-Bahá, *The Promulgation of Universal Peace,* 549–45.
11. "'The Purpose of the Covenant Was Simply to Ward off Differences,' Address delivered by Abdul-Baha at the home of Corinne True, Chicago, November 1, 1912," 230–31.
12. Ibid., 234.
13. Ibid.
14. Ibid.
15. Maḥmúd-i-Zarqání, *Maḥmúd's Diary,* 367–68.
16. "Instructions Given by Abdul Baha at the Home of Mrs True, Friday Evening, November 1, 1912, to the Members of the Spiritual Meeting," in "Report of the Bahai Committee of Investigation, 1917–1918," at http://www.h-net.org/~bahai/docs/vol5/RCI/RCI.html (accessed April 19, 2011).
17. Maḥmúd-i-Zarqání, *Maḥmúd's Diary,* 370–71.
18. Ibid., 372.
19. "Abdul-Baha's Message to the People of America," *Star of the West* 6, no. 11 (Sept. 27, 1912): 81–82; cf. 'Abdu'l-Bahá, *The Promulgation of Universal Peace,* 547–48. Maḥmúd's description of the talk is quite different from the "stenographic notes" in *Promulgation,* and both the *Star of the* West and *Promulgation*

texts says the talk was on November 5, so most likely the talk was given in the morning.

20. Maḥmúd-i-Zarqání, *Maḥmúd's Diary,* 373.
21. Smith, "The American Bahá'í Community, 1894–1917: A Preliminary Survey," 186. The total number of talks 'Abdu'l-Bahá gave in Washington has been added up from mentions in *Maḥmúd's Diary.*
22. "'Through the Teachings of Baha'o'llah the Eastern Horizon was Made Radiant': Address by Abdul Baha at the Church of Our Father (Universalist), Washington, D.C., Wednesday evening, November 6, 8:15 P.M.," 198; Maḥmúd-i-Zarqání, *Maḥmúd's Diary,* 378.
23. Maḥmúd-i-Zarqání, *Maḥmúd's Diary,* 379.
24. http://www.whctemple.org/our_history.htm (accessed April 20, 2011); "'My Purpose and Intention is to Remove from Amongst Men this Enmity and this Religous Hatred,' Address by Abdu'l Baha at Eighth Street Temple (Jewish Synagogue) Washington, D. C., November 8, 1912," 3. An edited version of this talk was published in 'Abdu'l-Bahá, *The Promulgation of Universal Peace,* 567–78.
25. "'My Purpose and Intention is to Remove from Amongst Men this Enmity and this Religous Hatred,' Address by Abdu'l Baha at Eighth Street Temple (Jewish Synagogue) Washington, D. C., November 8, 1912," 4.
26. "'My Purpose and Intention is to Remove from Amongst Men this Enmity and this Religous Hatred,' Address by Abdu'l Baha at Eighth Street Temple (Jewish Synagogue) Washington, D. C., November 8, 1912," 6–8; Parsons, *'Abdu'l-Bahá in America: Agnes Parsons' Diary,* 131; Maḥmúd-i-Zarqání, *Maḥmúd's Diary,* 380.
27. "'My Purpose and Intention is to Remove from Amongst Men this Enmity and this Religous Hatred,' Address by Abdu'l Baha at Eighth Street Temple (Jewish Synagogue) Washington, D. C., November 8, 1912," 9.
28. "'My Purpose and Intention is to Remove from Amongst Men this Enmity and this Religous Hatred,' Address by Abdu'l Baha at Eighth Street Temple (Jewish Synagogue) Washington, D. C., November 8, 1912," 10.
29. Parsons, *'Abdu'l-Bahá in America: Agnes Parsons' Diary,* 132; Maḥmúd-i-Zarqání, *Maḥmúd's Diary,* 380.
30. "Talk by Abdul Baha At the home of Mrs. Parsons, Washington, D.C., November 9, 1912," 16. An edited version of the same talk is available in 'Abdu'l-Bahá, *The Promulgation of Universal Peace,* 579–84.
31. Prothero, *American Jesus,* 236.
32. Parsons, *'Abdu'l-Bahá in America: Agnes Parsons' Diary,* 10, note 11; Maḥmúd-i-Zarqání, *Maḥmúd's Diary,* 381–82; Parsons, *'Abdu'l-Bahá in America: Agnes Parsons' Diary,* 133–35.

33. "'It is proved that the existence of phenomena is effected through the Eternal Will,' Talk by Abdul Baha at the home of Mrs. Parsons, Washington, D.C., November 19, 1912," 24. An edited version of the talk appears in 'Abdu'l-Bahá, *The Promulgation of Universal Peace*, 594–99.
34. Maḥmúd-i-Zarqání, *Maḥmúd's Diary*, 383–84.
35. Clark, "The Bahá'ís of Baltimore, 1898–1990," 114–15; Stockman, *The Bahá'í Faith in America*, vol. 2, 344–45; Clark, "The Bahá'ís of Baltimore, 1898–1990," 126–28.
36. Clark, "The Bahá'ís of Baltimore, 1898–1990," 129; Maḥmúd-i-Zarqání, *Maḥmúd's Diary*, 386.
37. "Abdul Baha Going Away," *New York Tribune*, Nov. 24, 1912, quoted in Ward, *239 Days*, 188; Parsons, *'Abdu'l-Bahá in America: Agnes Parsons' Diary*, 141; Maḥmúd-i-Zarqání, *Maḥmúd's Diary*, 402. It should be added that Juliet Thompson says in her diary, page 376, that 'Abdu'l-Bahá had planned to sail on the *Mauretania* but visited Montclair overnight on November 23 and missed his chance to reserve berths.
38. Thompson, *Diary of Juliet Thompson*, 365–66.
39. Maḥmúd-i-Zarqání, *Maḥmúd's Diary*, 390; Thompson, *Diary of Juliet Thompson*, 367–68.
40. Maḥmúd-i-Zarqání, *Maḥmúd's Diary*, 393, 400–401; Thompson, *Diary of Juliet Thompson*, 370–71.
41. Thompson, *Diary of Juliet Thompson*, 371–72.
42. Maḥmúd-i-Zarqání, *Maḥmúd's Diary*, 393, 400–401; Thompson, *Diary of Juliet Thompson*, 371–72.
43. Maḥmúd-i-Zarqání, *Maḥmúd's Diary*, 393, 400–401; Thompson, *Diary of Juliet Thompson*, 371–72.
44. Stockman, *The Bahá'í Faith in America*, vol. 2, 207–9; Thompson, *The Diary of Juliet Thompson*, 369; 'Abdu'l-Bahá to Howard MacNutt, Aug. 14, 1909, Howard MacNutt Papers; Gail, *Arches of the Years*, 116–25.
45. Maḥmúd-i-Zarqání, *Maḥmúd's Diary*, 405–6, 410–11; 'Abdu'l-Bahá, *The Promulgation of Universal Peace*, 642–43. Most likely, the Day of the Covenant celebration was held on a Saturday because many Bahá'ís were not available on Tuesday, November 26.
46. Maḥmúd-i-Zarqání, *Maḥmúd's Diary*, 406–7.
47. Ibid., 384–429.
48. Ibid., 414–16.
49. Ibid., 402, 409; Thompson, *The Diary of Juliet Thompson*, 387; Ives, *Portals to Freedom*, 167–68.

50. Thompson, *The Diary of Juliet Thompson,* 387; Maḥmúd-i-Zarqání, *Maḥmúd's Diary,* 386, 445.
51. Maḥmúd-i-Zarqání, *Maḥmúd's Diary,* 402, 422; Thompson, *The Diary of Juliet Thompson,* 375.
52. "'We must arise to accomplish that which is required by the Lord,' Talk Given by Abdul Baha, Tuesday morning, December 3, 1912, at 780 West End Avenue, New York City," 123–24. The same talk appears in 'Abdu'l-Bahá, *The Promulgation of Universal Peace,* 649–51.
53. Maḥmúd-i-Zarqání, *Maḥmúd's Diary,* 422.
54. Ibid., 429–32. The translation has been approved by the Bahá'í World Center. The oldest version of the text may be found in *Star of the West* 3, no. 18 (Feb. 17, 1913): 3–4 and was published in edited form in 'Abdu'l-Bahá, *The Promulgation of Universal Peace,* 660–63.
55. Maḥmúd-i-Zarqání, *Maḥmúd's Diary,* 432; Thompson, *The Diary of Juliet Thompson,* 393.

12 / "The call of God has been raised in all the cities of America"

The chapter title is taken from Maḥmúd-i-Zarqání, *Maḥmúd's Diary,* 345.

1. Shoghi Effendi, *God Passes By,* 467, 468, 288; *Century of Light,* 21.
2. "Addresses by Abdul Baha in California"; "Informal Talks"; "Tablets[,] Interviews and Personal Talkes [*sic*]," Ella Cooper Papers.
3. GhaneaBassiri, *A History of Islam in America,* 133, 98.
4. Mullick, *The First Hindu Mission to America,* 192–209.
5. Adiswarananda, *Vivekananda: World Teacher,* xi–xiv; Jackson, *Vedanta for the West,* 32–34; Vivekananda, "Hinduism," in Barrows, *The World's Parliament of Religions,* vol. 2, 968–78.
6. Anagarika Dharmapala, "The World's Debt to the Buddha," in Barrows, *The World's Parliament of Religions,* vol. 2, 862–80; Tessa J. Bartholomeusz, *Women Under the Bo Tree: Buddhist Nuns in Sri Lanka* (Cambridge: Cambridge Univ. Press, 1994), 48, 56.
7. 'Abdu'l-Bahá, quoted in Maḥmúd-i-Zarqání, *Maḥmúd's Diary,* 381.
8. "Certain New Teachings of the Bahai Revelation Not Found in the Religious Books of the Past," 254–55; also see 'Abdu'l-Bahá, *The Promulgation of Universal Peace,* 639–44.
9. 'Abdu'l-Bahá to Martha Root, trans. Shoghi Rabbani, July 20, 1919; *Star of the West* 10, no. 12 (Oct. 16, 1919): 234.

10. William Ernest Hocking, "Recollections of Swami Vivekananda," quoted in Burke, *Swami Vivekananda in the West: New Discoveries, His Prophetic Mission, Part One,* 117–18. Hocking was also a speaker at a World Unity Conference in 1927, which was organized by a Bahá'í-inspired institute set up by the National Spiritual Assembly; see *World Unity Magazine* 1, no. 1 (Oct. 1927): 68.
11. "MEMORIAL RESOLUTION: ALBERT LEON GUÉRARD (1880–1959)" at http://histsoc.stanford.edu/pdfmem/GuerardAL.pdf; Albert Guérard, "The International Language Problem Today," *World Order* 4, no. 7 (Oct. 1938): 245–49; Preliminary Draft of a World Constitution," *Bulletin of the Atomic Scientists* 4, no. 5 (May 1948): 144–50, at http://books.google.com/.
12. Louise Waite, "My Visits with and Instructions from Abdul Baha while He was in Chicago from April 30th to May 6th 1912," 31–32.
13. 'Abdu'l-Bahá, *The Promulgation of Universal Peace,* 455, 457–58; Maḥmúd-i-Zarqání, *Maḥmúd's Diary,* 127–128, 132, 135, 137, 166–67, 268, 277, 339–41, 346–47, 371, 390, 392; Shoghi Effendi, *God Passes By,* 288; Dahl, "American Bahá'í Publishing: 1896–1922," 46; "Minutes of the Eleventh Annual Mashrekol-Azkar Convention," *Star of the West* 10, no. 18 (Feb. 7, 1920): 334.
14. Shoghi Effendi, *God Passes By,* 288.
15. Marion Holley, "May Ellis Maxwell," *The Bahá'í World: A Biennial International Record, Vol. VIII, 1938–1942,* 642; Morrison, *To Move the World,* 247–51, 217; Whitehead, *Some Bahá'ís to Remember,* 143–44.
16. Shoghi Effendi, *God Passes By,* 281; Stockman, *The Bahá'í Faith in America,* vol. 2, 379–81.
17. Roger Dahl, personal communication.
18. Morrison, *To Move the World,* 28; Whitehead, *Some Early Bahá'ís of the West,* 148–52; Randall-Winckler, *William Henry Randall,* 252–53; "Ruth J. Moffett," *The Bahá'í World: An International Record, vol. XVII, 1976–79,* 464.
19. Whitehead, *Some Early Bahá'ís of the West,* 42; Morrison, *To Move the World,* 134–35.
20. Whitehead, *Some Bahá'ís to Remember,* 137–39; Edna True, "Saichiro Fujita," *The Bahá'í World: An International Record, Vol. XVII, 1976–1979,* 406–8.
21. Hassall, "Dunn, Clara (1869–1960), and Dunn, John Henry Hyde (c. 1855–1941)," http://www.bahai-encyclopedia-project.org/ (accessed Dec. 6, 2011).
22. Historical Record Card for Monroe Charles Ioas, Bahá'í National Archives, Wilmette, IL.
34. Tablet to the American Friends from 'Abdu'l-Bahá, translated by Mírzá Ahmad Sohrab on April 28, 1911, in *Star of the West* 2, no. 4 (May 17, 1911): 7; Thompson, *The Diary of Juliet Thompson,* 395.
24. "The Most Important Work: Words of Abdul-Baha to a little group of Americans in Paris," *Star of the West* 4, no. 15 (Dec. 12, 1913): 256.

BIBLIOGRAPHY

Works of 'Abdu'l-Bahá

The Promulgation of Universal Peace: Talks Delivered by 'Abdu'l-Bahá during His Visit to the United States and Canada in 1912. Compiled by Howard MacNutt. Wilmette, IL: Bahá'í Publishing Trust, 2007.

Tablets of Abdul Baha Abbas. Chicago: Bahai Publishing Society, 1909–16.

Works of Shoghi Effendi

The Advent of Divine Justice. New ed. Wilmette, IL: Bahá'í Publishing Trust, 2006.

God Passes By. Rev. ed. Wilmette, IL: Bahá'í Publishing Trust, 1974.

Compilations

Bahá'u'lláh, the Báb, and 'Abdu'l-Bahá. *Bahá'í Prayers: A Selection of Prayers Revealed by Bahá'u'lláh, the Báb, and 'Abdu'l-Bahá.* Wilmette, IL: Bahá'í Publishing Trust, 2002.

Other Works

Abdo, Lil. *Religion and Relevance: The Bahá'ís in Britain, 1899–1930.* PhD dissertation, University of London School of Oriental and African Studies, 2004.

"Abdul-Baha's 'Welcome' to California." *Star of the West* 4, no. 11 (Sept. 27, 1913): 190–91, 194.

"Address by Abdul Baha at Leland Stanford Junior University, Palo Alto, California." *Star of the West* 3, no. 10 (October 16, 1912): 10–14.

Adiswarananda, Swami, ed. *Vivekananda: World Teacher, His Teachings on the Spiritual Unity of Humankind.* Woodstock, VT: Skylight Paths Publishing, 2006.

Alkan, Necati. *Dissent and Heterodoxy in the Late Ottoman Empire: Reformers, Babis, and Baha'is.* Piscataway, NJ: Gorgias Press, 2010.

Allen, Frances Orr. "Abdul-Baha in San Francisco, California." *Star of the West* 3, no. 12 (Oct. 16, 1912): 9–10.

———. "Abdul-Baha in San Francisco, California. Continued from last issue of the Star of the West." *Star of the West* 3, no. 13 (Nov. 4, 1912): 11–13.

"A Pioneer at the Golden Gate." *Star of the West* 13, no. 8 (Nov. 1922): 203–7.

Ashraf, Ghodiyeh. "Ghodsiyeh Ashraf's Memoirs." In Houshang Mahmoudi, *Notes About 'Abdu'l-Bahá* [*Yád-dáshthá-yi dar báriy-i-Hazrat-i-'Abdu'l-Bahá*]. Bundoora, Australia: Century Press Publications, 2009.

Bahá'í Yearbook: Volume One—April, 1925–April, 1926. Wilmette, IL: Bahá'í Publishing Trust, 1980.

Balyuzi, Hasan M. *'Abdu'l-Bahá: The Centre of the Covenant.* Oxford: George Ronald, 1971.

Barrows, John Henry. *The World's parliament of religions: An illustrated and popular story of the World's first parliament of religions, held in Chicago in connection with the Columbian exposition of 1893.* 2 vols. Chicago: Parliament Publishing Company, 1893.

Bartholomeusz, Tessa J. *Women Under the Bo Tree: Buddhist Nuns in Sri Lanka.* Cambridge: Cambridge University Press, 1994.

Bartlett, Edward E. "'Abdu'l-Bahá in Chicago." *Bahá'í News* 558 (Sept. 1977): 2-8.

Bass, Dorothy C., ed. *Practicing Our Faith: A Way of Life for a Searching People.* Hoboken, NJ: John Wiley & Sons, 2010.

Brookshaw, Dominic Parviz, and Seena B. Fazel. *The Baha'is of Iran: Socio-Historical Studies.* London: Routledge, 2008.

Brown, Ramona Allen. *Memories of 'Abdu'l-Bahá: Recollections of the Early Days of the Bahá'í Faith in California.* Wilmette, IL: Bahá'í Publishing Trust, 1980.

Buck, Christopher. *Alain Locke: Faith and Philosophy.* Los Angeles: Kalimat Press, 2005.

Burke, Marie Louise. *Swami Vivekananda in America: New Discoveries, His Prophetic Mission, Part Two.* Calcutta: Advaita Ashrama, 3rd ed., 1984.

———. *Swami Vivekananda in the West: New Discoveries, A New Gospel, Part Two.* Calcutta: Advaita Ashrama, 1987.

———. *Swami Vivekananda in the West: New Discoveries, The World Teacher, Part One.* Calcutta: Advaita Ashrama, 1985.

———. *Swami Vivekananda in the West: New Discoveries, The World Teacher, Part Two.* Calcutta: Advaita Ashrama, 1996.

Bushrui, Suheil, and Joe Jenkins. *Kahlil Gibran: Man and Poet.* Oxford: Oneworld, 1998.

Campbell, Helen. *Bahaism in its Social-Economic Aspect.* Chicago: Bahai Publishing Society, 1910.

Caton, Peggy. "A History of the Sacramento Bahá'í Community, 1912–1991." In *Community Histories*, edited by Richard Hollinger, 241–80. Vol. 6 of *Studies in Bábí and Bahá'í History.* Los Angeles: Kalimat Press, 1992.

Century of Light. Prepared under the supervision of the Universal House of Justice. Haifa: Bahá'í World Center, 2001.

"Certain New Teachings of the Bahai Revelation Not Found in the Religious Books of the Past." *Star of the West* 4, no. 15 (Dec. 12, 1913): 253-55, 258.

Chase, Thornton. "Impressions of 'Abdu'l-Bahá and His Station." Compiled by Robert H. Stockman. *World Order* 25, no. 1 (Fall, 1993): 13-22.

Clark, Deb. "The Bahá'ís of Baltimore, 1898–1990." In *Community Histories*, edited by Richard Hollinger, 111-50. Vol. 6 of *Studies in Bábí and Bahá'í History.* Los Angeles: Kalimat Press, 1992.

Cobb, Stanwood. *Memories of 'Abdu'l-Bahá.* Washington, D.C.: Avalon Press, n.d.

Collins, William P. "Kenosha: The History of the second Bahá'í community in the United States." *Bahá'í News,* no. 553 (April 1977): 1-9.

Dahl, Roger M. "A History of the Kenosha Bahá'í Community, 1897–1980." In *Community Histories,* edited by Richard Hollinger, 1–64. Vol. 6 of *Studies in Bábí and Bahá'í History.* Los Angeles: Kalimat Press, 1992.

———. "American Bahá'í Publishing: 1896–1922." In *World Order,* 29, no. 3: 31–47.

D'Evelyn, Dr. [Frederick]. "The Coming of Abdu'l Baha to California." In *Herald of the South,* no. 3 (Aug.–Sept. 1926): 5.

Dharmapala, Anagarika. "The World's Debt to the Buddha." In vol. 2 of Barrows, *The World's parliament of religions,* 862–80. Chicago: Parliament Publishing Company, 1893.

Dodge, Wendell Phillips. "Abdul-Baha's Arrival in America." *Star of the West* 3, no. 3 (Apr. 28, 1912): 3-6.

Ebbert, Doris, and Olga Finke. "Victoria Bedekian." In vol. XIII of *The Bahá'í World: An International Record, 1954–63,* 884-85. Haifa, Israel: The Universal House of Justice, 1970.

Ford, Bahiyyih Randall. "Experiences with 'Abdu'l-Bahá of the Randall Family." Typescript by Kay Zinky of a recorded talk Ford gave in Colorado, June 11, 1953, Kay Zinky papers.

Fowler, James. *Stages of Faith: The Psychology of Human Development and the Quest for Meaning.* San Francisco: Harper and Row, 1981.

Gail, Marzieh. "Ali-Kuli Khan." In vol. XIV of *The Bahá'í World: An International Record, 1963-1968,* 351-53. Haifa, Israel: Bahá'í World Centre, 1974.

———. *Arches of the Years.* Oxford: George Ronald, 1991.

Garis, Mabel. *Martha Root: Lioness at the Threshold.* Wilmette, IL: Bahá'í Publishing Trust, 1983.

GhaneaBassiri, Kambiz. *A History of Islam in America: From the New World to the New World Order.* New York: Cambridge University Press, 2010.

Grundy, J. G. and H. MacNutt. "Taking of the Moving Picture of Abdul-Baha, The Centre of the Covenant." *Star of the West* 3, no. 10 (Sept. 8, 1912): 3–4.

Haney, Mariam. "Mrs. Agnes Parsons." In vol. V of *The Bahá'í World: A Biennial Record, 1932–1934*, 410–14. Wilmette, IL: Bahá'í Publishing Trust, 1936.

Hannen, Joseph. "Abdul-Baha in Washington, D.C." *Star of the West* 3, no. 3 (Apr. 28, 1912): 6–8.

———. "With Abdul-Baha in Dublin, New Hampshire." *Star of the West* 3, no. 11 (Sept. 27, 1912): 3–6.

———. "The Public Meeting of the Fourth Annual Convention of Bahai Temple Unity." *Star of the West* 3, no. 4 (May 17, 1912): 3–5, 32.

Harmon, W. W. *Divine Illumination.* Boston, MA: The Bahai Movement, 1915.

Hassall, Graham. "Dunn, Clara (1869–1960), and Dunn, John Henry Hyde (c. 1855–1941)." http://www.bahai-encyclopedia-project.org/.

Hatch, Willard P. "'Abdu'l-Bahá and the Rabbi." *The Bahá'í Magazine* 20, no. 4 (July 1929): 109–11.

Hogenson, Kathryn Jewett. *Lighting the Western Sky: The Hearst Pilgrimage and the Establishment of the Bahá'í Faith in the West.* Oxford: George Ronald, 2010.

Holley, Horace. "George Orr Latimer." In vol. XI of *The Bahá'í World: A Biennial International Record, 1946–1950*, 511–12. Wilmette, IL: Bahá'í Publishing Trust, 1952.

Holley, Marion. "May Ellis Maxwell." In vol. VIII of *The Bahá'í World: A Biennial International Record, 1938–1940*, 631–42. Wilmette, IL: Bahá'í Publishing Trust, 1981.

Hutchison, William R. *Religious Pluralism in America: The Contentious History of a Founding Ideal.* New Haven: Yale University Press, 2003.

"Interview of W. H. Short, Secy N.Y. Peace Society and Hudson Maxim with Abdul-Baha at the Hotel Ansonia, New York City, April 15th, 1912," *Star of the West* 3, no. 7 (July 13, 1912): 4–5, 10–11.

"'It is proved that the existence of phenomena is effected through the Eternal Will,' Talk by Abdul Baha at the home of Mrs. Parsons, Washington, D.C., November 19, 1912." *Star of the West* 6, no. 3 (Apr. 28, 1915): 21–24.

Ives, Howard Colby. *Portals to Freedom.* Birmingham, UK: George Ronald, 1948.

Ives, Mabel Rice-Wray. "Grace Robarts Ober." In vol. VIII of *The Bahá'í World 1938–40*, 656–60. Wilmette, IL: Bahá'í Publishing Trust, 1981.

Jackson, Carl T. *Vedanta for the West: The Ramakrishna Movement in the United States.* Bloomington, IN: Indiana University Press, 1994.

Jasion, Jan Teofil. *'Abdu'l-Baha in the West: A Biographical Guide.* Paris: Librarie Baha'ie, 2012.

Jaxon, Honore J. "Dedication of the Mashrak-el-Azkar Site." *Star of the West* 3, no. 4 (May 17, 1912): 5–7.

Kazemzadeh, Firuz. "'Abdu'l-Bahá 'Abbás (1844–1921." Bahá'í Encyclopedia Project, http://www.bahai-encyclopedia-project.org/. Accessed May 15, 2011.

Kingdon, Geeta Gandhi. "Education of Women and socio-economic development." In *Reason and Revelation: New Directions in Bahá'í Thought,* edited by Seena Fazel and John Danesh, 231–43. Los Angeles: Kalimat Press, 2002.

Leonard, Levi W., and Josiah L. Seward. *The History of Dublin, N.H., Containing the Address by Charles Mason, and the Proceedings of the Centennial Celebration, June 17, 1852, with a Register of Families.* Dublin, NH: Town of Dublin, 1920.

MacNutt, Howard, comp. and ed. "Addresses Delivered by Abdul-Baha in New York City and Vicinity." *Star of the West* 3, no. 9 (Aug. 20, 1912): 3–7, 9–16.

———. "Addresses Delivered by Abdul-Baha in New York City and Vicinity." *Star of the West* 3, no. 10 (Sept. 8, 1912): 4–15, 17–32.

———. "Addresses Delivered by Abdul-Baha in New York City and Vicinity." *Star of the West* 3, no. 11 (Sept. 27, 1912): 6–7, 9–16.

"Martha Root's Travels in India, Burma and Australia—Her Death in Honolulu." In vol. VIII of *The Bahá'í World: A Biennial International Record, 1938–1940,* 60–73. Wilmette, IL: Bahá'í Publishing Trust, 1980.

McKinney, Edna. "Abdul-Baha's Visit to Philadelphia." *Star of the West* 5, no 6 (June 24, 1914): 83–87, 89–90.

"Message to the Church: Address by Abdul Baha, Unitarian Church, Palo Alto, California, (Mr. Clarence Reed, Minister), Tuesday, 8 P.M., October 8, 1912." *The Palo Altan* X, no. 43 (November 1, 1912): 4.

"Message to the Jews: Address by Abdul-Baha Abbas before Congregation Emma-nu-El, San Francisco, Cal., (Martin A. Meyer, Rabbi) Saturday, October 12, 1912." *Star of the West* 3, no. 13 (Nov. 4, 1912): 3–7, 10–11.

Mírzá Maḥmúd-i-Zarqání. *Maḥmúd's Diary.* Translated by Mohi Sobhani with the assistance of Shirley Macias. Oxford: George Ronald, 1998.

Morrison, Gayle. "Gregory, Louis George." *The Bahá'í Encyclopedia Project,* http://www.bahai-encyclopedia-project.org (accessed December 9, 2010).

———. *To Move the World: Louis G. Gregory and the Advancement of Racial Unity in America.* Wilmette, IL: Bahá'í Publishing Trust, 1982.

Mortensen, Fred. "When a Soul Meets the Master." *Star of the West* 14, no. 12 (Mar. 1924): 365–67.

Mullick, Sunrit. *The First Hindu Mission to America: The Pioneering Visits of Protap Chunder Mozoomdar.* New Delhi: Northern Book Center, 2010.

"'My Purpose and Intention is to Remove from Amongst Men this Enmity and this Religious Hatred,' Address by Abdu'l Baha at Eighth Street Temple (Jewish Synagogue) Washington, D. C. November 8, 1912." *Star of the West* 6, no. 1 (March 21, 1915): 3–10.

National Spiritual Assembly of the Bahá'ís of the United States and Canada, comp. *The Bahá'í Centenary, 1844–1944: A Record of America's Response to Bahá'u'lláh's Call to the Realization of the Oneness of Mankind.* Wilmette, IL: Bahá'í Publishing Committee, 1944.

Ober, Harlan F. "Louis G. Gregory." In vol. XII of *The Bahá'í World: A Biennial International Record, 1950–54*, 666–70. Wilmette, IL: Bahá'í Publishing Trust, 1981.

Ong, Rose. *Vignettes from the Life of Shirin Fozdar.* N.p. 2000.

Paulson, Ross E. "Campbell, Helen Stuart." *Notable American Women, 1607–1950: A Biographical Dictionary*, 280–81. Cambridge, MA: Belknap Press of Harvard University Press, 1971.

Perry, Anne Gordon, Robert Atkinson, Rosanne Adams-Junkins, Richard Grover, Diane Iverson, Robert H. Stockman, Burton W. F. Trafton, Jr. *Green Acre on the Piscataqua: A Centennial Celebration.* Eliot, ME: Green Acre School Council, 2nd ed., 2005.

Perry, Mark. "Pioneering Race Unity: The Chicago Bahá'ís, 1919–39." *World Order* 20, no. 2 (winter 1985–86): 41–60.

Pew Research Center. *Muslim Americans: Middle Class and Mostly Mainstream.* Pdf available at http://pewresearch.org/assets/pdf/muslim-americans.pdf (accessed May 9, 2011).

"Pinchot, Gifford." *Funk & Wagnalls New Encyclopedia.* Funk & Wagnalls, 1983.

Prothero, Stephen. *American Jesus: How the Son of God Became a National Icon.* New York: Farrar, Straus and Giroux, 2003.

———. *The White Buddhist: The Asian Odyssey of Henry Steel Olcott.* Bloomington: Indiana University Press, 1996.

Rabbání, Rúḥíyyih. *The Priceless Pearl.* 2nd ed. Haifa: Bahá'í World Centre, 2000.

Randall-Winckler, Bahiyyih, and Mabel Garis. *William Henry Randall.* Oxford: Oneworld, 1996.

"Record of the Fourth Annual Convention of the Bahai Temple Unity, Chicago, April 27–May 1, 1912," *Star of the West* 3, no. 5 (June 5, 1912): 2–7.

Remey, Charles Mason. "Reminiscences of My Visit to the Master in England the Summer of 1911." Typescript, Charles Mason Remey Papers, National Bahá'í Archives.

———. *Reminiscences of the Summer School Green Acre Eliot Maine.* Typescript, 1949. Accessible at http://h-net.org/~bahai/diglib/MSS/P-T/R/Remey/RGA.htm.

Report of the Baha'i Committee of Investigation, 1917–1918. Typescript. Available online at http://www.h-net.org/~bahai/docs/vol5/RCI/RCI.html.

"Report of the Eighteenth Annual Lake Mohonk Conference on International Arbitration, May 15th, 16th, and 17th, 1912." Lake Mohonk Conference on International Arbitration: 1912.

Root, Martha. "The Bahá'í Faith and Eastern Scholars." In vol. VII of *The Bahá'í World: A Biennial International Record, 1936–1938*, 682–92. Wilmette, IL: Bahá'í Publishing Trust, 1980.

Rosenbaum, Fred. *Visions of Reform: Congregation Emanu-El and the Jews of San Francisco, 1849–1999*. Berkeley, CA: Judah L. Magnes Museum, 2000.

Rothman, Sheila. *Woman's Proper Place: A History of Changing Ideas and Practices, 1870 to the Present*. New York: Basic Books, 1978.

Ruhe, David. *Robe of Light: The Persian Years of the Supreme Prophet Bahá'u'lláh, 1817–1853*. Oxford: George Ronald, 1994.

"Ruth J. Moffett." In vol. XVII of *The Bahá'í World: An International Record, 1976–79*. Haifa: Bahá'í World Centre, 1981.

Rutstein, Nathan. *Corinne True: Faithful Handmaid of 'Abdu'l-Bahá*. Oxford: George Ronald, 1987.

Schmidt, Leigh Eric. *Restless Souls: The Making of American Spirituality*. New York: Harper Collins, 2005.

Seager, Richard Hughes. *Buddhism in America*. New York: Columbia University Press, 1999.

———. *The World's Parliament of Religions: The East/West Encounter, Chicago, 1893*. Bloomington: Indiana University Press, 1995.

Sheldon, Charles M. *In His Steps*. Grand Rapids, MI: Zondervan, 1967.

Smith, Peter. "The American Bahá'í Community, 1894–1917: A Preliminary Survey." In vol. 1 of *Studies in Bábí and Bahá'í History*, edited by Moojan Momen, 85–223. Los Angeles: Kalimát Press, 1982.

Sohrab, Mírzá Ahmad. "Abdul-Baha at the Grave of Thornton Chase. Los Angeles, California, October 19, 1912." *Star of the West* 3, no. 13 (Nov. 4, 1912): 14–15.

———. "A Glimpse of Abdul Baha at Green Acre, Maine." *Star of the West* 3, no. 15 (Dec. 12, 1912): 3–4.

Spicer-Simson, Theodore. *A Collector of Characters: Reminiscences of Theodore Spicer-Simson*. Miami, FL: University of Miami Press, 1962.

Stockman, Robert H. *The Bahá'í Faith and American Protestantism*. ThD dissertation, Harvard University, 1990.

———. *The Bahá'í Faith in America: Early Expansion, 1900–1912, vol. 2*. Oxford: George Ronald, 1995.

———. *Thornton Chase: First American Bahá'í*. Wilmette, IL: Bahá'í Publishing Trust, 2002.

Storch, Juanita. "You Are Happy Because You Have Seen 'Abdu'l-Bahá." *World Order* 25, no. 1 (Fall 1993): 25–42.

Taherzadeh, Adib. *The Covenant of Bahá'u'lláh.* Oxford: George Ronald, 1992.

"Talk by Abdul Baha At the home of Mrs. Parsons, Washington, D.C., November 9, 1912." *Star of the West* 5, no. 2 (Apr. 9, 1912): 11–13, 16.

Terry, Peter. "Rabindranath Tagore: Some Encounters with Bahá'ís." Typescript, author's personal papers (supplied by Peter Terry).

"The Feast of Rizwan." *Star of the West* 6, no. 5 (June 5, 1915): 35–37.

The Free Religions Association: Proceedings at the Forty-fifth Annual Meeting, Held in Boston, Mass., Thursday and Friday, May 23 and 24, 1912. Boston, MA: The Free Religious Association, 1912. Available on Googlebooks at http://books.google.com/.

The Official Guide of the Railways and Steam Navigation Lines of the United States, Puerto Rico, Canada, Mexico, and Cuba, Also Time Tables of Railroads in Central America, January 1910 (New York: National Railway Publication Co., 1910), available online at http://cprr.org/Museum/Books/I_ACCEPT_the_User_Agreement/Official_Rail_Guide_1910.pdf.

"'The Purpose of the Covenant Was Simply to Ward Off Differences,' Address delivered by Abdul-Baha at the home of Corinne True, Chicago, November 1, 1912." *Star of the West* 5, no. 15 (Dec. 12, 1914): 230–31, 234.

"The Visit of Abdul-Baha to Mr. Charles Tinsley." *Star of the West* 4, no. 16 (Oct. 16, 1913): 205.

True, Edna. "Saichiro Fujita." In vol. XVII of *The Bahá'í World: An International Record,1976–1979.* Haifa: Bahá'í World Centre, 1981, 406–8.

Thompson, Juliet. *The Diary of Juliet Thompson.* Los Angeles: Kalimat Press, 1983.

"'Through the Teachings of Baha'o'llah the Eastern Horizon was Made Radiant': Address by Abdul Baha at the Church of Our Father (Universalist), Washington, D.C., Wednesday evening, November 6, 8:15 P.M." *Star of the West* 5, no. 13 (Nov. 4, 1914): 195–99.

True, Edna. "Saichiro Fujita." *The Bahá'í World: An International Record* 17, 1976–79: 406–8.

Tussing, Phillip. "FINISHING THE WORK: 'Abdu'l-Bahá in Dublin, 1912." Unpublished typescript.

Van den Hoonaard, Will C. *The Origins of the Bahá'í Community of Canada, 1898–1948.* Waterloo, ON: Wilfrid Laurier Press, 1996.

Vivekananda, Swami. "Hinduism," in vol.1 of Barrows, *The World's parliament of religions,* 968–78.

Waite, Louise. "My Visits with and Instructions from Abdul Baha while He was in Chicago from April 30th to May 6th 1912." Manuscript, Louise Waite Papers. Bahá'í National Center, Evanston, IL.

———. "The Changed Man." *The Bahá'í Magazine: Star of the West* 17, no. 4 (July 1926): 107–11.

Ward, Allan L. *239 Days: 'Abdu'l-Bahá's Journey in America.* Wilmette, IL: Bahá'í Publishing Trust, 1979.

Watts, Evelyn Loft and Charles Jardine. "Alfred James Loft." In vol. 16 of *The Bahá'í World: An International Record, 1973–76,* 514–16. Haifa: Bahá'í World Centre, 1978.

Weber, Max. *From Max Weber: Essays in Sociology.* Edited by H. H. Gerth and C. Wright Mills. New York: Oxford University Press, 1946.

"'We must arise to accomplish that which is required by the Lord,' Talk Given by Abdul Baha, Tuesday morning, December 3, 1912, at 780 West End Avenue, New York City." *Star of the West* 7, no. 11 (Nov. 4, 1916): 123–24.

Whitehead, O. Z. *Some Early Bahá'ís of the West.* Oxford: George Ronald, 1976.

———. *Some Bahá'ís to Remember.* Oxford: George Ronald, 1983.

Whitmore, Bruce. *The Dawning Place: The Building of a Temple, the Forging of a North American Bahá'í Community.* Wilmette, IL: Bahá'í Publishing Trust, 1984.

Wilson, Samuel Graham. *Bahaism and Its Claims: A Study of the Religion Promulgated by Baha Ullah and Abdul Baha.* New York: Fleming H. Revell Co., 1915.

"Wisdom Talks of Abdul-Baha (Abbas Effendi) at Chicago, Illinois, April 30th to May 5th, 1912. Published as an appendix to *Star of the West* 3, no. 3 (Apr. 28, 1912).

Yazdi, Marion Carpenter. *Youth in the Vanguard: Memoirs and Letters Collected by the First Bahá'í Student at Berkeley and at Stanford University.* Wilmette, IL: Bahá'í Publishing Trust, 1982.

BIBLIOGRAPHY OF ARCHIVAL SOURCES

All sources are in the National Bahá'í Archives, Wilmette, IL.

Chase, Thornton, Papers.
Cooper, Ella, Papers.
Farmer, Sarah, Papers.
Goodall, Hellen, Papers.
Ioas, Joseph, Papers.
Parsons, Agnes, Papers.
MacNutt, Howard, Papers.
Remey, Charles Mason, Papers.
Waite, Louise, Papers.
Windust, Albert, Papers.
Zinky, Kay, Papers.

For more information about the Bahá'í Faith,
or to contact Bahá'ís near you,
visit http://www.bahai.us/
or call
1-800-22-UNITE

BAHÁ'Í PUBLISHING AND THE BAHÁ'Í FAITH

Bahá'í Publishing produces books based on the teachings of the Bahá'í Faith. Founded over 160 years ago, the Bahá'í Faith has spread to some 235 nations and territories and is now accepted by more than five million people. The word "Bahá'í" means "follower of Bahá'u'lláh." Bahá'u'lláh, the founder of the Bahá'í Faith, asserted that He is the Messenger of God for all of humanity in this day. The cornerstone of His teachings is the establishment of the spiritual unity of humankind, which will be achieved by personal transformation and the application of clearly identified spiritual principles. Bahá'ís also believe that there is but one religion and that all the Messengers of God—among them Abraham, Zoroaster, Moses, Krishna, Buddha, Jesus, and Muḥammad—have progressively revealed its nature. Together, the world's great religions are expressions of a single, unfolding divine plan. Human beings, not God's Messengers, are the source of religious divisions, prejudices, and hatreds.

The Bahá'í Faith is not a sect or denomination of another religion, nor is it a cult or a social movement. Rather, it is a globally recognized independent world religion founded on new books of scripture revealed by Bahá'u'lláh.

Bahá'í Publishing is an imprint of the National Spiritual Assembly of the Bahá'ís of the United States.

OTHER BOOKS AVAILABLE FROM BAHÁ'Í PUBLISHING

PORTALS TO FREEDOM
Howard Colby Ives
$16.00 US / $18.00 CAN
Trade Paper
ISBN 978-1-931847-99-5

A personal memoir that deals with spiritual transformation, and brings to life in warm and intimate detail the historical figure of 'Abdu'l-Bahá.

Portals to Freedom is an intimate portrait of one of the most significant religious figures in recent history, 'Abdu'l-Bahá—the son and appointed successor of the Prophet of the Bahá'í Faith. Author Howard Colby Ives offers us a remarkably candid and honest description of his own personal spiritual search as a Unitarian minister struggling with questions of faith and spirituality. His search ultimately led him to a discovery of the Bahá'í Faith just a short time before 'Abdu'l-Bahá arrived in North America in 1912 on a quest to share the teachings and vision of his father with the people of the West. In *Portals* we get not only Ives's personal reflections and inner struggles, but a fascinating eyewitness account of the words and actions of one who has been described by his Prophet-Father as "the Mystery of God," is considered by Bahá'ís to be the perfect exemplar of the Faith's teachings, and who emerged from a lifetime of exile at the hands of the Ottoman Empire to travel tirelessly and share the Faith's message of unity in a profound and loving manner that touched the hearts of all with whom he came in contact.

SPIRIT OF FAITH
THE HUMAN SOUL
Bahá'í Publishing
$12.00 U.S. / $14.00 CAN
Hardcover
ISBN 978-1-61851-000-6

A collection of uplifting prayers and writings that focuses on the human soul for spiritual seekers of all faiths.

Spirit of Faith: The Human Soul is a compilation of writings and prayers that focus on the human soul and the qualities of this remarkable and unique aspect of our existence. Spiritual seekers of all faiths will relish these uplifting passages that offer a great deal of insight into the nature and significance of the human soul—a subject that has never been so extensively explored in the religious texts of the past. This collection contains writings from Bahá'u'lláh, the Báb, and 'Abdu'l-Bahá.

The *Spirit of Faith* series explores a range of topics—such as the unity of humanity, the eternal covenant of God, the promise of world peace, and much more—by taking an in-depth look at how the writings of the Bahá'í Faith view these issues. The series is designed to encourage readers of all faiths to think about spirituality, and to take time to pray and meditate on these important topics.

TALKS BY 'ABDU'L-BAHÁ
THE EXISTENCE OF GOD
Bahá'í Publishing
$14.00 U.S. / $16.00 CAN
Hardcover
ISBN 978-1-61851-001-3

A spiritually uplifting and thought-provoking collection of talks that offers insight into the ability to know and worship God.

Talks by 'Abdu'l-Bahá: The Existence of God is a collection of talks given by 'Abdu'l-Bahá—the son and appointed successor of Bahá'u'lláh, the Prophet and Founder of the Bahá'í Faith—during his historic journey to Europe and North America in 1911 and 1912. Speaking in front of multiple audiences, 'Abdu'l-Bahá offered simple yet profound and logical proofs for the existence of God, and discussed humankind's relationship with its Creator. The talks included here present convincing and thought-provoking explanations for some of the weightiest and most complex theological questions we face when trying to untangle the mysteries of life.

THE PROMULGATION OF UNIVERSAL PEACE
TALKS DELIVERED BY ‘ABDU’L-BAHÁ DURING HIS VISIT TO THE UNITED STATES AND CANADA IN 1912
‘Abdu’l-Bahá
$25.00 U.S. / $27.00 CAN
Hardcover
ISBN 978-1-931847-98-8

A special centenary edition marking the 100th anniversary of the talks delivered by ‘Abdu’l-Bahá during his historic journey through North America in 1912.

The Promulgation of Universal Peace is a collection of 140 talks given by ‘Abdu’l-Bahá—the son and appointed successor of Bahá’u’lláh, the Prophet and Founder of the Bahá’í Faith—during his extensive tour of North America in 1912. This compilation touches on a wide range of subjects including the coming of age of the human race, the oneness and continuity of the Prophets of God, and the oneness of religion as a social force for establishing world order and peace. These talks serve as a priceless resource for studying the language and personal example of one of the most significant religious figures in recent history.